D0225822

LOS CAPITALISTAS

SUSAN CALAFATE BOYLE

Los Capitalistas

HISPANO MERCHANTS AND THE
SANTA FE TRADE

✠ ✠ ✠

University of New Mexico Press Albuquerque

© 1997 by the University of New Mexico Press

All rights reserved.

FIRST EDITION

Library of Congress Cataloging-in-Publication Data

Boyle, Susan C.

Los capitalistas : Hispano merchants and the Santa Fe trade/ Susan Calafate Boyle. — 1st ed.

p. cm.

Includes bibliographical references.

ISBN 0–8263–1789–8.

1. New Mexico — Commerce — Mexico.

2. Mexico — Commerce — New Mexico.

3. Merchants — New Mexico — History.

4. New Mexico — History — To 1848.

5. Santa Fe Trail — History.

6. Mexico — History — Spanish colony, 1540–1810.

I. Title.

HF3161.N6B69 1997

380.1'09789'0903 — dc20 96–35705

CIP

Frontispiece: Felipe Chávez

For Terry, Joe, and Gabe, who have brought joy to my life

Acknowledgments

More than thirty years ago, I fell in love with the state and the people of New Mexico. However, I did not have the opportunity to explore their history until the Southwest Regional Office of the National Park Service at Santa Fe made possible the initial research for this work (through Contract CX 7029-0-0011). Art Gómez and Neil Mangum, who at that time worked in the Santa Fe office, offered constant encouragement and supported the publication of an earlier version of this volume.

My deepest gratitude goes to Susan L. Flader, who recognized from the earlier drafts the importance of looking at the Santa Fe Trail from a broad geographical perspective. Her perceptive and thorough comments greatly enhanced the quality of the manuscript. I would like to acknowledge the help from Marc Simmons, an inspiration for all who care about the history of New Mexico and, particularly, the Santa Fe Trail. Marc made available to me materials from his exceptional library and offered guidance and support from the beginning. I greatly appreciate the assistance I received from Mark L. Gardner. For hours over the phone, he and I discussed every conceivable topic associated with the Santa Fe Trail, and he generously shared research notes and documents that have greatly strengthened this work. I wish to thank Daniel Tyler of Colorado State University, who provided essential advice during the early stages of the project. In addition, I owe a great debt to my friends from the Denver Service Center of the National Park Service, William Patrick O'Brien and Jere Krakow, who listened to me and commented on earlier versions, and Dana Kinsey, who assisted with the mapping.

I want to recognize those who in various degrees contributed to the formulation and refinement of the ideas presented in the manuscript: Thomas B. Alexander, Thomas Bentrup, Liston Leyendecker, Richard Forry, Oakah Jones, the late Myra Ellen Jenkins, John Paige, Ronald W. Johnson, Stanley Hordes, Sandra Jaramillo, Richard Salazar, and David Sandoval.

I am indebted to the excellent staffs of numerous research institutions and archives: Southwest Research Center at the University of New Mexico Zimmerman Library; New Mexico State Records Center and Archives at Santa Fe; Rio Grande Historical Collections at New Mexico State University; Special Collections at the University of Texas at El Paso; Special Collections at the Colorado State University; Denver Public Library; Museum of New Mexico at Santa Fe; Colorado Historical Society; National Archives at Denver; and Socorro County Historical Society, New Mexico. I also extend thanks to the University of New Mexico Press.

I would like to thank my parents, who taught me the importance of persistence and hard work. Most of all, I wish to acknowledge the support from my husband Terry and my sons Joseph and Gabriel, who helped me put everything into perspective.

Susan Calafate Boyle
Fort Collins, Colorado
January 21, 1997

Contents

Maps

Introduction

El adjunto expediente contiene una solicitud que Juan Esteban Pino por sí y a nombre de otros capitalistas del territorio . . . presentó a la Diputación Territorial.[1]

The attached document contains a request presented by Juan Esteban Pino in his name and that of other capitalists in the territory . . . presented to the Territorial Representation.

JUAN ESTEBAN PINO, SEPTEMBER 1837

The 1837 petition of Juan Esteban Pino for a continued exemption from import duties for New Mexicans carrying local merchandise into the Mexican territory was not unusual as New Mexicans had had to apply for such exemptions every ten years. However, Pino's choice of the term "capitalist" to describe himself and other Hispanos deserves notice. The term probably had a more limited meaning in 1837 than it does today; still, Pino aptly portrayed the role that New Mexican merchants would play in the economic system that was developing in the territory as a result of the Santa Fe trade.[2]

Pino's request and numerous other documents reveal that the extensive literature on the Santa Fe Trail has failed to examine important aspects of its history.[3] This account addresses some of these important yet neglected topics. First, it focuses on the commercial activities of Hispano merchants. The literature on the Santa Fe Trail tends to celebrate Americans (and some western Europeans) and often portrays them as the daring explorers and visionaries who initiated commercial relations between the United States and Mexico. Often overlooked is the equally significant role played by Hispanos.[4] After the Santa Fe Trail officially opened, New Mexicans contributed to its growth and geographical expansion, developing their own commercial networks or joining foreigners in the crossing of the Plains and in business transactions.[5] By 1835 they were the majority of those traveling into the Mexican territory, owned a substantial portion of all the goods freighted south, and specialized in hauling *efectos del país* (local merchandise). At the end of the 1830s wealthy Mexican and New Mexican merchants expanded their operations and traveled to the eastern United

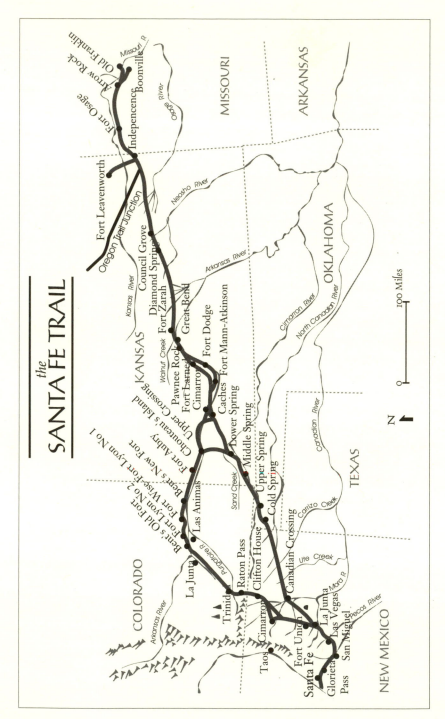

The Santa Fe Trade

States, where they developed direct relations with wholesalers and commission merchants. They established permanent businesses based on a well-calculated balancing of risks and took advantage of their resources, skills, and knowledge of the territory to develop a form of commercial capitalism well suited to the special circumstances of the New Mexican economy.

Second, this book examines the controversy regarding economic control of the Santa Fe trade before and after the Mexican War. Unfortunately, the lack of systematic information regarding ownership, the value and amount of merchandise, and its origin and final destination prevents a definitive analysis of the trade between New Mexico and the United States during the nineteenth century. Estimates of the value of the merchandise invested in the Santa Fe trade are crude and incomplete, and irregularities in record keeping by customs officials at Santa Fe also cast doubt on the nature of the transactions recorded. Thus, it is not possible to establish positively which ethnic group controlled the trade. However, it is clear that after 1839 Hispanos played a major role in the commerce between Mexico and the United States. The Mexican War did not stop commerce for long and had limited short-term detrimental impact on New Mexican commercial interests. Hispano merchants did not allow the armed confrontation to affect their economic transactions in the United States and they continued to trade heavily with Eastern and Midwestern cities, at least until the railroad brought an end to the Santa Fe Trail.

Third, this study explores how cultural and socioeconomic conditions in New Mexico contributed to the development and success of the Santa Fe trade. Isolated from Mexican markets both by distance and stifling commercial constraints, New Mexican merchants turned to the Santa Fe trade for survival and success. Fortunes were founded and augmented by this trade. Supplying products for transport on the trail provided some additional income for a broad segment of the population. The Hispanos' celebrated skill at packing and managing the cargo-carrying mules was widely sought. The *ricos* (wealthy) were the prime beneficiaries of the profits that resulted from a dramatic increase in merchandise entering the territory, but the working people also enjoyed some improvement in their standard of living.

One can argue that the theme of dependence is crucial to an understanding of the history of New Mexico. Although the forms and degree have varied, the territory has been continuously dependent, first on Mesoamerica, then on Spain, later on Mexico, and after 1846 on the United States. By the end of the Santa Fe Trail era (ca. 1880) it had become dependent on United States Army freighting and supply contracts. It is clear that the

Hispano elite was able to take advantage of the economic system it had established to maintain a position of privilege. However, the members of this elite were forced to rely on the advice of eastern commission merchants to buffer their holdings from the risks and wide economic fluctuations that characterized the period from 1860 to 1880. Those who were not as prosperous found it increasingly difficult to compete and continued to be dependent on their *patrones* (masters, bosses).[6]

Fourth, I demonstrate that the geographical boundaries of the Santa Fe Trail extended far beyond the more familiar stretch connecting Missouri and Santa Fe. This was but one segment of a complex network of commercial operations, which this study identifies as the Santa Fe trade (see figs. 1 and 2). This extensive pattern of economic relations involved two continents — North America and Europe — and several countries — Mexico, the United States, England, and France. Activities associated with the Santa Fe trade extended west to the California coast; south from the Arkansas River into Mexico; southeast to New Orleans; east beyond Missouri to New York, Baltimore, Pittsburgh, and other eastern cities; and across the Atlantic Ocean, particularly to England's Liverpool and London. By the 1850s the Santa Fe trade was linked to commercial hubs in Mexico, the United States, and Europe, where commission merchants, wholesalers, and agents completed intricate transactions, which required advanced planning and information on prices and demand, a complicated credit system, coordination of various types of transportation, and considerable risk taking and entrepreneurial skills.[7]

Fifth, I argue that the Santa Fe trade did not decline after the Mexican War. A new shorter and safer route through Texas carried a significant portion of the United States–Mexican trade; however, the volume and value of the merchandise that entered New Mexico increased steadily after the 1840s and climaxed during the 1870s, when it exceeded that of the previous five decades combined.[8] Wealthy New Mexican merchants contributed to this expansion. After the Mexican War they solidified their economic position as they refined a system that permitted them to take advantage of their geographical location and resources. The nature of their operations changed as they became aware of the need to diversify their activities and investments in an effort to minimize the risks that characterized the evolving trade.

Sixth, this work illustrates how the Santa Fe trade steadily evolved through time. Initially it was a simple operation involving a handful of individuals who drove a few wagon trains or pack mules. It required minimal capital and credit, and the risks were limited. As the size of the shipments grew, it became necessary to expand operations and to search for additional capital and credit, new sources of merchandise, competitive prices for goods, insurance, and transportation. Commission merchants became indispensable by providing information and facilitating the increasingly complex transactions. The number of owners of merchandise declined as trading required a financial investment that only the extremely wealthy could muster. As the volume of trade continued to expand, the profit from each individual sale declined. Conflict with the Indians, particularly after 1860, threatened mercantile operations that could not afford the periodic losses of valuable shipments. By this time only the extremely wealthy were able to profit from the purchase and sale of merchandise. Most merchants turned to freighting and supplying army posts as less risky activities that offered sizable earnings with a minimum of risk.

Finally, this study suggests a need to abandon racial and cultural stereotypes in order to understand the social and economic developments that took place. The documents clearly demonstrate that, contrary to the stereotypical depiction of Hispanos failing to possess a strong drive for material productivity, many members of the New Mexican mercantile elite conducted business in ways that closely resembled those of the German capitalists described by William Parish and the Santa Fe traders portrayed by Lewis E. Atherton. Many wealthy Hispanos behaved as such and even identified themselves as capitalistas as early as 1837. Although they did not always agree amongst themselves and in some cases strongly opposed the American presence, their economic activities and their behavior were quite analogous to those of the "entrepreneurial" Anglos and Jews.[9] The willingness of many leading Hispanos to join Anglos in wholesaling and retailing firms (Chick and Armijo, Otero and Sellar, Browne and Manzanares, Tully and Ochoa, for example) also demonstrates that racial differences did not prevent commercial cooperation.

This work includes eight chapters organized in the following manner. Chapter 1 provides a summary of trading activities and socioeconomic conditions in the New Mexican territory prior to independence from Spain in 1821. Chapter 2 focuses on social and economic problems New Mexicans faced after 1821 and the special concerns that leading citizens voiced regarding the need for help from Mexican authorities. Chapter 3 examines in detail the trade along *el Camino Real* (from New Mexico to Chihuahua and Mexico City) and those who made it possible. Chapter 4 explains the reasons for the illegal activities (mostly contraband) in which both Anglos and Hispanos participated. Chapter 5 explores the trade between New Mexico and the United States prior to the Mexican War, and sketches the mercantile system pioneered by merchants like Manuel Alvarez. Chapter 6 examines the mercantile activities of Felipe Chávez, one of the wealthiest and most influential of the New Mexican merchants during the second half of the nineteenth century. Chapter 7 summarizes the available information on other leading New Mexican traders and on *comerciantes* (merchants) of more moderate means. Chapter 8 analyzes census data for 1860 and 1870, and examines how the evolution of the Santa Fe trade with its ever-increasing dependence on United States Army contracts might explain the polarization of the New Mexican mercantile elite and the decline of some of its members.

Throughout this analysis the name of Josiah Gregg appears often. His account of the Santa Fe Trail through the early 1840s, *Commerce of the Prairies*, sometimes reflects the biases of the times. Nevertheless, it provides the most comprehensive history of the trade and such related subjects as geography, politics, economy, social customs, military activities, American Indians, natural resources, arts and sciences, religion, and many others. His narrative includes insightful observations and provides an invaluable background for anyone wishing to learn about the trade and the trail.

Although this study focuses on the involvement of the Hispanos in establishing and developing a network of commercial relations along various southwestern trails, one must not forget that other ethnic groups shared the work and the adventures. While the historical literature abounds with tales of the trip across the prairie, there is little information on foreign owners (particularly after the 1840s); the source, nature, amount and value of the merchandise they carried; the commission merchants who facilitated the purchase and delivery of the goods, and the credit system that allowed commerce to develop and thrive for almost sixty years. This book calls for a more systematic approach to the study of the commercial system that characterized the Santa Fe trade and its evolution. This would allow for a more adequate comparison of the commercial activities of Anglo merchants with those of their New Mexican counterparts and would illuminate an important aspect of the development of the west.

Other topics need attention. Little is known about the role of American Indians in the Santa Fe trade. The 1860s and 1870s censuses reveal that a substantial number of them worked for Hispanos, and it would be safe to assume that they participated in various capacities in trail-related activities. The contributions of women must also be more clearly identified — a difficult task because of the lack of information regarding their participation in social and commercial activities. New Mexican women are almost invisible in the official provincial records between 1821 and 1880. They appear almost exclusively as plaintiffs in cases of physical abuse against their husbands or other relatives.[10]

Travelers noted that Hispano *ciboleros* (buffalo hunters) were often accompanied by their wives and families. However, it is not clear whether they were referring to women working in the caravans that hauled goods from the east or in those that went south into the Mexican territory. When wealthy Hispano merchants went on vacation to New York, they certainly took their wives and stayed in fancy hotels where they enjoyed such luxuries as French champagne, but it is not possible to establish the degree to which wealthy New Mexican women participated in their families' commercial transactions. With the exception of Gertrudis Barceló none was listed as a merchant in any of the official documentation for the period 1821 to 1846. Neither was any woman identified as a comerciante in the 1860 and 1870 censuses, although the enumerations do sometimes show women's assets separate from those of their husbands. It is quite likely that even if they did not directly participate in the trade, women of all social levels played an important role in the development of the province's commercial economy. Their husbands' absences undoubtedly forced them to assume greater responsibilities and to act for their spouses while they were away.[11]

This book aims primarily to begin a systematic examination of New Mexican society during the nineteenth century. It stresses the need to conduct meaningful research and analysis "grounded on the materials forces and social relations of production which ultimately define the historic course of any group of people."[12] It explores economic activities and their development as the century progressed, and highlights the importance of placing them within a broad geographic context. It calls for a re-examination of the various roles that different ethnic groups played in the development of the west and challenges some of the stereotypes that have characterized Western history.

The documents examined during the course of this study contain a wide variety of spellings both for Hispano and Anglo personal names. These have been standardized, except in cases where there remains concern that two or more separate individuals are being described.

ONE

Isolation and Dependency

De esta adhesión y fidelidad acaso se hallan más penetrados los habitantes de los Estados Unidos que los de la antigua España. Inteligenciados del abandono con que ha sido mirada aquella provincia, han procurado atraerla a sí por varios medios. . . . han procurado ya con los halagos de un comercio ventajoso, ya convidándonos con unas leyes suaves y protectoras, unir esta preciosa porción de territorio al comprado de la Luisiana.[1]

Of this loyalty and faithfulness the United States are probably more aware than the citizens of Spain. Cognizant of the abandonment with which Spain has kept this province, they [United States] have tried to attract it through various means. . . . they have done this by means of a beneficial commerce, inviting us with benign and protective laws, to join this precious portion of territory to that of the Louisiana purchase.

PEDRO BAUTISTA PINO, 1812

Throughout the colonial period New Mexicans knew that the province's poverty and peripheral geographical situation condemned it to be neglected or forgotten. Pedro Bautista Pino, New Mexico's first deputy to the Spanish *Cortes* (legislative body), was among the first who dared to make public what others would later voice — that unless Spain addressed some of the problems facing the territory, it would be difficult to disregard for long the attention of the United States.

New Spain's northern frontier was distant and isolated, and its citizens struggled for their region to become an integral part of the Spanish empire. Almost seventeen hundred miles separated Santa Fe and Mexico City. This distance was made all the more formidable by the absence of a transportation system, and obstacles to travel, such as the rugged terrain of northern and central Mexico, discouraged communication and mutual understanding. New Mexicans searched for means to relieve their isolation and bring an end to their dependency on an economic system that was designed to benefit the mother country and ill-suited to the conditions that prevailed in their remote territory. A widespread network of trade activities involving various ethnic groups became the principal method of alleviating their problems. With time, New Mexicans came to rely on a variety of licit and illicit commercial strategies to circumvent the government policies that stifled the economic development of the province.[2]

Mission supply trains were officially sanctioned and became the standard link between Mexico City and its northernmost province. Starting in 1609, more than two centuries before William Becknell embarked on his famous journey to Santa Fe, New Mexico was the destination of an overland freight service. Every three years caravans traveled from Mexico City to Santa Fe to supply the missions of the remote province. They followed the Río Grande Pueblo Trail, one of three pre-Columbian routes that allowed for exchanges of merchandise among the Pueblos and their numerous Mexican counterparts.[3]

The mission supply trains were quite sizable, normally including thirty-two wagons, more than five hundred mules, herds of livestock, and even military escorts. Their main goal was to sustain the missions, but they played a significant role in other facets of provincial life. Settlers going out to New Mexico for the first time, traders, and local citizens returning home accompanied the trains. Officials used the service for the dispatch of mail, and royal and vice-regal decrees. On the return journey those going to Mexico on business, ex-governors and other officials, priests, and sometimes even prisoners joined the caravan.[4]

The mission supply service also affected the economic life of New Spain's far northern frontier. Lack of adequate transportation was one of the major impediments to economic development, and the mission supply wagons helped to transport local products to the mining centers of Nueva Vizcaya. A yearly caravan could not have provided an adequate outlet for the bulky products of the region, but it was the only sanctioned means of maintaining economic interaction with other communities of New Spain.[5] The most common efectos del país were *piñones* (pine nuts), salt, candles, buffalo hides, *gamuzas* (deer hides), weavings, blankets, and a coarsely woven cloth called *sayal*. The single most important export was livestock: largely sheep, along with relatively small numbers of oxen and cattle.

It is not clear if the use of the wagons to export goods from New Mexico was legal, although the governors frequently took the position that the wagons, being the property of the crown, were at their disposal after the supplies from New Spain had been delivered. James E. Ivey argues that it is unlikely that such an important resource as the supply wagons would have gone unutilized and returned to Mexico City empty, and he believes that any dispute was probably over how much space the governor could legitimately claim in the wagons.[6]

Contact with French traders was not licit, but it, too, became an important means of relieving the isolation of the province. Commercial exchanges between the Spanish settlements along the Río Grande and French communities in the Illinois country had started even before the eighteenth century. By the 1720s interaction was becoming more frequent. Spanish officials in Mexico City feared the presence of French traders, but local need for manufactured goods was such that authorities in New Mexico often looked the other way. The French traded with impunity, only occasionally suffering arrest or expulsion. At times their activities were temporarily curtailed, as in 1795, when the governor of New Mexico ordered the arrest of all French merchants and the confiscation of their goods.[7] However, restrictive policies did not last long and did not discourage Frenchmen determined to gain access to the New Mexico market. Late in the eighteenth century Jean Baptiste Lalande, Pierre Chouteau, Laurent Durocher, and Jules DeMun, among others, realized that economic opportunity awaited those who supplied the region with reasonably priced merchandise.[8]

Contact with Americans was sporadic until the 1780s but became more frequent as the ex-British colonists moved west looking for new hunting grounds, land, and opportunity. First, they came from the areas that would become Missouri, Kentucky, and Tennessee; later, they came from Natchez, Mississippi, and New Orleans and Natchitoches, Louisiana. After Zebulon Pike's adventures (1806–7) were made public, Americans' interest in New Mexico increased and so did the number of adventurers who were willing to risk imprisonment in order to gain access to the New Mexican market.[9]

The Spanish, themselves intent on consolidating their outposts in Texas and New Mexico and also aware of the need to widen the range of their commercial activities, encouraged a series of trips to investigate possible trade routes. In November 1786 Governor Juan Bautista de Anza requested permission to explore, at his own expense, a route from the province of Sonora to New California. Anza also claimed to have opened the road between Santa Fe and Arizpe in the province of Sonora. In 1787 José Mares went from Santa Fe to San Antonio and returned the following year. Five years later (1792) officials in New Spain promoted the search for a direct

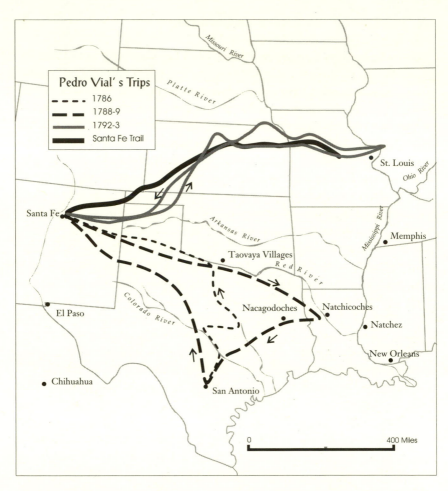

Pedro Vial's Trips
- - - - 1786
— — 1788-9
——— 1792-3
—— Santa Fe Trail

Missouri River

Platte River

St. Louis

Ohio River

Santa Fe

Arkansas River

Mississippi River

Memphis

Taovaya Villages

Red River

Colorado River

El Paso

Nacagodoches

Natchicoches

Natchez

New Orleans

Chihuahua

San Antonio

0   400 Miles

PEDRO VIAL'S PIONEER ROUTE CLOSELY RESEMBLES THE ROAD FOLLOWED
BY SANTA FE TRADERS IN THE NINETEENTH CENTURY.

trade route between Sonora and Santa Fe. The objective was to facilitate the exchange of goods between the two territories for their mutual benefit, since it appeared such a route would be shorter than the road through El Paso. This was an important project, which received the attention of the viceroy, the commandant general of the interior provinces, Pedro de Nava, and other officials. Another expedition was led by interpreter Joseph Miguel, who left Santa Fe in June 1800. Miguel was accompanied by two Indians from Taos and four *genízaros* (non-Pueblo Indian captives rescued by the Spanish settlers from various nomadic tribes), and was to explore the territory from New Mexico to the Missouri River. In 1808 Francisco Amangual embarked on a reconnaissance of the territory between Santa Fe and San Antonio, and he kept a detailed diary of his activities.[10]

The most famous expeditions were led by Pedro Vial, a French gunsmith and Indian trader. Vial traveled from San Antonio to Santa Fe in 1786, and from Santa Fe to Natchitoches and San Antonio and back to Santa Fe in 1788. Probably his most important trip took place in 1792, when he pioneered a route to St. Louis that closely resembled the one Santa Fe traders would follow during the next century (see fig. 3). This journey demonstrated that the distance between the Louisiana Territory and New Mexico was far from insurmountable. Vial claimed that he could have made the trip from St. Louis to Santa Fe in twenty-five days if the Indians had not captured him.[11]

Although Vial furnished officials detailed maps of the areas he reconnoitered, the government never developed the new routes. It is possible that the flourish of exploratory activities at the turn of the nineteenth century was part of the Bourbon policies that aimed to integrate the northern Mexican economy within a larger regional commercial system. Made possible by the halt of hostilities between the settlers and the Plains Indians, it was too brief to allow for these newly opened trade routes to develop officially.[12]

From the beginning, conflict characterized relations between the surrounding Indian tribes and New Mexicans, but trading was equally customary and widespread. In general, Spanish policy towards the Indians evolved from confrontation to pacification, but local ordinances regarding commercial relations with the *naciones bárbaras* (hostile Indian tribes) changed periodically as officials adopted new strategies: enemies became friends, and former allies became dreaded foes.[13]

New Mexicans were often willing to risk prosecution to trade with the Indians. Father Eusebio Kino, who died in 1711, claimed that even before his time New Mexicans had bartered with the Sobaipuris near the present site of Nogales, Arizona. Numerous proceedings throughout the colonial period reveal widespread and "embarrassing" trading with the "savage Indians."[14] As early as 1735 Spanish officials complained about the *alcalde* (mayor) of Taos bartering with Comanches before the time set for the regular trade. Various ordinances in the 1740s and 1750s specifically banned the sale of horses, animals, and arms to the Indians. By the 1780s large parties of New Mexicans were being arraigned for trading with the Utes.[15]

As the eighteenth century drew to a close, Spanish policy toward the Indians moved towards pacification, and the emphasis shifted to a distribution of liberal annual gifts in the name of the king. Expeditions frequently sent out for this purpose were also conducted to provide enough trade goods to keep the Indians satisfied and to supply them with an outlet for their furs and surplus crops. The 1786 peace talks with the Comanches included the promise of fairs and free trade. Spanish objectives also included winning and holding the allegiance of the Indian tribes of Louisiana and the Plains, keeping those tribes hostile to all foreigners (especially the English), excluding unlicensed traders, encouraging friendly tribes to pillage French traders, inducing friendly Indians to cross the Mississippi from the east and to establish posts to encourage those crossings, and controlling the Indians through carefully regulated trade. By the 1790s "extraordinary expenses incurred in the maintenance of friendly relations with the Indians" were substantial and provided ample opportunity for commercial interaction between Indians and Hispanos, the norm in New Mexico well into the nineteenth century.[16]

Even before the end of the eighteenth century, Taos and Pecos had become the leading trading centers where both Indians and traders congregated. Taos and Pecos were important because they were accessible both from the Rocky Mountains and the Great Plains. Annual fairs took place in July and August and attracted many merchants. Comanches, Arapahos, Pawnees, Utes, Navajos, and others brought buffalo hides, deer skins, blankets, and sometimes even captives to be sold or exchanged for slaves. They bartered for horses, knives, guns, ammunition, blankets, strong drink, and small trinkets. In 1786 Pedro Garrido y Durán reported that the Comanches exchanged more than six hundred hides, many loads of meat and tallow, fifteen riding beasts, and three guns.[17] French, Spanish, and American trappers carried pelts and trinkets, while Chihuahua merchants came laden with imported goods. All gained in the exchange, but the latter made most of the profit.

During the winters New Mexicans turned south to attend fairs at Chihuahua, one of the greatest events of the year. Villa San Felipe el Real de

Chihuahua had been established around 1707 when the exploitation of profitable mines in the Chuviscar Valley began on a large scale. The area grew rapidly, and by the middle of the eighteenth century, with almost eighteen thousand residents, it became the leading trading center of Nueva Vizcaya, the northern Mexican territory.[18]

The economic success of Chihuahua merchants was not surprising. They followed the example of comerciantes elsewhere in New Spain. Throughout Mexico *gachupines* (Spanish-born merchants) made large profits and virtually dominated the economy.[19] The lack of an effective monetary commercial exchange fostered this control. Large producers sent surplus agricultural products like sugar, cotton, cacao, livestock, and cereals on consignment to merchants in the capital. In exchange these merchants returned local and imported manufactures, resold the agricultural products at monopoly prices in the controlled markets of Mexico City and the mining centers, and gained from exchanging staples and primary products for manufactures and imported goods.[20]

The wealthy landowners who produced surpluses of basic agricultural products were at the mercy of the merchants, yet they earned substantial profits. Two factors contributed to their success. First, the merchants in the capital provided a sure outlet for the surplus production every year and were able to pay immediately for the merchandise, or, more commonly, give the producer merchandise or credit of equal value. Second, the large producers resold the clothing, textiles, shoes, and other manufactured goods to their own workers at a higher price. Often the *hacendados* (large landholders) opened stores and dealt with smaller producers on the same terms as Mexico City merchants did, taking agricultural products in exchange for manufactured articles (a practice that New Mexican merchants would successfully adopt in the 1830s and 1840s).[21]

Chihuahua merchants quickly gained regional economic preeminence, and by the middle of the eighteenth century they dominated the trade from their province to New Mexico. This monopoly continued until Americans began to supply New Mexico with abundant merchandise in the 1820s. In fact, Hispanos still complained about the "excessive monopoly" in 1829. Chihuahua merchants enjoyed the advantageous geographical situation of their town, on the "Camino Real de Tierra Adentro," which dominated the silver trade to the south and controlled the presidial supply system.[22]

Three major factors contributed to New Mexicans' dependence: the complex monetary system in use, the shortage of currency in the territory, and the practices of Mexican merchants. Four different monetary units existed. These were the official *peso de plata* (silver peso), which was worth eight *reales* but was practically nonexistent, and three "imaginary" coins employed in bookkeeping. A *peso a precio de proyecto* (peso at project price) was worth six reales, a *peso a precios antiguos* (peso at old prices) was worth four reales, and a *peso de la tierra* (peso of the land) was valued at only two reales. New Mexicans were victimized in a "vicious circle of swindles."[23] Max Moorhead described how these factors interacted to exploit traders:

> a merchant of Chihuahua could buy 32 yards of coarse woolen goods in the south for 6 *pesos de plata* and sell it in New Mexico at a *peso de la tierra* per yard, or a real value of eight *pesos de plata* in all. Since he was paid in local produce, he could accept remuneration in El Paso brandy, which was worth only one *peso de la tierra* per bottle when exchanged for manufactured goods, and thus acquire 32 bottles for the bolt of cloth. However, in reselling the brandy to other New Mexicans the merchants could charge a *peso de plata* a bottle and then eventually receive 32 *pesos de plata* for goods which had cost him only six. But again, since silver money did not circulate in the province, he must be paid in goods, and should the purchaser of the brandy wish to pay in corn from a future harvest, he was charged the prevailing *peso de precios antiguos* rate, four *reales* for each short bushel (*costal*) of grain, or 51 short bushels for the 32 bottles. After the harvest, when this was collected, he could sell it to the troops in the southern presidios for ten *reales* per short bushel, almost 84 *pesos de plata* in all, or more than ten times the original cost of his goods and freightage.[24]

This monopoly deeply affected New Mexicans. Chihuahua was the closest and most affluent market where they could exchange livestock and efectos del país for the manufactured goods they needed. New Mexicans had almost no access to hard currency and paid exorbitant prices, making their purchases on credit and pledging future crops, livestock, or merchandise. Fray Juan Agustín de Morfi, a Franciscan who visited New Mexico around 1778, noted that many sold their crops as much as six years in advance.[25] New Mexicans were in desperate need of metal tools, awls, shovels, and scissors. These items were so expensive and scarce that they remained out of the reach of the majority of the population for many decades.

The goods New Mexicans carried to Chihuahua were quite limited to a few crude manufactures, mostly the "produce of the soil": sheep, raw wool, buffalo and deer hides, *colchas* (quilts), homemade *serapes* [*sic*] and stockings, pine nuts, salt, brandy from El Paso, and Indian blankets. In exchange they received expensive manufactured goods, particularly iron tools and weapons, domestic and imported fabrics, boots, shoes, chocolate, sugar, tobacco, liquor, ink, and paper.[26]

Chihuahua merchants took advantage of the dependent New Mexicans, but it was Spain's colonial economic policy, heavily influenced by mercantilist doctrine, that was greatly responsible for the shortage of currency and the scarcity and high prices of manufactured goods throughout colonial Mexico.[27] Spain's policies attempted to regulate, restrict, and prohibit rather than to encourage. The Spanish crown, in its search for revenue, aimed to control all possible economic activities. Most manufactured goods were not made locally and were often of British, Dutch, or French origin. Articles that came through legitimate channels were expensive because of high freight rates, difficulties and delays in transportation, and the greed of merchants who often tried to make a fortune on the first cargo sent to Veracruz.[28]

Commercial transactions in Mexico were also extremely cumbersome because of the multitude of duties, fees, charges, commissions, royalties, licenses, and tributes. Furthermore, all trade to and from New Spain legally entered and exited through just one port—Veracruz. Taxes were easily levied in Spanish ports because of the power of local *consulados* (merchants' guilds). The treasury also imposed fees on internal trade by placing customs houses on the royal highways and by ordering that certain trades travel along one permitted route.[29]

The government did not have the bureaucrats, accounting system, or technology to tax systematically, so it attempted to impose general and simple taxes, hoping to obtain all that was possible rather than the optimum from any given tax. Much of the revenue came from the *almojarifazgo* (customs fee) required on all merchandise. The rates varied. Exports paid 2.5 percent, while imports were charged between 5 and 17.5 percent. The alcabala was originally set at 2 percent of the sale price of goods, but rose to double that amount by the seventeenth century. In times of crisis, higher rates were used, and they often lasted long beyond the emergency. By the eighteenth century, the tax had reached 6 percent. Smaller towns often managed to delay its imposition, and some areas or towns were able to obtain temporary exemptions. New Mexico was one of the provinces that was spared from paying the alcabala through the 1840s.[30]

Other taxes included the *sisa* (an excise on food), the *quinto* (a 20-percent royalty on bullion), the *derecho de fundidor* (originally a smelting charge, but it evolved into the quinto), the *palmeo* (a trade tax based on the bulk of the goods), the *bula de santa cruzada* (a tax on indulgences), the *mesada* (a tax on appointive offices that evolved into the *media añata* [half of the first year's salary of persons occupying official positions]), the *avería* (which aimed to cover all transportation costs and rose up to 14 percent), the *almirantazgo* (an import duty established as an endowment for the Admiral of the Indies Columbus, and his descendants), and several others.[31]

Reforms enacted during the reign of Carlos IV (1788–1808) modified some of these impositions, but they were later re-established, and prices in Mexico remained as high as ever. Foreign products were burdened 36 percent of their value upon their arrival at Veracruz, and because of colonial imposts the duties rose to 75 percent by the time they reached the consumers.[32]

In addition, the Spanish government monopolized articles of common necessity, like salt, fish, tobacco, mercury, playing cards, stamped paper, leather, gunpowder, snow brought from the mountains for refrigeration, alum, copper, lead, tin, alcohol, and cocks for fighting. All individuals were prohibited to trade in these products, since the profit from them belonged exclusively to the government. The evils of monopolies were increased by leasing them; usually the most powerful persons in the community became the contractors and worked for their own selfish interests to the disadvantage of consumers.[33]

In New Mexico the Spanish reformers faced a dilemma as they tried to fit the province into the larger fiscal and governmental reforms designed for New Spain. Authorities in Mexico City wanted strictly to enforce the newly created monopolies to recoup some of the losses incurred in fighting the Comanches and Apaches, but they realized that the collection of revenue of any kind would only add to local and regional economic troubles.[34]

It appears that New Mexicans enjoyed a brief period of relative prosperity between 1785 and 1810. The Spanish defeat of the Comanches and Apaches allowed for the growth of trade between New Mexico and the rest of northern New Spain. Ross H. Frank argues that a growing population, increased trade with Chihuahua and other settlements outside of the province, and regional policies that fostered trade and finance resulted in a full-fledged commercial economy driven by a "more intensive and extensive economic connection to the developing regional economy of northern New Spain."[35]

New Mexicans suffered economically as a result of Spanish mercantile policies, but not everybody in the province was equally affected. A few large landowners, particularly those from the Río Abajo (the portion of the Río Grande Valley south of La Bajada), were able to thrive by shipping south large quantities of sheep. Their prosperity, however, had a negative impact on the long-term development of the province. Heavy emphasis on sheep raising led to overgrazing and damage to the fragile ecosystems of the arid west and also effected a disregard for agriculture. Furthermore, massive sheep exports produced local shortages that left weavers unemployed and sharply limited the production of domestic textiles.[36]

At the beginning of the nineteenth century, New Mexicans were still isolated and dependent on Chihuahua merchants. Becoming increasingly aware of the need to foster the development of the area, a *junta* (council) met to discuss manufactures and mining in June 1805.[37] Within a decade, this council was able to gain a considerable measure of political autonomy as its members took advantage of the turmoil that accompanied the Napoleonic overthrow of Spain's Ferdinand VII. The Cortes not only resisted the French, but also restructured government at all levels. Liberal reforms included in the Spanish Constitution of 1812 provided, among others, guidelines for establishing *ayuntamientos* (town councils), which became popularly elected bodies. At the provincial level, reforms created a new institution, the *diputación*, a legislature of elected representatives.[38]

These changes affected even the most remote corners of the Spanish empire and in New Mexico produced a heightened awareness of the need to address some of the province's economic woes.[39] Pedro Bautista Pino was elected to represent New Mexico in the Spanish Cortes meeting at Cadiz in 1812. Pino compiled his concerns in a book which was published the same year. He eloquently presented the case for his province, briefing the Cortes on problems and making suggestions to remedy the situation. Pino expressed a common sentiment — New Mexico was threatened by Americans who were pressing upon her borders, seeking an excuse for invasion. According to Pino, Americans were aware of the neglect and impoverished circumstances affecting his province and hoped that promises of liberal laws and open trade would encourage New Mexicans to join the province of Louisiana.[40]

Pino was highly critical of Spain's economic policies, particularly the monopoly on tobacco, which prevented local production. He also stressed how distance, neglect, and the constant threat of Indian attacks made it difficult to earn a living from agriculture. Pino bemoaned the lack of manufactures. Coarse wool and cotton items, bridles, and spurs were the only goods produced. Although Pino acknowledged that the government had sent agents to instruct New Mexicans on techniques of finer weaving, he conceded that the products were still very coarse in comparison to those produced elsewhere.[41]

Pino stressed the physical and emotional cost that the province had borne in trying to fend off the thirty-three Indian nations. Since the central government did not provide enough funds for their protection, New Mexicans had been forced to bear the brunt of their defense, serving in the militia as well as furnishing the weapons, ammunition, and provisions necessary for the outfitting of the troops. Pino complained that serving in a campaign often meant economic ruin because volunteers had to sell their clothes and those of their families in order to be ready for the frequent operations against the salvajes. Pino believed that channeling resources towards the control of the Indians caused the economic backwardness of the province. He emphasized the difficulty of raising revenues because there was no customs house except for the one at Chihuahua. The only sources of income were the *estanco* (monopoly) on tobacco, gunpowder, and playing cards, but since these items were brought from Mexico City, the revenues obtained were insignificant, and, Pino noted, the province could profit greatly if it were allowed to produce its own tobacco.[42]

Pino's economic summary showed New Mexicans purchasing 112,000 pesos worth of goods a year from the south, but selling only 60,000 pesos worth in return. Even the government payroll, which brought in about 38,000 pesos, did not offset the imbalance, and the annual deficit of about 14,000 pesos not only drained the province of hard money, but kept its inhabitants indebted.[43] Pino lamented as well the almost total absence of educational facilities. Only those who could afford a private tutor were able to instruct their children. It was impossible even in the capital city of Santa Fe to retain one elementary school teacher.[44]

New Mexico was isolated geographically from Mexican markets and by administrative restriction from the advantages of trading with the Americans and French. The government mercantilist policy with its trade monopolies overlooked New Mexicans' need for ready currency to purchase essential tools and supplies. Mexican merchants, particularly those from Chihuahua, amassed profits because they had ready cash and controlled the markets. New Mexican dependence on Spain was guaranteed by the complex monetary system that handicapped the settlers. Many New Mexicans were forced to pledge crops years ahead to purchase goods because of the extreme shortage of cash.

Pino warned the Spanish government of the problems it was creating, but his presentation to the Cortes produced no immediate benefits. In fact, it is unlikely that the liberal Spanish government would have been interested in, or able to address, problems in so peripheral a region. At any rate the restoration of the Bourbon king in 1814 temporarily set aside liberal reforms, and it would be seven more years before the Mexican territory would be free of Spain.

On the eve of the revolution (1821), after more than two centuries of colonial rule, conditions had not changed, and New Mexico remained remote and destitute. The advent of political independence raised expectations and led its citizens to be more adamant in their frequent requests for government assistance. However, nearly a decade later, major problems were still unsolved, and aid had not materialized. New Mexicans searched for economic freedom elsewhere.

TWO

Poverty and Neglect

Sin dinero no hay tropas y faltando éstas está fuera de duda que peligra mi provincia. . . . No han faltado disidentes malvados que en mi provincia andan diseminando la especie de que le estaría mejor agregarse a los Estados Unidos del Norte.[1]

Without money there are no troops, and without them there is no doubt that my province is in danger. . . . There have been some wicked dissidents who in my province are spreading rumors that it would be better for it [my province] to join the United States.

JOSÉ RAFAEL ALARID, 1824

If New Mexicans in 1821 anticipated that the new Mexican government would address the concerns voiced by Pedro Bautista Pino during the previous decade, they were disappointed. Political freedom produced greater political autonomy, and autonomy was welcome, but it did not solve the major socioeconomic problems affecting the territory.[2] Local officials and leading citizens, like José Rafael Alarid, repeatedly requested authorities in Mexico City to furnish the territory adequate resources to halt its deterioration. Discontent was common during the first two decades after Independence and was not limited to New Mexico. Editorials in Chihuahuan newspapers lamented the government's lack of concern with the frontier provinces.[3]

Unfortunately the turmoil and instability common during the early decades of the republic did not allow the central administration to respond. Settlers along Mexico's northern frontier came to expect little from their government, except ill-suited laws, excessive regulations, and constant demands for additional revenue. Neglect was not limited to New Mexico, but the great distance between the capital and Santa Fe contributed to poor communication and growing apprehension and mistrust.

New Mexico's disappointment with Mexican officials is understandable, but so is the behavior of the central government as Mexico experienced a very violent and traumatic period. The presidency changed hands forty-nine times between 1824 and 1857. Equally important was the fact that by 1821 the whole country's economy was in ruins. Prosperity had always depended upon the mining industry, and during the long struggle for independence (1810–21) the production of silver had declined dramatically — according to some accounts more than 90 percent. Machinery had been wrecked and thrown down the mine shafts. The shorings had been pulled out when wood was needed. The abandoned mines soon filled with water that rotted timbers and collapsed tunnels, making mining impossible without extensive rehabilitation.[4] Capital, which was needed to resume production, was scarce.[5]

In 1821 the textile industry, producer of Mexico's most important manufacture, was on the verge of collapse, and the adoption of free trade threatened its extinction. Lack of modern transportation also contributed to the crisis. The cost of hauling cotton-mill machinery from Veracruz to Mexico City equaled the original price of the equipment in England. The expense of sending raw cotton from the coastal regions to Guadalajara was so high that the textile industry there faltered. Transportation costs also made it unprofitable to send the finished products to distant markets.[6]

The leaders of the independence movement enthusiastically supported economic liberalism, but the "free trade" policies they adopted produced few changes. In most cases they continued "quasi-mercantilist" practices established by Spanish colonial administrations. Most of the new statutes imposed high customs duties, and a profusion of internal taxes discouraged the movement of goods. State officials, hungering for additional revenues, invented "new tax horrors of their own."[7] Furthermore, economic policies changed often, reflecting an ambiguous attitude toward protectionism. The 1821 tariff, which went into effect in 1822, was hailed as a prime example of liberalism, but it placed heavy taxes on numerous products and excluded altogether trade in tobacco, hams, bacon, salt, tallow, cotton yarn, ready-made clothing, blankets, lace, skins, worked leather, wood, and bricks. At the same time the Mexican Congress appealed to the local populations for additional funds.[8]

Total import charges were quite high — 25 percent import duty, 1.5 percent consulado, 3.12 percent *avería*, and 15 percent *derecho de internación* (internation duty) (the tax on imports that replaced the alcabala).[9] Many states were dissatisfied with these rates, so the central government enacted new regulations in December 1824. It added foods, liquors, hides, worked metal, many fabric cloths, and clay crockery to the list, as well as the *derecho*

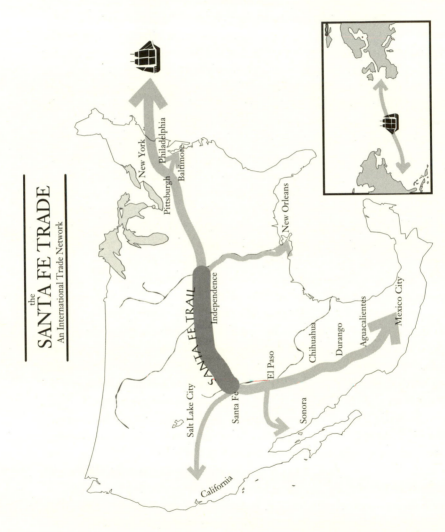

THE SANTA FE TRAIL: PART OF AN INTERNATIONAL TRADE NETWORK

de consumo, a 3-percent charge states levied on goods consumed within their boundaries. Exports could go out free, except for gold and silver objects, which were taxed 2–3.5 percent.[10] A new tariff schedule, ratified on 16 November 1827, imposed *ad valorem* (levied according to assessed value) duties of 40 percent on all articles, except some fifty-six that were prohibited, but this did not appreciably alter the general picture. By 1829 the government restored restrictions once again with a congressional decree prohibiting the importation of foreign goods that competed with artisan industries. In 1832 new calls were made for the reinstitution of prohibitions, but this did not happen until 1838. The constitutional law of 1843 included another rigid prohibitionist clause — no articles harmful to the national industry could be imported without the prior approval of two-thirds of the departmental assemblies.[11]

Foreigners were largely unaware of these regulations when they began trading with New Mexicans. Captain William Becknell of Missouri "opened" the Santa Fe Trail late in 1821, but he had little knowledge of the Mexican economic system. Becknell, accompanied by five associates, set out to trade with the Indians and go to Santa Fe. Although his party carried only a small amount of merchandise, the Americans were able to realize handsome profits.[12]

Becknell's account of his trip encouraged others to venture west. This decision made economic sense as foreigners were as eager to sell as New Mexicans were to buy. After 1821 American, French, and British traders introduced items previously not readily available in New Mexico and undersold the merchants from Chihuahua and Durango by perhaps two-thirds. Foreign goods were not only comparatively inexpensive, but as one New Mexican described them, "better merchandise than we had known."[13]

According to Max Moorhead, before the opening of the Santa Fe Trail the majority of New Mexicans went without any kind of clothing except leather and homespun, and without iron or steel tools of any kind. This was undoubtedly an exaggeration, yet there was not a single printing press in the province, and books and paper were extremely scarce. The trade changed conditions, and a few years after 1821 these items were available in large quantities as the market was flooded with textiles of almost every kind and implements for carpentry, housekeeping, farming, and hunting.[14]

The province of New Mexico, however, offered limited long-term opportunities. Cash was scarce and the population was small. Foreign merchants soon began to follow the advice of United States Indian agent R. Graham, who in 1824 recommended expanded trade to the south, particularly with "the more wealthy city of Mexico."[15] The following year

Missouri newspapers noted saturation of the market: "that country [New Mexico] cannot support the trade to the extent it is now carried on. Missouri alone can supply that country with twice the amount of goods it has the means to purchase."[16]

Soon foreigners were carrying large shipments to Chihuahua, Sonora, and Durango. Some, like Frenchman Charles Beaubien, sent the traditional assortment composed of a variety of items with a strong emphasis on textiles. In 1826 he hauled two thousand yards of various fabrics, but also five dozen mirrors, umbrellas, a hundred pairs of shoes, ribbons, buttons, leather combs, beads, and others—in all, thirty-eight different types of merchandise. In the same year, William Wilson carried a type of shipment that would become the norm among big traders: nineteen hundred yards of *manta* (coarse, cotton fabric) and *indiana* (calico), and twelve hats—only three types of goods. During the 1830s the variety of merchandise remained relatively low, but the size of the shipments increased dramatically. However, there were exceptions. For example, in 1831 James Harrison imported thirty thousand yards of cloth, close to 150 dozen shoes, twenty-two dozen socks, silk, scarves, ribbons, combs, hairpieces, mirrors, hairpins, parasols, lace, belts, thread, knives, pocket knives, razors, snaps, saws, files, scissors, tin boxes, soap boxes, inkstands, ink, stoneware, crystal, shawls, threads for sewing and embroidery, thimbles, needles, paper, cinnamon, and many other items.[17]

The trip to the interior provinces opened richer markets, yet it required additional encounters with customs officials. Most American traders, like Josiah Gregg and James Webb, eager to make quick and large profits, bitterly complained about the unfairness of the high import duties. The rates, however, appear to have been within the limits established by the current Mexican laws. Through the 1820s they were quite consistent—15 percent derecho de internación and 3 percent derecho de consumo. What Americans were unable or unwilling to understand were the periodic changes in the assessments and in the number and types of excluded items.[18]

There were reasons for the rates and the policies. The entire financial structure of the Mexican republic was dependent on income from foreign trade. Between 1821 and 1834, no new tax was levied on income, personal property, or real estate. Historians believe that this policy meant to diffuse discontent with the central government and promote political stability. Mexican import duties were supposedly high enough to produce sufficient revenues and low enough to discourage contraband.[19] In New Mexico they did neither. The province never made substantial contributions to the national treasury, and smuggling became widespread among all social groups.

Foreign businessmen complained about duties that reached 100 percent of invoice prices, and the local population and even public officials often helped them circumvent the encumbrances that Mexican law established.[20]

Throughout the period 1821–46, Mexican authorities continued to enact trade regulations that were difficult to enforce and required considerable administrative skills. Even if compliance had been feasible, the government at Santa Fe did not have the resources or the educated personnel necessary to enforce complex and ever-changing laws and regulations. For example, there were eight different types of wine identified in the tariff of 1822, and each one was assigned a different duty; it would have been difficult enough for custom officials to enforce such a variety of duties had they been the same throughout the period, but both the duties assessed and the categories of wine changed periodically.[21]

In addition, the great distance and poor communications between Santa Fe and the rest of the country made compliance burdensome. For example, Mexican law placed restrictions on all the merchandise brought into any part of the country's territory and designated certain locations, such as Santa Fe, as customs houses or ports of entry. After 1825, when any foreign merchant decided to take goods from Santa Fe to the interior of Mexico he had to obtain a *guía* from the customs officials.[22] This was not a human guide, but a sort of mercantile passport bearing the place and date where it was issued, name and signature of the merchant, number of packages in the cargo, specification of which items were of foreign and which were of domestic origin, value of the merchandise, its destination, name of the person to whom it was consigned, and the number of days allowed for remitting certification of its final arrival. The guía was required not only on leaving the port of entry, but also when taking goods from one state to another and from one town to another within a state. Merchants had to carry the guías with them at all times, were not allowed to go anywhere but the locations specified on it, and could not deviate from major roads. If a trader was found straying from the major roads, his merchandise could be confiscated as contraband. He could be thrown in jail and fined up to a quarter of the value of the goods. The *tornaguía*, a certification that the merchandise had reached its proper destination, had to be endorsed by another official at the point where the merchandise was sold, and returned within a specified time to the port of entry. Failure to meet this requirement subjected the endorser to a forfeiture equal to the full amount of the duties on the consignment.

Beginning in 1826 local customs officials at Santa Fe kept *cuadernos* (notebooks) where they recorded most of the information from the guías issued. The cuadernos provide the most accurate account of the names of the merchants, muleteers, guarantors, the type and value of the goods traded south, and their destination. Some guías were not registered in the cuadernos. Many have been lost. Still, these documents are excellent sources for the study of commercial activities associated with the Santa Fe Trail before the Mexican War.[23]

By 1831 the customs house at Santa Fe began to log the foreign goods introduced into the New Mexican territory. These documents, called manifests, appear less regularly than guías, but they are good records of the merchandise that came over the Santa Fe Trail. In a few instances, it is possible to compare manifests with guías. For example, in July 1831 Samuel Parkman, an agent of Jedediah Smith, hauled forty-nine *cajones* (big boxes), *tercios* (bales, bundles), and *baúles* (trunks). Two months later he obtained a guía for thirty-one *fardos* (bundles), *cajas* (boxes), and baúles for sale in Sonora and Chihuahua.[24]

Trade regulations were complex enough, but authorities in Mexico City continued to issue additional directives increasing the responsibilities of customs officials. A statute enacted in August 1822 ordered the maritime customs houses to communicate regularly with their terrestrial counterparts, providing them with lists of the guías issued to traders going in their direction. Customs houses had to keep one another informed of the fate of the merchandise, and equal attention had to be paid to the tornaguías. Customs officials were to maintain regular correspondence with each other, to read and constantly update the cuaderno de guías, and to note any discrepancies or failures to report the fate of every shipment of merchandise. Even if communications had been much better, it would have been difficult for New Mexican authorities to follow the dictates of such laws.[25]

The central government not only imposed an increase in the bureaucratic burden, but also solicited additional revenues, periodically at first, but almost on a regular basis as the century progressed. Identified by a variety of names, *subscripción voluntaria* (voluntary subscription), *préstamo forzoso* (forced loan), and *arbitrio extraordinario* (extraordinary excise tax), these unexpected levies became commonplace. The local population, which in most cases was unable or unwilling to pay, greatly resented them.[26]

New Mexican authorities repeatedly attempted to apprise officials in Mexico City of the gravity of the economic situation in the province and their inability to meet demands for additional funds. In 1821 Felipe González, the alcalde from Taos, explained to Governor Facundo Melgares that he had been unable to collect the required revenues for the subscripción voluntaria. After apologizing for having raised only four pesos, he noted that "the misery of these people reaches such a degree that I know that they have started to feed themselves with cow hides."[27]

Most New Mexicans were unable to pay, but some of their reluctance stemmed from their failure to understand the reasons for the levies, and they questioned the purpose of the unscheduled assessments. An 1825 letter addressed to *Alcalde Interino* (provisional mayor) Pablo García excused the people for not raising a stipulated sum because they were so poor they were having a hard time paying even the tithe. The letter added that the citizens "wonder what the purpose of these frequent contributions is."[28]

Unscheduled subsidies became the norm. In 1829 acting Governor José Antonio Chávez ordered all those likely to have personal assets worth 1,000 pesos or more to submit a sworn statement listing what they owned and the income produced by their holdings.[29] The declarations that survive indicate that nobody possessed enough property to pay this newly imposed tribute, although it is impossible to know if the ricos provided the governor with accurate lists of all their property.

In November 1835 the government established another subsidio extraordinario on those who owned real estate. The amount was based on the assessment of the land, but the documents show neither the size of the payments nor the extent of the compliance.[30] As additional requests for revenue became more common, resentment grew that probably contributed to the revolt of 1837, which led to the assassination of Albino Pérez, the governor of New Mexico at the time. In May 1837 Pérez had insisted that the province meet the 5,000-peso quota, which he felt the province could easily raise. Unfortunately only 3,600 pesos had been collected up to that time, and the governor admonished the alcaldes to ensure that all persons who did not pay fulfill their obligation in cash within twenty-four hours. No document records the reaction of the local population to this order, but even the wealthiest men in the province claimed to have trouble meeting the quotas set by the government. It is doubtful that Pérez's decision increased his popularity, and two months after this letter the governor was killed.[31]

In spite of the increasing number of duties placed on merchandise, chronic shortages of funds for the operation of the provincial government continued. Authorities in New Mexico were uneasy since they could not make even the payments disposed by the laws, such as salaries of public employees, pensions to widows and orphans, and, more importantly, the troops' wages.[32] On 31 August 1836, *escribiente* (scribe) Francisco Troncoso received ninety-nine pesos in back pay. His salary was fifteen pesos per month, but like many other officials, he had been forced to wait to collect his meager wages.[33] Others suffered even greater neglect. In January 1836 José Miguel Tenorio wrote to Governor Albino Pérez complaining that he had not been paid for three years.[34] To satisfy such legitimate requests and the basic needs of the troops stationed at Santa Fe, officials were forced to resort to their own private resources or those of their supporters or associates. By 1836 leading New Mexicans were regularly lending money to the treasury, and requests for additional funds continued. In 1838 prominent Spanish merchant Manuel Alvarez requested a certification that the late Governor Pérez and other members of his administration had regularly borrowed money from foreign merchants in Santa Fe to cover the expenses of the government and their own.[35] To make matters worse New Mexico seldom received from higher authorities the revenues to which it was entitled. For example, in 1836 the territory was scheduled to collect 6,000 pesos from the Mexican government for military expenses, but somehow only 1,000 pesos was received.[36]

Lack of adequate resources had a profound impact on education and defense. Mexican authorities recognized the importance of educational reform and the need to stress elementary education. Governor Albino Pérez had blamed lack of concern for education as the principal ill affecting the territory and had proposed a plan to improve public education in Santa Fe.[37] However, poor economic conditions made it impossible to retain teachers. The problem was widespread throughout the territory, and surviving census data for El Paso, Cochití, Santa Cruz de la Cañada, and Albuquerque show an inadequate number of educators. Almost 27 percent (3,619) of the reported population (13,434) was between the ages of seven and sixteen. Only three teachers were listed for Albuquerque, which had 632 children in this category. One teacher took care of educating the 288 children at Cochití. Santa Cruz de la Cañada was more fortunate: it had six teachers to serve 966 students. In El Paso the ratio was similar: eight educators for 1,753 youngsters. The 1823 census of Santa Fe listed only three teachers.[38]

In 1826 strict school regulations were imposed, and the provincial deputies asked that funds be collected from the citizens to cover the expenses of establishing elementary educational facilities. Sparse documentation indicates that the population was to be divided into three groups: the first was to pay four pesos; the second, two pesos; and the third, one peso. Since nobody seemed to have any cash, payment was to be accepted in sheep or corn, if collected during harvest time.[39] Local leaders were aware of the need to improve education, yet few changes took place, and the regulations described above were not enforced.

Inadequate funds to help the settlers in their struggle against the Indians also caused apprehension. The number of soldiers stationed at the capital city steadily declined, and those who remained lacked weapons, ammunition, and adequate clothing. They policed the streets, protected the governor, escorted the traders' caravans into Santa Fe to prevent smuggling, and searched wagons for contraband, yet they were unable to assist the settlers in the escalating war against hostile tribes.[40] The militia, made up mostly of poor farmers and Pueblo Indians who served under their own officers at their own expense, had always borne the burden of defense. They provided their own weapons, horses, and mules. Participating in campaigns against the salvajes often resulted in physical injuries and major economic losses, since crops and flocks were not properly tended and were frequently damaged during their absence.[41]

Growing conflict characterized relations between settlers in northern Mexico and the surrounding tribes. Indian raids were frequent and often resulted in considerable property damage. Less often, they ended with injuries or death. These attacks had a major impact on New Mexican sheep raisers. In 1837 Juan Esteban Pino claimed that sheep exports at the beginning of the decade had amounted to more than a hundred thousand animals, but, due to the bitter struggle with surrounding Indians, this number had declined to forty thousand in 1836 and to less than twenty thousand the following year. There was some truth in Pino's statement. Large flocks needed fresh pastures and were often kept at a distance from the more heavily populated settlements. The Indians ransacked the areas where the herders tended the sheep and stole large numbers of animals with relative impunity. Such depredations led to a push eastward from the traditional Río Grande ranges onto the Plains beyond the Sandía and Manzano Mountains, but the Indians were not deterred. In 1842 Charles Bent reported that the Utes had driven off about eight thousand head of sheep and some four hundred head of cattle from an area near Cerro de la Gallina.[42]

After 1821, Indian hostilities increased because the impoverished Mexican government was unable to pay the annual annuities Spain had given the tribes to keep them at peace.[43] Furthermore, until 1821 the naciones bárbaras had been dependent upon the Spanish population for trade, but with the coming of foreigners they were able to obtain good guns and powder, which they used to plunder settlements and steal livestock, principally sheep. They traded these back to the Americans for more arms and munitions, as well as whiskey and other items. Mexico's failure to mend these broken alliances and to strengthen its military posture emboldened the Indians, who created havoc for several decades. Tension between New

Mexicans and foreigners escalated, with the former accusing the latter of urging the Indians to steal cattle and supplying them with weapons to carry out their forays. Violence erupted over contraband cases, mostly the result of discontent among the troops who were not receiving their salaries regularly.[44]

Upheaval resulting from Indian raids became frequent. In 1822 the Comanches entered the plaza at Taos and terrified the citizens. Assured of their strength, they acted cockily, taking three boys as hostages and finally returning them unharmed. They left after taking a few chickens and hens.[45] Alcalde Manuel Martínez described a similar incident that took place in Taos in September 1827.[46] The Navajos continually stole from every community. Sometimes the thefts turned into more violent raids, which led to reprisals.[47] During certain periods hostilities escalated, and brutal encounters became common. In 1829 the Navajos stole and killed cows and sheep, and in general kept the populations of Jemez, San Isidro, and Villa de la Cañada in constant terror.[48] At the same time the Utes were harassing settlers around Taos.[49] Documents show that 1829 was a particularly bad year, and a long letter exists criticizing the authorities for doing very little about Indian atrocities.[50] In 1831 complaints abounded about the Navajos, Kiowas, Comanches, and Pawnees. Jemez, Abiquiú, and San José del Vado were the prime targets of these attacks.[51] During the following year the Navajos, Apaches, and Comanches committed atrocities.[52]

In the spring of 1833, the rural militia of Río Arriba was called out to fight the Navajos. The same year, the *jefe político* (political leader) encouraged wealthy New Mexicans to join the campaign against the Indians. He reminded them that it would be beneficial for them and it would also encourage the participation of the less fortunate.[53] In 1836 major incidents disrupted relations between the settlers and the Navajos, but many New Mexicans still proved unwilling to contribute the animals necessary for campaigns against the Indians. Almost a decade later, the same problem persisted, and lack of support made it impossible for the local troops to strike at the tribes who were menacing local populations.[54]

There were no resources to strengthen the troops at Santa Fe or to help the local militia, who often reported for duty with arrows for weapons. Periodically, Mexican authorities tried to alleviate tension by granting limited concessions, as they did in 1832 when they allowed New Mexico to use treasury funds not already designated for a special purpose to cover the expenses of the troops. However, it is not clear how much money, if any, was in fact freed for the purpose.[55]

In spite of the mounting violence and conflict, the desire, or need, to

trade with the Indians persisted. Central authorities discouraged such activities, but the records show that, as in the eighteenth century, Hispanos
continued to be willing to risk legal action to barter with the salvajes. New
Mexicans obtained furs from the Utes, illegally sold them to the Americans,
and in return received merchandise that they sold back to the Indians for
more furs.[56] In May 1840 citizens of Río Arriba requested permission to
exchange goods with the Comanches, "as has always been the style." Settlers at Socorro traded with the Apaches and those at Abiquiú did the same
with individual Utes through the 1840s, a decade characterized by hostility
and violent confrontations.[57]

Local leaders were quite aware of the problems affecting their province
and demanded action from the central government. In 1824 José Rafael
Alarid, New Mexico deputy to the Mexican Congress, wrote a bitter letter
to authorities in the capital city. He complained about the poverty affecting
the province and requested funds from the tithe to pay for the presidial
company and the public schools. Alarid believed that it was essential to
cover the 200-peso deficit of the troops stationed at Santa Fe because
"without money there are no troops, and without them there is no doubt
that my province is in danger."[58]

His letter also included a veiled threat, an indication that New Mexicans
were becoming impatient and expected the government to address their
concerns: "There have been some wicked dissidents who in my province
are spreading rumors that it would be better for it [my province] to join the
United States."[59] Mexico City officials appear to have acknowledged the
threat because less than three weeks later they authorized the use of revenues from state monopolies to pay for troops and public education if the
funds derived from the tithe were insufficient.[60]

Unfortunately the situation did not improve, and leading New Mexicans
wrote again in January 1825 complaining about the lack of an efficient
judicial system, the need for a jail, and the deplorable condition of the
educational system.[61] Nothing was done, and the complaints continued. In
1829 Juan Esteban Pino drafted a letter describing the problems and needs
of the province. He requested permission to establish *cátedras* (college-level
classes) in Spanish, Latin grammar, and philosophy to allow citizens to
attend major universities and become better able to discharge political,
civil, ecclesiastic, and military jobs.[62] There is no record of any reply.

In 1829 Jesús María Alarid, member of one of New Mexico's leading
families, vehemently responded to the ban on foreign goods that competed
with artisan industries. He admonished authorities in Mexico City for their
failure to understand that such a law would produce much hardship on the

New Mexican population who would have to travel to Chihuahua or Durango to obtain the necessary merchandise. He stressed that such trips would be harmful, for not only would they affect the local families, but they would also result in a reduced number of agricultural workers and available militiamen. Alarid continued that the excessive monopoly of the merchants from Chihuahua and Durango impeded the development of the area. He also noted that American merchants left in the territory at least a third of the merchandise they introduced and they employed many of the local citizens and paid them much more than they could normally earn. He finally requested that the central government help to establish textile industries in New Mexico, particularly for the manufacture of cotton and woolen fabrics. He concluded by pleading that New Mexico be granted the exclusive right of trading with the Americans.[63]

Grievances continued throughout the 1830s.[64] In 1831 several ayuntamientos supported a plan proposed by Juan Esteban Pino, Juan Felipe Ortiz, and Francisco Baca to make a new state out of New Mexico.[65] After describing the economic and personal sacrifices made by New Mexicans for many years, the authors proposed that the territory be transformed into a free and sovereign state to be called Hidalgo. They suggested a fifteen-year period during which the state would keep all the import duties paid by foreign traders, and recommended that a garrison of at least five hundred men be established near the Río Colorado. Finally, they requested that the new military command be independent from Chihuahua.[66]

In 1837 Juan Esteban Pino once again addressed the authorities. Speaking on his behalf and for the "other capitalists in the territory," he officially petitioned for the extension of the exemption from paying the alcabala on "efectos y frutos de producción natural e industria de este país" (local effects and fruits from the natural production and industry of this country). Most of the missive, however, focused on the damage the Indian raids had caused and the need for the territory to receive some material assistance from the central government.[67]

New Mexico was not alone in seeking help from authorities in Mexico City. Editors of the Chihuahua newspaper *El Fanal* shared similar concerns. They bitterly resented the lack of support from the central government in their struggle against the Apaches. *El Fanal* expressed feelings analogous to those of José Rafael Alarid: "For Chihuahua to survive it would be necessary to sever their ties to the Mexican nation and join the United States. That would be the only way to escape the deplorable conditions produced by the war with the gentiles and the neglect of the federal government."[68]

Mexico was too embroiled in its own problems to attend to those of New

Mexicans, however. By 1821 its silver-mining economy was in ruins, and textile manufacturing was on the verge of collapse. Capital disappeared as many took their fortunes back to Spain. Trade-hindering taxes increased. American traders realized generous profits from selling a great variety of higher-quality goods at prices up to two-thirds less than those charged by Mexican merchants. The financial structure of Mexico depended on income from foreign trade, and duties often equaled the invoice price of goods. Not surprisingly, smuggling became the means of survival for many settlers, further weakening the Mexican government.

Officials in Mexico City were unable to address the mounting discontent among the people in the northern provinces and failed to dispel the conviction expressed by the editors of *El Fanal* that "the government does not pay as much attention to the edges of the Republic as to its center."[69] Between 1821 and 1846 most New Mexicans remained destitute and continued to search for ways to improve their circumstances. Although they took advantage of the economic opportunities the Santa Fe trade offered, they preserved the patterns of trade of their ancestors. At the same time, wealthy local merchants developed strong economic relations with United States exporters, wholesalers, and bankers, establishing mercantile capitalism in the territory. New Mexico was politically still a part of Mexico, but it was slowly becoming dependent on the United States.[70]

THREE

Going Down the Royal Road

The trade to the South constitutes a very important branch of the commerce of the country, in which foreigners, as well as natives are constantly embarking.[1]

JOSIAH GREGG, *Commerce of the Prairies*

Economic dependence on the United States did not come about quickly. The opening of the Santa Fe Trail did not immediately revolutionize conditions in New Mexico, and the appearance of fine and inexpensive merchandise did not result in a stampede of Hispanos traveling east to purchase goods in the United States.[2] On the contrary, for more than a decade the majority of New Mexico's merchants maintained their traditional patterns of trade.

Such a strategy made sense in view of the local economic conditions. New Mexico had neither the population nor the resources to absorb the large amount of merchandise that foreigners were freighting across the Plains. Hard currency was extremely scarce. By 1825 Missouri traders were aware of saturation in the Santa Fe market, and on 25 January the *Franklin Intelligencer* noted that, sales being "effected very slowly," the goods "now on the way to that country [New Mexico] together with what are already there, will be more than adequate to the demand."[3]

During the following year Americans and other foreigners began to venture down the Royal Road, into the heart of the Mexican territory, looking for more profitable outlets for their goods.[4] The closest markets were in the province of Nueva Vizcaya, where Durango and Chihuahua were located. With a population of 232,000 (almost six times the forty thousand reported for New Mexico) and only sixty thousand of the people listed as Indians (almost 50 percent of the New Mexicans were classified in that category), rich mining operations that supported approximately thirty smelters, and a mint that stamped out more than 500,000 pesos worth of coins a year,

Nueva Vizcaya became a powerful magnet for foreign merchants and continued to attract growing numbers of New Mexican traders.[5]

The excess of foreign goods in Santa Fe relieved New Mexicans from their dependence on Mexican merchants. They now had access to merchandise of higher quality and cheaper price than that available in Chihuahua and other northern Mexican towns; they were no longer forced to accept the expensive and crude products they had been buying for decades, and they could demand better prices for their local goods and even obtain payment in cash. Although a few New Mexicans occasionally hauled foreign effects, the majority continued to use the Royal Road to Mexico City to transport sheep and local manufactures. American and foreign traders traveled down the Camino Real, but specialized in different merchandise.[6]

The nearly seventeen hundred miles separating Santa Fe and Mexico City were not as formidable an obstacle as the hardships of the trip. The terrain was rugged, the Indian threat was always present, and scarce water was found most often in "fetid springs or pools . . . only rendered tolerable by necessity." Historian Albert Bork remarked that the character of the territory between Missouri and New Mexico was ideal compared to the extremely difficult nature of the roads leading to the interior of Mexico.[7]

New Mexican traders seldom traveled alone. They formed caravans, as had been done on the Camino Real since the sixteenth century, to fend off robbers, marauders, and Indians. Local officials announced in advance the departure of the convoys with the intent of gathering a group respectable enough in size to discourage possible attacks. George Gibson noted that Mexicans traveled in large parties and were armed, "as well as Mexicans usually are."[8] Gregg believed that being armed to the teeth was a necessary precaution on the road to Chihuahua. New Mexican caravans along the Old Spanish Trail, which linked Santa Fe with southern California, however, carried relatively few firearms, most of which were in bad condition, the bulk of their weapons being bows and arrows.[9] Most merchants began their trip south during August or September. More than 75 percent of all guías (359) were issued during these months. In certain years (1836, 1837, 1839, and 1840) large groups also left in October (15 percent). A few ventured south during the winter (3.26 percent), but almost nobody journeyed in the spring.[10]

Large caravans were the rule. It is not clear if they moved in a single file, but they probably extended for a considerable distance, taking at least a day or two to pass through any specific location. In August 1835, twenty-three merchants traveled south; twenty-one went two years later. During 1838,

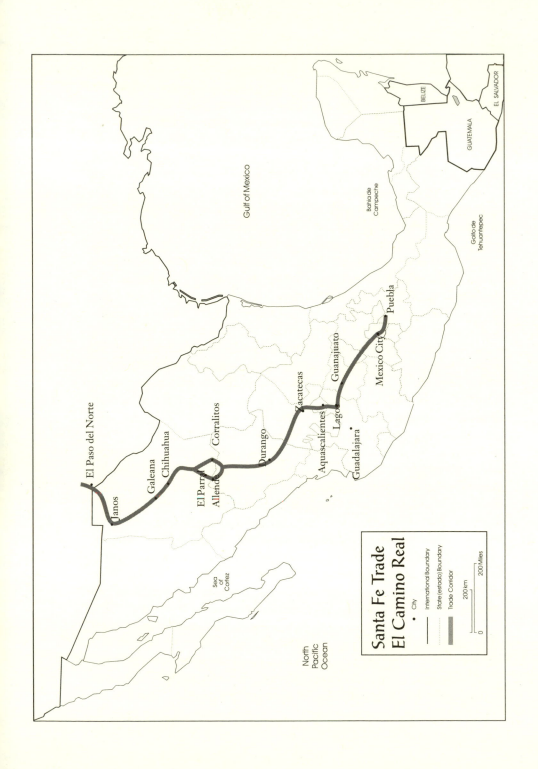

Santa Fe Trade
El Camino Real

● City
——— International Boundary
·········· State (estado) Boundary
▬▬▬ Trade Corridor

200 km
0   200 Miles

El Paso del Norte

Janos

Galeana

Chihuahua

Corralitos

El Parral
Allende

Durango

Zacatecas

Aquascalientes

Lagos

Guanajuato

Guadalajara

Mexico City

Puebla

Gulf of Mexico

Bahía de
Campeche

Golfo de
Tehuantepec

BELIZE

GUATEMALA

EL SALVADOR

North
Pacific
Ocean

Sea
of
Cortez

nineteen left in August, twelve in September, and eleven in October. The year 1839 saw considerable activity, with twenty-one trips in August, thirty-one in September, fifteen in October, and four in November. The same was true of 1843, when thirty-three merchants left in August, twenty-four in September, twelve in October, and two in November. The following year also witnessed significant movement, with thirty-one merchants leaving between 3 and 9 September, carrying 271 bundles. During two weeks in August 1840, thirty-eight New Mexican merchants sent 26,156 sheep, three carts with foreign merchandise, seventy pounds of wool, twenty-four *fanegas* (grain measure of about 1.6 bushels) of pinyon, and 833 bundles of domestic merchandise toward the interior of Mexico.[11]

Hundreds of mules were used to carry these goods, and a fairly substantial number of animals (either mules or horses) was necessary for the *arrieros* (muleteers), *conductores* (conductors), and *peones* (laborers) who accompanied the loads. New Mexicans also relied on ox carts to haul merchandise, but they appear to have been less popular than mules.[12]

A journey from Santa Fe to Chihuahua normally lasted close to forty days, as it was seldom possible to average more than fifteen miles per day. Even under ideal circumstances, it took twenty-six days for a letter mailed in Santa Fe to reach Chihuahua and forty more days for it to arrive at Mexico City.[13] Not only was the trip long and dangerous, it offered few amenities. Taverns with general accommodations were uncommon. However, the majority of traders had no need for such luxuries. Most of the conductores and the arrieros camped out with their *atajos* (strings) of pack mules. They often traveled with their cooks and *cantinas* (large wallets or leather boxes) filled with provisions. On top of these canteens they lashed a mattress and all the other "fixings" for bed furniture.[14] Travelers were astonished to see how little they managed to live upon. Gibson noted that they used every part of a hog or cow, including head, feet, and entrails. Their only meal — a small piece of meat, *chile colorado*, beans, and tortillas — lasted for twenty-four hours except for a cup of chocolate and a piece of bread.[15]

Hispanos had an excellent reputation as horsemen and muleteers. After watching two Mexicans lance two buffalos to death, Philip St. George Cooke reluctantly admitted that they were fine riders and "would be formidable as lancers."[16] Gregg marveled at the dexterity and skill with which they harnessed and adjusted packs of merchandise: "Half a dozen [men] usually suffice for 40 or 50 mules. Two men are always engaged at a time in the dispatch of each animal, and rarely occupy five minutes in the complete adjustment of his *aparejo* (pack saddle) and *carga* (load)."[17] David Lavender provided one of their most colorful descriptions:

> Ludicrous-looking they were. Conical hats covered with oilcloth peaked above their hair. Their dusky heads were thrust through holes in coarse, bright-hued blankets, and their leather pantaloons were split down the sides, revealing a loose pair of cotton drawers beneath. Enormous spur rowels jingled on their heels; their saddles bore sweeping leather skirts and wooden stirrups three inches broad.[18]

Experienced travelers suggested that Mexicans be used as teamsters for they "can catch up and roll up in half the time the average person does."[19] Traders relied on a mule pack system, which by the nineteenth century had become highly sophisticated, efficient, and remarkably well suited to conditions in the Mexican territory. The United States Army eventually adopted Mexican techniques for loading, names for the equipment, and uses of the mule (see fig. 4).[20]

The Mexican mule, although short in stature, had been bred exclusively for pack service. The average animal weighed between seven hundred and eight hundred pounds and could carry half its own weight. In addition to this incredible strength (much greater than that of a horse or ox), mules were able to travel over long distances and in areas where forage and water were scarce. Their physical ability and small hooves were well suited to the region's rugged terrain, and the Mexican mules became famous for a remarkable blend of physical characteristics, stamina, and intelligence. They were a highly prized asset in many areas of the western United States.[21]

In addition to the mule pack system, New Mexican traders used equipment that was designed for carrying heavy loads. The aparejo, the central piece of gear, was described by an expert packer from the Hudson's Bay Company as "nearer to what I consider to perfection in a pack saddle, than any other form of pack saddle yet invented."[22] The superiority of the aparejo stemmed from its capacity to carry heavy, odd-sized items safely over long distances without injuring the animal. It consisted of two leather bags stuffed with dried grass and joined at the top to form an arch or gable. It was designed to resist condensation and distribute the weight over the mule's rib cage and away from its back. New Mexicans have been known to custom-fit each mule with its own aparejo. Once fitted, pack saddles were not switched between animals for fear of injuring a loaded mule's back, or front or rear quarters. To identify each aparejo, packers embroidered a telltale sign on the *corona* (a blanket used with the saddle). Often the *grupera* (a leather band attached to the rear of the aparejo that prevented the load from shifting forward) was also distinctively sewn or inlaid with cut Mexican silver coins.[23]

The mules and the equipment were important, but they would have had little impact without men skilled in the task of packing. By the 1850s "Mexicans" represented the majority of packers in most of the West and were always in demand. Packers required a variety of skills. They had to secure loads with intricate knots, splices, and hitches; act as veterinarians and blacksmiths (Gregg marveled at their speed and efficiency in shoeing mules); estimate the safe carrying capacity of a mule; identify and treat an animal suffering from an improperly balanced load without detaining others; and they had to govern the length of the day's trip so as to stop at some meadow or creek bottom that would provide good grass for the animals. Packers also had to be able to lift heavy loads and "accomplish marvels with the axe, a screw key and a young sapling for a lever."[24] In spite of their superior skills, native New Mexicans were employed as teamsters mostly by other New Mexicans. When they were hired by foreigners, they received only $15.00 per month, roughly half of the $25.00 to $30.00 that their Anglo-American colleagues were paid.[25]

Guías reveal that packers used a series of terms to identify the type and size of the shipments and possibly their shape. The one most commonly used to describe loads of foreign merchandise was *tercio*. Domestic goods were most often carried in *bultos*, although sometimes they were hauled in tercios. Other loads were *cajones, fardos, baúles,* and *piezas* (pieces).[26]

Surviving guías, tornaguías, and *pases* (passes) provide the best and most complete documentation for identifying those involved in the trade with the interior of Mexico and the United States until the Mexican War. The information is very valuable, but it is marred by omissions and errors, and the officials themselves admitted that scribes often made mistakes.[27]

Ownership is not always clear. The guías were supposed to make a distinction between the proprietor and the conductor of the load, but in several cases the information is incorrect or missing. For example, a guía issued in 1838 lists Antonio Ballejos as the owner and Juan Otero as the conductor. An examination of the rest of the guías for that and following years reveals that Juan Otero probably owned the merchandise and that Ballejos was the conductor of the load. This is not the only case with inaccurate information. In November 1843 the cuaderno de guías indicated that Mariano Lucero took seven piezas of domestic goods to Chihuahua and Sonora as owner; however, the surviving guía shows Manuel Cisneros as the owner. There is not enough evidence to identify either as the true owner of that load.[28] On 26 August 1843 José Armijo received guías 18 and 19. They both indicate the same amount and value of merchandise (fourteen bultos valued at 133 pesos 2 reales); while a coincidence is possible, it is more likely that they reflect an error on the part of the scribe in charge of the cuaderno de guías.[29]

Additional confusion stems from the inability to differentiate between individuals. In 1843 Ambrosio Armijo is listed as the owner of three loads that left Santa Fe on 31 August, 1 November, and 10 November. The documents do not indicate whether a conductor accompanied any of these. It would have been impossible for Armijo to have completed three trips between August and November; it is likely that if he went to Mexico at all, he accompanied the later shipment, which included close to 9,000 pesos worth of foreign merchandise. Of course, there may have been be more than one Ambrosio Armijo operating at the same time. The records indicate that in 1843 Ambrosio Armijo hauled a substantial amount of foreign goods (valued at more than 8,200 pesos); it is highly unlikely that the same individual would have bothered to carry two shipments of domestic goods valued at 155 pesos and 403 pesos 4 reales, respectively, in 1845.[30] The identities of other traders are also unclear. Is Tomás Baca the same man as Francisco Tomás Baca? Is the Vicente Baca who traveled in 1829 and 1830 the same individual who journeyed south in 1841? Did Francisco García go down in 1835 and 1844? Is José Manuel Montaño the same man as José Montaño?[31]

Since New Mexicans were exempt from obtaining guías for local products until 1830, it is impossible to identify the amount, type, and value of the merchandise taken to Mexico before that year. Nevertheless, the surviving documents clearly indicate that the number of Hispano shipments increased steadily after 1830, and between 1835 and 1845 almost five hundred Hispano traders sent merchandise south (see table 1).[32]

New Mexicans' favorite destination was Chihuahua, with 349 traders listing the capital of Nueva Vizcaya as one end point of their trip. Durango and Sonora also attracted many merchants, with 221 and 175 mentions respectively. Other popular targets were Aguas Calientes, El Paso, Mexico City, Sinaloa, Guanajuato, Guadalajara, Allende, San Juan de los Lagos, Puebla, California, Jesús María, Puebla, Michoacán, and Zacatecas (see fig. 5). In certain cases specific destinations were not indicated. Instead the guías included comments such as "ferias" (fairs), "donde me convenga" (where it suits me), "otros puntos en el camino" (other points along the road), "provincias internas" (internal provinces), and others. Hispanos also did business in places like Hermosillo and Guaymas. While New Mexican

TABLE I

Trips to the Mexican Territory Undertaken by Hispanic Traders

Year	Number of Trips
1826	2
1827	1
1828	4
1829	0
1830	2
1831	7
1832	6
1833	1
1834	5
1835	31
1836	15
1837	28
1838	63
1839	78
1840	75
1841	[a]14
1842	[b]1
1843	76
1844	90
1845	25

[a]The decline is due to the temporary closure of the customs house at Santa Fe.
[b]The extremely low number for 1842 could have been caused by the aftermath of the Texan Santa Fe Expedition, but it also reflects the fact that a large portion of the cuaderno de guías for that year was lost.

guías never identified these particular communities as the destination of any shipment, documents issued in these communities indicate that New Mexicans bought loads of much-needed iron and steel there.[33]

All social classes participated in the trade down the Camino Real. More than three hundred individuals were listed as owners of merchandise. Some, like Agapito Albo, José Cordero, Francisco Elguea, and Manuel Escudero, were from the internal provinces, but the majority were New Mexicans. As Licenciado Antonio Barreiro remarked, the ricos (the wealthy settlers and political leaders of the province), mostly from the Río Abajo area, transported large numbers of often already consigned wethers and efectos del país; the less well-to-do hauled mostly hides, nuts, and a variety of local manufactures. Barreiro also noted that although a few individuals monopolized the sheep trade, even the middle and lowest classes benefited from the sale of hides and coarse woolen goods in Mexico's interior markets.[34]

His observations were accurate. The guías indicate that relatively few merchants sent large flocks of sheep to Mexico — only twenty-eight owners

TABLE 2

Destinations of Hispano Merchants Traveling to the Mexican Territory

Destination	Number of Trips
Abrafuerte	1
Aguas Calientes	14
Allende	4
California	4
Corralitos	1
Chihuahua	349
Durango	221
El Parral	3
El Paso	58
Galeana	7
Guadalajara	8
Guanajuato	7
Janos	1
Jesús María	2
Mexico City	42
Michoacán	1
Puebla	4
San Juan de los Lagos	48
Sinaloa	10
Sonora	175
Tierra Caliente	5
Vizcaya	4
Zacatecas	47
Unspecified	10

from sixteen families participated in this activity.[35] Ownership was even more concentrated, because three families (Chávez, Otero, and Sandoval) controlled over 60 percent of the nearly four hundred thousand sheep valued at 200,000 pesos that were herded south. The largest shipments date from 1835 with close to a hundred thousand animals. Sizable herds also traveled in 1844 (53,700 sheep), 1843 (47,492 sheep), and in 1837 (44,921 sheep).

There were considerable yearly fluctuations in the number of animals, and only one shipment per year was recorded for 1831, 1833, 1834, and 1836. In spite of sporadic losses, sheep raising continued to be a mainstay of the economic base of the ricos. The *Missouri Republican* estimated that fifty thousand sheep would leave New Mexico for California in 1853. However, losses were quite common, and Aubry reported that a large number of sheep belonging to Ambrosio Armijo failed to reach the market in 1852.[36]

Barreiro's perceptions regarding the middle and lowest classes also appear correct, as even those with relatively limited resources participated in

TABLE 3

Merchandise Carried by Hispano Merchants into the Mexican Territory

Number of Loads (N=420)	Range in Value of Individual Loads	Total Value of Loads (pesos and cents)
Lowest quartile (*N*=105)	20 pesos–133 pesos 3 reales	9,580.38
Second quartile (*N*=105)	133 pesos 4 reales–234 pesos	18,610.95
Third quartile (*N*=105)	234 pesos–1,143 pesos 2 reales	46,811.63
Highest quartile (*N*=105)	1,170 pesos–26,474 pesos 7 reales	347,904.75
Total value of all the merchandise		422,907.71

the trade. The value of the majority of the shipments was very small (see table 3). More than a hundred merchants (close to 25 percent) carried less than 133 pesos worth of merchandise, and 251 merchants (more than 50 percent), less than 250 pesos worth. In 1839 three traders carried less than fifty pesos worth. The year before, Guadalupe Santillanes hauled domestic goods valued at 23 pesos 4 reales. The load was so small that it was not even recorded in the guía notebook.[37]

Purchases of iron and steel in Guaymas and Hermosillo provide a good example of the limited amount of capital required to engage in trade. On 5 November 1842, Antonio Griego left from Guaymas en route to New Mexico carrying seven quintales (910 pounds) of steel valued at seven pesos.[38] A week later (12 November) Rumaldo Baca stopped at Hermosillo to buy eighteen piezas of iron, steel, and domestic merchandise valued at 247 pesos. Antonio Martínez purchased ten piezas of iron, steel, and domestic manufactures assessed at 54 pesos 56 cents, also at Hermosillo. Two days later (23 November) Antonio Montaño left Hermosillo having entered with a guía issued in Santa Fe on 14 September. He had acquired ten piezas of steel, iron, and foreign merchandise for sixty-two pesos. Diego Romero probably took a small load of domestic merchandise, possibly to Hermosillo, where on 29 November he received a guía for 15,060 pounds of iron. Two weeks later he arrived at Sonora where he purchased four piezas of iron, steel, and domestic merchandise valued at 108 pesos 6 reales.[39] Even though the value of iron and steel was ridiculously low, apparently it made sense to bring such goods back because they were so scarce that traders are likely to have made enough profit from their sale.

New Mexicans (as opposed to foreigners and other Mexicans) were exempt from paying the alcabala on efectos del país, and this undoubtedly helped them to make these trips more profitable. Although the province had to make a request for this exemption every ten years, trading down the Royal Road was beneficial even for those who took small shipments south

TABLE 4

Merchandise Carried by Hispano Traders to the Mexican Territory, 1826–46

Type of Merchandise	Number of Loads	Percentage of Loads
Domestic merchandise	296	56.38
Foreign merchandise	79	15.05
Foreign and domestic merchandise	8	1.52
Sheep	61	11.62
Sheep and domestic merchandise	20	3.81
Other (metal goods)	2	0.38
No information	59	11.24
Total number of loads	525	100

because they were paid in specie.[40] By the late 1820s and 1830s Mexican silver production was on the rise, and New Mexicans could demand cash as payment for their products. Guías indicate that most of those traveling south from Santa Fe intended to exchange the merchandise for silver or coins. Unfortunately, very few documents indicate what they brought back.

The majority of New Mexican merchants who traveled south hauled efectos del país — coarse weavings like sayal, gerga, sarapes, frazadas, ponchos, and medias (socks, stockings). They also transported a variety of hides — gamuzas, cíbolos (buffalo robes), osos (bear skins), nutrias (beaver skins), and antas (elk hides) — and colchas, sombreros (hats), and rebozos (shawls). Some individuals or families appear to have specialized in specific types of merchandise. The Sandovals traded sheep; the Archuletas traded either domestic goods or sheep; Cristóbal and José Armijo always took efectos del país; others hauled mostly blankets. Most traders, however, tended to include a variety of items in their shipments, like the fourteen bultos Felipe Romero took to Chihuahua and Durango on 9 September 1838. In his load, assessed at only 161 pesos, he carried seventy-one buffalo hides, 163 blankets, 114 pairs of socks, four elk hides, six sarapes, one bed blanket, thirteen bedspreads, seven deer hides, and two bear skins (see table 4).[41]

Hauling domestic goods became more common with time as there was a dramatic increase in both the number and the percentage of individuals involved in the activity. Between 1826 and 1838, eighty-two traders traveled south, but between 1839 and 1845 their number expanded to 236. The size of the shipments also increased, although there is little information on the value of the majority of them.[42]

Many individuals participated in hauling merchandise to the interior of

TABLE 5

Trips to the Mexican Territory by Hispanic Merchants, 1826–46

Number of Trips	Merchants in this Category
1	214
1 (multiple loads)	246
2	29
3	22
4	12
5	3
6	2
7	1
8	2

Mexico. Surviving guías between 1826 and 1846 identify 531 owners and eighty conductores. The documents do not include any information on the peones, who probably comprised the single largest group of men engaged in the trade. It is also difficult to learn much about the traders who made only one trip (214), and even those who carried multiple loads in a single year (246) (see table 5). It is, however, possible to learn some details about those (71) who made more than one trip. Some, like Agapito Albo from El Paso, came to Santa Fe periodically to purchase foreign goods. In 1834 and 1839 he acquired close to 5,000 pesos worth of foreign effects. Another famous New Mexican trader was Manuel Armijo. He obtained fourteen guías between 1835 and 1845. In eight cases he sent sheep—a total of 34,916 animals. In all other instances, he shipped domestic manufactures under the care of a conductor, who in most cases appeared to be a relative.[43]

Some traders seem to have made a profit from the trade down the Camino Real. Francisco Tomás Baca made a number of trips. In 1835 he carried thirty-six pesos worth of merchandise and twenty-two hundred sheep for a total value of 1,136 pesos. The following year he took three thousand sheep assessed at a value of 1,500 pesos. In 1838 he hauled both merchandise and sheep for a total of 675 pesos. There is no record for 1839, but by 1840 he was able to take 2,498 pesos worth of domestic manufactures in seventy-five bultos, the highest amount and value of domestic merchandise carried into the interior of Mexico for which guías still exist.[44]

Santiago Flores was another trader involved in at least four trips. It appears that he was not the owner but the conductor of a large load of foreign merchandise valued at 5,837 pesos in 1844. However, it is likely that he owned the fifty tercios appraised at 297 pesos that he carried in 1841, and the seventeen bultos assessed at 491 pesos 4 reales that he took in 1844.

His seems to be another success story, as records from Moctezuma, Mexico, indicate that in 1845 he received a guía for fifty-five bultos of domestic effects and 900 pesos in cash for a total value of 1,390 pesos.[45]

Baca and Flores appear to have done well, but it is less clear how others fared. Eugenio Archuleta made four trips down the Royal Road between 1835 and 1843. His shipments included only domestic merchandise and, in one case, sheep, but it is not possible to estimate his profits nor a pattern of the size or value of shipments. In 1835 he carried eighteen tercios, but no value was given. In 1838 he carried eighteen bultos priced at 183 pesos. The next year he hauled almost twice as much—thirty-three tercios, with a value of 220 pesos and 5 cents. He next appears in the records in 1843 driving fourteen hundred sheep assessed at a value of 700 pesos and carrying twelve bultos of domestic merchandise valued at 161 pesos and 4 cents. It is not possible to say positively that Archuleta had dramatically increased his assets, however, because the sheep may have belonged to Tomás Baca. Baca was listed as the conductor but was in all likelihood also the owner of the sheep. Archuleta could have been herding Baca's sheep and at the same time carrying his own efectos.[46]

In 1838 Fernando Aragón received two guías for twenty tercios of domestic goods valued at approximately 200 pesos with the destinations Chihuahua and Sonora. He left on 24 October. Three months later he left Hermosillo with 451 pesos worth of merchandise. Even though the net profit was small, proportionately he made a substantial gain over the original investment, particularly since the expenses associated with such trips were small, and payments to peones were minimal at best. A year later (16 October 1839) Aragón obtained another guía for 402 pesos and 5 cents worth of goods. Unfortunately no information survives about his return trip. In October 1840 he went south again, but this time he took only 130 pesos and 5 cents worth of merchandise.[47]

Diego Gómez took four bultos valued at ninety pesos in 1840, six priced at 187 pesos in 1843, and six again in 1844 assessed at only seventy-eight pesos. Salvador López made trips in 1838 and 1840 carrying 159 and 317 pesos worth of goods respectively. José Dolores Durán traded exclusively efectos del país, but the number and value of his goods varied considerably—six bultos valued at ninety-four pesos in 1838, fifteen valued at 234 pesos in 1840, and eleven valued at 200 pesos in 1844. Another merchant who made four trips was Juan Miguel Mascarenas. Like many of the others, he specialized in local manufactures and carried small loads—six tercios in 1838, five piezas in 1839, eight tercios in 1843, and a similar small load in 1845. The value of his goods varied slightly, from eighty-three pesos in

1838 to 144 pesos in 1845. Diego and José Antonio Lucero both made two trips, but the latter specialized in foreign merchandise, although he could have been the conductor of goods belonging to either New Mexico's ricos or foreign merchants. Three other members of the Lucero family frequently carried effects to Mexico—Blas, Pedro Antonio, and Mariano. Pedro Antonio made four trips, while Blas and Mariano made three and two respectively. In each case, the size and value of the shipments varied only slightly.[48]

The guías identify others who were essential to the system—the conductors. They were in charge of carrying the shipments sent by those who were unable to travel or who could afford to pay someone to travel in their place. At least eighty individuals were so listed, although many others might have been omitted.[49] Leading the caravans appears to have provided valuable experience for the sons or younger relatives of wealthy merchants. In twenty-nine instances the conductors shared the last name of the owners, and it is probable that in other cases familial relations were involved. The frequent intermarriages of the elite make identification of the relationships between owners and conductors quite difficult.

Many conductors did double duty. They were in charge of shipments sent by others, but they also took their own loads. In 1838 Pedro Armijo hauled his merchandise to Sonora, but he was also listed as the conductor of a load belonging to Manuel Armijo. In 1845 Rumaldo Baca herded four thousand sheep belonging to José María Gutiérrez to Durango. At the same time he took a thousand wethers of his own to the same destination. Juan José Sánchez was the conductor of a cargo of foreign merchandise belonging to Gerardo Miranda that left Santa Fe for El Paso in 1839. At the same time he hauled two shipments of his own—one to El Paso and the other one to Galeana.[50]

Was there an opportunity for conductors to become owners? Although not frequent, such progressions seem to have occurred. In 1840 Jesús María Ortiz led two loads belonging to Juan Gutiérrez. Four years later he carried his own bundles of foreign merchandise to Chihuahua and Sonora. In 1837 José María Martínez herded sheep belonging to Pedro José Perea to Durango, but by 1843 he was able to haul fifteen bundles of his own domestic merchandise to Chihuahua, Durango, and Zacatecas.[51]

New Mexicans maintained their traditional direction of trade (north/south) throughout the 1830s, but at the same time (1830–46) they established a similar network of commercial relations with California along the Old Spanish Trail (Santa Fe to California by way of the Great Basin [see fig. 1]). The process started in 1829 when acting Governor José Antonio Chávez authorized a caravan, quite similar to those traveling down the Royal Road, under the command of Antonio Armijo, to secure mules in exchange for efectos del país. Armijo also kept track of the Indian tribes the caravan encountered on its way and the distance that separated the province of New Mexico from California. He believed it important for the government to protect and foster the commerce between the two territories. The journey must have been quite arduous as the party left Santa Fe on 7 November 1829 and didn't arrive at Mission San Gabriel until 31 January 1830.[52]

Only four guías survive that document similar trips to California, but caravans apparently went west on a yearly basis. Francisco Esteban Quintana left in 1839 with six bundles assessed at seventy-eight pesos. Juan Arce carried more valuable merchandise in two bundles in 1843. Two merchants traveled to California in 1844 — Francisco Frantes and Francisco Rael. The latter was probably among the first to drive sheep to California.[53]

The records of the 1847–48 caravan to California reveal many similarities with those traveling south. The merchandise consisted mostly of bulky efectos del país weighing eight thousand to ten thousand pounds carried by 150 to 160 mules. Between seventy and eighty men were owners of the effects, but apparently there were "as many [again] interested in the concern." Like that of those going south, the value of the goods was relatively low — the greatest amount of property owned by any one trader did not exceed 300 or 400 pesos.[54]

The California caravans continued traditional patterns of trade, but in the late 1830s a dramatic change took place — the wealthiest New Mexicans began to travel east, in the direction of St. Louis, New York, and Philadelphia, to purchase goods directly from major wholesalers. Dealing in foreign goods was not new. Starting in 1826 a few traders had taken foreign merchandise down the Camino Real (16 percent of all shipments included such goods). Eliseo Sánchez and Ramón García were the first for whom records exist. Sánchez left Santa Fe on 27 August 1826, and was issued two guías. He carried in all a substantial amount of foreign merchandise — valued at 3,065 pesos 5 reales 6 granos. García left a few days later (9 September) and took a smaller load (valued at 676 pesos 5 reales 6 granos).[55]

In all, only a few New Mexican merchants followed the example of Sánchez and García in hauling *efectos extranjeros* (foreign merchandise) to Mexico during this period — only thirty-two individuals participated in this activity between 1826 and 1838. Although it is not possible to establish the size and value of many of these loads, in those cases where the assessment was included, it was quite low, averaging only 343 pesos and 75 cents. In

several instances the documents indicate that local merchants had purchased the merchandise from foreigners living in New Mexico.[56]

However, wealthy New Mexicans continued to acquire foreign products
in the interior provinces of Mexico for resale in their territory. Although
the records documenting such purchases are very sporadic, and it is impossible to establish the number of individuals involved, the frequency of the
trips, or the amount and value of the goods procured, it is clear that some of
the ricos made significant purchases until the late 1830s.[57] It is possible that
in exchange for these purchases they were able to obtain advantageous
prices for their local products. Perhaps Mexican dealers were temporarily
able to compete with traders selling foreign merchandise in Santa Fe due to
the astronomical mark-ups local merchants paid in the province's capital.[58]

After 1838 a transformation took place. The number of New Mexican
merchants carrying foreign goods into the Mexican territory remained
stable, but their identity changed and the value of the average shipment
increased to 3,781 pesos, with seven individuals each carrying loads valued
at more than 15,000 pesos. The leading New Mexico traders gradually
invested a larger portion of their assets in such purchases, although they
also continued to ship traditional local merchandise to the interior provinces of Mexico. For example, in 1843 José Chávez sent a monumental
shipment of foreign goods to Durango, Zacatecas, and San Juan de los
Lagos — more than 160 bundles — yet the following year he still sent sheep
and local manufactures to Chihuahua and Lagos. His brother Mariano
followed a similar pattern. In 1844 he sent 177 pieces of foreign goods
assessed at a value of 26,474 pesos to Chihuahua, but at the same time his
trusted *mayordomo* (steward) Cristóbal García herded six thousand sheep to
Durango and Zacatecas. The Oteros did the same. They shifted emphasis
from domestic to foreign goods, but they still drove large flocks of sheep to
the interior of Mexico.[59]

Those who controlled the sheep trade dominated the sale of foreign
merchandise as well. Five families (Armijo, Chávez, Otero, Perea, and
Yrizarri) owned 81.68 percent (148,248 pesos) of the 181,492 pesos worth
of foreign goods listed in the guías. Some of these shipments were quite
impressive. In 1843 José Chávez remitted over 105,000 yards of *lienzo*
(linen), 48,700 yards of indiana, and more than ten thousand yards of assorted fabrics. In addition, his conductor also carried 250 dozen scarfs and
handkerchiefs, thirteen dozen hats, twenty-nine dozen pairs of stockings,
thirty-six gross of buttons, five dozen razors, one box of needles, three gross
of thimbles, seven mirrors, four sets of pistols, fifty-four strings of beads,

one gross of pencils, one dozen brushes, ten dozen assorted necklaces, four dozen inkstands, three dozen pairs of scissors, seven dozen ivory combs, six boxes of ribbons, three accordions, seven silk hats, ten guns, one dozen muslin dresses, six dozen silk gloves, four dozen silk shoes, and additional single items.[60]

As soon as wealthy New Mexicans traveled east and began to trade directly with American wholesalers, most of them stopped purchasing foreign goods from their counterparts in Chihuahua and Durango, and began to develop a network of commercial relations outside their nation that would alter the economic structure of the province. Nevertheless, they continued to send consignments of local goods and sheep to the interior provinces of Mexico, possibly to ensure their advantageous sale and avoid unexpected fluctuations in the market.[61]

New Mexicans were cautious entrepreneurs who were reluctant to abandon traditional patterns of trade, but gradually they became aware that unless they modified their commercial strategies, only foreigners would enjoy the benefits associated with the Santa Fe trade. Realizing that they could expect little help from the Mexican authorities, they began venturing to major cities in the east. There, they slowly helped to create a widespread commercial network, establishing strong economic relations with major entrepreneurs in the United States and Europe. They searched for the most lucrative deals using extensive information networks. Back home they established stores where they bought or traded products of the countryside for imported goods.

The majority of New Mexicans received limited benefits from these activities. Trading down the Royal Road produced some economic gains for those who owned and hauled local merchandise, but it is doubtful that arrieros and peones made enough money substantially to improve their circumstances. Most continued to be dependent on patrones, who, by the middle of the nineteenth century, had accumulated massive fortunes. Increased trade also contributed to smuggling, as traders attempted to avoid taxes.

FOUR

Contraband and the Law

. . . seguí mi camino dividiéndome con las acciones que observaba entre los que venían espiando a ver si dejaban los Americanos algunos tercios. . . .[1]

. . . I continued my way watching those who were espying to see if the Americans were leaving any tercios. . . .

FRANCISCO PÉREZ SERRANO, 1828

Francisco Pérez Serrano's account highlights New Mexicans' attempt to profit from the widespread smuggling of the late 1820s. Finding the hidden merchandise would have meant at least temporary economic relief for people who lived in poverty. The increased economic activities associated with the Santa Fe trade produced few dramatic changes for the majority of New Mexicans, and economic opportunity continued to be limited to those who were well connected, owned a substantial amount of land, and raised large herds of sheep. Even the ricos apparently did not accumulate significant amounts of liquid capital or credit until the 1830s.

One of the major impacts of the Santa Fe trade was an increase in available jobs. This was partially the result of the large amount of fabrics introduced in the territory and the Mexican ban on the import of ready-made clothes. Between 1822 and the 1840s the number of *sastres* (tailors) and *costureras* (seamstresses) multiplied dramatically. There were also striking increases in the number of Hispanos working in trade-related occupations. This growth continued steadily. Between 1860 and 1870, for example, the number of freighters, teamsters, and wagon drivers rose from 203 to 307. Most of these workers resided in San Miguel, Doña Ana, Valencia, Socorro, and Bernalillo counties, which remained the centers of mercantile activities.[2] Additional employment and the availability of cheaper and better merchandise contributed to an improvement in the standard of living.

Wages, however, remained incredibly low—in the 1840s most peones earned only two pesos per month, although some managed to obtain the maximum remuneration of five pesos. Herders made even less — 1 peso and 75 cents a month. Work in the Santa Fe trade caravans possibly paid better. In the 1860s the going wage for a peón was six to eight dollars a month. However, a surviving account reveals that this might have applied only to highly skilled arrieros. Teenage boys, who were a significant element of the convoys, received considerably less. In 1867, sixteen-year-old José Librado Gurulé received eight dollars after working eleven months and traveling back and forth to the United States. There were few fringe benefits. The merchant who owned the goods (José Leandro Perea) furnished the meager food the boy consumed — one full meal during each day supplemented by two snacks of tortillas and onions — but Gurulé had to pay for his own clothes and shoes.[3]

Increased commercial activity offered a limited number of opportunities for those with certain skills. New Mexicans who enjoyed a well-deserved reputation as excellent muleteers and horsemen, became highly sought after for work in the caravans that traveled from Missouri to the interior of Mexico. Americans acknowledged their superlative skills in packing and handling beasts of burden, but it is not clear whether that recognition resulted in adequate wages.[4]

Packing mules, driving wagons, and freighting offered economic opportunities for some. Leading commission merchants and wholesaling firms, like Chick, Browne, and Co., and Otero and Sellar, relied on Hispanos' packing expertise to haul merchandise cheaply and effectively. Freighting was an attractive economic enterprise that required less capital and risk than trading. As Charles Raber noted after he and his partner failed to sell anything on a trading trip down the Río Grande, "This was the last time we hauled our own goods again. From then on we did a freighting business, and in this way got our pay at the end of each trip, and could put the money into more rolling stock, thereby increasing our earning capacity."[5] After the Civil War the United States Army provided others, like Epifanio Aguirre and the Romeros (Vicente, Miguel, Trinidad, and Eugenio), with a chance to capitalize on their reputation as excellent packers, by awarding contracts to carry freight and to supply military installations with flour, grain, and hay. The need to save the cost of transporting forage and food items across the Plains, particularly after the Civil War, resulted in a series of contracts to supply military installations in the west, but very few Hispanos were able to take advantage of this opportunity. It is possible, however, that many who did not obtain awards might have been able to work as subcontractors.[6]

Only a small portion of the population of New Mexico appears to have enjoyed significant improvements in economic circumstances in the nineteenth century. Even though the 1821–80 period witnessed substantial territorial expansion, making a living remained difficult.[7] The majority continued to farm and ranch; they were laborers who reported no assets. They lived in poverty, and many were driven into a system of debt peonage from which escape became difficult.[8]

Some searched for extra-legal means to enhance their economic conditions. The increased commercial activities associated with the Santa Fe Trail possibly raised the expectations of New Mexicans. They had resorted to contraband to ease their economic woes while under Spanish control, and in the 1820s they tried to profit from foreigners' interest in evading Mexican regulations. Smuggling was not a new activity for the foreigners operating in the territory either. Widespread contraband and disregard for British mercantilist policies had been one of the major factors leading to the American Revolution. Prevalent in the western frontier, it had involved British, French, Spanish, and Americans, and a variety of Indian groups, and had been rampant in Missouri.[9]

American merchants claimed to have been horrified at the New Mexican officials' willingness to accept bribes and subvert Mexican laws, but they engaged in similar illegal activities and took advantage of the local permissiveness when it was in their best interests. Gregg claimed that "the average gross return of the traders has rarely exceeded 50 percent, upon the cost of the merchandise, leaving a net profit of between 20 and 40 percent; though their profits have not infrequently been under 10 percent; in fact, as has been mentioned, their adventures have sometimes been losing speculations."[10] This became a good excuse to avoid paying the tariff duties imposed by Mexican laws and to lobby in the American Congress for the Drawback Act. This legislation, which was finally enacted in March 1845, allowed overland traders who re-exported European goods in their original packages to Santa Fe and Chihuahua to receive drawbacks (rebates) on their customs duties.[11]

The growing Santa Fe trade produced increased contact between Americans and New Mexicans. Unfortunately, this interaction did not result in mutual acceptance and tolerance. On the contrary, most Americans' observations reveal a profound misunderstanding of local culture, attitudes, and values. Josiah Gregg acknowledged some virtues, principally gratitude and hospitality. He also noted their "politeness and suavity," their charity, their moral courage, and concluded that "I am fain to believe and acknowledge that there are to be found among them numerous instances of uncompromising virtue, good faith, and religious forbearance."[12] Nonetheless, he seriously questioned the character of Mexicans and felt strong contempt for what he considered absolute disregard for legal institutions:

> The administration of the laws in Northern Mexico constitutes one of the most painful features of her institutions. Justice, or rather judgements, are a common article of traffic; and the hapless litigant who has not the means to soften the claws of the alcalde with a "silver unction" is almost sure to get severely scratched in the contest, no matter what may be the justice of his cause, or the uprightness of his character. It is easy to perceive, then, that the poor and humble stand no chance in a judicial contest with the wealthy and consequential, whose influence even apart from their facilities for corrupting the court and suborning witnesses, is sufficient to neutralize any amount of plebeian testimony that might be brought against them.[13]

He was not the only critic. Charles Bent, one of the most famous Americans to settle in the territory, described New Mexicans in the following manner:

> there is no stability in these people, they have no opinion of their own, they are entirely governed by the powers that be, they are without exception the most servile people that can be imagined. They are completely at the will of those in power lest these be as ignorant as may be they dare not express an opinion contrary to that of their rulers, they are not fit to be free, they should be ruled by others than themselves. Mexico has tried long enough to prove to the world that she is not able to govern herself . . . every species of vice in this country is a recommendation to public office; and such officers as they are corrupt, destitute of all principle, lazy, indolent, ignorant and base to the last degree. There is no confidence to be placed in them. . . . Officers and justices . . . equally ignorant insolent and avaricious are easily bribed. Justice is badly administered and is rendered with extreme delay, caused as much by the wrangling and subterfuge of advocates as the insufficiency of the laws and the innumerable ignorant pleasers who from their indolence and incapacity, and the extortion of the justices are always calculated to create delay. Fees are a grievous item they are always exacted according to the caprice of the justice. The Mexican character is made up of stupidity, obstinacy, ignorance, duplicity and vanity.[14]

Gregg and Bent were not alone in depicting New Mexicans in these terms. Other observers shared their animosity. James Ross Larkin noted in 1856, "the morals of the residents generally are very bad — the habits of the women very loose and the men addicted to gambling and stealing." George Rutledge Gibson's remarks about the man who offered him board and embraced him provide another good example of the profound distrust Americans felt: "Like all Mexicans he is tricky and I watched him closely without being able to discover anything."[15]

John P. Bloom, recording the perceptions of New Mexico by American troops, included comments from a Mormon youth who admitted that he was quite prejudiced against Mexicans; he had heard since infancy that they were a very savage and unprincipled people, his mother having particularly cautioned him against them when he enlisted.[16]

Americans found it hard to adjust to the legal system that operated in New Mexico. Local authorities often handled small legal matters by means of a system of verbal decisions, whereby the plaintiff and the accused got together with the justice of the peace and a pair of individuals who would speak for each of the parties. Conciliations were reached promptly and in most cases those involved appeared satisfied with the outcome. Little formality accompanied these hearings, which were devoid of the argumentation typical of traditional legal proceedings.[17]

Local officials tried to enforce the laws to the best of their ability and to avoid unjust and unusual punishments. Even the ricos were penalized for their excesses. José María Chávez, a member of one of the leading families in New Mexico, signed a contract with a carpenter named Ignacio Trujillo to build a series of shelves for Chávez's store. Trujillo was unable or unwilling to deliver the shelves. Chávez, believing that serious punishment was in order, sued Trujillo for breach of contract and convinced the local alcalde to order Trujillo's mother and brother to administer him a series of lashes. The carpenter was lashed, but he appealed the humiliating sentence to the governor, who declared the punishment cruel and unjust and sentenced Chávez to pay a fine.[18]

American observers, however, invariably ignored the positive aspects of New Mexican society. They focused on stereotypes that did not allow for the fact that local circumstances might provoke illegal activities, like contraband. In most cases smuggling was not symptomatic of a lack of morality, but a normal human response to a frontier situation where economic survival often depended on taking advantage of limited opportunities. Earning a living was difficult, and the prospect of realizing any economic gain en-

couraged disregard for laws that were troublesome to enforce and perceived as detrimental to local well-being. The increasing presence of foreigners and merchandise provided incentives and additional markets for
those with initiative.

The earliest and most widespread form of contraband involved furs.
Beaver skins had always attracted foreigners' interest, and French, British,
and American hunters had successfully operated along the Rockies during
the late eighteenth century. Spanish authorities had been aware of their
presence and remained quite wary about the infiltration of foreign trappers
along their northern frontier. These activities continued and increased
after Mexican independence from Spain.[19]

Mexicans looked at the foreigners operating in the back country with the
same suspicion as the Spanish, and they were reluctant to issue the required
permits for hunting. Difficulties arose as a result. Licenses were scarce, and
foreigners were seldom allowed to hunt legally. If unable to get a permit
for beaver directly, they purchased the furs from the locals, who in turn
claimed to have obtained them from a variety of Indian groups.[20] The
earliest recorded instances of this practice involved Frenchmen. Silvestre
Pratte was charged with illegal hunting of beaver. Although part of the
information is missing, surviving evidence reveals that Juan Bautista Vigil,
who had a legal license to hunt, had sold the pelts to Pratte. A similar case
involved two other Frenchmen, Vicente Guion and Jean Baptiste Trudeau.
In this instance the authorities confiscated three hundred pounds of beaver.
Guion claimed that he had never hunted and that he had obtained the furs
from Trudeau, who in turn testified that he had bought them from the
alcaldes of Taos and Abiquiú, their predecessors, and their children. Trudeau maintained that Guion paid him in fabrics, not in cash.[21] Americans
Richard Campbell and Philip Thompson were also involved. The alcalde of
Taos admitted selling beaver skins to merchants like Manuel Alvarez, but
professed to having obtained them from the Comanches.

Americans continued to hunt illegally until declining numbers of beaver
forced trappers to scout larger regions to obtain sufficient pelts and eventually put a halt to their activities. In 1832 Ewing Young hunted over a
considerable portion of Mexico's northern provinces along the Colorado
and the Salado Rivers, the Río Arriba (the Río Grande Valley north of La
Bajada), the San Francisco, the Río Abajo down to the Gila River, the
Maricopa, and from there to California.[22] His appears to be the last major
legal case involving the illegal acquisition of furs.

The most significant type of contraband activity, however, focused on
foreign goods. New Mexicans used a variety of methods. Sometimes they

made arrangements with foreigners to introduce merchandise illegally. The parties involved, usually a foreigner and a New Mexican, selected a rendezvous, where the former hid the merchandise. The latter waited until it was safe (when the militia dispatched to prevent fraud had disappeared), retrieved the cache, and met the owner at a prearranged location. Few documents record the identities of these partners. Manuel Armijo, for example, participated in such an incident in 1832. During the judicial proceedings, he did not deny that he had illegally introduced a tercio of foreign merchandise for an American merchant. The details became public only because Armijo was sued when he claimed to have lost the merchandise.[23]

Typically, New Mexicans furtively followed foreign caravans, hoping to see where the foreigners hid or left contraband merchandise.[24] Then they had two options. They could steal and try to sell the goods by themselves, or they could denounce the contraband to the official authorities. The first option had the potential to yield greater profits because there was no need to share the proceeds, but there were more risks involved. The merchandise had to be hidden until they could arrange for its sale, and during this period it was more susceptible to denunciation. Furthermore, it was hard to get high prices for contraband goods, so profits were smaller.[25]

The second option, made possible by Mexican law, entailed less risk and could be remunerative if the contraband was sizable. The Mexican government had carried on Spanish mercantilist policies, issuing strict regulations detailing the *comiso* (confiscation) process. Although the rules were periodically modified (as were the lists of prohibited merchandise), it was a simple operation. The law detailed every step — from the official declaration of contraband to the distribution of the profits resulting from its confiscation. Half of the proceeds from comiso was to go to the public treasury, while the other half was to be divided into thirds — one for the *denunciante* (denouncer), another for the *aprehensor* (apprehender), and the last to be shared among the local alcalde who declared the contraband, the *promotor fiscal* (district attorney), the commandant, and the *administrador* (political leader).[26]

In New Mexico the practice was somewhat different, and it changed over time and between various local administrations. In some cases the public treasury received close to the 50 percent stipulated by the law. However, in most instances it secured only 25 percent; the denouncer and the apprehender collected 35 percent each; and the remaining 5 percent was used for the expenses associated with the confiscation. In the 1820s the alcalde received roughly 10 percent; the *promovedores* (promoters), 20 percent; the public treasury, close to 45 percent; and the rest went to the denouncers.[27]

The documents reveal that some New Mexican officials made a con-

certed effort to curtail contraband, particularly during the late 1820s and
1830s. As soon as the Santa Fe Trail caravans approached, authorities dispatched troops to discourage fraud, particularly the common practice of
hiding merchandise along the road.[28] According to Gregg, about 150 miles
from Santa Fe, parties of customs house agents or clerks accompanied by a
military escort would come out to meet a caravan and accompany it to the
capital with the ostensible purpose of preventing smuggling. However, he
claimed that "any one disposed to smuggle would find no difficulty in
securing the services of these preventive guards, who, for a trifling *douceur*
(gift) would prove very efficient auxiliaries, rather than obstacles to the
success of any such designs."[29] Naturally, these agents and soldiers were
susceptible to bribes, and the local authorities might have been aware that
these encounters could produce a measure of economic relief for the under-
paid New Mexicans. In 1837 unrest flared among the troops in Santa Fe
after they denounced a load of contraband belonging to Daniel Workman
and the local officials authorized the return of the confiscated merchandise.
In 1845 securing enough funds to cover soldiers' salaries was still an important political issue.[30]

Still, evidence reveals determination on the part of some local authorities
to follow correct procedures. This was difficult because New Mexico's isolation delayed judicial appeals and impeded the prompt administration of
justice. Furthermore, officials were seldom adequately trained and often
ignorant of the legal system and the current judicial dispositions.

The most revealing case during this period involved a leading citizen
accused of smuggling. The prolonged proceedings (1828–31) are important for two reasons: they include valuable information on the mechanics of
contraband and on operating the legal system, and they reveal conflicting
perspectives between New Mexican and Mexican authorities regarding the
punishment of smugglers.[31]

In July 1828 Francisco Pérez Serrano, *primer vocal* (first deputy) for the
territory of New Mexico to the Mexican Congress, was accused of carrying
five tercios of contraband. Pérez Serrano was jailed and the confiscated
merchandise distributed. Of the total, assessed at a value of 816 pesos 2
reales 5 granos, close to 42 percent (342 pesos 6 reales 3 granos) went to the
treasury; the alcalde received 81 pesos 4 reales 2 granos; while the denouncers and promoters received 196 pesos each. According to Pérez Serrano's testimony, he had found the tercios on the side of the road along the
Cañada de los Alamos, a few miles east of Santa Fe, as he was riding with
José María Padilla. He immediately realized that fraud of some kind was
involved, so he and Padilla moved the tercios to a spot close by where they

waited to see if the owner would show up. Since nobody did, Pérez Serrano decided to take them to the aduana in Santa Fe on less-frequented roads. Corporal José Larrañaga and a detachment of soldiers dispatched for the purpose of preventing contraband stopped Pérez Serrano and Padilla and accused the former of trying to introduce merchandise illegally. Pérez Serrano told Larrañaga to take the merchandise back, but the officer refused and carried Pérez Serrano to the Santa Fe jail. The subsequent depositions indicate animosity between these two individuals, and it is possible that there was an underlying family feud behind much of what happened.[32]

Pérez Serrano sat behind bars as his plea for bail was not accepted. Juan Bautista Alarid, the *alcalde segundo* (vice-magistrate), mishandled the case as a result of his ignorance of correct legal procedures or perhaps antagonism toward Pérez Serrano. A month after the incident, New Mexican authorities requested legal advice from Licenciado Victoriano Guerra from Chihuahua. He severely chastised Alarid for not following exactly the provisions of the law. The comiso should have been declared within forty-eight hours of finding the merchandise. Only then would it have been possible to establish a legal action against Pérez Serrano. Depositions should have been obtained from the soldiers and the corporal immediately after they seized the property. Guerra also noted that there appeared to have been intent to harm the provincial deputy because Padilla was left free while Pérez Serrano stayed in jail. Most important, since the deputy had been held for more than seventy-two hours without being told the motive for his imprisonment, he would have to be released immediately.[33]

Soon after Guerra's pronouncement, Alarid acknowledged having made involuntary mistakes in his original handling of the case and proceeded to record the testimony from Larrañaga and his soldiers. They all concurred that upon apprehension Pérez Serrano had confessed that he was carrying the merchandise for an American. He asked the corporal to take the mules and the merchandise. Since Larrañaga would not agree, Pérez Serrano asked the corporal to shoot him to avoid the shame that such an action would bring upon his name.[34]

Miguel Sena, the promotor fiscal of the territory at the time, presented an eloquent case against Serrano. He claimed that Pérez Serrano used the "supposed" animosity of Larrañaga to hide his dishonorable behavior. Sena believed there were doubts about Pérez Serrano's innocence and was particularly incensed at the attempt to defraud the public treasury. He wanted a harsh punishment for Pérez Serrano because he was an *empleado público* (public employee) and as such he should have been worthy of the people's trust. Sena requested that in accordance with the Mexican law of 4 September 1823, Article 13, Serrano's name and crime be published in the newspapers declaring him to be unworthy of the public trust. Sena was particularly infuriated that a public servant like a deputy to the Mexican Congress, who might have voted for the comiso law enacted in 1823, should be involved in such an outrageous crime.[35]

A week later, Santiago Abreu presented a lengthy and articulate defense of Pérez Serrano. Abreu's argument rested on the hostility that existed between Pérez Serrano and Larrañaga and spoke of the intent to harm his client, although it is never clear why this was so. Abreu was quick to point out that Padilla was allowed to leave Santa Fe the day after the incident, but his client was forced to remain in jail and his offer of bail was not accepted.[36]

Alarid was unsure how to continue, so he sent all the documents associated with the case to authorities in Chihuahua, once again requesting legal advice. On 31 December 1828, Licenciado Juan Antonio Villaroel responded. His decision reached Santa Fe in February. By this time Alarid was no longer the magistrate, having been replaced by Francisco Trujillo. Villaroel pointed out that in the past when there had been no *audiencia* (high court), as was now the case in New Mexico, the alcaldes and lower judges did not have the authority to sentence, only to suspend a case. In such instances, they sent the closest audiencia the dossier and an explanation of why there was a disagreement. Villaroel decided that this was what had to be done, and New Mexican officials complied. However, upon receipt of the case, the circuit court in El Parral returned the materials. They had found a number of *nulidades* (corrections, crossouts, intercalated documents that nullify a legal act) throughout the proceedings and made Alarid responsible for the failure to handle the case correctly. The members of the circuit court warned Trujillo that the form and order of the documents had to be corrected before the appeal could continue.[37]

The tribunal at El Parral also requested officials to determine if Alarid had acted as substitute district judge or simply as alcalde. If Alarid had not acted as a judge, the materials relating the case were to be sent to a magistrate knowledgeable on such matters so that a decision could be reached in accordance with the law. Alarid confirmed that he had acted as primer alcalde, but was angered by the turn of events and left for Chihuahua and Sonora. The court at El Parral decided that since it was not the responsibility of the alcaldes of the territory to be knowledgeable on matters regarding the public treasury, Alarid had not had the authority to declare the comiso nor to distribute the smuggled merchandise as he did. The court also added that Alarid had only had the authority to place the merchandise in deposit and that the district judge should take care of the case.[38]

However, there were no district judges in New Mexico. After eighteen months (in December of 1830) the Parral circuit judges noted that a law enacted in May 1826 stipulated that the territory of New Mexico should have a district judge, and that if such a position could not be filled the government should appoint three *letrados* (lawyers) as substitutes. Failing that, it would have to appoint three of the most capable local individuals. Since none of these appointments had been made, the tribunal decided that there was no competent authority in the territory to handle matters pertaining to the national treasury. José Francisco Blanco, the head of the tribunal, conceded that Pérez Serrano was guilty of trying to smuggle merchandise, but ruled that the irregularities in the proceedings forced him to nullify the case.[39] An appeal finally went before the supreme court which upheld the ruling of the lower court. Mexico's highest judicial authority's verdict endorsed the notion that punishing smuggling was not as important as ensuring that the legal process operated without irregularities and that it follow strictly the dictates of the law. Local authorities had limited powers, and until the national judiciary was established they would be limited in their ability to enforce the laws.

Contraband cases were numerous in the late 1820s and early 1830s but declined during the following decade. Corporal Larrañaga participated in other smuggling incidents and seemed always ready to follow the dictates of the law. In one instance, a group of Americans was digging a large crater in the ground, supposedly for fifty-five adjacent tercios. The foreigners claimed that they were trying to cover the merchandise temporarily until two of their broken wagons were fixed. However, the corporal did not hesitate to inform the local authorities and request a decision on whether contraband was to be declared. Unfortunately, no records survive that document the outcome of this case.[40]

Denunciation of illegal merchandise was a common occurrence. In March 1831 the authorities seized contraband merchandise from a store operated by Americans.[41] Another interesting case involved José M. Martínez, the alcalde of Taos. In 1832 some Americans rented twelve mules from Martínez's brother. Apparently, he later found out that the Americans intended to introduce contraband and he tried to catch them. He was not successful, but later it appeared that the Americans had held the merchandise in the vicinity. Martínez later argued that since he was only a local official, he was not empowered to act.[42]

There is no doubt that contraband was common, and that many New Mexicans took advantage of the economic opportunity smuggling offered. The administration of justice was slow and ill-suited to a province like New

Mexico — large, distant, isolated, and lacking officials who were well educated and versed in judicial matters. Pérez Serrano was jailed but not fined,
and suffered only the loss of the merchandise, for which he had probably
paid nothing. The local officials, on the other hand, were chastised and
reprimanded by Mexican judicial authorities. Even though they attempted
to conduct the process carefully, their ignorance of proper procedures
caused them to spend a considerable time on this case for nought. It is not
surprising that relatively few were charged with contraband after 1831.
Even if there was a strong incentive to prosecute those who violated Mexican regulations, the province did not have the resources to take them to
court.

It is interesting to note that most cases of contraband for which documentation exists listed a limited amount of merchandise and — with a couple of exceptions — involved individuals who were not socially prominent.
Political authorities and the well-to-do were able to take advantage of their
position to avert any inconveniences that might hinder their illegal activities. Manuel Armijo, a relative of the famous governor, traveled east
several times. The records show that no guías for foreign merchandise were
ever issued to him, even though Missouri newspapers and customs house
records note that Armijo, like other merchants from the Río Abajo, regularly made substantial purchases of merchandise in the United States for
the Mexican market and brought them to New Mexico via the Santa Fe
Trail.[43] It is not clear what Armijo did with these goods, but it is probable
that, like other wealthy merchants, he succeeded in establishing a sophisticated system of mercantile operations.[44]

The main impact of the trail trade on most New Mexicans was an increase in job opportunities, although wages continued to be appallingly
low. Because of the Mexican ban on importing ready-made clothing, tailors
and seamstresses were in considerable demand. Hispanos were renowned
for their muleteer, horsemanship, and packing skills, and were sought for
packing and freighting services. Nonetheless, most of the population continued to live in poverty with little opportunity for betterment. Many were
driven into debt peonage, pledging crops years in advance. Contraband
offered economic relief that looked increasingly attractive to a neglected,
destitute population.

Most contraband cases show that authorities in Mexico City were unable
to pay adequate attention to the edges of the republic and failed to realize
that illegal trading was becoming a means of strengthening the economic
ties linking American traders to the struggling New Mexican population.

FIVE

New Mexican Merchants and Mercantile Capitalism

Está algo enredado, pero así se hace dinero.[1]

It is somewhat tangled, but it is a way to make money.

DAMASO ROBLEDO, 1846

Damaso Robledo, an agent for Manuel Alvarez, was scouting the New Mexican territory, buying grains and legumes from small farmers and selling merchandise that Alvarez had purchased in the eastern United States. His activities were typical of the commercial system that had developed in New Mexico by the time of the Mexican War and illustrate how New Mexican merchants took advantage of the economic opportunity their territory offered. Like Manuel Alvarez, New Mexican merchants had established stores throughout the countryside where the local population could buy their imported merchandise. Since most New Mexicans had no cash, they paid for these purchases with sheep or crops, which they often mortgaged years in advance.

It took time for the New Mexican mercantile system to mature. For almost two decades after the "opening" of the Santa Fe Trail in 1821, local merchants did not participate in any direct large-scale commercial activities with United States firms. By the end of the 1830s, however, they were venturing east to New York, Baltimore, Philadelphia, and Pittsburgh, where they invested the sizable capital they had accumulated. Slowly they became part of a widespread commercial network, which offered them substantial returns. Their complex transactions came to include merchants in the United States, Europe, and Mexico. Far from ending Hispano involvement, the changes that resulted from the Mexican War appear to have strengthened the economic relations between New Mexico's *comerciantes* and their counterparts in the United States, and allowed for the development of a powerful mercantile elite that controlled a substantial proportion of the territorial wealth.

By the mid-nineteenth century, New Mexicans regularly arranged for substantial purchases in the major commercial centers in the eastern United States, including European merchandise from Ireland, Great Britain, France, and Italy. American businesses and newspapers in Kansas, Missouri, and New York acknowledged the presence of large parties of Hispanos and, realizing their likely impact in the local economies, they published advertisements in Spanish, intended exclusively to attract their attention. The announcement of Francisco B. Rhodes and Co. provides an excellent idea of the variety of items that New Mexicans purchased in the United States.[2]

Hispano merchants might not have dominated the trade, but they owned a significant portion of the goods hauled across the prairies before and after the Mexican War. For example, out of the 956 wagons hauling freight from Council Grove to Santa Fe in 1859, more than half (526) belonged to Hispanos. It is not possible to determine the value of the merchandise carried by each ethnic group, but it is likely that it was in proportion to the volume. Records of caravans during the 1850s and 1860s indicate no major changes in this pattern, and carved inscriptions in Oklahoma (at such places as Autograph Rock) corroborate the presence of large numbers of New Mexican traders until the 1880s.[3]

During those four decades (1839–80) the nature of the Santa Fe trade evolved. Hispano merchants, like their American and European counterparts, stopped making yearly trips east to arrange orders of merchandise and began to use the services of commission merchants, such as Peter Harmony of New York, to manage their transactions in the United States. They designated trusted mayordomos to travel east and make the final purchases and freighting arrangements. They obtained goods from a variety of sources in an attempt to get the best prices. Enough evidence exists on Chávez family members to describe their business and its evolution with time.[4] Census data from 1860 and 1870 and scattered correspondence from Manuel Alvarez, the Delgado family, and others confirm its operation and success.

Hispanos began to trade sporadically in the United States in the early 1820s. The Escuderos, a couple of Chihuahuan traders, are often identified as the first to do so. In 1824 Governor Bartolomé Baca selected José Escudero to travel to Council Bluffs (present-day Iowa) with a delegation of twenty-six Spaniards. However, his primary purpose on that trip was to conclude a treaty with the Pawnees, and there is no evidence that Escudero purchased any merchandise in the United States.[5]

Another Escudero, Manuel Simón, a deputy to the Mexican Congress, journeyed east the following year. Commissioned by Governor Baca as well, his task was to visit the United States in the interests of international commerce and to seek protection from the Indians. Manuel Escudero stopped at St. Louis, Washington, and Franklin, Missouri.[6] His stay in the United States received considerable attention. The *Franklin Intelligencer* reported that Escudero had arrived with "six or seven new and substantial built waggons [*sic*] . . . heavily laden with merchandise." The article added that Escudero had expended a very large sum in the purchase of goods, wagons, and equipment, and concluded that the trip "may be considered as a new era in the commerce between Mexico and this country, and it is probable the example of Mr. Escudero will be followed by others of his rich countrymen who will bring hither large portions of their surplus wealth for the same purpose."[7]

The Escuderos made at least one more trip. In July 1827 Manuel received a guía that listed him as the owner of a modest amount of foreign merchandise (valued at 346 pesos 5 reales 6 granos) with the destination of Chihuahua. Luis Escudero was the recipient of the effects, and another Escudero, José Agustín, was the conductor of the load.[8]

Apparently the Escuderos' trading did not ignite the imagination of New Mexican merchants, however, as it would be more than ten years before the province's ricos decided to bring "large portions of their surplus wealth" to the United States.[9] It is possible that José Ignacio Ortiz, the alcalde of Santa Fe, traveled to Philadelphia in 1830 to arrange for the purchase of merchandise, but only one document records his stay, and unfortunately it does not reveal the purpose of his trip.[10]

New Mexicans continued to acquire large shipments of foreign goods from their traditional Mexican suppliers at least until 1837, when José Chávez purchased 7,680 pesos worth of merchandise from Durango.[11] However, commercial opportunities in Mexico appeared to be declining. A June 1838 letter from José Cordero to Manuel Armijo suggested the need to look for markets elsewhere. Cordero informed Armijo that it would be difficult to sell sheep in the Mexican territory and that prices would be lower than usual. He notified his business associate that he was thinking of leaving Chihuahua since it was no longer possible to make a good living there. The postscript of Cordero's letter also requested information on the merchandise brought on that year's caravan, their prices, and quantity.[12]

It is unclear if and how Cordero's assessment relates to the change in New Mexican patterns of trade that took place in 1839, but it is possible that Cordero and his New Mexican counterparts realized that in order to satisfy the growing demand for foreign goods they would have to acquire merchandise elsewhere. It is also difficult to ascertain the accuracy of Cordero's appraisal of the situation in Mexico, since an April 1840 report by Mariano de Valois (in response to a letter from United States Representative Edward Cross) indicated that Chihuahua, with a population of 140,000 and a consumption to the value of $2.5 million to $3 million a year, continued to be an ideal market for foreign goods.[13]

Why didn't New Mexicans trade directly with American wholesalers until the late 1830s? There are several possible explanations. First, New Mexicans might not have had enough cash on hand in the 1820s to get favorable credit terms. Second, as foreigners, they might not have been able to get loans to purchase merchandise in the eastern cities. Third, local New Mexican authorities may have imposed unofficial restrictions on their commercial activities in a foreign country. After all, the governor of the province (Baca) had had personally to authorize Escudero's trip. Fourth, it may have been a dramatic change in economic conditions within the Mexican territory in the late 1830s that made such trips profitable. Fifth, wealthy New Mexicans might have decided to stop paying substantial mark-ups on foreign products. Although it was cheaper to buy foreign merchandise in Santa Fe than from Mexican merchants, surcharges were still high. In 1834 local storekeepers Santiago and Ramón Abreu bought goods from Manuel Alvarez. They paid surcharges of 100 and 120 percent on most items. Such practices continued to be the norm as late as April 1845, when Juan Otero paid similar surcharges on the 7,800 pesos worth of goods he purchased from Manuel Alvarez at Santa Fe.[14]

Regardless of the reasons, 1839 witnessed a significant change in the direction of trade from New Mexico. Although Cordero did not leave Chihuahua in 1838, the following year he was among the first Hispanos who traveled east to establish direct commercial relations with commission merchants and suppliers of needed efectos extranjeros. Cordero was identified as one of the prominent "Mexicans" who were part of a large trading caravan of more than a hundred wagons crossing present-day Kansas en route to Santa Fe. The size of his shipment was substantial, although the official assessment of its total value, if it ever existed, has not survived. A manifest of the property he declared at the New Mexican customs house at Santa Fe indicates that he imported forty-two thousand yards of cotton textiles for which he paid more than 10,000 pesos in duties. He received two guías: a small one for 280 pesos worth of merchandise and a much larger one, including forty-two bundles, for which no value was indicated.

It is not clear if he carried back to Chihuahua all that he purchased in the United States.[15]

Cordero traveled with José Olivares, another Mexican merchant, who bought a smaller amount of merchandise. They were the earliest merchants, but not the only ones, who went east that year. José Chávez and other Mexican merchants left San Miguel del Vado, New Mexico, on 23 September and reached Independence, Missouri, on 30 October. Theirs was a five-wagon caravan, apparently composed entirely of New Mexicans. According to the *Niles' National Register*, the members of the group traveled again to St. Louis on 11 November, carrying $60,000 in specie.[16] These merchants spent the winter in the United States and left in May for Santa Fe where they arrived in July. Both official documents from the aduana at Santa Fe and American newspaper reports concur that these entrepreneurs freighted eleven wagons of merchandise back to New Mexico.

The Chávez brothers and the other merchants were wealthy and carried substantial amounts of cash on their trips to the United States. It seems, however, that American newspapers may have exaggerated the amount and value of the specie New Mexicans took. If we believe the *Weekly Picayune*, Chávez and his party managed to make a substantial profit in those five months. According to that newspaper, the "Mexican" merchants carried back merchandise valued at $75,000 — five times more than the $15,000 reported in November. The manifests for these goods survive, and it is unlikely that all the assessments together could have reached even the lower alleged sum.[17]

Nevertheless, the 1839 trip must have been successful because thereafter increasing numbers of New Mexican merchants traveled east every year to arrange for commercial transactions in the United States. They quickly adopted regular trading patterns. In general, their caravans departed from Santa Fe during April or the early part of May, reached Independence or St. Louis, Missouri, and then continued on to eastern industrial centers like Pittsburgh, Baltimore, Philadelphia, and New York. In June they started on the trip home, although weather sometimes delayed their activities, and they did not return until September or October.[18] Many probably followed the example of Gaspar Ortiz and José Chávez who added foreign goods to the merchandise they had been sending to the interior of Mexico for years. They both came back from the United States on 27 July 27 1843. Less than a month later, on 17 August, Ortiz sent two loads to Chihuahua and Sonora. Chávez postponed the shipment of his merchandise to Mexico until 25 August.[19]

In theory, manifests for caravans entering New Mexico had to account for all packages, their certified value, the persons to whom they were consigned, their destination, and their value. Historians agree, however, that the declared value of the merchandise bore little relation to what the owner had paid or even to what tariff the local officials collected. According to Moorhead, the customs records merely justified the amount of revenue actually sent to the national treasury, and the true value of the Santa Fe trade was never accurately reported.[20]

Gregg and other foreign merchants complained that unfair import duties favored New Mexicans, but the surviving documents reveal no special treatment from the authorities at the customs house in Santa Fe. In 1839 Cordero paid 7,897 pesos and 48 cents of derecho de internación, 459 pesos of derecho de consumo, and 1,673 pesos and 52 cents on a special fee placed on cotton textiles — four cents on each square vara (0.84 yards), and he was not the exception. Another Mexican merchant who traveled with Cordero, José Olivares, paid similar dues.[21]

In July 1840 two American traders, in addition to three New Mexicans, introduced merchandise into the territory. The locals paid a substantial share of the import duties — 4,647 pesos and 72 cents for derecho de internación, 895 pesos and 98 cents for derecho de consumo, and 9,555 pesos and 2 cents for a special temporary surcharge on cotton textiles. Their total amounted to 6,499 pesos and 21 cents. Americans did not pay the derecho de consumo, so their duties were relatively lower than those paid by the locals — 3,413 pesos. New Mexicans contributed 61 percent of the derecho de internación, but only 38.7 percent of the derecho de consumo. It is difficult to generalize on the basis of these figures because they included only merchandise introduced during the month of July, and unfortunately no additional records survive for that year. Undoubtedly, rumors about the Texan Santa Fe Expedition contributed to a temporary decreased interest in the trade.[22]

The following spring (May 1841) the Chávezes, the Armijos, possibly the Oteros, and others traveled east in the company of American traders. The *Daily Missouri Republican* noted that the caravan had twenty-two wagons, a large number of mules, and $180,000 to $200,000 in specie. A witness saw "about 20 Spanish Mexicans . . . led by Chávez." The New Mexicans apparently did not winter in the United States that year. Newspapers reported that by early October Armijo and Chávez had left Independence, Missouri, and were heading west with thirty wagons, seventy-two tons of merchandise, and around 350 mules. Most of the official customs documents for 1841 have been lost, and it is not possible to learn much more about this trip. Gregg listed fifteen merchants carrying $150,000 in goods for that year.[23]

During the early 1840s the size of New Mexican purchases in the United States increased substantially. Webb believed that "the [American] traders had some hand in deterring the Mexicans from going in for goods by exaggerating the danger and reporting rumors of a large expedition from Texas being organized for the purpose of making a raid upon the prairies and taking every Mexican train that should attempt to cross the plains that year."[24] Local merchants, however, were undeterred by the failed Texan Santa Fe Expedition.[25] In June 1842 Juan Perea introduced seventy bultos. Among them he brought 30,129.5 yards of fabrics, different types of sewing threads, ribbons, cotton socks, and a hundred hats. The most interesting aspect of this shipment, however, is the lack of variety — only twelve different types of goods. Four of these were fabrics, but most of the shipment — 26,589 yards (88 percent) — consisted of lienzo. Perea paid 4,910 pesos and 10 cents in duties. Lienzo was inexpensive and it only required one real per vara in import duties. Other fabrics carried higher tariffs: *paño* cost twelve reales per vara; woolen knittings, fifteen reales per vara. Luxury items were subject to more substantial duties: silk thread and ribbons cost two dollars per pound; socks, two and a half dollars per dozen; hats, three dollars each.[26]

Perea was not the only merchant who introduced large shipments with little variety. Antonio José Otero's purchases for 1842 included almost twice as much cloth as Perea's and showed the same lack of variety. Otero paid 9,321 pesos and 9 cents in import duties, reflecting the substantial size of his purchase.[27] New Mexican merchants were following the example of some foreign merchants, who since the early 1830s, had been introducing large quantities of selected items. However, not all traders relied on this strategy. For example, in 1843 Spanish-born Manuel Alvarez introduced a much wider assortment than those of Perea and Otero, a larger number of items costing higher import duties. John McKnight followed the pattern adopted by the Spaniard, while James Magoffin took a middle course. His manifest reflected less variety than Alvarez's but a lot more than either Perea's or Otero's.[28]

The year 1843 was very important for the Santa Fe Trail. Gregg reported thirty traders with 230 wagons carrying almost $500,000 worth of merchandise.[29] In spite of the murder of Antonio José Chávez, which took place in April, increasing numbers of New Mexicans began trading directly with United States wholesalers. In April, 180 men, forty-two wagons, and twelve hundred mules left Santa Fe for Independence, where they arrived in mid-May. Most were identified as Mexicans who carried between $250,000 and $300,000 in bullion and a substantial amount of furs. Witnesses reported that eleven traders continued to New York to make purchases. An account indicates that it was during this trip that Juan and José Leandro Perea and José Chávez brought young Francisco and Joaquín Perea and J. Francisco Chávez to be registered as students in a Jesuit college.[30]

By late June the merchants were back in Santa Fe. The manifests for the year document an expanding New Mexican presence and changes in the composition of the caravans. New families joined the trade for the first time as it became possible even for those with limited capital to participate in direct trade with the United States. Tomás González, for example, brought a modest load consisting of four different kinds of fabrics: five hundred yards of lienzo, forty-five yards of manta, 330 yards of indiana, and 120 yards of *mahón* (nankeen). Customs officials charged him 150 pesos in tariffs.[31] Juan Nepomuceno and José Mariano Gutiérrez returned with thirteen bundles of foreign merchandise. Together they paid 2,626 pesos and 22 cents in duties. Their goods included little variety and no luxury items. Juan introduced 2,817 yards of linen, 1,792 yards of calico, 450 yards of assorted fabrics, nine dozen knives, twelve dozen pairs of cotton socks, three dozen pairs of scissors, six dozen locks, and four dozen pocket knives. José Mariano's manifest showed even less variety, but large quantities: thirty-one hundred yards of linen, twenty-five yards of nankeen, thirty-three hundred yards of calico, 250 yards of other textiles, twenty-five dozen pairs of cotton socks, and sixteen pieces of handkerchief cloth.[32]

In general the economic resources of the owner determined the size, composition, and value of the shipments. The wealthier merchants introduced larger quantities of merchandise, but did not import a greater variety of items than those of more limited means. They concentrated instead on finer and more expensive merchandise. For example, Gaspar Ortiz introduced French and British calicos, top-quality cashmere, corduroy, velvet, silk gloves, and others. Mariano Chávez brought in close to forty thousand yards of textiles, and among these he included European luxury goods, such as cashmere, velvet, linen, calico, flannel, fancy shawls, satin, and silk ribbons.[33]

The manifests for 1844 suggest that each year New Mexican traders imported larger quantities of goods and more expensive foreign merchandise. Although the size of the shipments increased, their composition did not change. Juan C. Armijo, Antonio José Otero, Juan and José Perea, and Mariano Chávez together introduced close to $75,000 worth of merchandise. Shipments were composed almost exclusively of fabrics. In addition, Armijo's goods included combs, cotton socks, and handkerchiefs. Otero and the Pereas purchased the same kinds of effects, except no combs. Chávez's loads also included fur hats and scarfs.[34]

The records for 1845 appear incomplete, but that possibly reflects uncertainty as the clash between the United States and Mexico became inevitable. No manifests survive for this year, and the New Mexican shipments to the interior of Mexico were insignificant compared with the loads that foreigners carried. For example, the guías indicate that James Magoffin hauled 176 piezas assessed at a value of $26,000. The merchandise belonged to Kerford and Jenkin, who also sent more than a hundred thousand yards of various fabrics to the interior of Mexico under the care of other freighters. Albert Speyer dispatched 601 tercios valued at $68,948.[35]

The Mexican War did not stop commerce for long and appears to have had limited short-term detrimental impact on New Mexican commercial interests since merchants did not allow the armed confrontation to affect their economic transactions in the United States.[36] The Armijos, at least, seemed unconcerned, and New York newspapers recorded their presence late in 1845 "to purchase their winter outfit."[37] The following spring New Mexican merchants traveled east again to "acquire goods for the trade and Pittsburgh manufactures."[38]

There has been a lot of controversy regarding economic control of the Santa Fe trade before and after the Mexican War. Unfortunately the lack of systematic information regarding ownership, the value and amount of merchandise, and its origin and final destination prevents a definitive analysis of the trade between New Mexico and the United States during the nineteenth century. Estimates of the value of the merchandise invested in the Santa Fe trade are crude and incomplete.

Gregg provides the most often cited and possibly most reliable assessment prior to the Mexican War. With a few fluctuations, he identified a fairly steady increase in the value and volume of merchandise that culminated in 1843, with 230 men carrying $450,000 in merchandise in 230 wagons.[39] Later appraisals included fair indicators of volume, but the assessment of overall value is questionable. The reported average figure for the overland trade with Mexico for the period 1848 to 1858 was $1,138,000, nearly a quarter of the total American trade with Mexico. In 1858, S. M. Hayes and Company, located at Council Grove, recorded 2,440 men, 1,827 wagons, 429 horses, 15,714 oxen, 5,316 mules, 67 carriages, and 9,608 tons of goods for a total investment capital of $2,627,300. In 1859 the *Missouri Republican* reported that the trade had risen to a value of $10 million annually, as 2,300 men, 1,970 wagons, 840 horses, 4,000 mules, 15,000 oxen, 73 carriages, and over 1,900 tons of freight left for New Mexico. According to T. B. Mills, in 1860 even higher numbers of men (5,948), wagons (2,170), mules (5,933), and oxen (17,836) were carrying merchandise across the Plains. A decade later, even though the Civil War and mounting Indian hostilities had greatly disrupted commercial activities during the 1860s, it was estimated that the trade amounted to a value of over $5 million.[40]

Gregg claimed that by the 1840s Mexicans monopolized the trade. Cooke's statement in 1843 that "of about 200 wagon loads which I have escorted this year, I do not believe 10 have belonged to Americans who were resident citizens," appears to support this claim, but an analysis of surviving documents is far from conclusive.[41] Part of the difficulty stems from the incomplete nature of the records. Irregularities in record keeping by customs officials at Santa Fe also cast a doubt on the nature of the transactions recorded. For example, Missouri newspapers and witnesses agreed that Manuel Armijo procured considerable merchandise in the United States. However, no manifests identify such purchases, and even though the customs house records at Santa Fe show that Armijo received fourteen guías between 1835 and 1845, none of them declared foreign merchandise.[42]

Official records roughly agree with the number of shipments that Gregg reported, but his estimate of the value of the merchandise might be questionable. Any visual assessment of the value of the loads would have been subjective. Reporters referred to a wagonload as the standard unit of shipment, but carts were not necessarily the same size and were laden with different kinds of goods. Those carrying bulky, coarser textiles, such as bolts of lienzo and manta, paid lower duties than those carrying finer fabrics, such as silk or lace, or luxury items. Furthermore, during certain years some merchandise was exempt from import duties. For example, José Chávez and Antonio José Otero paid no duties on iron tools and coarse linens.[43] Assessments of the value of the trade were often based on newspaper accounts and eyewitnesses' reports. While these might be adequate indicators of the numbers of men, wagons, mules, and oxen, they should be considered as only rough estimates of the actual value of the merchandise hauled across the Plains.

Witnesses like Cooke might not have been able to identify with certainty the owners of the merchandise, since those who traveled with the goods did not necessarily own them. As the documents indicate and Gregg's figures suggest, by the 1840s foreign merchants did not always accompany their shipments. Furthermore, their reliance on the superior freighting skills of

New Mexicans probably accounts for the large number of Hispanos escorting the caravans to the United States during the 1840s. The information American newspapers presented regarding ownership was inconsistent. Sometimes they listed the real owner, even if he had not traveled east; sometimes the reported owner was the mayordomo in charge of organizing purchases and freighting the goods back home.[44]

Surviving documents, such as manifests and guías, do not allow an accurate and systematic comparison between American and New Mexican shipments. It is also impossible to establish the quantity and value of the merchandise that remained in the territory. Guías often do not provide information on the value of the goods. Customs officials seldom prepared complete manifests for an entire year, and, as Morehead noted, these documents bore little relation to either the number or the assessment of the imports. Although it is not possible to assert that New Mexicans controlled the trade on the eve of the Mexican War, it is accurate to maintain that during this period New Mexicans made up the majority of the traders traveling down the Royal Road to the interior of Mexico. In 1843 New Mexicans received seventy guías, compared with only twenty-one for Americans. However, only in ten cases did New Mexicans haul foreign goods. The other shipments included sheep and efectos del país. They were bulky and, in general, of much lower value than the shipments that foreigners sent. New Mexican merchants were trading alongside Albert Speyer, Henry Connelly, Louis Robidoux, George East, and other wealthy entrepreneurs who controlled sizable capital and had important commercial relations with major American financial institutions. It is not possible to establish who had ultimate control over the trade, but after 1839 New Mexicans certainly played a major role in the commerce between Mexico and the United States.[45]

The question of which ethnic group controlled the trade remains an issue of contention; there are neither descriptions nor analyses of the economic system that developed in New Mexico as a result. David Sandoval concludes that the changes following the Mexican War had an immediate detrimental impact on New Mexicans.[46] However, documents indicate that wealthy New Mexican merchants profited substantially from the trade in the decades immediately after the American occupation, as they continued to make large duty-free purchases in the United States. Many comerciantes suffered a decline, but this took place only in the years after the Civil War when the nature of trade operations changed dramatically. During the late 1830s, the 1840s, and 1850s the New Mexican elite developed a form of mercantile capitalism that took advantage of the conditions in the territory.

Unlike foreign merchants, they supplied the people in the countryside with the manufactured goods they needed. In exchange they obtained sheep, grains, and commodities as well as promissory notes.

Scholars have ignored the contributions New Mexicans made to the development of an economic system well suited to the special circumstances of their territory. Lewis E. Atherton's studies of Santa Fe traders include insightful observations, but these are concentrated exclusively on the activities of Missouri merchants before the Mexican War.[47]

William Parish wrote the most comprehensive study of the economic system that evolved in New Mexico as a result of the Santa Fe trade, yet he completely overlooked New Mexicans' contributions, focusing instead on the role of German Jews.[48] Parish identified three basic characteristics of mercantile capitalism in New Mexico. First, traveling merchants were replaced by sedentary merchants, who depended on regular deliveries and ordered ahead of time from Baltimore, Philadelphia, New York, and other eastern cities. Second, cash was a scarce commodity in the New Mexican economy, which had a strongly unfavorable balance of trade. This forced merchants to establish close connections with local institutions, such as United States Army forts, which paid for their badly needed local produce with cash. This was then converted into federal drafts on eastern banks and deposited with wholesaling houses and commission merchants in New York City. Third, the need to gain access to the produce of the countryside encouraged the establishment of stores in small rural towns.[49]

New Mexican merchants began to implement such a system before the Mexican War, and after 1845 they were quick to acquire much-needed credit through the sale of raw materials to industrial areas and of supplies to federal installations, such as United States Army posts, and possibly Indian reservations.

Parish's failure to examine Mexican documents accounts for his assessment that "He [the German Jewish merchant] had found the Mexican merchants, with few exceptions, to possess little drive for material productiveness."[50] Parish did not realize that wealthy New Mexicans shared many of the characteristics of their German counterparts, and, like them, did not enter the trade for speculative reasons, but sought to build a thriving and permanent business enterprise.

It is not possible to ascertain who was the first individual to implement mercantile capitalism in New Mexico. It is clear, however, that Hispanos had developed a fairly sophisticated system before the Mexican War. Manuel Alvarez was not a native New Mexican, but he should share at least partial credit for introducing mercantile capitalism to the province. Parish dismissed him as a minor figure because "his ledgers . . . show but three Eastern trips, some bartering in Taos and Abiquiú, but no signs of imports and exports on any scale."[51] It is unfortunate that Parish did not see how well Alvarez and other New Mexicans fit the model of the sedentary merchant who had gone beyond petty capitalism to introduce a more sophisticated mercantile system to the territory.

Alvarez, a Spaniard who sporadically acted as American consul in New Mexico, spent close to three decades in Santa Fe. His international contacts allowed him to interact with relative ease with Europeans, Mexicans, and Americans.[52] It is true that Alvarez only made three trips east, but one of them took him to Europe, from where he kept himself informed of business developments in the province and periodically forwarded instructions to his employees.[53] Alvarez was certainly not a traveling merchant. On the other hand, he seems to have matched perfectly Parish's idea of the sedentary merchant, "who sat down in administration . . . [and] became dependent on regular deliveries, ordered ahead of time, from distant areas."[54] Invoices from New York firms demonstrate that even though Alvarez himself did not travel east in 1845, he made substantial purchases from Alfred Edwards and Co., Francis B. Rhodes and Co., and Hyslop and Brothers.[55]

His ledgers might not reflect all his purchases, but they do show that until his death in 1856 he acted as a major wholesaler, retailer, commission merchant, and intermediary for both New Mexican merchants and their foreign counterparts. He had a large and varied clientele, and by 1834 he was already wholesaling merchandise to Santiago and Ramón Abreu and lending money to a wide range of individuals. His economic operations prospered, possibly because he took advantage of the continued local demand for foreign goods. On 24 April 1845, he sold close to $8,000 worth of merchandise to Juan Otero, among it twenty-seven thousand yards of fabric.[56]

Another characteristic of Alvarez's system was the establishment of branch stores in order to gain access to the produce of the countryside. Alvarez had stores in San Miguel del Vado, La Cañada, Mora, and El Paso. During the 1840s he employed at least two agents, Damaso and Francisco Paula de Robledo. They covered certain areas of the New Mexican territory collecting grains and legumes, and informed Alvarez of the result of their efforts and of fluctuations in local production and demand for specific merchandise.[57] In 1844 Francisco Robledo notified Alvarez that he was exploring the countryside looking for sarapes and hides as part of a scheme to introduce non-native cattle to the territory. From his official residence at San Miguel del Vado, Robledo made trips to neighboring communities where he sold the merchandise that Alvarez had ordered from the United States. As they traveled throughout the Río Arriba, the Robledos updated don Manuel on the types of goods that would be easy to sell. In November 1846, drinking glasses and metallic beads of various colors were in demand.[58] At the same time the Robledos purchased wheat, corn, beans, and other produce, which they probably sold to the United States Army, as the correspondence mentions contracts with, and payments from, the Quartermaster's Office.[59]

Parish might have overlooked New Mexican merchants because he focused on those who operated out of Santa Fe and San Miguel del Vado.[60] These were important ports of entry for the trade caravans and attracted influential foreigners. The wealthiest New Mexican merchants (Oteros, Pereas, Armijos, Yrizarris, and Chávezes), however, did not reside in that area, but at the time lived in Bernalillo and Valencia counties, the area referred to as the Río Abajo (see chapter 8, table 6). These astute entrepreneurs took advantage of the opportunities that the Santa Fe trade offered to develop a widespread network of commercial establishments, which by the 1850s allowed them to solidify their control of the provincial economy.

The economic success of the Río Abajo merchants is not difficult to explain. Most were members of wealthy families who participated in a variety of economic activities. They farmed, raised cattle and sheep, and mined. In addition, they owned retail businesses and acted as local and regional banks. Information before the 1850s survives for only one property, that of José and Mariano Chávez. This family would own several of the best stores in the territory. The biggest one was probably at Belén; the earliest, at San Miguel del Vado; and the most famous, at Santa Fe. Visitors remarked that the Santa Fe store on the southeast corner of the plaza managed by Juan Sena was "the second best store in town . . . floored with plank—the only plank floor in New Mexico."[61]

There are no available management records for this establishment, but it probably operated like the one at San Miguel del Vado. For several years after 1840, Pablo Delgado, the youngest son of another influential merchant, Manuel Delgado, managed the Chávez store in this community. Pablo's duties and the complex transactions in which he participated resembled those of Alvarez's agents. Young Delgado was responsible for a geographic area around the store, including a variety of communities around San Miguel: Antón Chico, Tecolote, Puertecito, Cuesta, San José, and Bernal. He sold whatever the locals needed. Pablo's correspondence with his father Manuel and his brothers Simón and Felipe reveals that repayment of debts was a prime concern in operating the business.[62] Pablo accepted grains, wheat, barley, and oats as payment for debts. Although the store owned some sheep, Delgado collected *carneros* (wethers) as reimbursement, in particular from the *partidarios* (individuals who signed agreements to look after sheep belonging to someone else).[63] Most of the leading New Mexican merchants took advantage of the partido system, which allowed them to increase the size of their herds without incurring much risk.[64]

The Chávez business at San Miguel del Vado was a diversified operation, designed to take advantage of the local shortages of cash to collect valuable local commodities: grains, *aguardiente* (alcoholic spirits), wine, sheep, and precious metals. The store records reveal that mining precious minerals was a significant factor in the creation of the family wealth. A notebook started on 20 November 1841 provides an almost daily account of the weight of the gold brought to this store. The entries stopped after 9 May 1842. Although it is incomplete and extremely hard to read, and it does not record who did the mining or who brought the ore to the store, the notebook shows that the province provided a significant source of the bullion that wealthy merchants took to the United States. This document also demonstrates that the Chávezes, like other New Mexican ricos, relied on a variety of economic activities to support and enhance the family business.[65]

Hispano merchants pioneered many of the activities that Parish associated with the German Jews. They were particularly successful in securing and arranging deliveries of merchandise from eastern markets, such as Baltimore, Pittsburgh, Philadelphia, New York, and — for bulkier goods — Independence and St. Louis. They were intent on building permanent businesses, and they realized that it was necessary to cultivate personal associations with suppliers if they were to receive high-quality merchandise at competitive prices. Initially, they selected the goods personally, since the eastern wholesalers had little "feel" for southwestern markets, but later on they were content to send agents to act in their behalf. New Mexicans learned that the most consistent, reliable, and profitable method of obtaining credit in the eastern United States was through the shipment of raw materials. To begin with, they carried metal ores and Mexican silver dollars, and later on they freighted hides and wool. To get cash for more far-flung ventures they also furnished United States Army installations with supplies that they obtained from their regional stores.[66]

Years before the Jewish merchant Charles Ilfeld moved to Taos in 1865, New Mexican merchants had put in practice an economic system based on the model Parish so aptly described. Several wealthy entrepreneurs participated in the evolution of a form of mercantile capitalism that allowed them to control the economic life of the province. Their commercial activities foreshadowed those that German Jews would carry out during the last decades of the nineteenth century. Extensive documentation appears to indicate that Felipe Chávez came to be among the most successful in implementing this economic system.

SIX

Felipe Chávez

. . . fue para mí el amigo más fino y más sincero que he conocido, pues no tengo suficientes palabras para manifestarle mi gratitud a un amigo como él, que siempre lo hayé listo cuando recurría a él en mis necesidades. . . . ruego y le suplico que me deje el dinero, si gusta con el seis por ciento como me lo tenía prestado su buen papá.[1]

. . . I will never forget him because for me he was the finest and most sincere friend that I have known; I do not have enough words to express my gratitude to a friend like him who was always ready to help me when I was in need. . . . I beg and plead with you that you continue to lend me the money, if you wish at 6 percent as your kind father, my boss, don Felipe, had done.

FELIPE DELGADO, 1906

Felipe Delgado's letter to José E. Chávez at the time of his father's death reveals the complex nature of *el millonario* (the millionaire). Felipe Chávez (1834–1906) seldom hesitated to lend money to relatives or acquaintances in need, yet at the same time he seldom failed to charge the prevailing interest for his loans.[2] A shrewd entrepreneur, his economic activities are an excellent example of mercantile capitalism and represent the culmination of the system that New Mexican merchants developed during the years prior to the Mexican War. His transactions reveal that during the second half of the nineteenth century Felipe Chávez took advantage of every opportunity that the Santa Fe trade offered to become one of the most prosperous and influential businessmen in the region.[3]

Chávez was able to build on the fortune he inherited from his father because he adopted a sound yet flexible commercial strategy. Diversification was crucial to his success. Chávez sold American and European manufactures, raised grains and sheep, shipped wool and precious metals, bought large amounts of merchandise, purchased real estate in the east (New York City), and acted as a banker, commissioner, wholesaler, and retailer. He maintained economic relations with merchants in Liverpool and Manchester (England, UK), New York, Philadelphia, St. Louis, Santa Fe, Albuquerque, El Paso, Chihuahua, Durango, Zacatecas, and Guadalajara; established partnerships with other New Mexicans; and was an intermediary between American and Mexican wholesalers. Although he was unable to organize Río Abajo freighters into an association to obtain government contracts, his accounts show that the United States Quartermaster's Office was one of the main sources of the funds he used to finance large purchases of merchandise. Cautious, but not reluctant to take risks, he regularly requested and received information on the prices of precious metals and commodities and on other investment opportunities. His decisions were often based on the advice he sought from business associates in New York, St. Louis, and Mexico. His meticulous record keeping ensured that losses due to carelessness and mistakes were kept to a minimum, and he was careful to invest capital where he could receive the highest possible return. At the same time he also appears to have been generous with kin and friends to whom he often lent large sums of money.

Felipe Chávez was the son of José María Chávez and Manuela Armijo. Born in 1834, he attended school at the *Seminario Conciliar de Guadalajara* (Conciliar Seminary of Guadalajara), Mexico, where he distinguished himself, receiving awards for his academic efforts. He completed his education in 1852.[4] Returning home, young Chávez began to help his father with the management of the family's thriving commercial operations and took charge of the entire business four years later. Felipe was smart, had a great deal of common sense, and was a meticulous record keeper. He kept *borradores* (onion-skin notebooks containing carbon copies) of most of his outgoing business letters.[5] He painstakingly checked all the shipments he received and was quick to note any discrepancies.

Until his father's death, Felipe made sure that their merchandise was kept separate. In September 1856, a wholesaler in New York apologized for a labeling error that mistakenly assigned Felipe's merchandise to his father. Felipe quickly noted the error and wrote to ensure that proper credit was assigned. For someone as wealthy as Chávez the sum was relatively small, and the incident is a good example of Felipe's careful record keeping and persistence. This was not an isolated episode either. Chávez always demanded full accountability from his associates. In 1859 a package of two thousand yards of lienzo, part of a shipment that included more than 150 such packages, was lost between New York and New Mexico. Upon discovering it was missing, Felipe dispatched letters to Peter Harmony and Nephews in New York, and Edward Glasgow in St. Louis. When he did not obtain a satisfactory reply, he wrote two additional letters until finally Harmony agreed to reimburse him for the cost of the lost cloth.[6]

Large-scale operations were becoming more common when Felipe took over the family business in 1856. He more than met Parish's criteria for the sedentary merchant who became dependent on regular deliveries and ordered from distant areas ahead of time.[7] His first documented major purchase dates from 1856, when he bought 172 tercios of merchandise weighing 42,964 pounds and valued at $14,167.33. To arrange the bulk of the purchase Chávez used the services of Peter Harmony and Nephews, a Spanish firm located in New York City that often did business with New Mexicans. Harmony acted as wholesaler, retailer, commission merchant, banker, real estate agent, answered Chávez's questions, and provided him sound business advice.[8]

In fact, Harmony was instrumental in arranging most of Felipe's major purchases for several decades. The transactions were complicated because they involved a variety of businesses and required the transportation of several tons of goods over thousands of miles. Chávez normally bought some merchandise directly from Harmony, but he often instructed his mayordomos to search for bargains, or items that were not available in New York or that could be obtained more favorably in Philadelphia, Pittsburgh, or elsewhere. Once the order was ready, Harmony consigned it to a firm in Independence or St. Louis, often Glasgow Brothers, that would oversee the final shipment to New Mexico.[9]

Massive purchases were the norm. An 1859 invoice listed eighty thousand yards of indiana, manta, and lienzo, 1,092 pairs of boots, 540 pairs of shoes, and 585 pairs of pants.[10] Another one from March 1860 included thirty-six pages of items: 135 *balas* (bolts) with close to two hundred thousand yards of fabric, 346 boxes, forty-eight bundles or packages, seventy-four large trunks, and two barrels, all valued at $36,237.77.[11] In 1863 Felipe arranged another order. A bill presented by W. H. Chick identified the expenses incurred in shipping merchandise to New Mexico. Chávez bought more than fifty thousand pounds of merchandise for which he paid $1,486.43 for storage and freight. He also bought seventy mules (each one cost six dollars) and a horse, and had to pay expenses for taking care of the animals. The order was so large that it took a month for the entire load to be processed and shipped. In addition, he arranged for the purchase of a variety of hardware, tools, and wagons from several dealers in St. Louis, and a standard order of dry goods from Glasgow Brothers.[12]

For many years the Glasgows arranged for the dispatch of merchandise when Chávez's caravans reached the moving railroad terminal. They sold

Chávez the groceries that normally completed these shipments.[13] Invoices from 1856 reveal that during the first week of May that year, Felipe bought 64,298 pounds of dry goods. Among them were 220 sacks of clarified sugar, seventy-one barrels of whiskey, one barrel of brandy, two boxes of cognac (listed apart from the brandy), ten boxes of claret, ten baskets of champagne, two boxes of oysters, two boxes of sardines, eighteen pounds of almonds, ten sacks of coffee, seventy boxes of sperm candles, forty boxes of white soap, three thousand cigars, and other miscellaneous items.[14]

This pattern continued throughout the next decade. During the first week of July 1871, Chick, Browne, and Co. prepared another order. Thirteen mule-drawn wagons under Francisco Chávez carried 64,866 pounds, and ox wagons led by Ambrosio Pino and Manuel Aragón hauled 5,704 and 18,675 pounds, respectively, for a total weight of 89,245 pounds. It is not possible to establish if Chávez's economic situation had improved by 1880, but it is clear that the weight of his shipments had not declined.[15]

In some years his purchases were more modest. In 1873 he received around twelve thousand pounds of goods, and in 1876 he bought only around $2,500 worth of merchandise from Samuel C. Davis and Co. of St. Louis, but this may not have been the only merchandise he acquired that year.[16] Chávez appeared to have bought additional commodities at the shipping terminals when his needs for merchandise were more limited. In many cases these were perishable goods, such as jams, ham, butter, crackers, pickles, corn, dried fruits, and potatoes, but sometimes the invoices included the occasional wagon, trunks, cups, and silverware.[17]

As Chávez set price limits for every item to be purchased, he often obtained substantial savings, which helped him to succeed in the highly competitive Santa Fe trade. In February 1860 he sent his mayordomo, Antonio Robles, to buy merchandise in New York. Chávez trusted Robles and authorized Harmony to make all the necessary funds available to facilitate his agent's task. Robles wrote to his *patrón* (boss) almost daily, informing him of the current prices and of the purchases he had made. The correspondence reveals how specific Chávez's instructions had been. Once, Robles bought too many capes, and he was afraid that they would not be the exact type Chávez had asked him to buy. Robles also provided Chávez with information on the quality and price of a variety of items, and kept him abreast of what he was about to buy.[18] At times this policy produced less favorable results. In 1859 Chávez gave specific instructions to Harmony regarding the purchase of items for the church. Harmony informed Felipe that out of the order for three crucifixes and six candle holders, he was only remitting one crucifix. He did not dare purchase more since he was unable to obtain them at less than forty dollars, and Chávez had set the upper limit at fifteen dollars.[19]

There were other risks in searching for the lowest prices. Anxious to please Chávez, Antonio Robles bought some items of clothing from less than respectable businessmen (not associated with Harmony), who offered him substantial discounts. Chávez was not satisfied with the quality of some of these items and complained to Harmony. The wholesaler replied that in his efforts to obtain the effects at the lowest possible price Robles had rejected those *almacenes* (warehouses) from whom Harmony normally made purchases and acquired merchandise from salesmen who did not have a sound reputation. Harmony warned that it was not possible to make a claim for a reimbursement. Chávez, still trying to recover some of his losses, complained again, but Harmony answered admonishing the New Mexican that it was common for outsiders to come to New York and listen to astute salesmen who promised merchandise at prices 4, 5, or even 20 percent cheaper and then delivered items of less than desirable quality. Harmony warned Chávez once again of the dangers involved in such dealings.[20] There is no record of his reply, but apparently he listened because on subsequent trips his agents dealt only with those businesses that had a reputation for honesty and reliability.

However, Chávez's search for the best available buys still led him to procure merchandise from a variety of wholesalers, and he continued this practice for decades. In 1858 another mayordomo, Atanacio Montoya, went to St. Louis, where he bought twenty carts from one dealer, mule harnesses from another, small carts from a third, fabrics from a fourth, guns and ammunition from H. E. Dimick, and groceries from Glasgow Brothers.[21] Similar purchases were made in 1861 and 1863.[22] In April 1867 he bought a shipment of fabrics from Charles Stern and Co. Amounting to $5,679.98, the order included close to twenty thousand yards of muslin, 2,540 shawls of various types, 144 yards of *alpaca* (wool or cloth), forty coverlets, eight grosses of handkerchiefs, three thousand yards of a variety of printed textiles, and five thousand yards of manta. In 1868 he received a letter of inquiry from Cuno, Bohms, and Co. from St. Louis, and he purchased $2,834 in boots and shoes from wholesale dealer Appleton, Noyes, and Co.[23] In June 1871 he acquired goods from at least four dealers: Glasgow Brothers, A. A. Mellier, Rodney D. Wells and Co., and B. and J. F. Slevin and Co.[24]

American merchants courted Felipe, trying to obtain his business. In

1865 S. P. Shannon of Kansas City offered him dry goods, shoes, boots, and ready-made clothes specially designed for the New Mexican market. Shannon informed Felipe that because the company had agents in New York it was able to offer the lowest prices and the greatest variety of goods, and promised discounts of 40 percent over the previous year's charges.[25] W. H. Chick followed suit in 1867 as he established new almacenes in Phil Sheridan, Kansas. When the firm became Chick and Browne, and moved to Granada, Colorado, Chávez received notification.[26] Other wholesalers tried to obtain Chávez's business and were extremely appreciative when they did, as were the Bartels Brothers.[27] Other American firms, like Pittsburgh's Black Diamond Steel Works, wrote advising him of the excellent quality of their products.[28]

The procedure for sending goods to New Mexico was quite complex. Merchandise from New York was usually sent via steamboat to St. Louis. Often it had to be stored while local purchases were readied. The shipper was responsible for checking that all items listed in invoices had arrived. This was a laborious task because merchandise — identified only with the initials of the owner — could easily be lost. Sometimes, the contents of the boxes did not quite match what was written on the invoices, and it was troublesome to trace the fate of some of these goods.

By the time the merchandise arrived in Missouri, one of Chávez's mayordomos was ready to help with the final shipment. This was not always easy. In 1860, Atanacio Montoya went to Kansas to help haul the merchandise that Robles had purchased in New York. From Westport, he wrote to Chávez explaining that it took a lot of work, time, and care to load each wagon with four thousand pounds of goods. He warned his patrón that in spite of his efforts he had been unable to load the entire 69,919 pounds that comprised the load.[29]

Hauling effects from New York to New Mexico was also very expensive. Merchants had to pay for packaging, carrying the merchandise to the almacén and from the almacén to the port, handling charges, insurance, and a 2.5-percent commission — in all about a 6.1-percent surcharge over the original purchase.[30] Railroad freight from New York to St. Louis was not cheap either, as it usually amounted to 3 percent of the value of the merchandise.[31] Freighting expenses declined very slowly as the railroad approached New Mexico, and Chávez searched for the best bargain. His correspondence with W. H. Chick documents his success in reducing the rates he paid. In June 1868, Chick informed him that part of the order would cost four cents per hundred pounds, but the rest, only three. Chick added that this was absolutely the best price available since freight to Fort

Union was two and a half cents per hundred pounds, and to Santa Fe, three cents per hundred pounds. Since the merchandise had to go to Los Lunas and Peralta (south of Albuquerque), Chávez was getting a special deal.[32]

Two years later the rates decreased. In July 1871 Chávez paid only two and a half cents per hundred pounds on a shipment from Kit Carson, Colorado, although in November, Chick, Browne, and Co. charged him three and half cents per hundred pounds for sending 1,540 pounds of coffee.[33] In April 1878, Francisco Manzanares explained to an impatient Chávez that competition between the railroad companies would result in lower rates, and he assured Felipe that when that time came he would be able to offer him the lowest available rates.[34]

He was right. Competition among the railroads did reduce freight rates almost by half. In 1878, Vicente M. Baca, Felipe's foster son, advised Chávez that the price of sending a hundred pounds to Las Vegas was down to half a cent, and that it was only three-quarters of a cent to Santa Fe and a cent and a quarter to Bernalillo.[35]

Insurance, normally a 1.25-percent surcharge, was virtually a necessity, even for relatively small purchases because losses and damages were quite common. In addition to the hazards of shipping tons of merchandise over thousands of miles, the Indian threat always had to be considered. In 1864 Chávez appeared concerned for the first time about the danger posed by Indian tribes.[36] In September 1868, one of his trains was forced to go back due to Indian hostilities.[37] The next year, during June, W. H. Chick congratulated Chávez on his luck because his train had arrived at New Mexico safely, while the Indians had attacked Phil Sheridan, Kansas, stealing thirty-four mules and a horse belonging to other New Mexican merchants who were getting ready to travel home.[38]

One of the keys to Chávez's success was his ability to take advantage of the information he received from his business associates. Harmony regularly kept him apprised of the prices of cotton fabrics, shoes, coffee, hides, and gold.[39] W. H. Chick and E. J. Glasgow also updated him on current prices of merchandise, freight, and gold. During the climax of the Civil War, the Glasgows forecast a dramatic increase in the price of cotton goods, and they mailed Chávez reports on the need for various types of wool.[40] In 1879 Benjamin Walker advised him of the financial trouble affecting Glasgow Brothers and warned him to transfer his shipments of wool to Gregg Brothers of Philadelphia.[41]

Chávez was willing to take risks, but he quickly realized his mistakes and did not repeat them. Early in his business career he purchased flannel directly from England. Two invoices survive documenting the transaction.

The first one, dated June 1856, records the sale of one thousand yards of flannel in Manchester, England. From Manchester, the fabric was sent to Liverpool. From there, it was shipped to New York, then to Kansas City, and finally to Santa Fe. The original cost of the flannel in Manchester, including shipping and commission fees, was $96.60, but by the time it reached New Mexico the total had risen to $661.04.[42] The next year Felipe tried again, but this time instead of sending the fabric to New York he shipped it through New Orleans. The result was not much different—he paid $662.18.[43] There is no record that he ever tried this type of transaction again.

The death of José María Chávez on 30 October 1858 meant that from then on Felipe was responsible for the well-being of his mother, as well as that of his sister Bárbara and numerous other relatives. Felipe always took this responsibility quite seriously, even though at times it probably became a heavy burden. His brother-in-law Nicolás Armijo, married to his sister Bárbara, regularly borrowed money. Armijo was apparently in charge of the Chávez family businesses in Chihuahua, and he appeared to be in constant economic trouble. Felipe's cousin, J. Francisco Chávez, became another chronic borrower. In 1865 he asked for $3,000. Francisco promised to insure the loan and pledged to handle the affair as a regular business transaction. He considered his economic prospects to be very positive and believed that his California property would return to him at least $50,000 in less than two years. There is no record that Francisco ever repaid this obligation.[44]

Other members of the family relied on Felipe's position and wealth to help them through bad times. In April 1867 Melquíades Chávez wrote to Felipe requesting funds to cover a *libranza* (draft) worth $5,000.[45] In 1879 J. Francisco Chávez informed Felipe that he was unable to settle his loan but would continue paying the annual interest and promised to repay the capital as soon as his situation improved. However, a month later Francisco requested an additional $3,000 to cover a debt to José Leandro Perea, promising ten carts with eight mules and ten thousand sheep as collateral on the new loan.[46]

Friends of his father and former employees also appealed to Felipe's generosity and asked for employment, loans, or delays in paying their accounts. In January 1868 José Gutiérrez wrote from Las Vegas that he had moved from Algodones hoping to receive a large sum of money that he had lent Francisco Perea; Perea was unable to pay, so Gutiérrez asked Chávez to sell him a train of mules which he had promised some time before. José did not have collateral for the loan and proposed to use the train of mules itself as security.[47]

Chávez received numerous requests for financial help, both from Hispanos and Anglos throughout the province, and he satisfied many of them.[48] He lent money to merchants and freighters, like Martín Amador, from Las Cruces and Hilario Romero, son of Miguel Romero.[49] When borrowers requested extensions in their loans, he often granted them.

It is not possible to know exactly how much profit Felipe made in his capacity as informal lending institution, since with few exceptions there is no information on the interest rates he charged, or if he regularly did so. On 26 June 1867 he lent A. and L. Zeckendorf $4,312.50. A month later Zeckendorf asked for an extension on the loan and a reduction in the interest. Felipe was charging the Albuquerque merchant 12 percent interest on this loan, and Zeckendorf reminded him that the going rate was 6 percent. If 12 percent was his standard charge, Chávez could have earned substantial sums, since commission merchants like Chick and Armijo, P. Harmony, and E. Glasgow paid only 5 percent on those funds left on account.[50] However, it is not clear that this was his customary rate. At the time of his death, he was charging Felipe Delgado 6 percent interest on a loan. Delgado's eager request for the continuation of the loan at the same rate may indicate that in cash-scarce New Mexico, Felipe Chávez's charges were quite reasonable.[51]

Besides, there were risks in lending. There is no evidence that any of Chávez's relatives ever repaid any of the principal they borrowed. Many of the other debtors also failed to fulfill their obligations. Collecting debts was time-consuming, and, depending on the economic circumstances of the debtor, it might not have been a worthwhile activity. In January 1868 Chávez sent José Felix Benavídez to Cubero and Cebolleta to collect from José Padilla, but he got nothing out of Padilla, who was apparently totally unable to pay.[52]

Chávez sometimes operated as an intermediary between local New Mexico merchants and eastern promoters like P. Harmony and W. H. Chick. For example, in 1867 a merchant from Las Cruces owed $2,400 in a libranza to a merchant from Sonora who had passed away, and Harmony wrote to Felipe requesting his help in straightening out the situation. This was not the only case in which commission merchants resorted to Chávez for help.[53] He also facilitated the economic ventures of many New Mexicans. In June 1860 he made it possible for José María Romero to purchase $7,925.13 worth of merchandise from Glasgow Brothers.[54]

Throughout his career, Chávez maintained economic relations with merchants in Guadalajara, Zacatecas, Durango, Chihuahua (Mexico), Manchester and Liverpool (England, UK), and Canada. In June 1858 Harmony made a $6,820 payment on Felipe's behalf to the account of Durango's Juan Flores; in August 1859 he credited José Cordero with $1,095.50 from Chávez's account. Felipe continued to make transactions with José Cordero for a number of years. Cordero relied on Chávez's accounts in New York to invest in United States government bonds, and when he sent his agents to the United States with the purpose of selling effects, he instructed them to do nothing before they got Chávez's advice. Cordero assumed responsibility for Chávez's libranzas in Durango, Mexico, and sold *piloncillo* (Mexican brown sugar in small pylon-shaped cakes) to the New Mexican as late as November 1862. The monthly accounts that Harmony prepared for Chávez often recorded transactions in which Cordero had participated.[55]

Associates in Zacatecas also relied on Felipe Chávez to act as intermediary with Peter Harmony, and in July 1861 P. Harmony made an interesting request. As the Civil War was disrupting commercial activities in the United States, Harmony asked Chávez to inquire among his business associates in Mexico, and particularly Chihuahua, if there would be any interest in purchasing several boxes of machinery.[56] During the next year (1862) the Delino Brothers from Durango also relied on Felipe Chávez to obtain a loan, which they backed with United States treasury notes.[57] Sixteen years later, Felix Francisco Maceyra, a leading merchant from Chihuahua, asked Felipe for a substantial loan and promised a high return — $40,000 to $50,000 at 12 percent.[58] Like his father, Chávez continued commercial relations with D. Duarte and Co. from Manchester, England, relying on the services offered by Guadalajara's Alvarez Araujo and the trusted Harmony.[59]

Chávez and other New Mexican merchants, particularly those from the Río Abajo, cooperated informally in commercial transactions. They often took care of each's other businesses. For example, Antonio José Otero acted as Chávez's intermediary in 1862, carrying correspondence from the Harmony store and money orders from Felipe to his business associates in New York.[60] Chávez also participated in more formal arrangements. During the 1850s he formed partnerships with other important New Mexico merchant. One of the most important and long-lasting was that with Simón and Felipe Delgado, who, besides being Chávez's associates, managed his store in Santa Fe, as their brother Pablo had done for Felipe's uncles Mariano and José during the 1840s.[61]

The earliest records for the partnership date from January 1857, when P. Harmony credited the account of Simón Delgado and Felipe Chávez with a $2,000 libranza from the United States Treasury.[62] The enterprise seemed remarkably successful, as the earnings for less than a year (November 1856 to May 1857) were $4,439.26, a substantial profit on the $25,902.32 that the partners had invested. The Delgados operated as special agents for Chávez, handling business affairs in Santa Fe and occasionally traveling east to arrange for purchases. In 1863 Simón Delgado was receiving payments from the Quartermaster of the United States Army to deposit in Chávez's account, but the records do not indicate the nature of the purchases. An 1865 invoice shows transactions with Fort Craig, but the cryptic entries do not present a clear picture either. In April 1867 Simón Delgado once again sent a libranza against the United States Subtreasury for $5,000, which Harmony credited to Chávez's account.[63] The next year Pablo Delgado credited Chávez with another libranza from the Quartermaster's Office against the treasury of New York, this time for $4,300. Delgado informed Felipe that Minister Shaw had paid $2,000 of the above sum.[64]

The two families maintained close relations as the Delgados continued to act as Chávez's agents or convoys throughout the century. During December 1868 Francisco A. Manzanares informed Felipe that he had sent $2,201.81 to St. Louis according to his wishes and that he had left copies of this transaction in Pablo Delgado's home in Santa Fe.[65] A few months later Pablo wrote to Chávez, updating him on the activities of Jacob Amberg, an important local merchant. Apparently Amberg had left New Mexico, and before leaving he had promised that he would cover all his debts.[66] However, Pablo found out that the day before, Amberg's brother and a commissioner from St. Louis had arrived at Santa Fe, and Pablo suspected something. He informed Chávez that he would keep his eyes open and get in touch with Chávez's lawyer if anything else happened. Delgado reassured Felipe that he was taking care of his affairs as if he (Chávez) were in town, and apparently he was. A June 1869 letter shows that Pablo was still handling finances for Chávez out of Santa Fe, sending a libranza for $13,643.56 to W. H. Chick and receiving payment from Chávez's debtors.[67] The partnership continued to operate at least through the 1870s.[68]

The relationship between the Delgados and Chávez is intriguing and spans many years. While strong economic interests were important elements that brought the two families together, the correspondence between Felipe and Pablo reveals a degree of trust that went beyond financial concerns. Pablo provided Felipe information regarding the misguided activities of his widowed mother in Santa Fe (where Pablo resided), and Felipe watched over Juanito, Pablo's son, and helped the young boy with his English.[69]

A more conventional partnership joined Felipe to a different wealthy family—the Oteros. In 1858 Manuel Antonio Otero and Felipe Chávez made two purchases from Glasgow Brothers in St. Louis. The first was made on 27 June and cost $5,985.13; the second was made on 18 November and cost $10,621.13. Invoices indicate that the partnership was still in operation during August 1859.[70]

Chávez normally paid for his purchases with libranzas, *letras de crédito* (letters of credit), or *letras de cambio* (letters of exchange) that had been deposited in his various accounts, but it was risky to send libranzas to New York. In August 1863 Harmony informed Chávez that he was trying to recover some of the losses resulting from the disappearance of various libranzas in the wreck of the steamboat *Tempest*. This was not an unusual occurrence.[71]

Sometimes Chávez's strategy was different. In 1858 he sent his mayordomo, Atanacio Montoya to Westport, Missouri, to collect $15,968.99 worth of merchandise. Chávez paid cash for this purchase—$14,420.00 in American coins, $432.00 in California gold, $31.00 in doubloons, $184.30 in sovereigns, $19.00 in French pieces, $146.00 in guilders, and $9.00 in odd pieces.[72] He tried to send specie to Missouri for safekeeping in 1861, but the Glasgow brothers asked Felipe not to because it was impossible to spend it and they did not want to be responsible for it. A few months later they repeated their warning against dispatching currency to St. Louis and suggested that it would be safer if they dealt with his agents in New York.[73]

It is difficult to identify a single source of Chávez's wealth. He inherited a significant fortune from his father, but he augmented it substantially. It is possible that mining activities in New Mexico (the Ortiz Mountains) contributed to his wealth.[74] He regularly remitted large drafts to P. Harmony, but it is not always clear how he earned this capital. The invoices indicate the date and the amount for libranzas credited to Chávez's accounts as well as the name of the individual or agency that authorized payment: the United States Subtreasury, the Quartermaster General, Americans, New Mexicans, or Mexican merchants. In settling his account with Harmony in August 1859, Chávez got $13,000 from an unclear source and $6,000 from Eugene Kelly. By October of that year, Kelly had paid an additional $2,000 and, by December, $6,400 more. Kelly continued to make sizable payments during the next year: $3,731 in August, $2,680.75 and $4,000 in September. Between October 1861 and June 1862, Chávez sent three *remesas* (remittances) to Harmony from the United States Subtreasury for a total of $37,987.09.[75] In August 1863, Chávez was credited with $6,652.05 from C. R. Morehead and Co. of Leavenworth. In another instance Chávez's account received a draft for $8,000 from C. P. Clever. A month later this note had not been paid, but by November of the same year the Assistant Treasurer of the United States in New York issued drafts in favor of Clever, which were also credited to Chávez's account.[76] His surviving papers do not show any official contract to supply army installations or to freight for them, but it is highly likely that he either freighted for the army or supplied army posts with flour, grains, or hay.

There is no easy way accurately to assess the wealth of Chávez. An 1857 invoice indicates that between May 1855 and August 1856 he had $56,400 tied up in various transactions, and that in August 1857 Harmony notified him that he had $24,326 in his account.[77] In spite of the voluminous correspondence, there exists only sporadic information on his total wealth. In the 1860 census he declared $5,000 in real estate and $62,575 in personal estate, indicating he owned a substantial amount of merchandise. At this time he was managing his mother's property, which was listed as $6,000 in real estate and $55,660 in personal estate. This made for a combined family total of $129,235.[78] By 1870 the listed family assets had increased to $40,000 in real estate and a $100,000 in personal estate.[79]

During the 1860s and 1870s Chávez maintained a sizable favorable balance with Peter Harmony, Glasgow Brothers, Otero and Sellar, Chick, Browne, and Co., and its successor Browne and Manzanares, as well as a substantial sum in the First Bank of Santa Fe. A statement from 1 January 1879, indicates that at that time he had $69,367.19 in his account with Glasgow Brothers. An invoice from Chick, Browne, and Co. shows that six months later his balance amounted to $12,616.14. By the end of the year (31 December 31 1879) his account with Harmony showed a favorable surplus of $39,289.99.[80]

Chávez was involved in a variety of economic activities. Sheep raising continued to be an important component of his business, particularly during the 1870s when his shipments of wool increased dramatically. His records indicate that through the 1880s, he had numerous partidarios who cared for nearly five hundred thousand sheep.[81] Even Americans tried to get involved in sheep raising. In 1869 Edwin Edgar asked Chávez if he would be willing to give him a partido contract. Edgar had kept a business at La Bajada for a number of months but was thinking of moving to Los Conejos, where according to reports it was ideal to raise sheep.[82]

Chávez sold most of his wool in Kansas, Missouri, and other points east. The system required several *fleteros* (freighters), who departed from New Mexico every other week. As soon as the carts reached their destination, the wool was unloaded, and merchandise targeted for New Mexico was loaded.[83] In 1869 W. H. Chick assured Chávez that he would sell his wool at the best possible price and would report back as soon as he firmed up the sale. By 1879 Glasgow was paying between eleven and thirteen cents per pound depending on the quality. Chávez incurred other expenses in selling this product — two cents per pound for freight and $1.15 per bale, as well as storage and commission charges (normally 4 percent) — but with the advent of the railroad, the freight charges were reduced slightly to 1.75 cents per pound, and it is possible that expenses were even lower since wool was no longer shipped in bales, but in tercios, each one holding close to five hundred pounds.

During the 1870s wool shipments became a significant part of Chávez's operations, growing steadily in size from 7,642 pounds (shipped to Philadelphia) in 1869 to 192,668.5 pounds nine years later. In 1878 his account with Glasgow Brothers indicated an income of $11,266.55 from the sale of wool. However, Glasgow was only one of the buyers of Chávez's wool, and it is safe to assume that he made at least twice as much. He made a profit on these sales only because the partido system ensured a risk-free wool production and because the wages Chávez paid to those handling the wool were quite low.[84] His account with P. Harmony indicates that in 1879 he earned $10,414.96 from the activity.[85] His growing interest in wool appears wise since during the 1870s there was a steady increase in prices — the earlier shipments brought about eleven to twelve cents a pound, but by 1879 Chávez was obtaining between eighteen and twenty-two cents per pound.[86]

Sometimes Chávez sent herds of sheep east. This type of operation appeared riskier as indicated in one of Vicente Baca's letters. From Dodge City, Kansas, he informed his foster father that he had lost eight hundred animals since leaving Belén. Nevertheless, he was still optimistic and felt that he would make enough on the trip to pay what he owed.[87]

Chávez also raised crops, but it is unclear how he managed his agricultural operations. A letter from José Chávez Ballejos identified the amount of wheat and corn to which Ballejos was entitled, but additional information on Chávez's agricultural activities has not been found. He probably produced a significant amount of grains as demonstrated by the purchase of a flour mill (*máquina de calórico de Ericson*), which according to Harmony would grind five bushels of wheat an hour.[88] Additional evidence also suggests substantial production. In June 1868 Z. Staab asked Chávez whether he could deliver a hundred thousand or two hundred thousand pounds of corn for his firm at Fort Fauntleroy and if so at what price.[89]

Throughout his life Chávez operated as a local retailer and wholesaler. Many of his customers charged their purchases, and it is unclear if and how they paid interest on their outstanding debts. Scattered correspondence appears to indicate that he was more lenient with the local population than with his business associates.[90] Chávez acted as wholesaler for many of the small New Mexican merchants and also as their banker. The partial account of José Miguel Baca, between 1868 and 1873, shows that Baca borrowed $217.50 in cash. In addition he charged $469.925 in groceries and supplies.[91] All the fabrics that Chávez and others like him introduced into the territory provided job opportunities for *modistas* (dressmakers). The records indicate the amounts paid, but there is no indication how many women worked, for how long, and what they produced.[92]

Chávez's ability to prosper was also the result of varied investment strategies. During the 1860s he became involved in real estate. He first asked Harmony for information, who, acting as real estate broker, advised Chávez that it would be best to acquire houses (as opposed to lots) since they were easy to lease and would immediately start making profit (about 4 percent per year). Chávez had already sent his mayordomo Castillo to New York with libranzas amounting to $42,911.36. Upon his arrival on 31 September 1864, Harmony prepared a list of houses for sale, and five days after his arrival Castillo examined them with care. Three months later Chávez was the owner of two houses, having paid $20,500 for one, and $18,000 for the other.[93] These properties produced a sizable monthly income. The larger one rented for $358.75 per three months; the smaller one, for $315.00 per three months. Some expenses were involved: Harmony charged a 0.5-percent commission to collect the rents, and Chávez also had to pay insurance and miscellaneous fees to inspectors and to file a legal form allowing Harmony to collect rent.[94] By 1866 the rents had been increased to $450.00 and $358.75, respectively.[95]

That year, Harmony began to look for a buyer for these properties. Chávez wanted to sell the smaller of the two, which was apparently located in an undesirable neighborhood. The renters did not want to move and offered to lease it for two or three additional years for $2,050 — 10 percent of the price that he had paid for the property — and that was the monthly rent that Chávez finally accepted. The same happened when he went to sell the other house. Harmony informed Chávez that he would be able to get the price he set for the first, $22,500, but Chávez wanted more money and asked for $25,000. He did not get it, and finally Harmony rented this property for $2,300 for three years.[96]

Before the leases' expiration approached, Harmony began to look for buyers. There is no record of the final sales, but Harmony informed Chávez in September 1869 that he could probably obtain $30,000 for the larger house and $26,500 for the smaller one, a 31-percent gain (not including rent) for a five-year investment.[97] However, Harmony's valuation was a little optimistic. The smaller house finally sold in 1871 for $25,000. After paying lawyers, fees, and other expenses, Chávez realized less than $24,000, but that still represented a considerable gain for a six-and-a-half-year investment.[98]

Chávez's financial strategies demonstrate his willingness to invest sizable capital in new ventures as well as his flexibility and commitment when changing investment fields. For example, during the 1870s he shifted away from real estate and began to purchase United States government bonds, probably as a result of advice he received from business associates like Peter Harmony. Although it is not possible to establish how much profit he made, he invested a sizable amount in a short period of time. He purchased the first bond ($10,000) in July 1878 and continued to purchase them on a regular basis, at least through the following year.[99]

Felipe Chávez, a successful entrepreneur, was one of the leading practitioners of early mercantile capitalism in New Mexico. His skillful management of personal resources, local products, and business connections, coupled with hard work, determination, informed risk taking, and some ruthlessness allowed him to strengthen his economic standing to become one of the richest men in the territory. Chávez's career was exceptional but not unique. Other New Mexican merchants rivaled him in wealth, influence, and skills. An examination of their commercial activities clearly reveals that many Hispanos possessed a strong drive for "the material productiveness" Parish found only among the German Jews. This drive allowed them to take advantage of the opportunities that Santa Fe trade offered to consolidate the comfortable economic conditions they had inherited.

SEVEN

New Mexican Capitalists

Usted se acordará que en nuestro viaje para Santa Fe, en el invierno pasado, usted adelantó la idea de formar una asociación de fleteros del Río Abajo para agarrar el contrato de los fletes del gobierno.[1]

You will remember that during our trip to Santa Fe last winter you suggested the idea of organizing a group of freighters from the Río Abajo to obtain the government's freighting contract.

HENRY HILGERT, 1867

Felipe Chávez's idea of organizing Río Abajo freighters was never implemented, although formal cooperation among Hispano merchants might have strengthened the economic position of some New Mexican comerciantes during the post-Civil War years. Most Hispanos had collaborated informally before the Mexican War, but after the American occupation a growing political schism between some members of the New Mexican elite polarized families and culminated with their support of opposing sides during the Civil War.[2]

It is likely that by 1867 Chávez realized that the evolving nature of the Santa Fe trade limited the profits to be made from buying merchandise in the east and selling it in New Mexico. He had diversified his business, but understood that increasing risks threatened his mercantile activities. Indian warfare, which broke out in Colorado after the Pike's Peak Gold Rush, began to take its toll on his shipments in the mid-1860s and may have affected many of the Santa Fe trade operations. In general, the years after the Civil War witnessed a great deal of economic upheaval and uncertainty in the west. Many commission merchants suffered similar consequences as they experienced major losses and in some cases went bankrupt.

By 1867 Chávez was aware of the potential benefits of consolidating the resources of the Río Abajo merchants to obtain freighting and supply con-

tracts, operations that required less capital and entailed less risk than purchasing merchandise in the east and bringing it back to New Mexico, and
he tried to bring together prominent Hispano merchants, like the Oteros,
Pereas, Yrizarris, and Armijos. For generations these families had intermar-
ried, participated in joint business ventures, and made possible the form of
mercantile capitalism that evolved in New Mexico, but by the 1860s cooperation was limited to a few individuals and appeared relegated to political
issues, such as selecting congressional representatives who would favor
individual interests. There is no evidence of support for Chávez's idea.[3]
Failure to work together might explain why only the extremely wealthy
maintained, and in only a few cases improved, their economic standing. For
those with more moderate assets, like the Delgados, commercial capitalism
meant continued dependency on the province's ricos.

Had the leading New Mexican merchants joined in an association, they
might have become a formidable economic block. They belonged to a
close-knit elite whose economic activities resembled those of Felipe Chávez. The Otero family was one of the most heavily involved in the Santa Fe
trade. Manifests at the customs house in the capital city indicate that the
Oteros were among the leaders in establishing direct commercial relations
with the United States before the Mexican War, but their achievements
extend well beyond economic prowess.

Descendants of a Spanish-born family who settled in New Mexico during the eighteenth century, Vicente Otero and his sons Antonio José, Manuel Antonio, and Miguel Antonio played important roles in the history of
New Mexico.[4] Oteros traveled east with Mariano and José Chávez at least
twice (1840 and 1844). A credit report from July 1856 listed Antonio José as
"enterprising" and worth between $75,000 and $100,000. The Otero name
does not appear in the very extensive lists of Santa Fc merchants who passed
Council Grove during June and July 1859, but census data for 1860 show
that two family members, enumerated as merchants, were among the richest New Mexicans: Manuel Antonio reported $164,550 in total assets, while
Antonio José declared $65,074. In 1870 Manuel Antonio claimed $174,500
in personal wealth and real estate, while Antonio José, who listed himself as
a farmer, assessed his property and that of his wife at a value of $22,000.[5]

Manuel Antonio Otero's partnership with Felipe Chávez and frequent
references to the Oteros throughout the Chávez papers confirm the similarity of their activities and interests. Like Felipe Chávez, Manuel Antonio
Otero maintained close economic ties to Chihuahua, as preparations for his
1867 trip suggest.[6] Also like Chávez, he became involved in banking ven-

tures. In December 1881 Jacob Gross of Gross, Kelly, and Company, forwarding and commission merchants, advised Manuel Antonio,

> When you organize your bank at Socorro, I would not advise a capital of over $50,000, that sum is plenty & it pays better when the capital is small. Get Lic. Perea interested or Felipe Chávez, or the present delegate Luna, if possible, then have some of the prominent people in Socorro to take a few shares, such men as Captain Abeita or Juan José Baca.[7]

The Oteros were successful politicians and businessmen. However, systematic information on their business operations is quite scarce. In the 1850s Antonio José erected a modern grist mill (the third one in the state) in Peralta. This is a clear indication that Otero had sufficient resources to take advantage of the military market and felt confident that he could obtain contracts to supply the army with an important commodity, such as flour.[8]

Antonio José was not the only member of the Otero family involved in such activities. Democrat Miguel Antonio Otero I was a delegate from New Mexico to the United States Congress between 1855 and 1861, but he abandoned his political career to devote his energy to "banking, outfitting, wholesaling, and retailing."[9] He and his family left New Mexico in 1862, when he became a partner in a commission merchant firm (Otero, Sellar, and Co.) that operated at the various terminal points of the Santa Fe Trail. The Oteros followed the changing railroad terminus from Westport to Fort Harker, then to Ellsworth, Hays City, Sheridan, Fort Wallace, Kit Carson, Granada, La Junta, and briefly back to New Mexico at El Morro, Otero, and Las Vegas.[10] Miguel Antonio Otero II's autobiography contains wonderful insights about life on the frontier and recounts the hectic activities of firms like those his father operated,

> [the business] remained open both day and night. This was necessary, since it usually took all day to load a large outfit, and after that there were many odds and ends that had to be attended to. The wagon-boss had to buy all his provisions for the trip, see that his wagons and animals were in good condition, sign the bills of lading for each wagon, obtain an advance of the money needed for incidental expenses on the trip, and give drafts to the merchants owning the goods. All this had to be done in time for the train of wagons to start at daybreak. To attend to these necessary details, the commission houses utilized two full sets

of bookkeepers, salesmen, clerks, and porters, one set working all day
and the other all night.[11]

Otero also revealed that his father, in addition to his regular line of business,
was a large government contractor, receiving and forwarding supplies to
different military posts and Indian reservations throughout the southwest.[12]
    Otero described the hacienda, La Constancia, the large estate of his
uncle Manuel Antonio, who according to his 1860 census declaration
was the fourth-richest man in New Mexico.[13] The hacienda was south of
Albuquerque:

> to the rear of the main house was the country store, which my uncle
> operated. It was a single room, about one hundred feet long and thirty
> feet wide, with shelves and a counter. One side of the room was de-
> voted to groceries, vegetables, fresh meats, chickens, milk, butter and
> eggs, while the other half was used for dry goods, hardware, leather
> goods, and the like.[14]

    The Pereas were also heavily involved in the Santa Fe trade. In 1844 Juan
and José Perea were among those New Mexicans who returned from the
United States with impressive shipments of American and European products. At the end of July of that year José remitted over $40,000 worth of
merchandise to Chihuahua, Zacatecas, and Aguas Calientes (see appendix
1).[15] Scattered documents confirm the size of the family business activities
after the Mexican War. The *Westport Border Star* reported that on 8 July
1859 the Pereas shipped thirty-five tons of merchandise, in fourteen wagons, to New Mexico. The caravan included sixteen men, two horses, four
mules, and 162 head of cattle.[16]
    In 1867 José Leandro Perea, by now one of the wealthiest men in New
Mexico, outfitted another large train that carried wool to Kansas City and
returned laden with merchandise, an operation that took place annually.[17]
Periodic financial summaries between 1851 and 1875 show that American
business firms considered him to be one of most prominent men in the territory. He had a top credit rating, and owned substantial real estate as well
as a series of stores, the most important at Bernalillo, where he resided. His
assessed wealth in 1875 was $800,000 with real estate valued at $100,000
and about seventy-five thousand sheep.[18] Census returns for 1860 and 1870
confirm the information presented in the credit reports. He was the richest
man in New Mexico, with assets listed at $225,000 in 1860, and $408,000 in
1870.[19]

There is no indication that José Leandro ever competed for army contracts. He had the reputation of being strongly anti-American and may have chosen to ignore the profit that obtaining such contracts would have meant for his business.[20] The richest man in New Mexico did not have to compete for the funds the army infused into the territorial economy.

Only one additional Perea in the 1860 census shared José Leandro's occupation—J. L. from Las Vegas with $36,500 in total assets. Other Pereas—Pedro José and Julián—declared themselves farmers but also owned substantial property. Pedro José reported $40,000 in personal estate, while Julián claimed $20,000. By the next census, José Leandro was the only member of the family listed as a merchant. However, five Pereas appeared as farmers. Together they held personal estate valued at $59,000, a substantial amount of property for farmers in New Mexico in 1870.[21] No records of a formal partnership linking José Leandro Perea with other Hispanos exist, but evidence suggests that he relied on assistance from the Delgado family to carry out transactions in the United States.

The Yrizarris were other New Mexicans who played an important role in the development of the Santa Fe trade. Mariano Yrizarri owned several stores, one of which was at Ranchos de Albuquerque, and at least until the 1870s he was heavily involved in bringing wagon trains of merchandise from Missouri. One surviving invoice from 1854 demonstrates a similarity in the buying strategy of the Yrizarris and the Chávezes. Mariano bought merchandise from nineteen different suppliers, including hats and caps from H. and K. Whittemore; fabrics from Eddy Jamison; ribbons from Pittman and Tennent; bandannas from T. W. Hoit; shoes from R. C. Shackleford and E. C. Yoste; pantaloons from Young Brothers; lace from Weil and Brother; miscellaneous items from A. J. McCreery and Co. and Hanford Thayer and Co.; and dishes from Noonan Tooly and Co. and O. S. Filley and Co. Like Chávez he purchased his groceries from Glasgow Brothers, who also handled his account. The *Westport Border Star* indicated in July 1859 that Mariano Yrizarri shipped sixty-three tons of merchandise to New Mexico in twenty-one wagons. Twenty-four men accompanied the load, which also included 210 head of cattle.[22]

Credit reports between 1868 and 1875 indicate that Yrizarri was also considered among the richest New Mexicans, with a total assessed wealth of $500,000 and a hundred thousand sheep. In 1873 they described him as, "carrying stock of $60,000 to $75,000 . . . a small mercantile business . . . owning real estate valued at $75,000 . . . has $50,000 or $60,000 in cash on deposit with Glasgow Brothers of St. Louis all the time and bushels of it buried." Apparently he was "too mean to have any less at any time."[23]

The same report noted that his son, Manuel, although worth only about $30,000, was a good businessman, prompt, reliable, and fair.

Those who rated Mariano were quite accurate, since the 1860 census information confirmed his economic status — he was the second-richest man in the territory with $213,000 in assets. Ten years later he no longer listed himself as a merchant, but as a farmer. Nevertheless his reported assets had grown slightly to $215,000. A substantial portion of his fortune was tied up in personal estate ($200,000), evidence that the change in occupation recorded in the census schedule does not necessarily indicate a change in his economic activities.[24] Yrizarri also received large payments from American sources, but it is not possible to establish whether they were from government contracts.

His son, Manuel appears to have lost some assets within a decade. In 1860, at twenty years of age, he held property valued at a total of $17,400, higher than the $15,000 that was the average reported for Hispano merchants that year. A decade later the value of his real estate had declined by half, to $1,000; his personal estate had dropped even more dramatically, from $15,400 to $3,000. Manuel had also changed his declared occupation — from merchant to freighter — perhaps suggesting that competing for army freighting contracts was becoming common among some members of the elite.[25]

The Armijo family needs little introduction to students of the Santa Fe Trail. Governor Manuel Armijo is probably one of the best known New Mexicans, but he was not the only entrepreneur in the family.[26] The Armijo name appears regularly among those of the merchants associated with the Santa Fe Trail, particularly those bringing American goods to New Mexico after the Mexican War. Cristóbal, Rafael, Nestor, and Juan Armijo owned 5 percent of all the wagons reported traveling through Council Grove in 1859. Combined, their caravans included 327 mules and eighty-four tons of merchandise.[27] Fifteen Armijos were listed in the 1860 census. Their reported assets ($458,500) were the largest for any family. A decade later the family's wealth remained high. Although only nine Armijos were listed as merchants, their declared property was worth over a quarter of a million dollars.[28]

Surviving documents suggest that the business strategies of the Armijos were quite similar to those of other Río Abajo ricos. Brothers Rafael and Manuel, cousins of the governor, were reported to have had the largest store of goods in Albuquerque during the 1850s. The 1860 census data confirm this, as each brother reported $74,000 in assets. Rafael, who apparently preferred to live in the southern part of the territory, also had retail

and wholesale businesses in Mesilla and Las Cruces. The records from one
of his stores — very much like the one owned by José and Mariano Chávez,
and operated by Pablo Delgado in San Miguel del Vado — reveal that during 1856 Armijo kept a blue notebook wherein he recorded the amount of
grains several individuals owed him. The majority of the notebook included
a series of promissory notes like the following:

> I, Seferino Quesada, will be guarantor [*fiador*] for Juan Reyes for the
> sum of 13 bags [*costales*] of corn from next year's crop [1857] and for
> this purpose I sign the present document before the witnesses below
> . . . having understood that I ensure the said sum with my personal
> property and that if I were to lose my property I would work for the
> said gentleman [Armijo] until the obligation was fulfilled.[29]

The notebook periodically displayed the total amount of the debt.
Though most of the entries were for very small sums, by the end of the year
the total amounted to over $1,000.[30] This was not a significant sum for a
wealthy merchant, but it is indicative of one type of operation that helped
entrepreneurs like the Armijos to acquire hard cash or credit from eastern
commission merchants. It entailed limited risks and furnished a substantial
amount of produce, which was probably used to supply army troops stationed in western posts and distributed among the various Indian reservations. The revenue from these contracts and sales would become an important source of monetary exchange.

The Armijos also appear to have acted as an informal lending institution.
An account book for 1859 listed more than one hundred individuals who
owed Rafael and Manuel close to $4,000. The amounts varied substantially
from three dollars to $704.51. Similar records for 1860 and 1861 indicate
that lending continued and that the sums involved increased.[31]

The Armijos' business skills allowed them to regain their economic status after the total loss of their property, which resulted from their support
of the Confederacy during the Civil War. Some of their economic recovery
was undoubtedly the result of their widespread commercial connections,
both in the United States and in Mexico. Like other New Mexican merchants, they maintained close economic ties to Mexican firms in Guadalajara. Some of their transactions were quite substantial. For example, early
in 1859 the firm of Alvarez Araujo remitted Manuel 154 boxes with almost
$12,000 worth of merchandise.[32] Manuel and Rafael skillfully used the legal
system to reclaim a substantial portion of their confiscated property.[33]

Salvador Armijo, a cousin of Manuel and Rafael, was another influential member of this family. An astute and successful businessman, he became one of Albuquerque's wealthiest and most influential citizens and acquired a reputation for political savvy. The owner of a major store in the Albuquerque plaza, he was a progressive farmer and merchant who became involved in a variety of mercantile operations and who profited by selling provisions to the American troops stationed in the province after the Mexican War.[34]

In spite of the losses he suffered at the outset of the Civil War, when the Confederate forces seized his merchandise and stock, his holdings remained substantial. In 1864 he announced the formation of a partnership with his son-in-law Santiago Baca with estimated assets of $100,000. Baca may have helped with some of the more time-consuming activities and allowed Armijo the opportunity to expand his business by opening stores at Cebolleta, Cubero, Jarales, and Peralta. The census of 1870 shows a moderate increase in the value of his personal property, from $15,000 in 1860 to $26,000.[35] However, these census declarations do not provide an accurate assessment of Armijo's wealth and influence.

Other New Mexican merchants who participated in the trade with the United States owned substantial amounts of property. More than half (sixty-three out of 112) of the shipments that left Council Grove in 1859 belonged to Hispanos. Close to eight hundred men (779) accompanied these loads, which weighed nearly fifteen hundred tons (1,411.5) and were hauled in 556 wagons. Among the owners were such family names as Luna, Baca, González, and Barela. With combined assets of over half a million dollars ($514,744) as reported in the 1860 census, these families comprised the wealthy New Mexican elite. Below them, in terms of reported wealth, were the Delgado, Vigil, Ortiz, Gallegos, Sandoval, Gutiérrez, and Sánchez families. Other merchants of means included Miguel Córdoba, Manuel García, Prudencio López, Pablo Pino, and Antonio Ribera. A decade later their numbers and overall reported wealth declined drastically, but the same family names headed the list of the wealthiest merchants.[36]

Information on merchants who were not members of the elite is very scarce, but this does not diminish the importance of their contributions to the development of commercial capitalism in New Mexico. Even though a systematic analysis of their individual circumstances is not possible, sufficient records survive for the Delgado family to sketch the role merchants like them played in the development of the Santa Fe trade.

Although influential and prosperous, Manuel Delgado and his sons worked for José and Mariano Chávez during the 1840s, and for José Leandro Perea and Felipe Chávez later. In a letter to his son Pablo, who was managing the Chávez store at San Miguel del Vado during the early 1840s, Manuel Delgado advised him to take good care of the interests of their patrones, to whom they owed so many favors. Simón Delgado also advised his brother Pablo to handle the affairs of the Chávez brothers with care, to ensure that the wethers belonging to the store were well looked after, and to appoint someone to collect the debts. Simón, Pablo, and Felipe Delgado continued to have close economic ties with Felipe Chávez. During the 1850s the Delgados formed a partnership with Felipe. Specific details are not available, but the Delgados managed Chávez's store in the capital, and other business and family affairs, at least through the 1870s. They sent libranzas in Chávez's name, received payment from debtors, and occasionally traveled east to arrange for large shipments.[37]

The Delgados were also merchants in their own right and owned a substantial amount of property. At the time of Manuel's death in November 1854, his assets were $243 in cash, $3,469 in carts and merchandise, $2,517 in animals, $1,309 in debts, and $441 in real estate. At close to $8,000, this was an important sum, if modest when compared with the value of the property of the wealthiest Hispano merchants.[38] Manuel's children also did fairly well. In 1860 Simón declared $27,000, Felipe followed with $10,000, while Fernando and Pablo reported $6,000 and $5,000 respectively, for a total of $48,000. The family's assets declined during the next decade to thirty-nine thousand.[39]

Delgado family members, like their patrones, participated in a variety of commercial activities linked to the Santa Fe trade. Fernando sold silver and gold in St. Louis in 1856; Felipe ran a mercantile establishment in Santa Fe, at least through the first decade of the twentieth century. Felipe did not purchase his merchandise directly from commission merchants in the eastern United States, but relied on local dealers, like Zadock Staab, for a sizable amount of the goods he retailed.[40] Through the 1880s Felipe also worked for José L. Perea, arranging for the sale of produce, like flour, barley, and sheep. He also satisfied other Perea requests, such as finding an adequate tailor to fashion a special gift for his son, and making inquiries and remittances to businesses in New York.[41]

Felipe Delgado always maintained economic ties with businesses on the Mexican border and in the Mexican nation. His correspondence with Sol and Albert Schutz reveals that in the late 1870s his attempt to sell wines in El Paso was not very successful. Scarce United States dollars meant that buyers offered only Mexican pesos, which meant a 15-percent loss. Wine sales in large quantities were difficult, and the high cost of containers (a

small barrel cost five to six dollars) made it impossible to make a profit. The
Schutzes also informed Felipe that an attempt to exchange the wine for
efectos del país, like piloncillo and soap, had been unsuccessful.[42]

Juan Delgado, too, maintained close commercial relations with El Paso
merchants, like Cecilio Robles. His correspondence confirms that historic
patterns of trade along the Royal Road continued through the 1870s, although the volume and nature of the merchandise changed. Delgado was
procuring small shipments of efectos del país, such as soap, chicle, chocolate, and piloncillo, from Mexico. Had the trains from the Mexican capital
to the frontier been running, Robles would have sold Delgado Mexican
goods, such as cashmere from San Ildefonso. It is not clear what merchandise, if any, Delgado would have delivered in return, since Mexican import
duties priced out foreign goods. Unstable political circumstances within
the Mexican nation produced uncertainty and made regular commercial
transactions between merchants across the border cumbersome.[43] Juan and
Felipe Delgado do not appear to have been given adequate information on
market conditions at El Paso and within the Mexican territory to make
successful transactions. Unlike Felipe Chávez, they seem to have lacked
sufficient capital and an adequate communication network to keep them
up-to-date regarding local demand, supply, and fluctuations in price.

As the railroad brought an end to the Santa Fe Trail (1880), the Delgados
continued to participate in a variety of economic activities, maintained
relations with Mexican merchants, and, through wholesalers, with commission merchants from the United States. The Delgados also acted as intermediaries for wealthier New Mexicans. Holding moderate resources, these
merchants played an important role in the development of mercantile capitalism. Like Damaso Robledo, the agent for Manuel Alvarez in the 1840s,
they provided an essential link between the rich mercantile class and the
local population.

The Delgados continued to be economically dependent on the elite,
however. Felipe Delgado's urgent request at the time of Felipe Chávez's
death (1906) for an extension on the interest rates on his loans documents
this continued dependency.

The New Mexican mercantile elite managed to maintain economic he-
gemony at least through most of the nineteenth century. Adapting sound
yet flexible commercial strategies, they succeeded because they had enough
capital to diversify their operations and were able to withstand the fluctuations of the unstable western economy. Their failure to form an association
of freighters may not have had a major negative impact on individual operations, since they managed to increase or at least maintain their economic

standing. Nevertheless, their reluctance to cooperate might have affected those merchants of more moderate means who appear to have been unable to compete in the ever-evolving Santa Fe trade economy. New Mexicans' inability to obtain the large and profitable army contracts that fueled the New Mexican economy after the mid-1860s meant that many of the less affluent comerciantes experienced moderate to substantial losses and often abandoned mercantile operations. It is likely that their decline (see chapter 8, table 6) also affected other segments of the Hispano population that had been dependent on trade-related activities to earn a living.

EIGHT

Too Little Freighting for Uncle Sam

He is a good example of the Hispanic capitalist who tapped into the military reservoir of federal dollars.

DARLIS A. MILLER DESCRIBING EPIFANIO AGUIRRE IN
Soldiers and Settlers

By the 1860s the nature of the Santa Fe trade had changed dramatically. As the volume of trade increased, the prices of the merchandise declined. Profits per unit also plunged. The dislocations associated with the Civil War and its impact on the textile industry, as well as increasing Indian attacks on trade convoys, made it necessary to control large sums of money to continue the traditional mercantile operations that had characterized the Santa Fe trade up to that time.

Most merchants in New Mexico lacked the resources to engage in such activities, so they searched for other opportunities. One which would become very profitable was freighting goods for the United States Army. The capital required was limited and Hispanos had the skills and the initiative to get involved. Initially they met with success. In October 1864, the *Santa Fe New Mexican* referred to Epifanio Aguirre as the "first large Mexican contractor." Aguirre received an award to freight five million pounds of supplies in June 1864 and completed it by the end of January 1865. He was paid a handsome sum ($138,177), although it is not possible to know how much he cleared after expenses. Unfortunately, his next freighting bid was rejected in favor of the one submitted by William H. Moore, and shortly after, Aguirre moved to Arizona, where he briefly continued to freight for the army.[1]

Other Hispano contractors were less successful than Aguirre and failed to obtain any awards, although it is possible that some worked as subcontractors, and the contracts others received may not have survived. Darlis Miller's study shows that New Mexicans became a distinct minority of those supplying military installations and freighting for Uncle Sam. Of the 117 individuals who received contracts to freight and provide wheat, corn, and oats for the army between 1867 and 1880, only seven were Hispanos, and six of the seven were members of one family — the Romeros. Although it is impossible to prove a deliberate attempt to discriminate against Hispanos, it can be said that the widespread fraud that characterized the awards hurt many New Mexicans.[2]

The inability to win contracts to supply army installations is one of several factors that help to explain the changes Hispano merchants experienced between 1860 and 1870. Territorial census returns for these years reveal geographic shifts as well as a dramatic decline in the number of merchants and their assets.[3] In 1860 the majority of New Mexican merchants (ninety-five out of 154) lived in the Río Abajo: south of Santa Fe, in Valencia, Bernalillo, Socorro, and Doña Ana counties (see table 6). The remaining (fifty-nine) resided in the northern jurisdictions of Río Arriba: San Miguel, Santa Ana, Santa Fe, and Taos. Ten years later their combined number had declined to 112 (see table 6), and the number of those residing in the Río Abajo had decreased to fifty-three (the number living in the Río Arriba remained the same). Some counties witnessed significant declines: San Miguel, from twenty-three to thirteen; Bernalillo, twenty-four to ten; and Valencia, thirty-one to five. Río Arriba was the only county where the number of merchants increased: from one to nine.[4] Hispano merchants also reported a sharp decrease in total wealth, from more than $2.25 million to less than $1.5 million (see tables 6 and 7). This drop of more than 40 percent signifies major modifications to the economic circumstances of comerciantes of average and above-average wealth.[5]

At the same time, the rich became richer. In 1860 the wealthiest 20 percent of the merchants controlled 76 percent of the declared wealth; a decade later the same segment of the population controlled 86 percent of the territory's assets. José Leandro Perea and José Felipe Chávez saw a major increase in the value of their real estate and personal property. Perea's declared wealth rose from $225,000 to $408,000; Chávez's grew from $67,575 to $140,000. Together they accounted for 38 percent of all wealth declared by New Mexican merchants in 1870.[6]

The excessive concentration of wealth in the southern half of the state continued. Reported personal and real estate figures reveal that in 1860 Río Abajo comerciantes controlled a disproportionate share — 83 percent — of all declared assets. Those living in two counties, Bernalillo and Valencia, accounted for 66.5 percent of all assessed wealth. Thus, Río Abajo merchants maintained their economic dominance through the next decade,

TABLE 6

Hispano Merchants, 1860–70

(Reported Wealth and Residency)

Area	County	1860 Number	1860 Total Assets ($)	1870 Number	1870 Total Assets ($)
Río Abajo	Bernalillo	24	1,025,375	10	714,500
	Valencia	31	542,930	5	321,976
	Socorro	20	239,100	27	148,200
	Doña Ana	20	150,725	9	36,775
	Lincoln[a]	—	—	2	2,675
Total		95	1,958,130	53	1,224,126
		(61.68%)	(83.05%)	(47.32%)	(84.34%)
Río Arriba	Río Arriba	1	3,059	9	24,160
	San Miguel	23	93,295	13	34,111
	Santa Fe	25	261,700	25	125,125
	Taos	5	26,700	6	30,900
	Santa Ana	1	2,500	2	3,797
	Mora	4	12,129	4	9,082
Total		59	399,383	59	227,175
		(39.32%)	(16.95%)	(53.68%)	(15.66%)
Total for Territory		154	2,357,513 (mean=15,308)	112	1,451,301 (mean=12,958)

[a]Lincoln County was created in 1869 out of the eastern part of Socorro County. Colfax County was created out of Mora in the same year. Grant County had been created the year before (1868) out of the western fourth of Doña Ana County. Both Valencia and Bernalillo Counties ceded their eastern third to San Miguel County.

even though their numbers declined markedly. By 1870 their share had increased to 84.34 percent. Those who resided in Bernalillo and Valencia counties, which witnessed the sharpest decline in the number of merchants, still owned 71.4 percent of all the assets (see table 6).[7]

Additional evidence demonstrates that during the 1860s comerciantes experienced a downturn in their economic circumstances. The census returns reveal a decline in the value of the average holding from $15,309 to $12,959. The number of merchants who reported wealth between $10,000 and $100,000 dropped dramatically, from forty-four to fourteen, and only 15 percent (seventeen out of 112) declared more than $10,000 worth of property. The proportion of assets tied up in personal estate, in part a surrogate for the value of their merchandise, also decreased. In 1860 almost 81 percent of wealth was in personal property; ten years later that portion had declined to 76 percent.[8]

Tracing the careers of New Mexican merchants from one census to another is difficult. The returns indicate that only thirty-four (30.35 per-

TABLE 7

Non-Hispano Merchants, 1860–70
(Reported Wealth and Residency)

Area	County	1860		1870	
		Number	Total Assets ($)	Number	Total Assets ($)
Río Abajo	Bernalillo	8	285,725	6	131,550
	Valencia	3	26,650	8	45,450
	Socorro	5	63,950	6	26,000
	Doña Ana	31	273,150	17	369,500
	Lincoln	—	—	11	91,500
	Grant	—	—	13	45,100
Total		47	649,475	61	709,100
		(39.16%)	(31.05%)	(38.36%)	(28.21%)
Río Arriba	Río Arriba	—	—	6	24,000
	Colfax	—	—	12	339,900
	San Miguel	13	412,600	24	314,576
	Santa Fe	29	524,350	22	647,100
	Taos	5	35,510	10	93,400
	Santa Ana	—	—	—	—
	Mora	25	469,100	24	385,125
Total		73	1,441,560	98	1,804,101
		(60.83%)	(68.95%)	(61.63%)	(71.78%)
Total for Territory		120	2,091,035	159	2,513,201
			(mean=17,425)		(mean=15,642)

cent) of the 112 comerciantes enumerated in 1870 had been similarly listed in 1860. Thirteen showed an increase in the total value of their property, one remained static, and the rest registered losses. Furthermore, except for Felipe Chávez and José Leandro Perea, the gains were quite small — an average of less than $4,900.[9]

Hispanos were not the only ones affected by instability during the 1860–70 decade. Foreigners experienced even greater mobility. Only eighteen (11.25 percent) of the 159 merchants listed in the 1870 census had declared the same occupation a decade earlier. However, most of those who stayed in New Mexico and maintained the same occupation experienced substantial increases in their reported holdings: an average of $40,000. In twelve cases the value of their property increased, in three cases it showed no change, and in two cases it declined.[10]

Unlike the majority of New Mexicans, foreign merchants strengthened their position between 1860 and 1870. Their numbers increased from 120 to 159 (see table 7), as did the value of their reported property — by almost $400,000, from $2,091,035 to $2,513,201. Their average wealth, however, declined, from $17,425 to $15,806 (see table 7). This group was also con-

TABLE 8

Distribution of Wealth among Merchants in New Mexico, 1860–70

	Assets	Hispanos Percentage	Assets	Percentage
Percentile	Reported, 1860 ($)(N=154)	of Wealth	Reported, 1870 ($)(N=112)	of Wealth
Top 20	1,845,685	78.28	1,256,700	86.59
Second 20	338,345	14.35	101,483	6.99
Third 20	120,579	5.11	51,192	3.52
Fourth 20	43,820	1.85	29,635	2.04
Bottom 20	9,084	0.38	12,291	0.84
Total	2,357,513	99.97	1,451,301	99.98
		Non-Hispanos		
	(N=120)		(N=159)	
Top 20	1,381,300	66.06	1,768,149	70.35
Second 20	420,525	20.11	484,897	19.29
Third 20	199,250	9.53	172,550	6.87
Fourth 20	70,810	3.39	74,705	2.95
Bottom 20	19,150	0.92	16,200	0.54
Total	2,091,035	100.00	2,513,201	100.00

centrated geographically, with more than 60 percent residing in the Río Arriba. Their wealth was much more evenly distributed than that of the Hispanos, however. The ninety-eight foreigners who lived in the northern counties constituted 61.63 percent of the merchants and held 71.78 percent of their wealth; the fifty-three Hispanos who resided in the Río Abajo constituted 47.32 percent of the merchants and possessed 84.34 percent of the reported property (see tables 6 and 7).[11]

Some of these apparent shifts may be the result of using census data to explain evolving conditions in the territory. Although census information is quite valuable as a study tool, it has to be used judiciously. Misreporting is probably one of the most common mistakes. Changes in the criteria that census enumerators used in their reports is another. Errors are sometimes committed in transcribing manuscript materials or in adding them up. Comparing results across time is difficult because of the changing format of successive census questionnaires.[12] Careless mistakes are quite common. For example, in recording the individual's country of birth, enumerators in certain counties just repeated the same information page after page. It is possible that Albert Stephenson and his wife Eleanor, reported living in Mesilla in 1870, were born in New Mexico, but it is not likely. The same is true for William Lewis who resided in Peralta, and Juan Joseph living in Taos. The census schedule often lists individuals with no assets. This could mean that the information was not available or not provided, not necessarily that the respondent owned no property. For example, the wealth and power of Ceran and Vicente St. Vrain are well documented, but they reported neither personal nor real estate in the 1870 census.[13]

Double reporting clearly shows some of the inconsistencies in the census returns. Some individuals were enumerated twice, and neither their declared assets nor their names match. For instance, Nathan Eldadt was also listed as Nicholas Eldadt, but because of the names and ages of his wife and children, it is possible to establish that there was only one Nathan (or Nicholas) Eldadt living in San Juan in 1870. Louis Clark was reported as a resident of both Río Arriba County and San Juan Pueblo. As a Río Arriba resident, the census enumerators listed his assets as $1,000 in real estate and $8,000 in personal assets. As a San Juan Pueblo resident, they assessed his property at $4,000 for both real and personal estate.[14]

These errors notwithstanding, the changes in economic conditions of Hispano merchants that the censuses reveal are too extreme to be explained by human error. They suggest that New Mexicans were losing the advantages they had enjoyed through 1860, in terms of the number of merchants and the assets they controlled (see tables 6 and 7). However, the losses were more gradual than they appear. The 1870 census sometimes listed former 1860 merchants as farmers, although the reported value of their personal property implies that they had continued their mercantile activities. For example, Mariano Yrizarri, the second-wealthiest merchant in 1860 was listed as a farmer in 1870, but his assets had increased to $215,000, with most of it ($210,000) in personal property.[15]

Some New Mexican merchants abandoned full-time commercial operations. As they grew older, they may have lacked the energy or the large resources necessary for the complex and risky activities of the evolving Santa Fe trade. Instead, they may have turned their attention to facilitating the careers of their sons. Such was the case with Juan Cristóbal Armijo, who lost 40 percent of his assets, but had supported the Chihuahua business operations of his sons, Nestor and Nicolás.[16] Others channeled their energies into agricultural activities, supplying army posts with flour, grains, and hay, while allowing their sons to acquire experience in commercial enterprises requiring more limited capital, such as freighting. Mariano Yrizarri called himself a farmer in 1870, but the size of his personal estate suggests that he had continued to engage in mercantile activities. It is possible that his son Manuel, who listed himself as a fletero, helped him with the family business. The sons of other individuals who declared high personal property were enumerated as store clerks, freighters, or "working in warehouse." Such were the situations of Juan María Baca from Las Vegas (San Miguel) and Antonio José Otero from Peralta (Valencia). Baca, at fifty-two years of age, reported $5,000 in real estate and $40,800 in personal estate in the 1870 census; fifty-eight-year-old Otero and his wife Mercedes claimed combined assets of $24,000. No property was reported for their son Adolfo who worked as a store clerk. Similar cases exist. Given the range of values in personal estate declared in the New Mexico 1870 schedule, those who declared more than $5,000 in personal estate are likely to have participated in other activities besides agriculture. Their number was substantial. Sixty-nine individuals fell in this category. With a combined personal estate of $889,379 it is possible that they had taken the place of the "missing" 1860 merchants.[17]

An analysis of trail-related occupations helps to account for some of the decline in the number of comerciantes. The 1860 census enumerated 203 Hispanos in six trail-related occupations: 151 teamsters, twelve wagon owners, three wagon masters, twenty-eight wagon drivers, five ox drivers, and four mule drivers. There were no freighters. Ten years later the enumeration included a total of 307: seventy-one freighters, 183 teamsters, nine wagon owners, six wagon masters, thirty wagon drivers, four ox drivers, and four mule drivers. Twelve of the freighters had called themselves merchants in 1860. Six of them reported losses for a total of $59,824 (an average of almost $10,000 per freighter). The gains were more modest. They amounted to $17,950 for an average of almost $3,000.[18]

Like the comerciantes, freighters were concentrated in the Río Abajo. More than half (forty-eight out of a total of seventy-one) resided south of La Bajada and only twenty-three in the Río Arriba. Three counties attracted the bulk of the freighters. Valencia County was the leader with twenty-eight. Socorro and San Miguel Counties followed with fourteen fleteros each.[19] Their assets, however, were much more moderate than those reported by merchants in 1860 and account for only a small portion of the losses Hispanos experienced during this decade. The Río Abajo freighters listed $129,826, and those from the Río Arriba recorded $38,062, for a total of $167,188 and an average wealth of $2,354.76.[20]

The growth of freighting as an occupational category among Hispanos signals their willingness to adapt to the evolving nature of the Santa Fe trade, but the much lower property values reported for the freighters in the 1870 census indicate that Hispanos who participated in trade activities did not fare well in this decade. Furthermore, the growth in trail-related occupations took place in categories, such as teamstering, that required no assets. Most teamsters were quite young and with very few exceptions reported no property. Wagon drivers, ox and mule drivers, and most of the wagon masters also listed few, if any, assets.[21]

Changes in residency also help to explain the declining number of Hispano merchants. Some individuals moved out of the New Mexican territory to Colorado. In certain cases they owned considerable property, for example Miguel Antonio Otero. Others were of more moderate means, like Juan Manuel Salazar and Julián Gallegos who together established a store in San Luis (Colorado) in 1857. Still others, like the Aguirres, may have gone west to Arizona. A few, like Nestor and Nicolás Armijo (the latter who married Bárbara Chávez, Felipe Chávez's sister), moved to Chihuahua for a decade (ca. 1868–78) where they continued the family's commercial activities.[22]

After 1860 few Hispano merchants followed Anglos into the newly created Lincoln, Grant, and Colfax Counties. In 1870 these three counties listed thirty-six foreign merchants but only two Hispanos, both of them in Lincoln County. New Mexicans appear to have missed the opportunity of establishing businesses in areas that would grow noticeably in a brief period of time. The assets that Anglos held in these new counties ($476,500) accounted for most of the growth in their overall wealth between 1860 and 1870 (see table 7). Comerciantes may have been reluctant to move because they preferred to settle where they could maintain their culture and where they expected less competition from Anglos.[23]

Some of the losses in numbers and their assets resulted from aging or death. In 1860 the average age of New Mexican merchants was 36.37, but twenty-one merchants were fifty years old or older. Most of them (out of a total of eighteen) were not listed in the census ten years later. Some could have gone to live with their children. Those who continued to act as merchants reported sharp losses in their property. In 1860 José Miguel Baca, a resident of Socorro County, at sixty years of age, reported $11,000 in assets. Ten years later his property had declined to a value of $550. Pedro Baca, who had been fifty in 1860, lost close to 40 percent during the decade; Guadalupe Miranda, who was the same age, lost almost 50 percent.[24]

Other demographic factors account for the losses experienced by New Mexican merchants during this decade. As the daughters of wealthy merchants married, they received their share of the family's fortune. If they married farmers or lawyers, the census would not have included their wealth among personal estate. Furthermore, when census schedules identified wives' property as separate, as in the case of Salvador Armijo's wife Nieves, it was because of marital problems.[25]

Cross-cultural marriages of the daughters of the New Mexican elite also contributed to the dispersal of Hispano personal wealth. For example, the

1870 census reveals that among the fifty wealthiest non-Hispano merchants, twenty had Hispano wives (twenty-one were single, and nine had married non-Hispano women). The trend is even more pronounced among the extremely wealthy Anglos. Three of the five richest (Lucien Maxwell, William Moore, and Henry Bierbaum) had Hispano wives. Since maiden names were listed only in certain precincts, it is difficult to identify all the brides' family names and so confirm the relationship between cross-cultural marriages and the decline in the wealth of the Hispano merchants.

It is also possible that comerciantes were less able than Anglos to withstand the economic dislocations caused by the Civil War. The experience of the Armijo family demonstrates that supporting the wrong side in that conflict could have a serious detrimental impact on personal fortunes.[26] The extensive Indian warfare that erupted after the Pike's Peak Gold Rush also caused major losses of merchandise at least in 1864 and 1868.[27]

As the Santa Fe trade developed, most New Mexican merchants lost the position of prominence they had enjoyed until the 1860s. The elite declined in number and grew ever more divided. Some of its members continued to accumulate power and influence, but others, as well as merchants of more moderate means, lost a substantial portion of their assets and influence, and struggled to maintain their financial standing.

In spite of their awareness of the need to cooperate and maintain fluid lines of communication, New Mexican merchants seem to have been reluctant to expand into new ventures at a time when expansion was necessary to survive. Their inability to obtain large government freighting contracts restricted their opportunities even more. It is also possible that as the railroad grew nearer to New Mexico, Hispanos lost the advantages they had enjoyed in transporting merchandise, distributing it in the territory, and exchanging it for local commodities. By the 1870s, most of the merchants associated with the Santa Fe trade were dependent on the expenditures of the federal government to supply army installations and the various Indian tribes. Most New Mexicans did not have the resources to continue the type of mercantile activity required by the unfolding Santa Fe trade. The margin of profit had become so small that they were unable to make a profit.

Howard Lamar notes that by 1865 "the once exotic and occasional wagon trains that meandered down the familiar rutted trail had given way to an everyday freighting business of 5,000 teams a year and an enterprise of national importance."[28] Only those who were major capitalists, like José Leandro Perea and Felipe Chávez, had the resources to enjoy continued economic success in a system of such magnitude. Their large holdings, their investment strategies, their diverse businesses, and their connections in St. Louis, New York, and other commercial centers allowed them not only to endure the fluctuations of the territorial economy, but also to enhance their circumstances. Although it is not clear if they were ever awarded government contracts, both Perea and Chávez received substantial payments from the Quartermaster's Office. They were astute entrepreneurs, but their continued success after the Civil War was primarily the result of the size of their assets and the way in which they managed their businesses.

Conclusion

This study emphasizes the prominence of New Mexicans in the Santa Fe trade. New Mexicans were well suited to their roles as international merchants since their ancestors had made commercial activities an important focus of the provincial economy. For decades they had traded with French, British, Americans, Mexicans, and a number of Indian tribes.

With the opening of the Santa Fe Trail, New Mexicans' dependence on Chihuahuan merchants slowly began to weaken. By the 1830s their shipments of efectos del país and sheep to the interior of Mexico rivaled in frequency and bulk those of the wealthy foreigners. Late in the same decade, wealthy New Mexican merchants had acquired sufficient cash and credit to venture into the United States to purchase manufactured goods directly from American suppliers and commission merchants.

The pattern of trade that evolved was complex. It required large capital, sound credit, coordination of the delivery of merchandise that often originated hundreds of miles away, and reliable up-to-date information on prices, demand, and supply. Diversification became essential. Those New Mexican merchants who did well economically participated in a variety of economic activities. They farmed, raised sheep, mined, shipped wool and precious metals, introduced large amounts of American and European merchandise, and acted as intermediaries for other businessmen, bankers, wholesalers, and retailers. They developed close relations with merchants and commission agents in Mexico, the United States, and Europe. They had scattered stores where they exchanged manufactured goods for efectos del país and produce. They were cautious, but understood that in order to thrive economically it was important to adapt and to take some measured risks. They delayed for more than a decade the establishment of direct commercial relations with businesses in the United States until they were moderately assured that the enterprise would be rewarding. Once they made the decision to trade east, they invested a substantial portion of their assets in this business.

New Mexican merchants took advantage of their knowledge of local conditions to gain access to important cash-producing products, such as grains, that were overlooked by foreign merchants who tended to be interested in quick profits. Between 1820 and 1880 wealthy *comerciantes* showed a remarkable ability to adapt to the unstable circumstances that affected the southwestern trade during this period. The rebellion of Texas (a former Mexican province) and its subsequent annexation to the United States, the Mexican War, the Civil War, and Indian warfare all contributed to make commercial enterprises uncertain and risky. Major business ventures, even those of American commission merchants like the Glasgow brothers, went bankrupt. Economic success, or even survival, in such circumstances was an indication of exceptional talent, resources, and hard work. New Mexican merchants with more moderate means did not fare as well after the 1860s, because large amounts of capital were required to succeed in the Santa Fe trade as it was evolving. Some became freighters; others put greater emphasis on agricultural activities, hoping to obtain contracts or subcontracts to supply the territorial army posts.

Other members of New Mexican society participated in the success of the Santa Fe trade and were in turn affected by it. Commercial activities contributed to a slight improvement in the standard of living of all segments of the population, as scarce and expensive manufactured goods became cheaper and more readily available. Contraband provided a few with a measure of temporary economic relief. Trade-related occupations expanded. They were not remunerative, but they allowed even peones, the poorest element of the population, the chance to become teamsters or drivers and earn scarce cash. New Mexicans' skills as packers brought them recognition as master muleteers, if very limited financial rewards. With the exception of wagon owners and freighters, those who worked in menial trade occupations reported almost no assets. However, without the skills and the labor of these people, the development and success of the Santa Fe trade would not have been possible.

The form of mercantile capitalism that evolved in New Mexico was dependent on cooperation between the various ethnic groups that participated in the trade. Hispano merchants tended to travel together, but they often joined foreign caravans because of common ventures or because they

hoped that larger trains might deter Indian attacks. New Mexicans understood that mutual support and cooperation were essential for success. They
were not reluctant to lend money, take care of each other's children, act on
each other's behalf, and provide necessary information and advice. They
developed strong familial alliances through marriages and business partnerships in an attempt to strengthen their social and economic position.
After the Mexican War some members of the elite felt strong animosity
toward Americans, yet many wealthy New Mexicans did not hesitate to
accept foreigners as their partners or sons-in-law. The need to maintain a
position of preeminence led Anglos and Hispanos alike to disregard their
cultural differences and work together on those activities that offered ample
rewards to individuals with capital and initiative. Willingness to push aside
animosity in favor of collaboration made sense at a time when competition was forcing merchants out of business. Had Hispano merchants and
freighters from the Río Abajo joined together to compete for army contracts, the decline many of them experienced might not have happened.

This study emphasizes the need to scrutinize the Santa Fe Trail from a
broad geographical perspective. The portion linking Missouri with New
Mexico was only one segment of a complex transportation network of
economic and cultural exchange that brought together two continents, and
several countries. The Santa Fe trade reached east well beyond Missouri to
include New Orleans, New York, Baltimore, Pittsburgh, and other major
cities; west, it extended as far as the California coast; and south, it stretched
deep into the Mexican territory to incorporate most of its western and
central provinces. The merchandise hauled across the prairies was often
European in origin and arrived in the southwest as a result of the involvement of commission merchants in England, France, Italy, Spain, and Por-
tugal, as well as the United States and Mexico.

In trying to place the economic activities of Hispanos within an adequate
context, it is apparent that certain aspects of the trade require further analysis. The endeavors of non-Hispano merchants, particularly those who
settled in New Mexico Territory, have to be examined in greater detail.
How did their operations compare to those of José Leandro Perea or Felipe
Chávez? Did they rely on the same strategies as their Hispano counterparts? Did they tend to establish businesses in areas where there was little
competition from wealthy New Mexicans? How did they relate to the less
affluent population? Were they more or less benevolent patrones than the
native elite? Equally important would be a study of the career of important
Mexican merchants, such as José Cordero and Francisco Elguea.[1] It would
be helpful to understand how well foreign merchants adjusted to the evolv-

ing nature of the trade. More successful than the Hispanos as a group, their high mobility rates might hide a substantial number of business failures.

It is critical to conduct a systematic study of wholesale and commission merchants, such as Peter Harmony and Nephews. The nature of these businesses varied as a result of their geographic location and possibly their financial networks in the United States. Commission merchants greatly facilitated trade, but their activities have yet to be systematically documented. They were fundamental to the success of New Mexicans. It is not clear, however, if they assisted other entrepreneurs to the same degree, and if and how their role evolved with time.

It would be valuable to examine American and New Mexican economic relations with Mexico before and after the Mexican War. These long-term, far-reaching commercial ties were not severed in 1846. Although large shipments were never discussed in the correspondence between merchants from northern Mexico and their New Mexican counterparts, there is evidence of continuous exchange, but it is not possible to ascertain its volume and value. The presence of business agents in Chihuahua and Durango, and the substantial drafts handled by commission merchants on behalf of Mexicans suggest that mercantile associations remained close at least until 1880.

There are other issues specifically related to New Mexicans that need clarification. How did the comerciantes manage to obtain substantial credit with United States agencies and commission merchants? What did they sell in addition to grains and wool? Both products are bulky, and, like the efectos del país, they would have to have been produced in enormous quantities to account for the drafts deposited in eastern accounts. Besides, wealthy merchants did not start sending large shipments of wool to the east until the late 1850s.

The sources of New Mexican wealth need to be identified more clearly. How significant was mining? Who was mining and where? What did they mine? How much ore did they get? To what extent were New Mexican merchants associated with mining? This last question is extremely important because the silver and gold bullion they carried to the United States during the late 1830s and early 1840s seemingly provided the basis for their mercantile operations. If they obtained bullion from Mexico, what did they sell in exchange? Throughout the 1830s the only goods sent to the interior of Mexico were sheep and domestic manufactures, neither one in sufficient volume to explain the substantial amount of bullion Missouri newspapers reported New Mexicans were carrying on their trips to the eastern United States.

Even more pressing is the need to study the less wealthy, to try to obtain a better understanding of how their participation in the Santa Fe trade changed with time and how their lives were modified as a result of trade with the United States. It would be valuable to explore the impact of the Santa Fe trade on the culture and the expectations of New Mexicans. How did their lives change as a result of the presence of additional goods? Was it a positive change? Did the Santa Fe trade result mostly in increasing dependence on patrones who cared little for their peones and were intent only on making a large profit? Were New Mexican merchants willing to help financially those dependent on them? Most of these issues defy easy analysis since source material is not readily available to shed light on them.

The contributions of various Indian tribes to the development of the Santa Fe trade need to be assessed. In general their participation has been viewed in negative terms, and Indians are considered mostly as physical threats to mercantile operations. However, they played a significant role in "opening" trade routes, even before the period of Spanish occupation. Historians acknowledge that they became key recipients of weapons, but it is also likely that they played a role as consumers of the merchandise hauled across the prairies.

Finally, this work is not a definitive study of the Santa Fe trade. It is an analysis of important yet mostly neglected sources that reveal crucial information about nineteenth-century New Mexicans, an ethnic group that has never received the notice it deserves. It encompasses almost six decades of New Mexican history and examines developments after the Mexican War during the territorial years, a period that has received little attention from historians.

Appendix 1

Mexican Merchants who Received Guías from the Customs House at Santa Fe, 1826–45[1]

Abeita, Aniceto (roll 40, frame 286, 6 September 1845). Guía 24. 18 bultos of domestic and foreign merchandise. Value: 152 pesos 6.25 reales. To: Chihuahua.

Abeita, Juan de Jesús (roll 34, frame 1209, 5 September 1843). Guía 44. 6 tercios of domestic merchandise. Value: 144 pesos. To: Chihuahua, Durango, and Zacatecas. [Guía exists: roll 34, frame 1246.]

Abeita, Juan de Jesús (roll 37, frame 400, 5 September 1844). Guía 6. 3 bultos of domestic merchandise. Value: 91 pesos 6 reales. To: Chihuahua and Tierra Caliente. [Guía exists: roll 37, frame 479.]

Abreu, Santiago (roll 21, frame 282, 20 September 1835). Guía 31. 1 *alambique* (still). To: de Palacios, Francisco; Chihuahua. Conductor: [?], Eduardo L.

Aguilar, Luis (roll 21, frame 357, 27 September 1840). Guía 59. Domestic merchandise. Value: 115 pesos 4 reales. To: Sonora. Conductor: Serrano, Miguel. [Guía exists: roll 28, frame 795.]

Aguilar, Luis (roll 21, frame 358, ca. 27 October 1840). Guía 68. [The rest of the entry is blank.]

Aguilar, Luis (roll 21, frame 359, 27 October 1840). Guía 71. 8 bultos of domestic merchandise. Value: 142 pesos 3 reales. To: Sonora. Conductor: Chávez, Juan Cristóbal.

Alarid, José Ramón (roll 21, frame 303, 24 August 1837). Guía 32. 3 tercios of domestic merchandise. Value: ca. 45 pesos. To: El Paso. [Guía exists: roll 24, frame 796.]

Alarid, Juan Bautista (roll 14, frame 258, 24 October 1831). Guía [?]. 3 tercios of foreign merchandise. To: Durango, Sonora, and Chihuahua.

Albán, Dionisio (roll 21, frame 316, 1 August 1839). Guía 115. 1 tercio of foreign merchandise. Value: 89 pesos. To: El Paso.

Albo, Agapito (roll 19, frame 323, 18 August 1834). Guía 48. Foreign merchandise. To: El Paso.

Albo, Agapito (roll 21, frame 318, 17 August 1839). Guía 122. 16 bultos. Value: 2,554 pesos 1 real. To: Ronquillo, José Ignacio; El Paso.

Albo, Agapito (roll 21, frame 318, 17 August 1839). Guía 123. 15 piezas of foreign merchandise. Value: 1,505 pesos. To: El Paso.

Albo, Agapito (roll 21, frame 318, 17 August 1839). Guía 124. 3 piezas. Value: 938 pesos 0.5 real. To: Velarde, Juan María; El Paso.

Ara, Eduardo (roll 21, frame 282, 5 October 1835). Guía 32. 21 tercios of foreign merchandise. To: Chihuahua and Sonora.

Ara, Eduardo (roll 21, frame 282, 5 October 1835). Guía 33. 20 tercios of foreign merchandise. To: Chihuahua, Sonora, and Durango.

Ara, Eduardo (roll 21, frame 283, 5 October 1835). Guía 34. 12 tercios. To: Chihuahua, Sonora, and Durango.

Aragón, Fernando (roll 21, frame 314, 24 October 1838). Guía 104. 4 tercios of domestic merchandise. To: Chihuahua and Sonora.

Aragón, Fernando (roll 21, frame 314, 24 October 1838). Guía 105. 16 tercios of domestic merchandise. Value: ca. 150 pesos. To: Chihuahua and Sonora. [Guía exists: roll 25, frame 1453.]

**Aragón, Fernando (roll 27, frame 643, 29 January 1839). Hermosillo, guía 27. 8 bultos. Value: 451 pesos 3 reales. To: New Mexico.

Aragón, Fernando (roll 21, frame 337, 16 October 1839). Guía 196. 25 bultos of domestic merchandise. Value: 402 pesos 4 reales. To: Sonora.

Aragón, Fernando (roll 21, frame 360, 16 October 1840). Guía 77. 20 bultos of domestic merchandise. Value: 130 pesos 4 reales. To: Chihuahua and Sonora.

Aragón, José (roll 21, frame 297, 15 February 1837). Guía 108. Domestic merchandise. To: El Paso. [Guía exists: roll 24, frame 767. There is a discrepancy between dates and guía numbers in the cuaderno and the guía itself.]

Aragón, Juan Antonio (roll 21, frame 353, 24 August 1840). Guía 43. 14 bultos. Value: 272 pesos 4 reales. To: Durango and San Juan de Lagos. [Guía exists: roll 28, frame 783. The prices of the items do not add up to the total as shown in the guía. Accounting seems to indicate that the real value was 230 pesos 4 reales.]

Aragón, Ramón (roll 21, frame 295, 27 October 1836). Guía 97. 2 baúles and 2 tercios. To: El Paso. Conductor: Perea, Baltazar. [Guía exists: roll 22, frame 1167. It is possible that the merchandise belonged to Baltazar Perea.]

Aranda, Pedro (roll 30, frame 324, 8 September 1841). Parida, New Mexico, guía 8. 14 bultos of domestic merchandise. To: Chihuahua and Sonora.

[Arce], Juan (roll 34, frame 1202, 7 August 1843). Guía 1. 2 bultos. Value: 487 pesos 46 cents. To: California.

Archuleta, Antonio Cayetano (roll 21, frame 313, 11 September 1838). Guía 96. 4 bultos of domestic merchandise. To: Chihuahua, Durango, and Sonora.

Archuleta, Eugenio (roll 21, frame 279, ca. 31 August 1835). Guía 25. 18 tercios. To: "Those states which are most convenient."

Archuleta, Eugenio (roll 34, frame 1206, 26 August 1843). Guía 26. 1,400 sheep. Value: 700 pesos. To: Chihuahua and Durango. Conductor: Baca, Tomás.

Archuleta, Eugenio (roll 34, frame 1207, 29 August 1843). Guía 33. 12 bultos of domestic merchandise. Value: 161 pesos 4 reales. To: Chihuahua and Durango.

Archuleta, José Eugenio (roll 21, frame 311, 3 September 1838). Guía 89. 19 bultos of domestic merchandise. Value: ca. 183 pesos 2 reales. To: Chihuahua, Durango, and Sonora. [Guía exists: roll 25, frame 1443.]

Archuleta, José Eugenio (roll 21, frame 332, 10 September 1839). Guía 179. 33 tercios of domestic merchandise. Value: 220 pesos 6 reales. To: Zacatecas and Guadalajara.

Archuleta, Pablo (roll 21, frame 353, 24 August 1840). Guía 42. 6 bultos of domestic merchandise. Value: 78 pesos 2 reales. To: Chihuahua and Durango.

Arellano, [?] (roll 21, frame 343, 27 March 1840). Guía 1. 10 bultos of foreign and domestic merchandise. Value: 1,011 pesos 4 reales. To: Durango, Zacatecas, and Mexico.

Armijo, Ambrosio (roll 21, frame 305, 10 February 1838). Guía 53. 20 bultos of domestic merchandise. To: Chihuahua and Sonora. [Property appears to be jointly owned with Cristóbal Armijo.]

Armijo, Ambrosio (roll 21, frame 358, 13 October 1840). Guía 64. 26 tercios of domestic merchandise. Value: 140 pesos 4 reales. To: Chihuahua and Sonora. Conductor: Armijo, José.

Armijo, Ambrosio (roll 34, frame 1208, 31 August 1843). Guía 37. 6 tercios of domestic merchandise. Value: 146 pesos. To: Chihuahua and Sonora.

**Indicates that the guía or tornaguía was issued outside the territory of New Mexico.

Armijo, Ambrosio (roll 34, frame 1215, 1 November 1843). Guía 109. 32 piezas of foreign merchandise. Value: 4,367 pesos 64 cents. To: Chihuahua and Sonora.

Armijo, Ambrosio (roll 34, frame 1215, 10 November 1843). Guía 115. 29 piezas of foreign merchandise. Value: 3,843 pesos 64.75 cents. To: Chihuahua and Sonora.

Armijo, Ambrosio (roll 37, frame 399, 1 September 1844). Guía 45. 26 piezas of foreign merchandise. Value: 267 pesos 3 reales. To: Chihuahua and Sonora. Conductor: Armijo, José. [Guía exists: roll 37, frame 472.]

Armijo, Ambrosio (roll 40, frame 283, 2 September 1845). Guía 7. 28 piezas of domestic merchandise. Value: 403 pesos 4 reales. To: Chihuahua, Sonora, and Sinaloa. [Guía exists: roll 49, frame 313.]

Armijo, Ambrosio (roll 40, frame 318, 10 September 1845). Guía 12. 15 bultos of domestic merchandise. Value: 155 pesos 2 reales. To: Chihuahua, Sonora, and Durango.

Armijo, Antonio José (roll 34, frame 1211, 12 September 1843). Guía 61. 4 bultos of domestic merchandise. Value: 221 pesos 6 reales. To: Chihuahua, Durango, and San Juan de los Lagos.

Armijo, Cristóbal (roll 21, frame 305, 10 February 1838). Guía 53. 20 bultos of domestic merchandise. To: Chihuahua and Sonora. [Property appears to have been be jointly owned with Ambrosio Armijo.]

Armijo, Cristóbal (roll 21, frame 351, 27 August 1840). Guía 32. 25 bultos of domestic merchandise. Value: 494 pesos. To: Chihuahua and Sonora. [Guía exists: roll 28, frame 775.]

Armijo, Cristóbal (roll 21, frame 356, 28 August 1840). Guía 54. 18 bultos. Value: 175 pesos. To: Chihuahua and Sonora.

**Armijo, Cristóbal (roll 32, frame 1645, 24 November 1842). Guaymas, pase. 2 cajas and 3 quintales of steel. To: New Mexico.

Armijo, Cristóbal (roll 34, frame 1206, 26 August 1843). Guía 27. 12 bultos of domestic merchandise. Value: 127 pesos 4 reales. To: Chihuahua and Sonora.

Armijo, José (roll 21, frame 358, 13 October 1840). Guía 63. 18 [?] of domestic merchandise. Value: 117 pesos 4 reales. To: Chihuahua and Sonora.

Armijo, José (roll 30, frame 318, 30 August 1841). Guía 133. 32 bultos of domestic merchandise. Value: 363 pesos 2 reales. To: Chihuahua and Sonora.

Armijo, José (roll 34, frame 1205, 26 August 1843). Guía 18. 14 bultos of domestic merchandise. Value: 133 pesos 2 reales. To: Chihuahua and Sonora. [The cuaderno shows the same information for guía 19. It might be a mistake.]

Armijo, José (roll 34, frame 1205, 26 August 1843). Guía 19. 14 bultos of domestic merchandise. Value: 133 pesos 2 reales. To: Chihuahua and Sonora.

Armijo, José (roll 37, frame 398, 29 August 1844). Guía 42. 25 bultos of domestic merchandise. Value: 340 pesos 4 reales. To: Chihuahua, Sonora, and Durango. [Guía exists: roll 37, frame 470.]

**Armijo, Juan (roll 27, frame 629, 21 January 1839). Chihuahua, guía 14. 12 bultos. Value: 411 pesos 2 reales. [This guía is a good indicator of how much goods cost in Mexico. It also shows what they brought back.]

Armijo, Juan (roll 21, frame 325, 27 August 1839). Guía 151. 1,200 common blankets. Value: 300 pesos. To: Zacatecas and Guanajuato.

Armijo, Juan (roll 21, frame 354, 25 August 1840). Guía 47. 20 bultos of domestic merchandise. Value: 189 pesos. To: Chihuahua, Durango, and Lagos. [Guía exists: roll 28, frame 787.]

Armijo, Juan (roll 30, frame 316, 23 August 1841). Guía 124. 16 tercios of domestic merchandise. Value: ca. 191 pesos 4 reales. To: Guanajuato and Zacatecas.

Armijo, Juan C. (roll 37, frame 395, 1 August 1844). Guía 19. 89 piezas of foreign merchandise. Value: 18,049 pesos 14 cents. To: Chihuahua, Durango, and Aguas Calientes.

Armijo, Juan Cristóbal (roll 21, frame 349, 22 August 1840). Guía 23. 1,400 sheep and domestic merchandise. Value: 800 pesos. To: Chihuahua and Durango. [Guía exists: roll 28, frame 766.]

Armijo, Julián (roll 21, frame 294, 27 October 1836). Guía 96. 54 bultos. To: Vizcaya or Sonora.

Armijo, Julián (roll 21, frame 306, 12 August 1838). Guía 60. 22 bultos of domestic merchandise. To: Chihuahua and Sonora.

Armijo, Manuel (roll 21, frame 274, 10 August 1835). Guía 4. 9,400 sheep and 20 tercios of blankets. Value: ca. 4,800 pesos. To: Mexico. Fiador: Abreu, Santiago.

Armijo, Manuel (roll 21, frame 275, 18 August 1835). Guía 8. 3,000 sheep. Value: ca. 1,500 pesos. To: Mexico City. [Guía exists: roll 21, frame 366.]

**Armijo, Manuel (roll 22, frame 1179, 2 January 1836). Durango, guía 515. 20 bultos. Conductor: García, Cristóbal.

Armijo, Manuel (roll 21, frame 294, 27 October 1836). Guía 95. 1 baúl of merchandise. To: Lucero, José Antonio; Chihuahua. Conductor: Apodaca, Ramón.

Armijo, Manuel (roll 21, frame 299, 12 August 1837). Guía 11. 4,100 sheep. Value: ca. 2,050 pesos. To: El Paso, Durango, and Mexico. Conductor: García, Antonio María.

Armijo, Manuel (roll 21, frame 305, 10 February 1838). Guía 54. 9 bultos of domestic merchandise. To: Sonora. Conductor: Armijo, Pedro. [Guía exists: roll 25, frame 1429.]

Armijo, Manuel (roll 21, frame 325, 31 August 1839). Guía 152. 1,800 common blankets and 6 tercios of pinyons. Value: 459 pesos. To: Zacatecas and Guanajuato. Conductor: Armijo, Rafael.

Armijo, Manuel (roll 21, frame 348, 20 August 1840). Guía 19. 5,116 sheep. Value: 5,116 pesos. To: Durango and Zacatecas. Conductor: Ortiz, Gaspar. Fiador: Chávez, José Antonio. [Guía exists: roll 28, frame 762.]

Armijo, Manuel (roll 21, frame 349, 20 August 1840). Guía 20. To: Chihuahua. Conductores: Ortiz, Gaspar and González, Mario.

Armijo, Manuel (roll 21, frame 354, 25 August 1840). Guía 46. 34 bultos. Value: 300 pesos. To: Chihuahua, Durango, and Lagos. Conductor: Armijo, Rafael. [Guía exists: roll 28, frame 786.]

Armijo, Manuel (roll 37, frame 393, 29 July 1844). Guía 11. 19 bultos of domestic merchandise. Value: 197 pesos. To: Chihuahua. Conductor: Ruiz, Marcos.

Armijo, Manuel (roll 37, frame 393, 27 July 1844). Guía 10. 4,500 sheep. Value: 2,500 pesos. To: Durango and Mexico. Conductor: Sánchez, Felix.

Armijo, Manuel (roll 40, frame 282, 2 September 1845). Guía 6. 4,000 sheep. Value: 2,000 pesos. To: Urquide, Juan N.; Chihuahua, Durango, and Mexico. Conductor: Suárez, Mateo.

Armijo, Pedro (roll 21, frame 305, 31 January 1838). Guía 50. 44 bultos of domestic merchandise. To: Sonora.

Armijo, Pedro (roll 21, frame 362, 26 October 1840). Guía 103. 30 tercios of domestic merchandise. Value: 375 pesos. To: Chihuahua and Sonora.

Armijo, Santiago (roll 14, frame 236, 14 September 1831). Guía 56. Foreign and domestic merchandise. Value: ca. 200 pesos. To: Sonora and Chihuahua. Conductor: Ortiz, Ignacio. [Guía indicates Ortiz is carrying for his (brother?) Santiago Armijo.]

Armijo, Vicente (roll 6, frame 509, ca. 2 September 1828). Guía 17. 8 tercios. To: Chihuahua and Sonora.

Armijo y Mestas, Manuel (roll 21, frame 303, 27 August 1837). Guía 35. 2,200 sheep. Value: ca. 1,100 pesos. To: Durango or Zacatecas, Mexico. Conductor: Vergara, Vicente. [Guía exists: roll 24, frame 798.]

Armijo y Mestas, Manuel (roll 21, frame 301, 18 August 1837). Guía 25. 2,600 sheep. Value: ca. 1,300 pesos. To: Zubiría, Francisco; Mexico.

Armijo y Ortiz, Ambrosio (roll 21, frame 325, 31 August 1839). Guía 153. 30 tercios of domestic merchandise. Value: 489 pesos. To: Sonora and Sinaloa.

Armijo y Ortiz, Ambrosio (roll 28, frame 774, 25 August 1840). Guía 31. 32 bultos of domestic merchandise. Value: 312 pesos 4 reales. To: Vizcaya and Sinaloa.

[Ascarante], Anastasio (roll 40, frame 344, 21 September 1845). Guía 61. Foreign merchandise. Value: 4,023 pesos 18.75 cents. To: Galeana, Corralitos and Janos. Fiador: Scolley, John.

Baca, Antonio (roll 34 frame 1206, 30 August, 1843). Guía 24. 3 bultos of domestic merchandise and 2,757 sheep. Value: 1,408 pesos 4 reales. To: Chihuahua and Durango.

Baca, Francisco Tomás (roll 21, frame 278, 29 August 1835). Guía 20. 2,200 sheep. Value: ca. 1,100 pesos. To: Yzurrieta, José María; Durango and Federal District. [Guía exists: roll 21, frame 371.]

Baca, Francisco Tomás (roll 21, frame 279, 29 August 1835). Guía 21. Domestic merchandise. Value: 36 pesos 6 reales. To: Chihuahua and Durango. [Guía exists: roll 21, frame 372.]

Baca, Francisco Tomás (roll 22, frame 1180, 2 January 1836). Durango, guía 516. Conductor: García, José. [Merchandise was possibly jointly owned with Juan Yzurrieta.]

Baca, Francisco Tomás (roll 21, frame 311, 3 September 1838). Guía 86. 50 bultos of domestic merchandise. Value: ca. 400 pesos. To: Chihuahua, Durango, and Sonora. [Guía exists: roll 25, frame 1440. In 1840 he is at Peña Blanca: roll 27, frames 1049–51.]

Baca, Francisco Tomás (roll 21, frame 311, 3 September 1838). Guía 87. 550 sheep. Value: ca. 275 pesos. To: Zuviría, Francisco; Durango. [Guía exists: roll 25, frame 1441.]

Baca, Francisco Tomás (roll 30, frame 319, 30 August 1841). Guía 138. 56 tercios of domestic merchandise. Value: 360 pesos. To: Chihuahua and Durango.

Baca, José (roll 21, frame 320, 23 August 1839). Guía 133. 40 baúles of domestic merchandise. To: Chihuhua, Durango, and Zacatecas.

Baca, Juan (roll 34, frame 1214, 30 October 1843). Guía 108. 4 bultos of domestic merchandise. Value: 185 pesos 4 reales. To: El Paso.

Baca, Juan Antonio (roll 6, frame 508, 22 August 1828). Guía 14. 4 tercios. To: Chihuahua and Sonora. Conductor: Baca, Juan.

Baca, Juan Bautista (roll 21, frame 294, 26 October 1836). Guía 94. 460 blankets. Value: ca. 115 pesos. To: Chihuahua and Sonora.

Baca, Juan de Jesús (roll 21, frame 314, 12 September 1838). Guía 103. 7 tercios. Value: 109 pesos 4 reales. To: Chihuahua and Durango.

Baca, Juan de Jesús (roll 21, frame 354, 26 August 1840). Guía 48. 6 bultos. Value: 143 pesos 2 reales. To: Chihuahua and Durango. [Guía exists: roll 28, frame 788.]

Baca, Juan de Jesús (roll 34, frame 1207, 30 August 1843). Guía 35. 6 bultos of domestic merchandise. Value: 122 pesos. To: Chihuahua and Durango.

Baca, Luis (roll 21, frame 304, 28 August 1837). Guía 36. 12 bultos of domestic merchandise. To: Sonora.

Baca, Pedro (roll 21, frame 333, 10 September 1839). Guía 181. 4 bultos of domestic merchandise. Value: 94 pesos 2 reales. To: Zacatecas and Guadalajara.

Baca, Pedro (roll 21, frame 355, 26 August 1840). Guía 50. 8 bultos of domestic merchandise. Value: 125 pesos 6 reales. To: Chihuahua and Durango. [Guía exists: roll 28, frame 790.]

Baca, Pedro (roll 37, frame 403, 7 September 1844). Guía 27. 4 bultos of domestic merchandise. Value: 150 pesos 2 reales. To: Chihuahua, Durango, and Lagos.

Baca, Pedro M. (roll 34, frame 1207, 30 August 1843). Guía 34. 6 bultos of domestic merchandise. Value: 128 pesos 6 reales. To: Chihuahua, Durango, and Zacatecas.

**Baca, Romualdo (roll 32, frame 1658, 12 November 1842). Hermosillo, guía 427. 18 piezas (iron, steel, and domestic merchandise). Value 247 pesos. To: New Mexico.

Baca, Romualdo (roll 34, frame 1205, 30 August 1843). Guía 22. 16 bultos of domestic merchandise and 791 sheep. Value: 541 pesos. To: Chihuahua and Durango.

Baca, Romualdo (roll 40, frame 283, 2 September 1845). Guía 9. 1,000 sheep. Value: 500 pesos. To: Chihuahua.

Baca, Tomás (roll 21, frame 302, 25 August 1837). Guía 31. 3,000 sheep. Value: ca. 1,500 pesos. To: Pescador, Antonio; Mexico. Conductor: Baca, Domingo.

Baca, Tomás (roll 21, frame 346, 18 August 1840). Guía 12. 75 bultos of domestic merchandise. Value: 2,498 pesos. To: Chihuahua, Durango, and Lagos. [Guía exists: roll 28, frame 758.]

Baca, Vicente (roll 10, frame 382, 18 November 1829). Guía 14. 1 tercio of foreign merchandise bought in the country. To: Sonora. [Baca is possibly arriero for Antoine Robidoux.]

Baca, Vicente (roll 12, frame 1155, 20 November 1830). Guía 32. To: Sonora. [Baca is possibly arriero for Antoine Robidoux.]

Baca, Vicente (roll 30, frame 320, 1 September 1841). Guía 143. 17 tercios of domestic merchandise. Value: 449 pesos. To: Chihuahua and Durango.

Baca y Pino, Juan José (roll 21, frame 308, 27 August 1838). Guía 70. 4,200 sheep and 4 bultos of domestic merchandise. Value: ca. 2,140 pesos. To: Chihuahua, Durango, and Mexico.

Ballejos, Antonio (roll 21, frame 306, 12 August 1838). Guía 63. 12 bultos and 600 sarapes. To: Chihuahua and Durango. Conductor: Otero, Juan.

Ballejos, Antonio (roll 21, frame 307, 12 August 1838). Guía 64. 3,800 sheep. Value: ca. 1,900 pesos. To: Chihuahua and Durango. Conductor: Otero, Juan. [It is not clear if the owner of the sheep is Ballejos or Otero.]

Barceló, José (roll 21, frame 345, 11 August 1840). Guía 6. 100 bultos of domestic merchandise. Value: 815 pesos. To: Sonora. Fiador: Madrid, Dolores. [Guía exists: roll 25, frame 754.]

Barceló, José (roll 21, frame 346, 14 August 1840). Guía 9. 46 bultos. Value: 348 pesos 1 real. To: Sonora. Fiador: Ortiz y Delgado, Francisco. [Guía exists: roll 28, frame 757.]

Barceló, Trinidad (roll 40, frame 352, 10 October 1845). Guía 65. Foreign merchandise. Value: 106 pesos 20 cents. To: El Paso.

Barela, Francisco (roll 21, frame 295, 7 November 1836). Guía 98. 1 small and 3 big tercios. To: Ponce de León, Juan María; El Paso. Conductor: Valencia, Tomás. [Guía exists: roll 22, frame 1168. It appears that Barela is also an arriero carrying merchandise which belongs to Ponce de León.]

Bazán, J. A. (roll 37, frame 402, 7 September 1844). Guía 16. 5 bultos of foreign merchandise. Value: 342 pesos 2 reales. To: Chihuahua and Sonora.

Benavídez, Sebastián (roll 19, frame 230, 16 August 1834). Guía 46. Foreign merchandise. To: El Paso.

Blanco, Miguel (roll 21, frame 344, 11 August 1840). Guía 5. 4 bultos. Value: 229 pesos 6 reales. To: Barrio, Lorenzo; El Paso. Fiador: Miranda, Guadalupe. [Guía exists: roll 28, frame 753.]

[Brena], Francisco (roll 21, frame 350, 23 August 1840). Guía 25. 24 fanegas of pinyon. To: Sonora.

Bustamante, Juan (roll 21, frame 294, 18 October 1836). Guía 91. 2 tercios of foreign merchandise. To: "The localities down south up to El Paso." Fiador: Valencia, Tomás. [Guía exists: roll 22, frame 1166.]

Bustos, Antonio (roll 21, frame 330, 10 September 1839). Guía 173. 12 bultos of domestic merchandise. Value: 179 pesos. To: Zacatecas and Guadalajara.

Bustos, Francisco (roll 21, frame 362, 26 October 1840). Guía 102. 3 bultos. Value: 67 pesos 2 reales. To: Chihuahua.

Cabeza de Baca, Luis María (roll 21, frame 303, 28 August 1837). Guía 36. 12 bultos of domestic merchandise. Value: ca. 117 pesos 4 reales. To: Chihuahua and Sonora [Guía exists: roll 24, frame 799.]

Candelaria, José Rafael (roll 34, frame 1211, 15 September 1843). Guía 63. 8 bultos of domestic merchandise. Value: 111 pesos 2 reales. To: Chihuahua, Durango, and San Juan de los Lagos.

Carbajal, Ventura (roll 21, frame 276, ca. 19 August 1835). Guía 13. 1 bulto of foreign merchandise. To: El Paso.

Carrillo, Juan Felipe (roll 21, frame 360, 16 October 1840). Guía 76. 2 piezas of foreign merchandise bought in S[an]ta Fe. Value: 201 pesos 2 reales 1 grano. To: Chihuahua and Sonora.

Chávez, Antonio (roll 21, frame 305, 31 January 1838). Guía 49. 24 bultos of domestic merchandise. To: Sonora.

Chávez, Antonio José (roll 21, frame 352, 30 August 1840). Guía 35. 20 bultos of foreign merchandise. Value: 2,337 pesos 6 reales. To: Chihuahua and Durango. Conductor: Chávez, José. [Guía exists: roll 28, frame 775, but the first page is mostly illegible and partially torn. Most of the value can be accounted from fabrics.]

Chávez, Antonio José (roll 34, frame 1204, 25 August 1843). Guía 16. 5,400 sheep. Value: 2,700 pesos. To: Durango and Mexico. Conductor: Chávez, José.

Chávez Castillo, José (roll 37, frame 394, 1 August 1844). Guía 15. 5,500 sheep. Value: 2,750 pesos. To: Urquide, Juan Nepomuceno; Chihuahua. Conductor: Chávez, Diego.

Chávez Castillo, José (roll 37, frame 398, 29 August 1844). Guía 40. Domestic merchandise. To: Chihuahua, Durango, and Lagos. [Guía exists: roll 37, frame 468. Guía indicates that Francisco Ortiz y Delgado signed for his father, but it is not clear if he is acting as conductor or fiador. Amount of merchandise is quite small — around 60 pesos. Amount of salt carried is not indicated.]

Chávez, Francisco (roll 21, frame 349, 25 August 1840). Guía 22. 14 bultos of domestic merchandise. Value: 150 pesos. To: Chihuahua and Durango. [Guía exists: roll 28, frame 765.]

Chávez, José (roll 21, frame 275, 18 August 1835). Guía 7. 11,000 sheep. Value: ca. 5,500 pesos. To: Mexico City.

Chávez, José (roll 21, frame 323, 26 August 1839). Guía 147. 5,000 sheep. Value: 2,500 pesos. To: Márquez, Juan de Dios; Durango. Conductor: Pino, José.

Chávez, José (roll 34, frame 1204, 25 August 1843). Guía 17. 12 tercios of foreign merchandise. To: Sonora, Durango, and Zacatecas.

Chávez, José (roll 34, frame 1205, 25 August 1843). Guía 18. 160 bultos of foreign merchandise. To: Durango, Zacatecas, and San Juan de los Lagos. Fiador: Pino, Miguel Estanislao. [Guía exists: roll 34, frame 1233. This was a very impressive shipment. It was one of the largest going to Mexico. Among the merchandise there were 100,169 yards of lienzo and 43,963 yards of indiana.]

Chávez, José Antonio (roll 21, frame 352, 28 August 1840). Guía 36. 1 *carro* (cart). Value: 3,390 pesos 4 reales. To: Chihuahua and Durango.

Chávez, Josefa (roll 30, frame 319, 30 August 1841). Guía 140. 2,400 sheep. Value: 1,200 pesos. To: Cordero, José; Chihuahua and Durango. Conductor: Gallegos, Julián.

Chávez, Juan de Dios (roll 21, frame 310, ca. 30 August 1838). Guía 84. Domestic merchandise. To: Chihuahua and Durango.

Chávez, Mariano (roll 15, frame 1035, 12 July 1832). Guía 97. 30,000 sheep and 600 frazadas corrientes. Value: ca. 15,150 pesos. To: Durango.

Chávez, Mariano (roll 21, frame 274, 18 August 1835). Guía 6. 26,000 sheep. Value: ca. 13,000 pesos. To: Mexico. Conductor: Chávez, José.

Chávez, Mariano (roll 21, frame 310, 30 August 1838). Guía 85. To: Durango, Mexico, and Puebla.

Chávez, Mariano (roll 21, frame 318, 23 August 1839). Guía 134. 500 sheep. Value: ca. 250 pesos. To: Chihuahua and Zacatecas. Conductor: García, Gregorio.

Chávez, Mariano (roll 21, frame 356, 29 August 1840). Guía 58. 5,500 sheep. Value: ca. 2,750 pesos. To: Zubiría, Francisco; Durango. Conductor: García, Gregorio, mayordomo. [Guía exists: roll 28, frame 794. It is signed by Mario Sandoval who does so for Mariano Chávez.]

Chávez, Mariano (roll 30, frame 319, 30 August 1841). Guía 139. 14 tercios of domestic merchandise and 7,000 sheep. Value: 3,554 pesos 4 reales. To: Zuviría, Francisco; Chihuahua, Durango, and Mexico. Conductor: García, José [this is possibly a mistake; the first name should be Gregorio].

Chávez, Mariano (roll 34, frame 1204, 25 August 1843). Guía 14. 4,400 sheep. Value: 2,200 pesos. To: Durango and Mexico. Conductor: García, Gregorio, mayordomo.

Chávez, Mariano (roll 37, frame 395, 2 August 1844. Guía 20. 177 piezas of foreign merchandise. Value: 26,474 pesos 79.5 cents. To: Chihuahua. Conductor: Sandoval, Mariano.

Chávez, Mariano (roll 37, frame 395, 2 August 1844). Guía 21. 6,000 sheep. Value: 3,000 pesos. To: Durango, Zacatecas, and Mexico. Conductor: García, Gregorio.

Chávez, Vicente (roll 21, frame 326, 31 August 1839). Guía 154. 18 bultos of domestic merchandise. Value: 254 pesos. To: Sonora and Chihuahua.

Chávez, Vicente (roll 21, frame 348, 20 August 1840). Padillas, New Mexico, guía 17. 17 bultos of domestic merchandise. Value: 212 pesos 4 reales. To: Chihuahua and San Juan de Lagos. [Guía exists: roll 28, frame 761.]

Chávez, Vicente (roll 30, frame 315, 22 August 1841). Guía 123. 15 tercios of domestic merchandise. Value: 162 pesos 4 reales. To: Chihuahua and Sonora.

Chávez, Vicente (roll 34, frame 1204, 25 August 1843). Guía 15. 9 bultos of domestic merchandise. Value: 110 pesos. To: Chihuahua and Sonora.

Chávez y Chávez, José (roll 21, frame 349, 21 August 1840). Guía 21. 14 bultos of domestic merchandise. Value: 150 pesos. To: Chihuahua and Durango. [Guía exists: roll 28 frame 764.]

Cisneros, Manuel (roll 21, frame 360, 18 October 1840). Guía 79. 16 piezas of domestic merchandise. Value: 250 pesos. To: Chihuahua and Sonora.

Cisneros, Manuel (roll 34, frame 1215, 6 November 1843). Guía 113. 1 bulto of foreign merchandise. Value: 193 pesos 5 reales. To: Chihuahua.

Cisneros, Manuel (roll 36, frame 1267, 7 November 1843). Guía 114. 7 bultos of domestic merchandise. Value: 261 pesos 4 reales. To: Chihuahua and Sonora. [The cuaderno lists Mariano Lucero as the owner of the merchandise (roll 34, frame 1215).]

Contreras, Jesús (roll 15, frame 1028, 2 August 1832). Guía 93. 1 tercio of foreign merchandise. To: El Paso. [He purchased goods from Solomon Houck.]

Contreras, Manuel (roll 21, frame 337, 16 October 1839). Guía 197. 7 bultos. Value: 80 pesos. To: El Paso.

Cordero, José (roll 21, frame 341, 7 November 1839). Guía 212. Bultos of foreign merchandise. Value: 280 pesos. To: Chihuahua, Durango, and Sonora.

Cordero, José (roll 21, frame 342, 7 November 1839). Guía 215. 42 bultos of foreign merchandise. To: Chihuahua, Durango, and Zacatecas.

Córdoba, Felipe (roll 25, frame 1463, 16 November 1838). Guía 121. 8 tercios of domestic merchandise. Value: ca. 134 pesos 4 reales. To: Chihuahua. [There is no record of this guía in the guía notebook of 1835.]

Córdoba, Felipe (roll 34, frame 1210, 6 September 1843). Guía 55. 6 tercios of domestic merchandise. Value: 146 pesos. To: Chihuahua, Durango, and Zacatecas.

Córdoba, José (roll 34, frame 1214, 30 October 1843). Guía 106. 15 bultos of domestic merchandise. Value: 268 pesos. To: Chihuahua and Sonora.

Córdoba, José del Espíritu Santo (roll 21, frame 332, 10 September 1839). Guía 177. 14 bultos of domestic merchandise. Value: 163 pesos 7 reales. To: Chihuahua, Durango, and Zacatecas.

Córdoba, José María (roll 21, frame 275, 19 August 1835). Guía 10. 1 bulto. To: El Paso

Córdoba, José María (roll 37, frame 532, 12 February 1844). El Paso, guía 21. 30 piezas of domestic merchandise. Value: 100 pesos. To: New Mexico.

Córdoba, José María (roll 37, frame 406, 9 November 1844). Guía 38. 10 bultos of domestic merchandise. Value: 88 pesos. To: Chihuahua. [Guía exists: roll 37, frame 495.]

Córdoba, José Rafael (roll 34, frame 1213, 24 October 1843). Guía 79. 6 bultos of domestic merchandise. Value: 105 pesos 6 reales. To: Chihuahua and Sonora.

Córdoba, Pedro (roll 21, frame 312, 10 September 1838). Guía 93. 5 tercios of domestic merchandise. To: Chihuahua and Durango.

Córdoba, Pedro (roll 37, frame 401, 6 September 1844). Guía 12. 8 bultos of domestic merchandise. Value: 218 pesos 2 reales. To: Chihuahua, Durango, and Lagos. [Guía exists: roll 37 frame 485.]

Córdoba, Pedro (roll 40, frame 332, 9 September 1845). Guía 47. 10 bultos of domestic merchandise. Value: 252 pesos. To: Chihuahua, Durango, and Lagos.

Cortez, José Manuel (roll 34, frame 1213, 30 October 1843). Guía 102. 6 bultos of domestic merchandise. Value: 137 pesos 4 reales. To: Chihuahua and Sonora.

Cortez, José Manuel (roll 37, frame 406, 11 November 1844). Guía 40. 2 bultos of domestic merchandise. Value: 95 pesos 3 reales. To: Chihuahua. [Guía exists: roll 37 frame 497.]

Cuarón, Juan (roll 37, frame 531, 13 February 1844). El Paso, guía 23. Domestic merchandise. Value: 186 pesos. To: New Mexico.

**Delgado, Juan José (roll 24, frame 802, 20 November 1837). Durango, guía 352. 50 piezas. Value: 7,680 pesos. To: Chávez, José; Padillas, New Mexico

Delgado, Simón (roll 21, frame 339, 28 October 1839). Guía 205. 25 bultos of domestic merchandise. Value: 211 pesos 6 reales. To: Chihuahua and Sonora.

**Delgado, Simón (roll 41, frame 832, 2 June 1846). Chihuahua, guía 81. 12 piezas of domestic and foreign merchandise. Value: 11,117 pesos 7 reales. To: Santa Fe. Conductor: Araujo, Angel.

Díaz de la Serna, Ramón (roll 21, frame 275, 19 August 1835). Guía 9. 1 tercio of foreign merchandise. Value: ca. 53 pesos. To: El Paso. [Guía exists: roll 21, frame 367.]

Domínguez, José (roll 21, frame 297, 11 February 1837). Guía 107. To: El Paso.

Durán, José Dolores (roll 21, frame 312, 10 September 1838). Guía 95. 6 bultos of domestic merchandise. Value: 94 pesos 7 reales 6 granos. To: Chihuahua and Durango. [Guía exists: roll 25, frame 1446.]

Durán, José Dolores (roll 21, frame 353, 24 August 1840). Guía 41. 15 bultos of domestic merchandise. Value: 234 pesos. To: Chihuahua and Durango. Fiador: Archuleta, Pablo. [Guía exists: roll 28, frame 781.]

Durán, José Dolores (roll 37, frame 401, 6 September 1844). Guía 9. 11 bultos of domestic merchandise. Value: 200 pesos. To: Chihuahua, Durango, and Lagos. [Guía exists: roll 37, frame 482.]

Elguea, Francisco (roll 21, frame 341, 3 November 1839). Guía 213. 33 bultos of foreign merchandise. To: Chihuahua and Guadalajara.

Elguea, Francisco (roll 21, frame 341, 3 November 1839). Guía 214. 78 bultos of foreign merchandise. To: Olivares, Pedro; Chihuahua.

Elguea, Francisco (roll 37, frame 408, 19 December 1844). Guía 48. 32 bultos of foreign merchandise. Value: 3,926 pesos 20 cents. To: Ronquillo, Ignacio; Chihuahua and other points along the way. Conductor: Castillo, Simón.

Elguea, Francisco (roll 37, frame 408, 19 December 1844). Guía 49. 22 bultos of foreign merchandise. Value: 2,395 pesos 49 cents. To: Chihuahua, El Paso, and El Parral. Conductor: Killman, Enrique.

Elguea, Francisco (roll 37, frame 408, 19 December 1844). Guía 50. 21 bultos of foreign merchandise. Value: 2,165 pesos 17 cents. To: Chihuahua, Jesús María, and Parral. Conductor: Castillo, Simón.

Escudero, Manuel (roll 6, frame 486, 1 July 1827). Guía 30. Foreign merchandise. Value: 346 pesos 5 reales 6 granos. To: Escudero, Luis; Chihuahua. Conductor: Escudero, José Agustín.

Esquivel, Diego (roll 37, frame 403, 7 September 1844). Guía 30. 7 bultos of domestic merchandise. Value: 145 pesos 4 reales. To: Chihuahua, Durango, and Lagos.

[Fentre], Nicolás (roll 37, frame 407, 15 November 1844). Guía 45. 150 fanegas of domestic pinyon. Value: 300 pesos. To: Chihuahua and Durango.

Fernández, José (roll 21, frame 304, 27 October 1837). Guía 44. 1 bulto of domestic merchandise. To: El Paso.

Flores, Santiago (roll 30, frame 320, 1 September 1841). Guía 141. 50 tercios of domestic merchandise. Value: 297 pesos 6 reales. To: Durango, Zacatecas, and San Juan de los Lagos.

Flores, Santiago (roll 37, frame 397, 23 August 1844). Guía 37. 47 bultos of foreign merchandise. Value: 5,837 pesos 88.75 cents. To: Chihuahua, Durango, and Sonora. [Guía exists: roll 37, frame 463.]

Flores, Santiago (roll 37, frame 398, 23 August 1844). Guía 38. 17 bultos of domestic merchandise. Value: 491 pesos 4 reales. To: Chihuahua and Sonora. [Guía exists: roll 37, frame 466.]

Flores, Santiago (roll 40, frame 314, 28 August 1845). Guía 9. Domestic merchandise. Value: 397 pesos 1 real. To: Durán, Ramón; Huepaca, Sonora. Conductor: Figueroa, Joaquín. [This guía is not listed in the cuaderno, which lists guía 9 as being issued to Rumaldo Baca on 2 September 1845.]

**Flores, Santiago (roll 40, frame 316, 1845. Moctezuma, guía [?]. 55 bultos of domestic merchandise and 900 pesos *en dinero* (in cash). Value: 1,390 pesos. To: New Mexico.

[Frantes], Francisco (roll 37, frame 405, 8 November 1844). Guía 36. 7 bultos of domestic merchandise. Value: 100 pesos. To: California. Fiador: Robidoux, Louis. [Guía exists: roll 37, frame 494.]

Gallegos, Antonio (roll 21, frame 294, 18 October 1836). Guía 92. 1 tercio of domestic merchandise. To: El Paso.

Gallegos, Isidro (roll 21, frame 361, 26 October 1840). Guía 98. 6 bultos of domestic merchandise. Value: 103 pesos. To: Chihuahua and Sonora.

Gallegos, José de la Luz (roll 34, frame 1210, 6 September 1843). Guía 52. 9 bultos of domestic merchandise. Value: 196 pesos 7 reales. To: Chihuahua and Durango. [Guía exists: roll 34, frame 1251.]

Gallegos, José Gabriel (roll 37, frame 401, 6 September 1844). Guía 13. 4 bultos of domestic merchandise. Value: 100 pesos 6 reales. To: Chihuahua, Durango, and Lagos. [Guía exists: roll 37, frame 486.]

Gallegos, José Pablo (roll 21, frame 330, 10 September 1839). Guía 171. 14 bultos of domestic merchandise. Value: 214 pesos 6 reales. To: Chihuahua and Durango.

Gallegos, Juan (roll 21, frame 336, 15 October 1839). Guía 191. 7 bultos of domestic merchandise. Value: 75 pesos. To: Chihuahua.

Gallegos, Saturnino (roll 21, frame 311, 3 September 1838). Guía 88. 2 bultos of domestic merchandise. Value: ca. 119 pesos 7 reales. To: Sonora. [Guía exists: roll 25, frame 1442. It indicates that Gallegos was carrying 15 tercios.]

Gallegos, Tranquilino (roll 34, frame 1210, 6 September 1843). Guía 51. 12 bultos of domestic merchandise. Value: 123 pesos 2 reales. To: Chihuahua, Durango, and Lagos. [Guía exists: roll 34, frame 1250.]

García, Andrés (roll 37, frame 403, 6 September 1844). Guía 20. 6 bultos of domestic merchandise. Value: 153 pesos 4 reales. To: Chihuahua, Durango, and Lagos.

García, Francisco (roll 21, frame 277, 20 August 1835). Guía 15. 1 bulto of foreign merchandise. To: El Paso.

García, Francisco (roll 37, frame 402, 6 September 1844). Guía 14. 9 bultos of domestic merchandise. Value: 208 pesos 4 reales. To: Chihuahua, Durango, and Lagos. [Guía exists: roll 37, frame 487.]

García, Hilarión (roll 21, frame 287, 6 December 1835). Guía 51. 4 tercios of foreign merchandise. To: Sonora. [Guía exists: roll 21, frame 395.]

García, Juan (roll 37, frame 398, 29 August 1844). Guía 41. 18 bultos of domestic merchandise. Value: 300 pesos. To: Chihuahua, Durango, and Lagos. [Guía exists: roll 37, frame 469.]

García, Juan B. (roll 37, frame 401, 5 September 1844). Guía 8. 7 bultos of domestic merchandise. Value: 234 pesos. To: Chihuahua, Durango, and Lagos. [Guía exists: roll 37, frame 481.]

García, Rafael (roll 34, frame 1210, 6 September 1843). Guía 53. 5 bultos of domestic merchandise. Value: 131 pesos. To: Chihuahua. Conductor: Montoya, Rafael. [Guía exists: roll 34, frame 1252.]

García, Ramón (roll 6, frame 477, 9 September 1826). Guía 10. Foreign merchandise. Value: 676 pesos 5 reales 6 granos. To: Chihuahua. [Guía exists: roll 6, frame 463.]

**Garibay, José María (roll 14, frame 306, 24 November 1831). Aguascalientes, guía 1193. 29 bultos of foreign and domestic merchandise. Value: 3,203 pesos. To: New Mexico. Conductor: Otero, Vicente.

Gil, Santiago (roll 21, frame 288, 26 April 1836). Guía 60. 7 tercios of domestic merchandise. To: Chihuahua.

Gómez, Diego (roll 21, frame 361, 26 October 1840). Guía 99. 4 bultos of domestic merchandise. Value: 90 pesos. To: Chihuahua and Sonora.

Gómez, Diego (roll 34, frame 1214, 30 October 1843). Guía 103. 6 bultos of domestic merchandise. Value: 187 pesos 4 reales. To: Chihuahua and Durango.

Gómez, Diego (roll 37, frame 407, 11 November 1844). Guía 43. 6 bultos of domestic merchandise. Value: 78 pesos. To: Chihuahua. [Guía exists: roll 37, frame 500.]

Gómez, Mariano (roll 34, frame 1214, 30 October 1843). Guía 104. Domestic merchandise. Value: 252 pesos 2 reales. To: Chihuahua and Sonora.

González, Ambrosio (roll 25, frame 1458, 15 November 1838). Guía 116. 6 bultos of domestic merchandise. Value: ca. 72 pesos 5 reales. To: Sonora. [There is no record of this guía in the guía notebook of 1835.]

González, Dionisio (roll 37, frame 401, 6 September 1844). Guía 10. 6 bultos of domestic merchandise. Value: 123 pesos 4 reales. To: Chihuahua, Durango, and Lagos. [Guía exists: roll 37, frame 483. Guía lists the owner as Patricio González.]

González, Hilarión (roll 34, frame 1213, 29 October 1843). Guía 80. 18 bultos of domestic merchandise. Value: 280 pesos 6 reales. To: Chihuahua. [Guía exists: roll 34, frame 1262.]

González, Hilarión (roll 37, frame 399, 4 September 1844). Guía 49. 16 bultos of domestic merchandise. Value: 171 pesos. To: Chihuahua, Durango, and Lagos.

González, José (roll 21, frame 338, 23 October 1839). Guía 199. 12 bultos of domestic merchandise. Value: 209 pesos 4 reales. To: Sonora.

**González, Juan José (roll 32, frame 1639, 17 November 1842). Hermosillo, guía 317. 5 quintales of iron. To: New Mexico.

González, Juan José (roll 37, frame 403, 7 September 1844). Guía 24. 12 bultos of domestic merchandise. Value: 230 pesos. To: Sonora. [Guía exists: roll 37, frame 488. There is a discrepancy in the value indicated. The cuaderno shows 230 pesos; the guía itself shows 232 pesos. Computation indicates that value should be 239 pesos.]

González, Sabino (roll 21, frame 336, 16 October 1839). Guía 192. 7 bultos of domestic merchandise. Value: 87 pesos. To: Sonora.

González, Santiago (roll 25, frame 1459, 15 November 1838). Guía 117. 18 tercios of domestic merchandise. Value: ca. 94 pesos 6 reales. To: Sonora. [There is no record of this guía in the guía notebook of 1835.]

González, Santiago (roll 21, frame 338, 23 October 1839). Guía 200. 6 bultos of domestic merchandise. Value: 99 pesos. To: Sonora.

**Griego, Antonio (roll 32, frame 1660, 5 November 1842). Guaymas, pase [?]. 7 quintales of steel. Value: 7 pesos. To: New Mexico.

**Griego, Manuel Victorio (roll 32, frame 1646, 20 December 1842). Moctezuma, guía 61. 12 piezas. Value: 126 pesos. To: New Mexico.

Griego, Saturnino (roll 21, frame 290, 30 August 1836). Guía 72. To: El Paso.

Griego, Victoriano (roll 21, frame 305, 12 February 1838). Guía 56. 12 bultos of domestic merchandise. To: Sonora.

Gutiérrez, José María (roll 30, frame 317, 29 August 1841). Guía 132. 50 tercios of domestic merchandise. Value: 2,062 pesos 4 reales. To: Chihuahua and Durango.

Gutiérrez, José María (roll 37, frame 393, 21 July 1844). Guía 6. Sheep. To: Chihuahua and Durango. Conductor: Baca, Romualdo.

Gutiérrez, José María (roll 40, frame 283, 2 September 1845). Guía 8. 4,000 sheep. Value: 2,000 pesos. To: Urquide, Juan N.; Chihuahua, Durango, and Mexico. Conductor: Baca, Rumaldo.

Gutiérrez, Juan (roll 21, frame 356, 28 August 1840). Guía 57. 18 bultos. Value: 175 pesos. To: Chihuahua, Durango, and Sonora. Conductor: Ortiz, Jesús María.

Gutiérrez, Juan (roll 21, frame 356, 28 August 1840). Guía 56. 8 bultos. To: Chihuahua, Durango, and Sonora. Conductor: Ortiz, Jesús María.

Guzmán, José Dolores (roll 21, frame 332, 10 September 1839). Guía 178. 6 bultos of domestic merchandise. Value: 115 pesos 7 reales. To: Chihuahua and Durango.

Herrera, Antonio José de (roll 25, frame 1461, 16 November 1838). Guía 119. 9 tercios of domestic merchandise. Value: ca. 125 pesos 2 reales. To: Chihuahua. [There is no record of this guía in the guía notebook of 1835.]

Herrera, Carpio (roll 34, frame 1210, 6 September 1843). Guía 54. 8 tercios of domestic merchandise. Value: 183 pesos 6 reales. To: Chihuahua and Durango.

Herrera, José de Jesús (roll 37, frame 400, 5 September 1844). Guía 7. 9 bultos of foreign merchandise. Value: 308 pesos. To: Chihuahua, Durango, and Lagos. [Guía exists: roll 37, frame 480.]

Huerta, Aniceto (roll 40, frame 320, 6 September 1845). Guía 24. 9 bultos of domestic and foreign merchandise. Value: 152 pesos 61.5 cents. To: Chihuahua.

Huerta, Rafael (roll 21, frame 345, 11 August 1840). Guía 7. 56 bultos. Value: 226 pesos 4 reales. To: Chihuahua and Michoacán. Fiador: Alarid, [Bautista]. [Guía exists: roll 28, frame 755.]

[Iconamio], Manuel (roll 32, frame 1630, 26 October 1842). Guía 24. Domestic merchandise. Value: 158 pesos 1 real. To: Chihuahua and Sonora.

Jaquez [Xaquez], José de la Luz (roll 19, frame 228, 16 August 1834). Guía 45. Foreign merchandise. To: El Paso.

Jaquez [Xaquez], José de la Libra (roll 21, frame 317, 16 August 1839). Guía 118. 18 tercios of foreign merchandise. Value: 1,680 pesos 13.5 cents. To: El Paso.

Jaramillo, Manuel (roll 21, frame 337, August 1839. Guía 194. 10 bultos. Value: 105 pesos. To: Sonora.

Llanes, José María (roll 21, frame 346, 14 August 1840). Guía 10. 22 bultos. Value: 157 pesos 2 reales. To: Sonora.

Lobato, Buenaventura (roll 34, frame 1214, 30 October 1843). Guía 105. 8 bultos of domestic merchandise. Value: 207 pesos. To: Chihuahua and Durango.

López, Francisco (roll 37, frame 400, 4 September 1844). Guía 1. 12 bultos of domestic merchandise. Value: 92 pesos. To: Chihuahua, Durango, and Lagos.

López, Salvador (roll 21, frame 312, 9 September 1838). Guía 92. 4 carros and 78 tercios of domestic merchandise. Value: 159 pesos 4 reales. To: Chihuahua, Durango, and Zacatecas. [Guía exists: roll 25, frame 1444.]

López, Salvador (roll 21, frame 355, 26 August 1840). Guía 52. 2 carros and 5 mules with domestic merchandise. Value: 317 pesos 4 reales. To: Chihuahua and Durango. Fiador: Madrid, Dolores. [Guía exists: roll 28, frame 792.]

Loya, Jesús (roll 40, frame 354, 13 October 1845). Guía 73. Foreign and domestic merchandise. Value: 486 pesos 39.25 cents. To: El Paso.

Lucero, Andrés (roll 21, frame 304, 31 January 1838). Guía 47. 40 bultos of domestic merchandise. To: Sonora.

Lucero, Blas (roll 21, frame 304, 22 January 1838). Guía 46. 60 bultos of domestic merchandise. To: Sonora.

Lucero, Blas (roll 21, frame 333, 18 September 1839). Guía 182. 50 bultos. Value: 512 pesos 4 reales. To: Sonora and Sinaloa.

Lucero, Blas. roll 34 frame 1207, Aug 28, 1843. Guía 30. 22 bultos of domestic merchandise. Value: 269 pesos. To: Chihuahua and Sonora. [Guía exists: roll 34, frame 1241.]

Lucero, Diego (roll 37, frame 403, 7 September 1844). Guía 25. 16 bultos of domestic merchandise. Value: 235 pesos 2 reales. To: Durango.

Lucero, Diego Antonio (roll 21, frame 330, 10 September 1839). Guía 170. 13 bultos of domestic merchandise. Value: 157 pesos 3 reales. To: Chihuahua, Durango, and Zacatecas.

Lucero, José Antonio (roll 21, frame 278, 24 August 1835). Guía 19. 2 bultos of foreign merchandise. To: El Paso. [Guía exists: roll 21, frame 370.]

Lucero, José Antonio (roll 21, frame 316, 1 August 1839). Guía 114. 1 tercio of foreign merchandise. Value: 125 pesos 2 reales. To: El Paso. Fiador: Madrid, Dolores.

Lucero, José Benito (roll 21, frame 295, 7 November 1836). Guía 99. 1 tercio of merchandise. To: El Paso.

Lucero, Mariano (roll 21, frame 305, 10 February 1838). Guía 55. 18 bultos of domestic merchandise. To: Sonora.

Lucero, Mariano (roll 34, frame 1215, 13 November 1843). Guía 114. 7 piezas of domestic merchandise. Value: 261 pesos 4 reales. To: Chihuahua and Sonora. [The cuaderno lists Lucero as the owner of the merchandise; the guía indicates Mariano Cisneros was the owner.]

Lucero, Pedro (roll 21, frame 329, 10 September 1839). Guía 167. 13 bultos of merchandise and 140 pesos en dinero. Value: 268 pesos. To: Zacatecas and Guanajuato.

Lucero, Pedro (roll 34, frame 1209, 5 September 1843). Guía 45. 22 bultos of domestic merchandise. Value: 238 pesos 4 reales. To: Chihuahua, Durango, and Lagos. [Guía exists: roll 34, frame 1247.]

Lucero, Pedro Antonio (roll 21, frame 352, 28 August 1840). Guía 38. 23 bultos of domestic merchandise. Value: 288 pesos 4 reales. To: San Juan de Lagos. Fiador: Abeita, Diego. [Guía exists: roll 28, frame 779.]

Lucero, Pedro Antonio (roll 37, frame 403, 8 September 1844). Guía 23. 20 bultos of domestic merchandise. Value: 234 pesos 4 reales. To: Chihuahua, Durango, and Lagos.

Lucero, Ricardo (roll 34, frame 1209, 6 September 1843). Guía 50. 18 bultos of domestic merchandise. Value: 103 pesos 3 reales. To: Chihuahua, Durango, and Lagos.

Luján, Antonio (roll 21, frame 328, 9 September 1839). Guía 163. 8 bultos of domestic merchandise. Value: 65 pesos 3 reales. To: Chihuahua.

Luján, José de Jesús (roll 21, frame 355, 28 August 1840). Guía 53. 4 bultos. Value: 88 pesos 4 reales. To: Chihuahua.

Luna, Juan de Jesús (roll 25, frame 1465, 16 November 1838). Guía 123. 6 tercios of domestic merchandise. Value: ca. 173 pesos 4 reales. To: Chihuahua. [There is no record of this guía in the cuaderno.]

Luna, Pedro (roll 34, frame 1209, 6 September 1843). Guía 49. 10 piezas of domestic merchandise. Value: 137 pesos. To: Chihuahua and Durango.

Luna, Ramón (roll 34, frame 1211, 13 September 1843). Lunas, N. M., guía 57. 500 sheep at 4 reales and 11 bultos of domestic merchandise. Value: ca. 499 pesos 4 reales. To: Chihuahua and Sonora. [Guía exists: roll 34, frame 1255.]

Mares, Juan de Jesús (roll 34, frame 1208, 5 September 1843). Guía 41. 11 tercios of domestic merchandise. Value: 287 pesos 5 reales. To: Chihuahua, Durango, and Zacatecas.

Márquez, Gerónimo (roll 21, frame 346, 14 August 1840). Guía 11. 76 bultos. Value: 586 pesos 4 reales. To: Sonora.

Márquez, Pedro Ignacio (roll 25, frame 101, 12 September 1838). Guía 101. 4 bultos of domestic merchandise. Value: 66 pesos 7 reales. To: Chihuahua and Durango. [Guía exists: roll 25, frame 1450. Cuaderno lists owner's surname as Martínez; guía indicates the surname was Márquez.]

Márquez, Salvador (roll 37, frame 403, 7 September 1844). Guía 26. 10 bultos of domestic merchandise. Value: 77 pesos. To: Durango and Lagos.

Martín, Juan Nepomuceno (roll 37, frame 403, 7 September 1844). Guía 28. 6 bultos of domestic merchandise. Value: 181 pesos. To: Chihuahua, Durango, and Lagos. [Guía exists: roll 37, frame 489.]

Martín, Ramón (roll 34, frame 1208, 5 September 1843). Guía 39. 8 tercios of domestic merchandise. Value: 147 pesos. To: Chihuahua and Zacatecas.

**Martínez, Antonio (roll 32, frame 1656, 21 November 1842). Hermosillo, guía 432. 10 piezas (steel, iron, and domestic merchandise). Value: 54 pesos 56 cents. To: New Mexico.

Martínez, Antonio (roll 34, frame 1209, 6 September 1843). Guía 48. 12 bultos of domestic merchandise. Value: 115 pesos 4 reales. To: Chihuahua, Durango, and Lagos.

Martínez, Francisco (roll 21, frame 330, 10 September 1839). Guía 172. 7 bultos of domestic merchandise. Value: 156 pesos 4 reales. To: Chihuahua. [Guía exists: roll 27, frame 624.]

Martínez, José Antonio (roll 21, frame 311, 3 September 1838). Guía 90. 15 tercios of domestic merchandise. To: Chihuahua and Durango.

**Martínez, José Antonio (roll 32, frame 1640, 21 November 1842). Hermosillo, tornaguía 267. [Document indicates that Martínez arrived on 2 November 1842 with guía 14, issued in Santa Fe on 13 September 1842.]

Martínez, José María (roll 34, frame 1209, 6 September 1843). Guía 47. 15 bultos of domestic merchandise. Value: 196 pesos 6 granos. To: Chihuahua, Durango, and Zacatecas.

Martínez, Juan Antonio (roll 21, frame 313, 11 September 1838). Guía 98. 4 tercios of domestic merchandise. Value: 54 pesos 3 reales. To: Chihuahua, Sonora, and Durango. [Guía exists: roll 25, frame 1447.]

Martínez, Juan Antonio (roll 21, frame 355, 26 August 1840). Guía 51. 2 bultos of domestic merchandise. Value: 81 pesos 2 reales. To: Chihuahua and Durango. [Guía exists: roll 28, frame 791.]

Martínez, Pascual (roll 21, frame 331, 10 September 1839). Guía 175. 13 bultos of domestic merchandise. Value: 205 pesos 6 reales. To: Chihuahua and Tierra Caliente.

Martínez, Pascual (roll 37, frame 406, 11 November 1844). Guía 39. 16 bultos of domestic merchandise. Value: 126 pesos 0.5 real. To: Chihuahua. [Guía exists: roll 37, frame 496.]

Martínez, Pedro Ignacio (roll 21, frame 314, 12 September 1838). Guía 101. 4 tercios. Value: 66 pesos 7 reales. To: Chihuahua and Sonora. [Guía exists: roll 25, frame 1450. Cuaderno listed owner's surname as Martínez; guía indicated the surname was Márquez.]

Martínez, Tomás M. (roll 34, frame 1202, 14 August 1843). Guía 3. 27 bultos. Value: 2,057 pesos 43 cents. To: Chihuahua, Durango, and Zacatecas.

Mascarenas, Juan Miguel (roll 25, frame 1467, 16 November 1838). Guía 25. 6 tercios of domestic merchandise. Value: ca. 83 pesos 2 reales. To: Chihuahua and Sonora. [There is no record of this guía in the guía notebook of 1835.]

Mascarenas, Juan Miguel (roll 21, frame 326, 2 September 1839). Guía 155. 5 piezas of domestic merchandise. Value: 138 pesos. To: Chihuahua and Sonora.

Mascarenas, Juan Miguel (roll 34, frame 1208, 1 September 1843). Guía 38. 8 tercios of domestic merchandise. Value: 96 pesos 7 reales. To: Chihuahua and Durango.

Mascarenas, Juan Miguel (roll 40, frame 324, 6 September 1845). Guía 30. Domestic merchandise. Value: 144 pesos 4 reales. To: Chihuahua, Durango, and Guadalajara.

Medina, Mateo (roll 21, frame 313, 11 September 1838). Guía 97. 8 bultos. To: Chihuahua, Durango, and Sonora.

Medina, Mateo (roll 21, frame 326, 3 September 1839). Guía 156. 10 bultos of domestic merchandise. Value: 93 pesos. To: Chihuahua and Durango.

Mestas, Francisco Antonio (roll 21, frame 329, 10 September 1839). Guía 169. 3 bultos of domestic merchandise. Value: 90 pesos. To: Sinaloa and Guanajuato.

Mestas, Francisco Antonio (roll 21, frame 361, 26 October 1840). Guía 101. 6 bultos of domestic merchandise. Value: 82 pesos 6 reales. To: Chihuahua.

Mestas, Francisco Antonio (roll 34, frame 1207, 31 August 1843). Guía 36. 12 bultos of domestic merchandise. Value: 207 pesos. To: Chihuahua and Durango. Fiador: Bustos, José María. [Guía exists: roll 34, frame 1244.]

Mestas, Francisco Antonio (roll 37, frame 403, 8 September 1844). Guía 21. 14 bultos of domestic merchandise. Value: 177 pesos 4 reales. To: Chihuahua, Durango, and Lagos.

Mestas, José Benito (roll 37, frame 403, 7 September 1844). Guía 29. 6 bultos of domestic merchandise. Value: 159 pesos. To: Chihuahua and Durango. [Guía exists: roll 37, frame 490.]

Mestas, Ramón (roll 34, frame 1208, 5 September 1843). Guía 43. 6 tercios of domestic merchandise. Value: 124 pesos 3 reales. To: Chihuahua, Durango, and Lagos. [Guía exists: roll 34, frame 1245. The listed value of the merchandise is 109 pesos.]

Miranda, [Gerardo] (roll 21, frame 316, 16 August 1839). Guía 117. 1 tercio of foreign merchandise. Value: 191 pesos 4 reales. To: del Villar, Tomás; El Paso. Conductor: Sánchez, Juan José.

Miranda, Guadalupe (roll 39, frame 1215, 3 November 1843). Guía 111. 3 bultos of domestic merchandise. Value: 308 pesos 2.5 cents. To: Sonora. Conductor: [Feller], Richard. Fiador: Larragoiti, Anselmo. [Guía exists: roll 34, frame 1266.]

Miranda, Guadalupe (roll 39, frame 1215, 3 November 1843). Guía 112. 16 bultos of foreign merchandise. Value: 1712 pesos 11.25 cents. To: El Paso.

Monge, Luis (roll 21, frame 307, 22 August 1838). Guía 67. 17 bultos of merchandise. To: Sonora.

Montalvo, Pablo (roll 21, frame 283, 15 October 1835). Guía 37. 2 tercios of domestic merchandise. To: Chihuahua and Sonora.

**Montaño, Antonio (roll 32, frame 1641, 23 November 1842). Hermosillo, tornaguía 275. [Montaño entered with guía 25 issued on 14 September 1842.]

**Montaño, Antonio (roll 32, frame 1654, 23 November 1842). Hermosillo, guía 441. 10 piezas (steel, iron, and foreign merchandise). Value: 62 pesos 3 reales. To: New Mexico.

Montaño, José (roll 21, frame 304, 31 January 1838). Guía 48. 25 bultos of domestic merchandise. To: Sonora.

Montaño, José (roll 21, frame 307, 22 August 1838). Guía 66. 25 bultos of domestic merchandise. To: Sonora and Vizcaya. [Guía exists: roll 25, frame 1429.]

Montaño, José (roll 21, frame 336, 16 October 1839). Guía 193. 20 bultos of domestic merchandise. Value: 253 pesos 4 reales. To: Sonora.

Montaño, José Manuel (roll 21, frame 314, 6 November 1838). Guía 106. 24 tercios of domestic merchandise. Value: ca. 150 pesos. To: Chihuahua and Sonora. [Guía exists: roll 25, frame 1454.]

Montaño, José Manuel (roll 21, frame 336, 15 October 1839). Guía 190. 27 bultos of domestic merchandise. To: Sonora.

Montaño, José Manuel (roll 32, frame 1651, 29 November 1842). Hermosillo, guía 442. 2 piezas of domestic merchandise. Value: 46 pesos 6 reales. To: New Mexico.

Montes, Jesús Donaciano (roll 21, frame 276, 19 August 1835). Guía 12. 1 tercio of foreign merchandise. To: El Paso.

Montoya, Diego (roll 21, frame 314, 24 October 1838). Guía 104. 4 tercios of domestic merchandise. Value: ca. 64 pesos 1 real. To: Chihuahua and Sonora. [Guía exists: roll 25, frame 1452. Fernando Aragón signed for Montoya.]

Montoya, Ermenegildo (roll 21, frame 303, 25 August 1837). Guía 34. 2 tercios of domestic merchandise and 25 sheep. To: El Paso. [Guía exists: roll 27, frame 620. Montoya is from El Paso. He brought 3 loads of wine and aguardiente.]

Montoya, Faustino (roll 21, frame 303, 25 August 1837). Guía 33. 2 tercios of domestic merchandise. Value: ca. 55 pesos 6 reales. To: El Paso. [Guía exists: roll 24, frame 797.]

Montoya, [Hugo] (roll 21, frame 361, 26 October 1840). Guía 100. 6 bultos of domestic merchandise. Value: 147 pesos. To: Chihuahua and Durango.

Montoya, Jesús María (roll 37, frame 397, 11 August 1844). Guía 34. 16 bultos of domestic merchandise. Value: 104 pesos 6 reales. To: Chihuahua, Durango, and Lagos. [Guía exists: roll 37, frame 460.]

Montoya, José (roll 21, frame 338, 21 October 1839). Guía 198. 28 bultos of domestic merchandise and 100 sheep. Value: 299 pesos 4 reales. To: Sonora. Conductor: Montoya, Miguel.

Montoya, José Nicolás (roll 21, frame 352, 28 August 1840). Guía 37. 13 bultos of domestic merchandise. Value: 480 pesos. To: San Juan de los Lagos. Conductor: Montoya, Miguel. Fiador: Madrid, Benito. [Guía exists: roll 28, frame 778.]

Montoya, José Nicolás (roll 30, frame 320, 1 September 1841). Guía 142. 34 tercios of domestic merchandise. Value: 571 pesos 6 reales. To: Chihuahua and Durango. Conductor: Montoya, José Miguel.

Montoya, Juan (roll 21, frame 337, 16 October 1839). Guía 195. 10 bultos of domestic merchandise. Value: 100 pesos. To: El Paso.

Montoya, Juan Bautista (roll 21, frame 334, 20 September 1839). [Not a guía, but a pase]. 4 bultos of domestic merchandise. Value: 46 pesos. To: Sonora.

Montoya, Juan de Dios (roll 37, frame 403, 6 September 1844). Guía 22. 5 bultos of domestic merchandise. Value: 134 pesos 6 reales. To: Chihuahua, Durango, and Lagos.

Montoya, Mariano (roll 34, frame 1211, 12 September 1843). Guía 59. 8 bultos of domestic merchandise. Value: 102 pesos 4 reales. To: Chihuahua and Sonora. [Guía exists: roll 34, frame 1256.]

Montoya, Mariano (roll 34, frame 1211, 14 September 1843). Albuquerque, guía 62. 1 bulto of foreign merchandise. Value: 119 pesos 68 cents. To: Chihuahua and Sonora. [Guía exists: roll 34, frame 1259.]

**Montoya, Miguel (roll 28, frame 799, 10 November 1840). Durango, guía 673. 24 bultos of domestic merchandise. Value: 502 pesos. To: New Mexico.

Montoya, Miguel (roll 34, frame 1205, 28 August 1843). Guía 20. 18 bultos of domestic merchandise and 750 sheep. Value: 730 pesos. To: Chihuahua and Durango.

Montoya, Ramón (roll 21, frame 329, 10 September 1839). Guía 168. 7 bultos of domestic merchandise. Value: 133 pesos 3 reales. To: Sinaloa and Guanajuato.

Moreno, Antonio (roll 21, frame 344, 3 August 1840). Guía 4. 18 bultos of domestic merchandise. Value: 222 pesos 4 reales. To: Sonora.

Ortega, Francisco (roll 21, frame 362, ca. 26 October 1840). Guía 104. 12 bultos of domestic merchandise. Value: 102 pesos. To: Chihuahua and Sonora.

Ortega, Gervasio (roll 37, frame 402, 6 September 1844). Guía 18. 8 bultos of domestic merchandise. Value: 108 pesos. To: Chihuahua, Durango, and Zacatecas.

Ortiz, Antonio (roll 21, frame 323, 26 August 1839). Guía 146. 10 bultos of domestic merchandise. To: Chihuahua and Zacatecas. Conductor: Ortiz, Rafael.

Ortiz, Antonio M. (roll 34, frame 1207, 29 August 1843). Guía 32. 7 bultos of domestic merchandise. Value: 1,575 pesos 2 reales. To: Chihuahua and Durango. [Guía exists: roll 34, frame 1243.]

Ortiz, Antonio Matías (roll 21, frame 354, 26 August 1840). Guía 45. 13 bultos of domestic merchandise. Value: 629 pesos 4 reales. To: Chihuahua and Durango. [Guía exists: roll 28, frame 785.]

Ortiz, Antonio Matías (roll 37, frame 396, 4 August 1844). Guía 29. 12 bultos of domestic merchandise and sheep. Value: 1,143 pesos 4 reales. To: Chihuahua and Durango. Conductor: Sánchez, José María. [Guía exists: roll 37, frame 459.]

Ortiz, Fernando María (roll 21, frame 305, 6 February 1838). Guía 52. 4 bultos of domestic merchandise. To: Sonora.

Ortiz, Francisco (roll 21, frame 279, 29 August 1835). Guía 22. 7 tercios of domestic merchandise. To: [Abrafuerte].

Ortiz, Francisco (roll 21, frame 279, 29 August 1835). Guía 23. 4,000 sheep. Value: ca. 2,000 pesos. To: "The capital of Mexico." Conductor: Ortiz, Francisco.

Ortiz, Gaspar (roll 21, frame 323, 26 August 1839). Guía 144. 8 tercios of domestic merchandise. Value: 160 pesos. To: Chihuahua and Durango.

Ortiz, Gaspar (roll 30, frame 319, 30 August 1841). Guía 137. 36 tercios of domestic merchandise. Value: 710 pesos 4 reales. To: Chihuahua and Durango.

Ortiz, Gaspar (roll 34, frame 1203, 17 August 1843). Guía 10. 23 bultos of foreign merchandise. Value: 3,138 pesos 33.25 cents. To: Chihuahua and Sonora. Conductor: Ortiz, Ignacio.

Ortiz, Gaspar (roll 34, frame 1204, 17 August 1843). Guía 11. [1] bulto of foreign merchandise. Value: 87 pesos 12 cents. To: Chihuahua and Sonora. Conductor: Ortiz, Ignacio. [On the margin it says "se tacha por haber pedido el remitente pase y no llegar la cantidad a 100 pesos" (crossed out for having requested the sender a pass and not reaching the value of the merchandise 100 pesos).]

Ortiz, Gaspar (roll 34, frame 1212, 1 October 1843). Guía 76. 5,500 sheep @ 4 reales. Value: 2,750 pesos. To: Cordero, José; Chihuahua.

Ortiz, Ignacio (roll 40, frame 319, 4 September 1845). Guía 17. 11 bultos. Value: 2,102 pesos 7 reales 7.5 granos. To: Chihuahua.

Ortiz, Ignacio (roll 40, frame 286, 5 September 1845). Guía 23. 11 piezas of foreign merchandise. Value: 2,102 pesos. To: Chihuahua.

Ortiz, Ignacio Ricardo (roll 14, frame 241, 27 September 1831). Guía 62. Domestic merchandise. Value: 486 pesos 2 reales. To: Sonora. [This is the first guía that includes prices for domestic merchandise.]

Ortiz, Isidro (roll 21, frame 335, 14 October 1839). Guía 188. 20 bultos of foreign merchandise. Value: 181 pesos 4 reales. To: Chihuahua and Sonora.

Ortiz, Isidro (roll 21, frame 360, 16 October 1840). Guía 78. 20 bultos of domestic merchandise. Value: 290 pesos. To: Chihuahua.

Ortiz, Jesús María (roll 37, frame 402, 7 September 1844). Guía 17. 3 bultos of foreign merchandise. Value: 255 pesos 40 cents. To: Chihuahua and Sonora.

Ortiz, José Francisco (roll 8, frame 1342, 14 October 1828). Guía 33. Foreign merchandise. To: Chihuahua and Sonora. [Guía indicates that Ortiz purchased merchandise from foreign merchant, Z. Nolan.]

Ortiz, José María (roll 21, frame 291, 30 August 1836). Guía 73. 6,000 sheep. Value: ca. 3,000 pesos. To: Mexico.

Ortiz, José María (roll 21, frame 301, 18 August 1837). Guía 24. 206 sarapes. Value: ca. 50 pesos. To: "The internal provinces."

Ortiz, Juan Rafael (roll 15, frame 1034, 12 August 1832). Guía 96. Domestic merchandise and sheep. Value: ca. 741 pesos 6 reales. To: Chihuahua and Durango. Conductor: Ortiz, Francisco [son].

Ortiz, Mateo (roll 21, frame 304, 26 October 1837). Guía 43. 2 bultos of domestic merchandise. Value: ca. 158 pesos 4 reales. To: El Paso. [Guía exists: roll 24, frame 800.]

Ortiz, Tomás (roll 21, frame 349, 22 August 1840). Guía 24. 9 bultos of domestic merchandise and 1,330 sheep. Value: 1,170 pesos. To: Chihuahua and Durango. Conductor: Rendón, Tomás, arriero. [Guía exists: roll 28, frame 767.]

Otero, Antonio José (roll 21, frame 301, 21 August 1837). Guía 26. 3,800 sheep. Value: ca. 1,900 pesos. To: Yzurrieta, Juan; Mexico.

Otero, Antonio José (roll 21, frame 302, 21 August 1837). Guía 28. 4,000 sheep. Value: ca. 2,000 pesos. To: Chihuahua, Durango, and Mexico. [Guía exists: roll 24, frame 794.]

Otero, Antonio José (roll 21, frame 350, 22 August 1840). Guía 29. 22 bultos of domestic merchandise. Value: 435 pesos. To: Chihuahua and Durango. Conductor: Otero, Manuel Antonio. [Guía exists: roll 28, frame 772.]

Otero, Antonio José (roll 21, frame 351, 22 August 1840). Guía 30. 4,800 sheep. Value: 2,200 pesos. To: Chihuahua and Durango. Conductor: Otero, Manuel Antonio. [Guía exists: roll 28, frame 773.]

Otero, Antonio José (roll 21, frame 358, [ca. October 1840]). Guía 67. [The rest of the entry is blank.]

Otero, Antonio José (roll 21, frame 358, 27 October 1840). Guía 69. 32 bultos of foreign merchandise. Value: 3,032 pesos 6 reales. To: Sonora.

Otero, Antonio José (roll 34, frame 1204, 24 August 1843). Guía 13. 9,500 sheep. Value: 4,750 pesos. To: Durango and Mexico.

Otero, Antonio José (roll 37, frame 392, 1 March 1844). Guía 1. 12 bultos of foreign merchandise. Value: 1,313 pesos 54 cents. To: Chihuahua. Conductor: Diviny, Juan.

Otero, Antonio José (roll 37, frame 395, 3 August 1844). Guía 22. 118 piezas of foreign merchandise. Value: 17,878 pesos 16.25 cents. To: Chihuahua, Durango, and Aguas Calientes.

Otero, Antonio José (roll 37, frame 395, 3 August 1844). Guía 23. 166 piezas of foreign merchandise. Value: 16,991 pesos 38.75 cents. To: Allende, Zacatecas, and Aguas Calientes.

Otero, Antonio José (roll 37, frame 395, 3 August 1844). Guía 24. 16 piezas of foreign merchandise. Value: 2,485 pesos 41.75 cents. To: Chihuahua, Galeana, and Aguas Calientes.

Otero, Antonio José (roll 37, frame 396, 3 August 1844). Guía 28. 13,000 sheep. Value: 6,500 pesos. To: Chihuahua, Durango, and Mexico.

Otero, Francisco Antonio (roll 17, frame 1107, 16 August 1833). Guía 2. 4,200 sheep. Value: ca. 2,100 pesos. To: Durango and Mexico.

Otero, Francisco Antonio (roll 21, frame 273, 16 August 1835). Guía 2. 4,200 sheep. Value: ca. 2,100 pesos. Fiador: Gutiérrez, Juan Nepomuceno. To: Yzurrieta, Juan; Durango.

Otero, Francisco Antonio (roll 21, frame 301, 21 August 1837). Guía 27. 4,000 sheep. Value: ca. 2,000 pesos. To: Yzurrieta, Juan; Chihuahua, Durango, and Mexico. [Guía exists: roll 24, frame 793.]

Otero, Francisco Antonio (roll 21, frame 302, 21 August 1837). Guía 29. 3,600 sheep. Value: ca. 1,800 pesos. To: Yzurrieta, Juan; Chihuahua, Durango, and Mexico. [Guía exists: roll 24, frame 795.]

Otero, Francisco Antonio (roll 21, frame 302, 21 August 1837). Guía 30. 26 bultos of domestic merchandise. To: Durango.

Otero, Francisco Antonio (roll 34, frame 1205, 28 August 1843). Guía 21. 28 bultos of domestic merchandise. Value: 384 pesos. To: Chihuahua and Durango.

Otero, José (roll 37, frame 396, 3 August 1844). Guía 26. 14 piezas of foreign merchandise. Value: 2,341 pesos 11.5 cents. To: Chihuahua, Allende, and Aguas Calientes. Conductor: Diviny, Juan.

Otero, José Antonio (roll 15, frame 1027, 24 July 1832). Guía 90. Domestic merchandise. Value: ca. 400 pesos. To: Zacatecas.

Otero, Juan (roll 21, frame 306, 12 August 1838). Guía 62. 6 bultos and 300 sarapes. To: Chihuahua and Sonora. Conductor: Chávez, Antonio.

Otero, Juan (roll 21, frame 306, 12 August 1838). Guía 63. 12 bultos and 600 sarapes. To: Chihuahua and Durango. Conductor: Ballejos, Antonio.

Otero, Juan (roll 21, frame 307, 12 August 1838). Guía 64. 3,800 sheep. Value: ca. 1,900 pesos. To: Chihuahua and Durango. Conductor: Ballejos, Antonio.

Otero, Juan (roll 21, frame 306, 13 August 1838). Guía 61. 800 sheep. Value: ca. 400 pesos. To: Durango, Chihuahua, and Mexico. Conductor: Perea, Manuel.

Otero, Juan (roll 21, frame 321, 23 August 1839). Guía 136. 5,000 sheep. Value: ca. 2,500 pesos. To: Chihuahua, Durango, and Zacatecas.

Otero, Juan (roll 37, frame 405, 16 October 1844). Guía 33. 10 bultos of domestic merchandise. Value: 125 pesos. To: Chihuahua and Sonora. [Guía exists: roll 37, frame 491.]

Otero, Manuel (roll 21, frame 273, 10 August 1835). Guía 3. 10,500 sheep. Value: ca. 5,250 pesos. Fiador: Sarracino, Rafael. To: Flores, Manuel; Mexico. [Guía exists: roll 21, frame 364.]

Otero, Manuel Antonio (roll 37, frame 396, 3 August 1844). Guía 27. 16 bultos of foreign merchandise. Value: 2,326 pesos 2.5 cents. To: Chihuahua, Allende, and Aguas Calientes.

Otero, Vicente (roll 6, frame 508, 2 September 1828). Guía 15. 5 tercios. To: Chihuahua and Sonora. Conductor: Otero, Antonio.

**Otero, Vicente (roll 15, frame 1023, 23 January 1832). Chihuahua, guía 8. 16 piezas of foreign merchandise. Value: 1,541 pesos 4 reales 9 granos. To: New Mexico. [These prices appear awfully low; they are probably not indicative of the value of the merchandise, but of duties imposed on foreign goods.]

Pacheco, Antonio Alejandro (roll 21, frame 313, 12 September 1838). Guía 100. 7 bultos of domestic merchandise. Value: 94 pesos 6 reales. To: Chihuahua and Durango. [Guía exists: roll 25, frame 1449.]

Pacheco, Antonio Alejandro (roll 21, frame 327, 5 September 1839). Guía 158. 9 piezas of domestic merchandise. Value: 143 pesos. To: Durango and Zacatecas.

Pacheco, Antonio María (roll 37, frame 400, 5 September 1844). Guía 3. 10 bultos of foreign merchandise. Value: 142 pesos. To: Chihuahua, Durango, and Lagos. [Guía exists: roll 37, frame 476.]

Pacheco, Juan Rafael (roll 34, frame 1208, 5 September 1843). Guía 40. 10 tercios of domestic merchandise. Value: 190 pesos. To: Chihuahua, Durango, and Zacatecas.

Pacheco, Ramón (roll 37, frame 400, 5 September 1844). Guía 2. 8 bultos of domestic merchandise. Value: 91 pesos 6 reales. To: Chihuahua, Durango, and Lagos. [Guía exists: roll 37, frame 475.]

Padilla, Blas (roll 21, frame 327, 5 September 1839). Guía 159. 6 bultos of domestic merchandise. Value: 71 pesos 4 reales. To: Durango and Zacatecas.

Padilla, Blas (roll 21, frame 354, 26 August 1840). Guía 49. 5 bultos of domestic merchandise. Value: 106 pesos 4 reales. To: Chihuahua and Durango. [Guía exists: roll 28, frame 789.]

Padilla, Jesús (roll 40, frame 355, 29 September 1845). El Paso, guía 97. Domestic merchandise. Value: 22 pesos. To: New Mexico.

Padilla, Juan Blas (roll 21, frame 313, 12 September 1838). Guía 99. 4 tercios. Value: 65 pesos 67 cents. To: Chihuahua and Durango. [Guía exists: roll 25, frame 1448.]

Perea, Baltazar (roll 21, frame 295, 27 October 1836). Guía 97. 2 baúles and 2 tercios. To: El Paso. Conductor: Aragón, Ramón. [Guía exists: roll 22, frame 1167.]

[Perea], José (roll 21, frame 348, 20 August 1840). Guía 16. 28 bultos. Value: 434 pesos 4 reales. To: Sonora.

Perea, José (roll 34, frame 1202, 17 August 1843). Guía 5. 4,500 sheep. Value: 2,250 pesos. To: Cordero, José; Chihuahua and Mexico. Conductor: Gallegos, Julián.

Perea, José (roll 37, frame 393, 27 July 1844). Guía 7. 104 bultos of foreign merchandise. Value: 15,207 pesos 42.75 cents. To: Chihuahua, Zacatecas, and Aguas Calientes.

Perea, José (roll 37, frame 393, 27 July 1844). Guía 8. 4,000 sheep. Value: 2,000 pesos. To: Urquide, Juan Nepomuceno; Chihuahua. Conductor: Cisneros, Mariano.

Perea, José (roll 37, frame 393, 27 July 1844). Guía 9. 5,000 sheep. Value: 2,500 pesos. To: Urquide, Juan Nepomuceno; Chihuahua. Conductor: Carbajal, Miguel. [Tornaguía exists: roll 37, frame 523. It was issued at Río Florido, annexed to the Administration of Allende. The document indicates that no duties were paid.]

Perea, José (roll 37, frame 394, 29 July 1844). Guía 13. 165 piezas of foreign merchandise.

Value: 25,128 pesos 48 cents. To: Chihuahua, Zacatecas, and Aguas Calientes. Conductor: Perea, Juan.

Perea, Juan (roll 21, frame 320, 23 August 1839). Guía 135. 5,000 sheep and 28 fanegas of pinyons. Value: ca, 2,584 pesos. To: Chihuahua, Durango, and Zacatecas. Conductor: Perea, Julián.

Perea, Julián (roll 21, frame 298, 2 August 1837). Guía 8. 5 tercios of foreign and domestic merchandise. To: Yzurrieta, José María; Sonora. Conductor: Leyba, Pedro. Fiador: Gallegos, Ignacio. [Guía exists: roll 24, frame 771.]

Perea, Julián (roll 34, frame 1203, 17 August 1843). Guía 9. 2,350 sheep. Value: 1,175 pesos. To: Cordero, José; Chihuahua and Mexico. Conductor: Gallegos, Julián.

Perea, Pedro José (roll 24, frame 769, [21] July 1837). Guía 2. 3,000 sheep. Value: ca. 1,500 pesos. To: Yzurrieta, Juan; Durango. Conductor: Martínez, José María.

Perea, Pedro José (roll 21, frame 352, 28 August 1840). Guía 39. 3,480 sheep. Value: 1,740 pesos. To: Chihuahua and Durango.

**Pescador, Juan Antonio (roll 22, frame 1177, 3 January 1836). Durango, guía 4. To: Ortiz, Francisco; New Mexico. Conductor: Rendón, Tomás.

Pino, Manuel (roll 21, frame 280, 31 August 1835). Guía 24. 17,000 sheep. Value: ca. 8,500 pesos. To: Chávez, Mariano. Conductor: Baca y Pino, José Francisco.

Pino, Manuel Doroteo (roll 14, frame 188, 28 July 1831). Guía 38. Domestic merchandise and 14,000 sheep. Value: ca. 7,000 pesos. To: Chihuahua and Durango. Conductor; Chávez, Ermenegildo.

**Pino, Manuel Doroteo (roll 14, frame 305, 6 September 1831). Durango, guía 318. 26 bultos of domestic merchandise. To: New Mexico. Conductor: Flores, Mark.

Pino, Manuel Doroteo (roll 21, frame 277, 24 August 1835). Guía 16. 2 tercios of foreign merchandise. Value: 300 pesos. To: Albo, Agapito; El Paso. Conductor: Sánchez, Juan José. [Guía exists: roll 21, frame 368.]

Pino, Manuel Doroteo (roll 21, frame 322, 26 August 1839). Guía 143. 9 tercios domestic merchandise and 4,000 sheep. Value: 4,387 pesos. To: Chihuahua and Durango.

Ponce de León, Juan María (roll 21, frame 316, 13 July 1839). Guía 113. 7 bultos of foreign merchandise. Value: 1,207 pesos 2 reales. To: El Paso.

Quintana, Francisco Esteban (roll 21, frame 334, 24 September 1839). Guía 185. 6 bultos of domestic merchandise. Value: 78 pesos 4 reales. To: California.

Quintana, José Vicente (roll 37, frame 397, 23 August 1844). Guía 35. 6 bultos of domestic merchandise. Value: 138 pesos 4 reales. To: Chihuahua, Durango, and Lagos. [Guía exists: roll 37, frame 461. Miguel Quintana signed the guía.]

Quintana, Ramón (roll 37, frame 400, 5 September 1844). Guía 4. 4 bultos of domestic merchandise. Value: 71 pesos. To: El Paso. [Guía exists: roll 37, frame 477. The cuaderno indicates that value of the merchandise was 75 pesos.]

Rael, Francisco (roll 37, frame 403, 28 September 1844). Guía 31. 5 bultos of domestic merchandise and sheep. Value: 1,748 pesos. To: California.

Rascón, Francisco (roll 21, frame 276, 19 August 1835). Guía 11. 1 bulto of foreign merchandise. To: El Paso.

Robledo, Damaso (roll 34, frame 1207, 29 August 1843). Guía 31. 20 bultos of domestic merchandise. Value: 250 pesos 2 reales. To: Chihuahua and Durango. [Guía exists: roll 34, frame 1242.]

Robledo, Damaso (roll 37, frame 398, 22 August 1844). Guía 39. 33 bultos of domestic merchandise. Value: 353 pesos 4 reales. To: Chihuahua and Sonora. [Guía exists: roll 37, frame 467.]

Robles, José María (roll 40, frame 284, 3 September 1845). Guía 11. 11 tercios of domestic merchandise. Value: 193 pesos 2 reales. To: Robles, Nicomedes; San Juan de los Lagos. Conductor: González, Desiderio, arriero.

Rodríguez, José Manuel (roll 21, frame 346, 20 August 1840). Guía 15. 70 pounds of wool. Value: 70 pesos. To: Sonora. Fiador: Provencio, Jesús. [Guía exists: roll 28, frame 759.]

Romero, Diego (roll 21, frame 335, 15 October 1839). Guía 189. 16 bultos of domestic merchandise. Value: 159 pesos.

**Romero, Diego (roll 32, frame 1652, 29 November 1842). Hermosillo, guía 448. 4 piezas (iron, steel, and domestic merchandise). Value: 108 pesos 6 reales. To: New Mexico.

**Romero, Diego (roll 32, frame 1648, 13 December 1842). Sonora, guía 133. 12 quintales of iron. Value: 84 pesos. To: New Mexico.

Romero, Domingo (roll 21, frame 307, 24 August 1838). Guía 69. 20 tercios. To: Chihuahua.

Romero, José Miguel (roll 21, frame 283, 8 October 1835). Guía 35. 8 tercios of domestic merchandise. To: Chihuahua. [Guía exists: roll 21, frame 378.]

Romero, Juan Felipe (roll 21, frame 312, 10 September 1838). Guía 94. 14 bultos. Value: ca. 161 pesos. To: Chihuahua and Durango. [Guía exists: roll 25, frame 1445.]

Roybal, Juan Antonio (roll 21, frame 314, 12 September 1838). Guía 102. 7 tercios of domestic merchandise. Value: 140 pesos 3 reales. To: Chihuahua and Durango.

Roybal, Juan Antonio (roll 21, frame 326, 5 September 1839). Guía 157. 14 bultos of domestic merchandise. Value: 202 pesos 4 reales. To: Chihuahua and Durango.

Roybal, Juan Antonio (roll 37, frame 401, 6 September 1844). Guía 11. 13 bultos of domestic merchandise. Value: 251 pesos 4 reales. To: Chihuahua, Durango, and Lagos. [Guía exists: roll 37, frame 484.]

Ruiz, Marcos (roll 37, frame 398, 1 September 1844). Guía 44. 26 bultos of domestic merchandise. Value: 230 pesos. To: Chihuahua. [Guía exists: roll 37, frame 471. Gaspar Ortiz signed for Ruiz.]

Saavedra, Francisco (roll 21, frame 346, 19 August 1840). Guía 13. 34 bultos and 300 sheep. Value: 400 pesos. To: Chihuahua and Durango.

Saavedra, Francisco (roll 21, frame 356, 28 August 1840). Guía 55. 18 bultos of domestic merchandise. Value: 207 pesos. To: Chihuahua and Sonora. Conductor: Saavedra, Miguel [his son]. [Guía exists: roll 28, frame 793.]

Salas, Pablo (roll 19, frame 294, 29 June 1834). Guía 96. 1,800 sheep. Value: ca. 900 pesos. To: Puebla.

Salazar, Antonio de José María (roll 21, frame 352, 28 August 1840). Guía 40. 17 bultos of domestic merchandise. Value: 213 pesos. To: Chihuahua and Durango. Conductor: Salazar, Diego. [Guía exists: roll 28, frame 780.]

Salazar, Damasio (roll 37, frame 399, 4 September 1844). Guía 47. 22 bultos of domestic merchandise. Value: 212 pesos 2 reales. To: Chihuahua and Durango.

Salazar, José (roll 21, frame 338, 23 October 1839). Guía 201. 40 bultos of domestic merchandise. Value: 349 pesos. To: Sonora and Sinaloa.

Salazar, José (roll 37, frame 396, 3 August 1844). Guía 25. 6 piezas of foreign merchandise. Value: 592 pesos 84 cents. To: Chihuahua, Zacatecas, and Aguas Calientes.

Salazar, Pablo (roll 15, frame 1029, 29 June 1832). Guía 93. 3,000 sheep. Value: ca. 1,500 pesos. To: Durango and Mexico.

Salazar, Pablo (roll 21, frame 334, 5 October 1839). Guía 186. Domestic merchandise. Value: 422 pesos 4 reales. To: Chihuahua and Sonora.

Salazar, Pablo (roll 21, frame 359, 27 October 1840). Guía 70. 18 bultos of domestic merchandise. Value: 352 pesos 4 reales. To: Chihuahua, Durango, and Sonora.

**Salazar, Pablo (roll 32, frame 1638, 4 November 1842). Durango, tornaguía 1091. [The document indicates that Salazar had guía 21 issued in New Mexico on 28 August 1842. He arrived at Durango on 27 October 1842.]

Salazar, Pablo (roll 34, frame 1213, 28 October 1843). Guía 78. 12 bultos of domestic merchandise. Value: 142 pesos 2 reales. To: Sonora. Conductor: Abreu, José. [Guía exists: roll 34, frame 1261.]

Salazar, Romualdo (roll 37, frame 402, 6 September 1844). Guía 15. 3 bultos of domestic merchandise. Value: 55 pesos. To: Chihuahua, Durango, and Lagos.

Salinas, Agapito (roll 37, frame 402, 6 September 1844). Guía 19. 5 bultos of domestic merchandise. Value: 120 pesos. To: Chihuahua, Durango, and Lagos.

Sánchez, Eliseo (roll 6, frame 474, 27 August 1826). Guía 3. 13 tercios of foreign merchandise. Value: 1,540 pesos 2 reales. To: Chihuahua and Sonora. [This is the first guía issued to a merchant with a Hispanic surname.]

Sánchez, Eliseo (roll 6, frame 475, [?] August 1826). Guía 6. 10 tercios of foreign merchandise. Value: 1,525 pesos 3 reales 6 granos. To: Chihuahua and Sonora.

Sánchez, Felix (roll 37, frame 398, 1 September 1844). Guía 43. 57 piezas of salt from New Mexico. Value: 134 pesos. To: Chihuahua.

Sánchez, Francisco (roll 21, frame 305, 31 January 1838). Guía 51. 4 bultos of domestic merchandise. To: Chihuahua.

Sánchez, Francisco Antonio (roll 30, frame 321, 1 September 1841). Guía [?]. 25 bultos of domestic merchandise. Value: 324 pesos 2 reales. To: Sonora and Vizcaya.

Sánchez, Gregorio (roll 21, frame 360, 18 October 1840). Guía 80. 6 bultos of domestic merchandise. Value: 117 pesos. To: Chihuahua.

Sánchez, José Manuel (roll 40, frame 285, 4 September 1845). Guía 18. 2 piezas of foreign merchandise bought locally. Value: 312 pesos 5 reales. To: El Paso. Conductor: Sánchez, Mauricio.

Sánchez, José Manuel (roll 40, frame 285, 4 September 1845). Guía 19. 2 tercios of foreign merchandise bought locally. Value: 416 pesos 1.5 reales. To: El Paso.

Sánchez, Juan José (roll 21, frame 317, 16 August 1839). Guía 120. 2 bultos. To: Galeana.

Sánchez, Juan José (roll 21, frame 317, 17 August 1839). Guía 121. 3 bultos. Value: 328 pesos 1 real 6 granos. To: El Paso.

Sánchez, Manuel (roll 21, frame 283, 15 October 1835). Guía 36. 15 tercios of domestic merchandise. To: Chihuahua and Sonora. Conductor: Montalvo, Pablo.

Sánchez, Manuel (roll 21, frame 303, 29 August 1837). Guía 37. 16 bultos of domestic merchandise. To: Chihuahua and Sonora.

Sánchez, Manuel Antonio (roll 21, frame 328, 9 September 1839). Guía 162. 3 bultos of domestic merchandise. Value: 72 pesos 2 reales. To: Chihuahua.

**Sánchez, Ramón (roll 37, frame 529, 18 November 1844). Durango, guía [?]. Domestic merchandise. To: New Mexico.

Sánchez, Victor (roll 21, frame 312, 3 September 1838). Guía 91. 14 tercios of domestic merchandise. To: Chihuahua, Sonora, and Durango.

Sánchez, Victor (roll 34, frame 1209, 6 September 1843). Guía 46. 11 bultos of domestic merchandise. Value: 181 pesos 6 reales. To: Chihuahua, Durango, and Sonora. [Guía exists: roll 34, frame 1248.]

Sandoval, [?] (roll 11, frame 1138, 16 October 1830). Guía 18. Foreign and domestic merchandise. To: Chihuahua. [Guía exists: roll 11, frame 1138. It indicates that in the previous year Sandoval had brought several tercios of *mercería* (haberdashery) from Chihuahua and was taking one of them back. This is the first guía that identifies domestic manufactures.]

Sandoval, Anastasio (roll 21, frame 327, 7 September 1839). Guía 160. 14 bultos of domestic merchandise. Value: 38 pesos. To: El Paso.

Sandoval, Antonio (roll 21, frame 274, 17 August 1835). Guía 5. 10,000 sheep. Value: ca. 5,000 pesos. To: Durango. Conductor: Ortiz, José María, arriero. Fiador: Abreu, Santiago. [Guía exists: roll 21, frame 365.]

Sandoval, Antonio (roll 21, frame 300, 18 August 1837). Guía 20. 3,800 sheep. Value: ca. 1,900 pesos. To: Márquez, Juan de Dios; Puebla.

Sandoval, Antonio (roll 21, frame 300, 18 August 1837). Guía 21. 3,621 sheep. Value: ca. 1,810 pesos 5 reales. To: Márquez, Juan de Dios; Durango.

Sandoval, Antonio (roll 21, frame 301, 18 August 1837). Guía 22. 3,300 sheep. Value: ca. 1650 pesos. To: Márquez, Juan de Dios; Zacatecas.

Sandoval, Antonio (roll 21, frame 301, 18 August 1837). Guía 23. 3,900 sheep. Value: ca. 1,950 pesos. To: Márquez, Juan de Dios; Mexico.

Sandoval, Antonio (roll 21, frame 310, 30 August 1838). Guía 83. 4,000 sheep. Value: ca. 2,000 pesos. To: Durango. Conductor: [?], José María.

Sandoval, Antonio (roll 21, frame 324, 27 August 1839). Guía 148. 5,000 sheep, 14 tercios of pinyons, and 80 blankets. Value: 2,546 pesos. To: Márquez, Juan de Dios; Durango. Conductor: Gómez, Lucas, arriero.

Sandoval, Antonio (roll 21, frame 346, 19 August 1840). Guía 14. 5,000 sheep. Value: ca. 2,500 pesos. To: Durango and Mexico. Conductor: Luera, José.

Sandoval, Antonio (roll 34, frame 1270, 30 August 1843). Guía [?]. 4,442 sheep. Value: 2,221 pesos. To: Cordero, José. Conductor: Santillanes, Guadalupe.

Sandoval, Antonio (roll 40, frame 283, 2 September 1845). Guía 10. 5,500 sheep. Value: 2,750 pesos. To: Urquide, Juan N.; Chihuahua, Durango, and Mexico.

Sandoval, Francisco (roll 30, frame 320, 1 September 1841). Guía 144. 20 tercios of domestic merchandise. Value: 198 pesos. To: Chihuahua and Sonora. Conductor: Sandoval, Jesús.

Sandoval, Juan (roll 37, frame 405, 9 October 1844). Guía 34. 4 bultos of domestic merchandise. Value: 212 pesos. To: Chihuahua and Sonora. [Guía exists: roll 37, frame 492.]

Sandoval, Juan Simón (roll 25, frame 1462, 16 November 1838). Guía 120. 3 tercios of domestic merchandise. Value: ca. 30 pesos. To: Chihuahua or Sonora. [There is no record of this guía in the guía notebook of 1835.]

Sandoval, Mateo (roll 15, frame 1023, 7 February 1832). Guía 88. 16 tercios of foreign merchandise. To: Chihuahua and Sonora.

Sandoval, Nepomuceno (roll 21, frame 353, 25 August 1840). Guía 44. 3 bultos of domestic merchandise. Value: 59 pesos 4 reales. To: Chihuahua and the fairs. [Guía exists: roll 28, frame 784.]

Sandoval, Simón (roll 21, frame 339, 28 October 1839). Guía 204. 6 bultos of domestic merchandise. Value: 55 pesos 6 reales. To: Chihuahua.

Santillanes, Guadalupe (roll 25, frame 1460, 15 November 1838). Guía 118. 3 tercios of domestic merchandise. Value: ca. 23 pesos 4 reales. To: El Paso. [There is no record of this guía in the guía notebook of 1835.]

Serrano, Juan Antonio (roll 37, frame 399, 3 September 1844). Guía 48. 18 bultos of domestic merchandise. Value: 189 pesos. To: Chihuahua and Sonora. [Guía exists: roll 37, frame 473.]

Silva, Jesús María (roll 21, frame 348, 20 August 1840). Guía 18. 20 bultos of domestic merchandise. Value: 133 pesos 4 reales. To: Chihuahua and Durango. Fiador: Jerres, José Francisco Baca. [Guía exists: roll 28, frame 762.]

Silva, Jesús María (roll 37, frame 397, 24 August 1844). Guía 36. 27 tercios of domestic merchandise. Value: 315 pesos. To: Chihuahua, Durango, and Lagos. [Guía exists: roll 37, frame 398. Tornaguía was issued at Durango on 16 November 1844.]

Silva, Jesús María (roll 40, frame 286, 6 September 1845). Guía 25. 18 piezas of domestic merchandise. Value: 214 pesos 4 reales. To: Chihuahua and Sonora. [Guía exists: roll 40, frame 321.]

Silva, Juan (roll 21, frame 327, 7 September 1839). Guía 161. 2 bultos of domestic merchandise. Value: 35 pesos 2 reales.

Soto, José (roll 21, frame 344, 28 July 1840). Guía 3. 7 bultos. Value: 83 pesos 2 reales. To: Montez, Josefa [his female boss (*su patrona*)]; El Paso.

Tafoya, José Dolores (roll 37, frame 406, 11 November 1844). Guía 41. 9 bultos of domestic merchandise. Value: 121 pesos. To: Chihuahua. [Guía exists: roll 37, frame 498.]

Tenorio, Juan (roll 21, frame 309, 27 August 1838). Guía 80. 5 bultos and 250 blankets. To: Chihuahua, Sonora, and Durango.

Tenorio, Juan (roll 21, frame 333, 18 September 1839). Guía 183. 40 bultos. Value: 227 pesos 4 reales. To: Sonora and Sinaloa.

Tenorio, Julián (roll 21, frame 309, 27 August 1838). Guía 78. 6 bultos and 300 blankets. To: Chihuahua, Sonora, and Durango.

Tenorio, Julián (roll 21, frame 308, 27 August 1838). Guía 79. 4 bultos and 200 blankets. To: Chihuahua, Sonora, and Durango.

Tenorio, Julián (roll 21, frame 357, 4 October 1840). Guía 60. 8 bultos. Value: 77 pesos. To: Sonora.

Tenorio, Julián (roll 21, frame 357, 4 October 1840). Guía 61. 25 bultos. Value: 241 pesos 4 reales. To: Sonora.

Tenorio, Julián (roll 37, frame 399, 28 September 1844). Guía 46. 18 bultos of domestic merchandise. Value: 572 pesos 4 reales. To: Chihuahua, Durango, and the fairs of San Juan.

Torres, Tomás (roll 34, frame 1213, 30 October 1843). Guía 101. 6 bultos of domestic merchandise. Value: 207 pesos 7 reales. To: Chihuahua and Durango.

Trujillo, Faustín (roll 21, frame 333, [10 September] 1839). Guía 180. 6 bultos of domestic merchandise. Value: 131 pesos 2 reales. To: Zacatecas and Guadalajara.

Trujillo, Juan Bautista (roll 37, frame 407, 11 November 1844). Guía 44. 6 bultos of domestic merchandise. Value: 58 pesos 4 reales. To: Chihuahua.

Trujillo, Juan de Jesús (roll 34, frame 1208, 5 September 1843). Guía 42. 10 tercios of domestic merchandise. Value: 217 pesos 2 reales. To: Chihuahua, Durango, and Tierra Caliente.

[Turnia], Manuel (roll 37, frame 399, 4 September 1844). Guía 50. 16 bultos of domestic merchandise. Value: 189 pesos 4 reales. To: Chihuahua and Sonora.

[Uvado], Miguel (roll 21, frame 277, 24 August 1835). Guía 17. 5 tercios of foreign merchandise. To: El Paso.

Valdez, Celedonio (roll 40, frame 285, 5 September 1845). Guía 20. 13 bultos of domestic merchandise. Value: 206 pesos 4 reales. To: Chihuahua, Sonora, and Tierra Caliente.

Valdez, Desiderio (roll 21, frame 334, 20 September 1839). Guía 184. 5 bultos of domestic merchandise. Value: 62 pesos 4 reales. To: Sonora.

**Valdez, Ignacio Díaz (roll 34, frame 1271, 7 November 1843). Chihuahua, guía 101. 970 *naipes* (playing cards) in 80 packages. To: New Mexico.

Valdez, Ignacio Díaz (roll 37, frame 396, 8 August 1844). Guía 30. 16 bultos of foreign merchandise. Value: 2,853 pesos 5.5 reales. To: Cordero, José; Allende.

Valdez, Ignacio Díaz (roll 37, frame 396, 8 August 1844). Guía 31. 52 piezas of foreign merchandise. Value: 9,184 pesos 0.75 reales. To: Chihuahua.

Valdez, Ignacio Díaz (roll 37, frame 397, 8 August 1844). Guía 32. 18 piezas of foreign merchandise. Value: 2,665 pesos 7.5 reales. To: Zuloaga, José María; Presidio de Galeana. Conductor: Torres, Cenovio.

Valdez, Ignacio Díaz (roll 37, frame 397, 8 August 1844). Guía 33. 12,500 sheep. Value: 12,500 pesos. To: Chihuahua, Zacatecas, and Durango.

Valdez, Juan de Jesús (roll 37, frame 406, 11 November 1844). Guía 42. 6 bultos of domestic merchandise. Value: 79 pesos 2 reales. To: Chihuahua. [Guía exists: roll 37, frame 499.]

Valencia, Domingo (roll 21, frame 307, 24 August 1838). Guía 68. 12 bultos of domestic merchandise. To: Chihuahua.

Valencia, Tomás (roll 21, frame 294, 4 October 1836). Guía 91. 2 tercios of foreign merchandise. To: El Paso. Conductor: Bustamante, Juan. [Guía exists: roll 22, frame 1166.]

Valencia, Tomás (roll 21, frame 295, 7 November 1836). Guía 100. 6 tercios of foreign merchandise. To: Ponce de León, Juan María; El Paso. Conductor: Barela, Francisco, arriero. [Guía exists: roll 22, frame 1170.]

Valencia, Tomás (roll 21, frame 304, 8 November 1837). Guía 45. 2 bultos of domestic merchandise. Value: ca. 255 pesos. To: Ponce de León, Juan María; El Paso. Conductor: Labbaddie, Pablo. [Guía exists: roll 24, frame 801.]

Valerio, Juan Pedro (roll 25, frame 1466, 16 November 1838). Guía 124. 6 tercios of domestic merchandise. Value: ca. 20 pesos. To: Chihuahua and Sonora. [There is no record of this guía in the guía notebook of 1835.]

Valverde, Francisco (roll 21, frame 316, 16 August 1839). Guía 116. 29 tercios of foreign and domestic merchandise. Value: 1,143 pesos 1.75 reales. To: El Paso.

Valverde, José Francisco (roll 14, frame 250, 3 October 1831). Guía 65. Foreign merchandise. To: El Paso. Conductor: Leal, José Gerónimo. [A large amount of the merchandise came from the United States, but some was purchased in Santa Fe from John E. Hardman. The tornaguía (roll 14, frame 254) indicates that goods were consigned to Valverde at El Paso.]

Valverde, José (roll 19, frame 234, 18 August 1834). Guía 49. 9 tercios, 2 cajones, and 2 baúles of foreign merchandise. To: El Paso.

Vasquez, José (roll 21, frame 278, 24 August 1835). Guía 18. 3 tercios of foreign merchandise. To: El Paso. Fiador: Madrid, Dolores. [Guía exists: roll 21, frame 369.]

Velarde, José Vicente (roll 37, frame 400, 5 September 1844). Guía 5. 3 bultos of domestic merchandise. Value: 70 pesos 6 reales. To: Chihuahua and Tierra Caliente. [Guía exists: roll 37, frame 478.]

Vigil, José Esquipulo (roll 25, frame 1464, 16 November 1838). Guía 122. 4 tercios of domestic merchandise. Value: ca. 67 pesos 4 reales. To: Chihuahua. [There is no record of this guía in the guía notebook of 1835.]

Vigil, José Francisco (roll 21, frame 331, 10 September 1839). Guía 174. 34 bultos of domestic merchandise. Value: 901 pesos 4 reales. To: Chihuahua, Durango, Zacatecas, and Guadalajara.

Vigil, José Francisco (roll 21, frame 332, 10 September 1839). Guía 176. 10 bultos of domestic merchandise. To: Zacatecas and Guadalajara. Conductor: Vigil, Juan de Jesús.

Vigil, José Miguel (roll 34, frame 1210, 6 September 1843). Guía 56. 9 tercios of domestic merchandise. Value: 123 pesos 2 reales. To: Chihuahua and San Juan de los Lagos. [Guía exists: roll 34, frame 1253.]

Vigil, Juan Bautista (roll 34, frame 1214, 30 October 1843). Guía 107. 4 bultos of domestic merchandise. Value: 148 pesos. To: Chihuahua.

Vigil, Ramón (roll 21, frame 328, 9 September 1839). Guía 164. Domestic merchandise. Value: 83 pesos 2 reales. To: Zacatecas and Guanajuato. Conductor: Mestas, Benito.

Vigil, Ramón (roll 21, frame 328, 9 September 1839). Guía 165. Domestic merchandise. Value: 210 pesos. To: Sonora and Sinaloa. Conductor: Martín [Marín], José Antonio.

Vigil, Ramón (roll 21, frame 329, 9 September 1839). Guía 166. Value: 135 pesos. To: Zacatecas and Guanajuato. Conductor: Seledón, José.

Vizcarra, Juan (roll 14, frame 294, 28 November 1831). Guía 80. Foreign merchandise purchased from Luis Robidoux. To: Chihuahua.

Yrizarri, Mariano (roll 21, frame 335, 5 October 1839). Guía 187. 30 bultos of domestic merchandise. Value: 655 pesos. To: Chihuahua and Sonora.

Yrizarri, Mariano (roll 21, frame 350, 22 August 1840). Guía 26. 900 sheep. Value: 450 pesos. To: Durango and Mexico. Fiador: Otero, Antonio José. [Guía exists: roll 28, frame 769.]

Yrizarri, Mariano (roll 21, frame 350, 22 August 1840). Guía 28. 36 bultos of domestic merchandise. Value: 383 pesos 1 real. To: Durango and Chihuahua. Fiador: Otero, Antonio José. [Guía exists: roll 28, frame 771.]

Yrizarri, Mariano (roll 34, frame 1204, 22 August 1843). Guía 12. 7 bultos of foreign merchandise. Value: 1,475 pesos 5 reales. To: Chihuahua and Durango. [Guía exists: roll 34, frame 1232.]

Yrizarri, Mariano (roll 34, frame 1206, 26 August 1843). Guía 29. 38 bultos of domestic merchandise. Value: 2,970 pesos. To: Chihuahua and Durango.

Yrizarri, Mariano (roll 37, frame 394, 1 August 1844). Guía 16. 16 bultos of domestic merchandise and 2,800 sheep. Value: 1,722 pesos 2 reales. To: Chihuahua, Durango, and Aguas Calientes.

Yrizarri, Mariano (roll 37, frame 394, 1 August 1844). Guía 17. 23 bultos of foreign merchandise. Value: 3,313 pesos 43.5 cents. To: Chihuahua, Durango, and Aguas Calientes.

Yrizarri, Mariano (roll 37, frame 394, 1 August 1844). Guía 18. 22 bultos of foreign merchandise. Value: 2,603 pesos 11.75 cents. To: Chihuahua, Sonora, and Durango. [Tornaguía exists: roll 37, frame 524. Issued at Allende on 24 August 1844. Yrizarri did not pay any duties because he sold the merchandise at the domestic fair.]

Yrizarri, Mariano (roll 40, frame 286, 5 September 1845). Guía 21. 3,000 sheep and 4 tercios of domestic merchandise. Value: 1,563 pesos. To: Chihuahua, Durango, and San Juan de los Lagos. Conductor: Aranda, Pedro.

Yrizarri, Pablo (roll 21, frame 310, 30 August 1838). Guía 82. 14 bultos of domestic merchandise and 200 sheep. To: Chihuahua and Durango.

Yrizarri, Pablo (roll 34, frame 1206, 26 August 1843). Guía 28. 40 bultos of domestic merchandise. Value: 530 pesos. To: Chihuahua and Sonora.

Yrizarri, Pedro (roll 40, frame 286, 5 September 1845). Guía 22. 26 piezas of domestic merchandise. Value: 209 pesos 4 reales. To: Chihuahua, Durango, and San Juan de Los Lagos.

**Yzurrieta, Juan (roll 22, frame 1178, 2 January 1836). Durango, guía 515. 20 bultos of domestic and foreign merchandise. To: Armijo, Manuel. Conductor: García, Cristóbal, arriero. [Guía exists: roll 22, frame 1179.]

**Yzurrieta, Juan (roll 22, frame 1180, 2 January 1836). Durango, guía 516. 10 tercios of domestic merchandise. Conductor: García, Cristóbal, arriero. [Guía exists: roll 22, frame 1180.]

Zubía, José Felix (roll 37, frame 408, 19 December 1844). Guía 47. 62 bultos of domestic merchandise. Value: 165 pesos 4 reales. To: Chihuahua, Durango, and Mexico.

Zuloaga, José M. (roll 40, frame 349, 22 September 1845). Guía 62. Foreign merchandise purchased in the United States and in "the area." Value: 9,370 pesos 96 cents. To: Galeana.

Appendix 2

Manifests of Merchandise Presented to the Customs House in Santa Fe Belonging to Hispano Merchants.[1]

1840   Chávez, José, 11 bultos (roll 28, frame 730).
1840   Chávez, Mariano (roll 28, frame 750).
1840   Otero, Antonio José, 30 bultos (roll 28, frames 736–38).
1842   Otero, José Antonio (roll 32, frames 1607–28).
1842   Perea, Juan, 70 bultos (roll 32, frames 1598–603).
1843   Chávez, Mariano, 34 bultos (roll 34, frames 1193–99).
1843   Chávez y Castillo, José, 5 bultos (roll 34, frames 1182–83).
1843   González, Tomás, 2 bultos (roll 34, frame 1171).
1843   Gutiérrez, José Mariano, 8 bultos (roll 34, frame 1190).
1843   Gutiérrez, Juan Nepomuceno, 5 cajas and bultos (roll 34, frames 1180–81).
1843   Ortiz, Gaspar, 22 bultos (roll 34, frames 1176–77).
1843   Sandoval, Antonio, 14 bultos (roll 34, frames 1191–92).
1844   Armijo, Juan C. (roll 37, frames 437–42).
1844   Chávez, Mariano (roll 37, frames 443–55).
1844   Otero, Antonio José (roll 37, frames 456–58).
1844   Perea, Juan and José (roll 37, frames 418–36).
1846   Armijo, Juan, 5 bultos (roll 41, frames 811–13).

Appendix 3
Hispano Merchants Listed in the 1860 Census
(Sorted according to total assets)

Name	County of Residence: Precinct or Town	Age	Real Estate ($)	Personal Estate ($)	Total Assets ($)
Perea, José Leandro	Bernalillo	38	25,000	200,000	225,000
Yrizarri, Mariano	Bernalillo: Los Ranchos	45	20,000	193,000	213,000
Otero, Manuel A.	Valencia: Valencia	38	10,000	154,550	164,550
Armijo, Juan Cristóbal	Bernalillo: Valencia	50	10,000	100,000	110,000
Armijo, Cristóbal	Bernalillo: Albuquerque	40	12,000	70,000	82,000
Armijo, Manuel	Bernalillo: José Leandro	47	14,000	60,000	74,000
Armijo, Rafael	Bernalillo: Albuquerque	42	14,000	60,000	74,000
Chávez, Felipe	Bernalillo	24	5,000	62,575	67,575
Luna, Antonio José	Valencia: José Leandro	52	4,000	63,500	67,500
González, Navarro	Santa Fe: La Ciénaga	41	13,000	53,000	66,000
Otero, Antonio J.	Valencia: Valencia	48	21,000	44,074	65,074
Barela, Anastasio	Doña Ana: Mesilla	43	15,000	50,000	65,000
Jaramillo, José	Valencia: Los Lunas	36	2,700	52,714	55,414
Baca, Luis	Socorro: Limitar	30	6,000	40,000	46,000
Vigil, Manuel	Socorro: Limitar	48	4,000	38,000	42,000
Perea, J. L.	San Miguel: Las Vegas	42	500	36,000	36,500
Gallegos, José M.	Santa Fe: Santa Fe	43	16,000	20,000	36,000
Sandoval, Anastasio	Santa Fe: Santa Fe	44	12,000	22,000	34,000
Luna, Ramón	Valencia: Los Lunas	50	1,000	31,000	32,000
Ortiz y Alarid, Gaspar	Santa Fe: Santa Fe	36	25,000	6,000	31,000
Montoya, Juan	Socorro: Limitar	39	800	28,000	28,800
Gutiérrez, Rafael	Valencia: Casa Colorada	45	2,600	25,800	28,400
Armijo, Ambrosio	Bernalillo: Albuquerque	32	8,000	20,000	28,000
Delgado, Simón	Santa Fe: Santa Fe	44	20,000	7,000	27,000
Salazar, José	Valencia: Valencia	32	2,800	21,027	23,827
Armijo, Nestor	Bernalillo: Griegos	28	2,500	20,000	22,500
Torres, Agustín	Doña Ana: Mesilla	46	3,000	19,000	22,000
Sánchez, Juan J.	Valencia: Valencia	60	4,000	16,545	20,545
Armijo, Salvador	Bernalillo: Albuquerque	37	5,000	15,000	20,000
Baca, Pedro	Socorro: Socorro	55	2,000	17,000	19,000
Lerma, Antonio	Bernalillo: Alameda	31	7,000	12,000	19,000
Montoya, Nestor	Bernalillo: Albuquerque	33	4,000	14,180	18,180
Romero, Miguel	Valencia: Los Lunas	23	500	17,000	17,500
Romero, Toribio	Valencia: Los Lunas	35	500	17,000	17,500

Yrizarri, Manuel	Bernalillo: Los Ranchos	20	2,000	15,400	17,400
Luján, Wensilao	Socorro: Limitar	36	1,000	15,000	16,000
Ribera, Antonio	Santa Fe: Santa Fe	51	3,500	11,000	14,500
Meléndez, Pablo	Doña Ana: Mesilla	60	10,000	4,000	14,000
Córdoba, Miguel A.	Taos: El Llano	46	3,900	10,000	13,900
Armijo, Francisco	Bernalillo: Albuquerque	20	10,000	3,800	13,800
Armijo, Juan	Socorro: El Sabinal	60	2,500	10,000	12,500
Barrientos, Saturnino	Doña Ana: Mesilla	40	12,000	1,000	12,100
Montoya, Stanislao	Socorro: San Ignacio	40	2,000	10,000	12,000
Armijo, José	Bernalillo: Gallegos	30	1,800	10,000	11,800
Baca, José Miguel	Socorro: La Panda	60	1,000	10,000	11,000
Ancheta, Nepomuceno	Doña Ana: Mesilla	33	2,000	8,000	10,000
Delgado, Felipe	Santa Fe: Santa Fe	32	4,000	6,000	10,000
Romero, José Miguel	San Miguel: Las Vegas	61	6,000	4,000	10,000
Romero, José María	Valencia: Los Lunas	27	1,000	8,900	9,900
López, Prudencio	San Miguel: San José	35	2,500	7,095	9,595
González, Ignacio	Bernalillo: Albuquerque	32	2,500	6,000	8,500
García, Manuel	Bernalillo: Albuquerque	36	7,000	1,470	8,470
Pino, Pablo	Valencia: Cubero	60	800	7,500	8,300
González, Tomás	Bernalillo: Albuquerque	37	2,000	6,000	8,000
Baca, Antonio María	Socorro: El Pago	60	1,000	6,000	7,000
Barela, Nestor	Doña Ana: Mesilla	32	2,000	5,000	7,000
Larragoiti, Benito	Santa Fe: Santa Fe	48	6,000	1,000	7,000
Silva, Mariano	Socorro: Sabinal	57	1,000	6,000	7,000
Abeita, Manuel	Socorro: Socorro	26	—	6,800	6,800
Ortiz y Delgado, Francisco	Santa Fe: Santa Fe	46	4,600	2,000	6,600
Chávez, Rumaldo	Valencia: Belén	39	1,000	5,000	6,000
Delgado, Fernando	Santa Fe: Santa Fe	33	1,000	5,000	6,000
García, Vicente	Santa Fe: Santa Fe	30	2,000	4,000	6,000
Jaramillo, Dionisio	Socorro: Socorro	30	3,000	3,000	6,000
Abeita, Antonio	Socorro: Socorro	36	1,000	4,500	5,500
Sena y Quintana, Miguel	San Miguel: La Extrañosa	—	1,500	4,000	5,500
Baca, Gregorio	Socorro: El Pago	26	450	5,000	5,450
Gallegos, José Guadalupe	San Miguel: Antón Chico	32	1,200	4,000	5,200
Barela, Jesús María	Mora: Santa Gertrudis	37	2,000	3,000	5,000
Delgado, Pablo	Santa Fe: Santa Fe	37	1,000	4,000	5,000
Sarracino, Clemente	Valencia: Cubero	48	500	4,500	5,000
Romero, Vidal	San Miguel: Las Vegas	25	500	4,000	4,500
Constante, Antonio	Doña Ana: Las Cruces	47	4,000	200	4,200
Baca, Francisco	Socorro: El Pago	26	600	3,500	4,100
Armijo, José Francisco	Taos: Arroyo Seco	35	1,000	3,000	4,000
Ulibarri, Felix	San Miguel: Chaperito	34	2,000	2,000	4,000
Martín, José	San Miguel: Antón Chico	36	3,000	700	3,700
Saenz, Manuel	Doña Ana: Pinos Altos	40	100	3,500	3,600
Salazar, Manuel	Valencia: Valencia	22	—	3,600	3,600
Chávez, Pablo	Valencia: Casa Colorada	25	350	3,050	3,400
Cuellar Medina, Celso	Socorro: Fray Cristóbal	34	250	3,000	3,250
Trujillo, Severo	Río Arriba: Precinct 9	26	1,400	1,659	3,059

Chávez, Ambrosio	Valencia: Valencia	26	1,000	2,020	3,020
Martínez, Leandro	Taos: Los Córdobas	26	—	3,000	3,000
Ortiz, Miguel	Taos: Río Colorado	38	1,000	2,000	3,000
Sandoval, Manuel	Santa Fe: Santa Fe	33	500	2,500	3,000
Miranda, Guadalupe	Doña Ana: Mesilla	50	1,300	1,500	2,800
Sánchez, Pedro	Taos: Fernando	28	800	2,000	2,800
Montoya, Lorenzo	San Miguel: Las Tuzas	28	300	2,400	2,700
Armijo, Reyes	Socorro: El Sabinal	60	600	2,000	2,600
García, Candelario	Socorro: Valverde	30	600	2,000	2,600
Baca, Bernardo	Santa Ana: Algodones	28	2,000	500	2,500
Montoya, Juan	Doña Ana: Mesilla	35	—	2,500	2,500
Gutiérrez, José	Mora: San Antonio	30	600	1,800	2,400
Armijo, José	Valencia: Valencia	20	1,500	800	2,300
Montoya, Francisco	Bernalillo: Albuquerque	38	1,500	600	2,100
López, Juan	Doña Ana: Mesilla	45	1,000	1,000	2,000
Ortiz, Antonio	Santa Fe: Santa Fe	29	1,500	500	2,000
Trujillo, Vicente	San Miguel: Las Manuelitas	31	800	1,200	2,000
González, Manuel	San Miguel: Las Manuelitas	31	1,000	900	1,900
Jaramillo, José	Valencia: San Fernando	44	500	1,200	1,700
Naranjo, Desiderio	Mora: Guadalupe	40	800	870	1,670
Herrera, Antonio	San Miguel: Las Manuelitas	38	1,000	600	1,600
Romero, Bonifacio	Santa Fe: Agua Fría	28	300	1,300	1,600
Griego, José Tomás	Bernalillos: Griegos	54	600	950	1,550
Abreu, Francisco	Santa Fe: Santa Fe	28	400	1,000	1,500
Chávez, Jesús María	Socorro: Socorro	28	1,000	500	1,500
Contreras, Reyes	Doña Ana: Las Cruces	40	500	1,000	1,500
Nevares, Ramón	Doña Ana: Las Cruces	42	1,000	300	1,300
Gallegos, Dolores	Valencia: Tajique	40	250	1,000	1,250
Abeita, Antonio	Santa Fe: Santa Fe	23	500	700	1,200
Baca, Ramón	San Miguel: Las Manuelitas	56	400	800	1,200
Robles, Antonio	Valencia: Manzano	35	200	1,000	1,200
Sánchez, Desiderio	Valencia: Los Chávez	25	200	1,000	1,200
Vigil, Agapito	San Miguel: Las Gallinas	28	200	1,000	1,200
Sánchez, Manuel	Valencia: Manzano	27	600	500	1,100
Luna, Venislao	Valencia: Los Lunas	22	500	500	1,000
Ochoa, Jesús	Doña Ana: Las Cruces	60	—	1,000	1,000
Robles, Cecilio	Santa Fe: Santa Fe	35	—	1,000	1,000
Baca, Tomás	San Miguel: Las Vegas	21	—	800	800
Oceáno, Segundo	Doña Ana: Mesilla	33	—	800	800
Sena, José	San Miguel: Las Vegas	23	—	800	800
Salas, Higinio	Valencia: Los Chávez	31	200	550	750
Salazar, José Trujillo	Santa Fe: Pojoaque	21	—	700	700
Apodaca, Marcos	Doña Ana: Mesilla	47	400	200	600
Crespín, José	San Miguel: San Gerónimo	34	200	340	540
Armijo, Pablo	San Miguel: Antón Chico	27	400	100	500
Colomo, Rosalía	Bernalillo: Albuquerque	31	—	500	500

Sánchez, Jesús	Valencia: Valencia	20	—	500	500
Silva, Bautista	Santa Fe: Santa Fe	27	—	500	500
Márquez, Leonardo	Valencia: El Bosque	30	100	300	400
Ortiz, Juan Luis	Santa Fe: Santa Fe	65	400	—	400
Ortiz, Teodoro	Santa Fe: Santa Fe	28	100	200	300
González de Rueda, J. D.	San Miguel: Antón Chico	39	180	100	280
López, Miguel	San Miguel: Los Luceros	61	—	250	250
Mes, Lupes	San Miguel: San Gerónimo	31	—	240	240
Ariscón, David	Doña Ana: Las Cruces	26	—	200	200
Roibal, Albino	Santa Fe: Santa Fe	24	—	200	200
Segura, Simón	Santa Fe: Santa Fe	28	100	100	200
Leivas, Basilio	San Miguel: San Gerónimo	25	—	190	190
Dena, Gemelo	Doña Ana: Mesilla	50	125	—	125
Baca, Victoriano	San Miguel: Las Vegas	37	100	—	100
Armijo, Nicolás	Bernalillos: Gallegos	18	—	—	—
Barela, Carlos	Doña Ana: Mesilla	38	—	—	—
Estrada, José	Doña Ana: Mesilla	46	—	—	—
García, Felipe	Bernalillo: Alameda	29	—	—	—
Luna, Jesús María	Valencia: Los Lunas	23	—	—	—
Mayagoitia, Eleuterio	Santa Fe: Santa Fe	36	—	—	—
Montoya, José Pablo	Bernalillo: Albuquerque	48	—	—	—
Otero, Vicente	Valencia: Valencia	21	—	—	—
Salazar, Jesús María	Valencia: Valencia	23	—	—	—
Salazar, Juan	Valencia: Valencia	23	—	—	—
Valdez, Pablo	Mora: Santa Gertrudis	23	—	—	—
Velásquez, José M.	Socorro: Fort Craig	20	—	—	—

Hispano Merchants Listed in the 1870 Census
(Sorted according to total assets)

Name	County of Residence: Precinct or Town	Age	Real Estate ($)	Personal Estate ($)	Total Assets ($)	Listed Occupation[a]
Perea, José Leandro	Bernalillo: Bernalillo	47	48,000	360,000	408,000	merchant & farmer
Otero, Manuel Antonio	Valencia: Tomé	47	24,500	150,000	174,500	dry goods merchant
Chávez, José Felipe	Valencia: Belén	35	40,000	100,000	140,000	dry goods merchant & retailer
Armijo, Ambrosio	Bernalillo: Albuquerque	50	15,000	85,000	100,000	merchant & farmer
Armijo, Cristóbal	Bernalillo: Albuquerque	50	6,000	60,000	66,000	wholesale merchant
Armijo, J. C.	Bernalillo: Los Griegos	60	8,000	58,000	66,000	wholesale merchant & farmer
Vigil, Manuel	Socorro: Socorro	58	8,000	38,000	46,000	general merchant
Lerma, Antonio	Bernalillo: Alameda	43	6,000	25,000	31,000	dry goods retailer

Name	Location	Age				Occupation
Ortiz, Gaspar	Santa Fe: Santa Fe	45	28,000	3,000	31,000	retail merchant
Baca, Nepomuceno	Socorro: Socorro	36	10,000	20,000	30,000	general merchant
Armijo, Salvador	Bernalillo: Albuquerque	47	5,000	21,000	26,000	merchant & farmer
Santiesteban, Juan	Taos: El Rancho	37	2,000	18,500	20,500	general merchant & retailer
Sandoval, Anastasio	Santa Fe: Santa Fe	54	16,000	2,000	18,000	merchant & retailer
López, Rafael	Santa Fe: Santa Fe	43	13,700	2,000	15,700	merchant & retailer
Delgado, Felipe	Santa Fe: Santa Fe	41	6,000	7,000	13,000	merchant & retailer
Baca, Pedro	Socorro: Socorro	60	3,000	9,000	12,000	general merchant
Delgado, Fernando	Santa Fe: Santa Fe	44	10,000	2,000	12,000	retail merchant
Abeita, Anastasio	Socorro: Limitar	43	5,000	5,000	10,000	general merchant
Armijo, Jesús	Doña Ana: Las Cruces	25	5,000	3,000	8,000	dry goods merchant & retailer
Baca, Vivian	Socorro: Precinct 1	35	2,000	6,000	8,000	general merchant
Chávez, Francisco	Bernalillo: Pajarito	33	1,000	7,000	8,000	manufacturer of flour
Roybal, Antón	Río Arriba: Santa Cruz	59	1,700	5,000	6,700	retail dry goods merchant
González, Ignacio	Doña Ana: Mesilla	45	1,300	5,000	6,300	dry goods merchant & retailer
Chávez, Sixto	Río Arriba: El Rito	22	1,000	5,000	6,000	retail dry goods merchant
Sánchez, Juan	Taos: Picuris	60	3,000	3,000	6,000	merchant
González, Ramón	Doña Ana: Mesilla	44	1,300	4,275	5,575	grocer & retailer
Aledo, José	Doña Ana: Las Cruces	42	1,500	4,000	5,500	dry goods merchant & retailer
Pino, José	Socorro: Alamosita	38	1,000	4,500	5,500	general merchant
García, Vicente	Santa Fe: Santa Fe	42	3,500	1,500	5,000	retail merchant
Luján, Vicente	Valencia: Valencia	41	1,000	4,000	5,000	dry goods merchant & retailer
Montoya, Nestor	Bernalillo: Albuquerque	44	3,000	2,000	5,000	retail merchant
Armijo, Perfecto	Doña Ana: Las Cruces	26	2,000	2,500	4,500	dry goods merchant & retailer
Delgado, Pablo	Santa Fe: Santa Fe	47	4,000	400	4,400	general merchant
Brito, Antonio	San Miguel: Sapillo	22	1,000	3,329	4,329	dealer in general merchandise
Robledo, Ramón	San Miguel: Sapillo	24	1,000	3,329	4,329	dealer in general merchandise
Armijo, Juan	Mora: Loma Parda	43	4,000	100	4,100	retail grocer & merchant
Martínez, Eduardo	San Miguel: Antón Chico	33	1,000	3,040	4,040	dealer in general merchandise
Jaramillo, Pedro J.	Río Arriba: El Rito	21	1,000	3,000	4,000	retail merchant
Tafoya, Rafael	Socorro: Alamosita	37	2,000	2,000	4,000	general merchant
Sánchez, José	San Miguel: Antón Chico	35	1,200	2,413	3,613	dealer in general merchandise
Abeita, Manuel	Socorro: Socorro	38	500	3,000	3,500	general merchant
Castillo, Pedro	Bernalillo: Bernalillo	22	500	3,000	3,500	store clerk
Delgado, Felipe	Santa Fe: Santa Fe	28	500	3,000	3,500	merchant
Montoya, Juan	Socorro: Limitar	43	1,000	2,500	3,500	general merchant
Ramírez, Candido	San Miguel: Chaperito	26	3,000	300	3,300	dealer in general merchandise

Sandoval, Florencio	Santa Ana: Algodones	30	550	2,747	3,297	merchant
Trujillo, Anastasio	Mora: Mora	35	1,600	1,592	3,192	retail merchant
Baca, Juan José	Socorro: Socorro	27	1,500	1,500	3,000	general merchant
Córdoba, Pablo	Socorro: La Joya	43	1,000	2,000	3,000	general merchant
Arranda, Francisco	Santa Fe: Santa Fe	65	2,100	800	2,900	merchant & retailer
Trujillo, Tomás	Río Arriba: El Rito	30	400	2,500	2,900	retail merchant
Gutiérrez, José	Santa Fe: Santa Fe	40	600	2,000	2,600	merchant & retailer
Baca y Baca, Antonio	San Miguel: San José	39	2,000	500	2,500	merchant in dry goods
Barello, Blaza	Doña Ana: Mesilla	40	2,000	400	2,400	grocer retailer
Montoya, Julián	Socorro: Alamosita	35	400	2,000	2,400	general merchant
Chávez, Tomás	San Miguel: Upper Las Vegas	30	300	2,000	2,300	dealer in general merchandise
Sena, Luis	Santa Fe: Santa Fe	21	2,000	300	2,300	clerk in store
Quintana, Miguel	Santa Fe: Santa Fe	34	2,000	100	2,100	retail merchant
Baca, Antonio José	San Miguel: Antón Chico	43	400	1,600	2,000	dealer in general merchandise
Baca, Severo	Socorro: Socorro	23	1,000	1,000	2,000	general merchant
López, Romano	San Miguel: San José	23	—	2,000	2,000	merchant in dry goods
Moreno, Juan	Doña Ana: Mesilla	45	1,000	1,000	2,000	dry goods merchant & retailer
Ortiz, Ambrosio	Santa Fe: Santa Fe	31	1,500	500	2,000	clerk in store
Romero, Maximiano	Taos: San Fernando	22	500	1,500	2,000	clerk in store
Sales, Sabino	Santa Fe: Santa Fe	45	2,000	—	2,000	retail merchant
Velarde, Pedro	Socorro: Alamosita	46	1,000	1,000	2,000	general merchant
Chávez, Blas	Socorro: Alamosita	33	800	1,000	1,800	general merchant
Rivera, José L.	San Miguel: La Cuesta	24	1,000	800	1,800	dealer in general merchandise
Luján, Leuterio	Santa Fe: Santa Fe	27	1,500	200	1,700	merchant
Pantaleón, Estes	Santa Fe: Santa Fe	23	200	1,500	1,700	merchant
Peralta, Felipe	Socorro: La Joya	31	500	1,200	1,700	general merchant
Armijo, Diego	Socorro: Limitar	34	500	1,000	1,500	general merchant
Gabaldón, Dionisio	Valencia: Los Lunas	32	500	1,000	1,500	dry goods merchant & retailer
González, Tomás	Santa Fe: Santa Fe	46	500	1,000	1,500	retail merchant
Miranda, Guadalupe	Doña Ana: Doña Ana	60	—	1,500	1,500	dry goods merchant (retired)
Montana, José	Lincoln: Fort Stanton	32	—	1,500	1,500	dry goods merchant
Mora, Jesús H	San Miguel: Antón Chico	37	500	1,000	1,500	dealer in general merchandise
Pino, Esquipulo	Socorro: Socorro	29	500	1,000	1,500	general merchant
Torres, Isidro	Socorro: Alamosita	27	1,000	500	1,500	general merchant
Vigil, José Armijo	Socorro: Limitar	28	500	1,000	1,500	general merchant
Abreu, Francisco	San Miguel: Chaperito	38	1,000	300	1,300	dealer in general merchandise
Ortiz, Esquipulo	Santa Fe: Pojoaque	46	500	700	1,200	trader
Sánchez, Jacinto	Lincoln: Fort Stanton	28	175	1,000	1,175	dry goods merchant
Baca, Juan María	Socorro: Socorro	37	1,000	150	1,150	general merchant
Romero, Benigno	San Miguel: Antón Chico	20	300	800	1,100	clerk in store

Valdez, Manuel	Río Arriba: San Juan	48	700	400	1,100	merchant (retired)
Romero, Lorenzo	Mora: La Cueva	40	500	510	1,010	retail merchant & grocer
Anglada, José de	Taos: San Fernando	33	1,000	—	1,000	clerk in store
Chávez, Juan B.	Bernalillo: Los Ranchos	25	500	500	1,000	retail merchant
González, Tomás	Socorro: Contadera	34	500	500	1,000	general merchant
González, Tomás	Santa Fe: El Paraje	34	500	500	1,000	general merchant
Villa, Juan	Doña Ana: Mesilla	41	—	1,000	1,000	dry goods merchant & retailer
Salazar, Manuel	Valencia: Tomé	35	600	376	976	clerk in store
Chávez, Juan	Socorro: Sabinal	40	400	500	900	general merchant
Ortiz, Teodoro	Río Arriba: San Juan Pueblo	33	400	500	900	merchant
Ortiz, Teodosio	Río Arriba: San José	33	450	450	900	merchant's clerk
Rodríguez, José G.	Taos: Río Colorado	50	250	650	900	general merchant
Córdoba, Ramón	Río Arriba: Yunque	80	400	460	860	grocer (retired)
García, Juan	Río Arriba: San Juan Pueblo	38	300	500	800	merchant
Gallegos, Dolores	Mora: La Cueva	50	100	680	780	retail merchant, groceries & dry goods
Valdez, Antonio	Santa Fe: Santa Fe	53	600	—	600	retail merchant
Baca, José Miguel	Socorro: Socorro	70	150	400	550	retail merchant
Valdez, Manuel	Santa Fe: Santa Fe	23	300	225	525	clerk in store
Montoya, José Andrés	Santa Ana: Jemez	21	—	500	500	merchant
Trujillo, Guillermo	Taos: San Fernando	30	300	200	500	clerk in store
Quintana, [Ireneo]	Santa Fe: Santa Fe	80	300	—	300	retail merchant
Bustamante, Bonifacio	Socorro: Contadera	40	100	100	200	general merchant
Durán, Facundo	Santa Fe: Santa Fe	44	100	—	100	retail merchant
Armijo, Jesús	Socorro: Contadera	26	—	—	—	general merchant
Pino, Leandro	Socorro: Contadera	25	—	—	—	general merchant
Rivera, Guadalupe	Santa Fe: Santa Fe	48	—	—	—	merchant (retired)
Sánchez, Juan	Santa Fe: Santa Fe	48	—	—	—	merchant

[a] Occupational classification varies among the various counties and precincts. The differences between some of the labels are not clear. Is a general merchant the same as a retail merchant? What is the difference between a dry goods merchant and retailer and a grocer? Some listings, like flour manufacturer, are included because the sale of flour was an important economic activity associated with the Santa Fe trade. Liquor dealers, hotel keepers, brewers, and druggists are not included.

Appendix 4
Non-Hispano Merchants Listed in the 1860 Census
(Sorted according to total assets)

Name Origin	County of Residence: Precinct or Town	Age	Real Estate ($)	Personal Estate ($)	Total Stated Assets ($)
St. Vrain, Cerain St. Louis	Mora: El Rancho	59	58,000	153,000	211,000
Moore, W. H. New York	San Miguel: El Tecolote	42	15,000	150,000	165,000
Connelly, Henry Kentucky	Bernalillo: Albuquerque	59	58,000	84,000	142,000
Gold, Andrés Germany	San Miguel: Las Vegas	34	1,500	75,000	76,500
Gold, John Germany	San Miguel: Las Vegas	40	1,500	75,000	76,500
Spiegelberg, Levi Prussia	Santa Fe: Santa Fe	29	15,000	50,000	65,000
Hersch, Joseph Poland	Santa Fe: Santa Fe	36	40,000	20,000	60,000
Hover, Oliver P. Vermont	Santa Fe: Santa Fe	33	18,000	35,000	53,000
McGroskey, William Ireland	Doña Ana: Mesilla	35	1,000	49,000	50,000
Brewster, Samson Prussia	Mora: San Fernando	30	3,600	41,000	44,600
Pley, Joseph Cadiz, Spain	Mora: San Fernando	40	12,000	32,000	44,000
Bull, Thomas Ohio	Doña Ana: Mesilla	35	7,000	30,000	37,000
Boyce, Stephen Canada	San Miguel: Las Vegas	42	15,000	20,000	35,000
Clark, C.B. New York	Bernalillo: Albuquerque	32	—	35,000	35,000
Joseph, Pedro Portugal	Mora: San Fernando	44	8,000	25,000	33,000
Huning, Charles Hanover, Germany	Bernalillo: Albuquerque	27	200	30,000	30,200
Clever, C. P. Prussia	Santa Fe: Santa Fe	30	—	30,000	30,000

Johnson, James Massachusetts	Santa Fe: Santa Fe	35	—	30,000	30,000
Metzger, Frank Prussia	Mora: Santa Gertrudis	41	30,000	—	30,000
Seligman, S. Hesse	Santa Fe: Santa Fe	30	—	30,000	30,000
Bucheau, Alfred New York	Doña Ana: Las Cruces	25	1,500	25,000	26,500
Amberg, Jacob Prussia	Santa Fe: Santa Fe	34	1,000	25,000	26,000
Stapleton, Robert H. Ireland	Socorro: Valverde	30	6,000	20,000	26,000
Amberg, Gustave Prussia	Santa Fe: Santa Fe	31	—	25,000	25,000
Rosé, L. D. Bavaria	Santa Fe: Santa Fe	33	10,000	15,000	25,000
Kingsbury, John M. Massachusetts	Santa Fe: Santa Fe	31	4,000	20,000	24,000
Duval, Alexander Virginia	Socorro: Río Bonito	41	2,500	21,200	23,700
Rosenstein, Simon Hanover	Bernalillo: Albuquerque	45	500	22,000	22,500
Beark, Charles Illinois	Valencia: Manzano	25	7,000	15,000	22,000
Wood, E. M. Ohio	Santa Fe: Santa Fe	38	2,500	18,000	20,500
Kroning, William Germany	Mora: Las Golondrinas	35	10,000	10,000	20,000
Mercure, Joseph Canada	Santa Fe: Santa Fe	41	—	20,000	20,000
Zeckendorf, Louis Hanover, Germany	Bernalillo: Albuquerque	22	—	20,000	20,000
Wheeler, H. M. England	Bernalillo: Albuquerque	31	2,500	15,525	18,025
Blummer, Charles Prussia	Santa Fe: Santa Fe	54	8,000	10,000	18,000
O'Neil, Henry Ireland	Santa Fe: Santa Fe	33	6,000	12,000	18,000
Bramford, Edward England	Bernalillo: Albuquerque	38	10,000	7,000	17,000
Cochran, Robert Virginia	Doña Ana: Mesilla	26	—	17,000	17,000
Desmarais, Miguel Canada	San Miguel: Las Vegas	54	—	15,000	15,000
Elsberg, Albert Prussia	Santa Fe: Santa Fe	27	—	15,000	15,000
Geck, Louis Poland	Doña Ana: Mesilla	48	6,000	9,000	15,000
Morrison, A. Hesse	San Miguel: Bernal	32	1,000	13,000	14,000
Posthoff, William Germany	Taos: Costilla	29	6,000	8,000	14,000

Augustine, A. Germany	Doña Ana: Mesilla	27	3,000	10,000	13,000
Zamowsky, J. Poland	Socorro: Ft. Craig	45	800	12,000	12,800
Birmbaum, Henry Germany	Mora: Santa Gertrudis	35	4,000	8,000	12,000
Bramford, William A. Virginia	Mora: Santa Gertrudis	48	4,000	8,000	12,000
Groton, James Pennsylvania	Doña Ana: Mesilla	27	8,000	4,000	12,000
Loeb, Randolph Germany	Mora: Río Colorado	39	3,000	9,000	12,000
Whitlock, F. M. Kentucky	San Miguel: El Tecolote	36	3,000	8,000	11,000
Zeckendorf, Aaron Hanover	Santa Fe: Santa Fe	25	500	10,000	10,500
Generet, Jules Switzerland	Doña Ana: Mesilla	28	—	10,000	10,000
Lacomb, Agustín France	Taos: Arroyo Hondo	48	2,000	8,000	10,000
Meyer, Lipman Bavaria	Santa Fe: Santa Fe	29	10,000	—	10,000
Smith, Stephen Maryland	Doña Ana: Pinos Altos	30	—	10,000	10,000
Webb, Nathan Boston	Mora: Las Golondrinas	32	—	10,000	10,000
Staab, Zadock Prussia	Santa Fe: Santa Fe	25	—	9,000	9,000
Tully, P. H. Tennessee	Doña Ana: Ft. Thorn	37	1,000	8,000	9,000
Martin, L. J. Mississippi	Doña Ana: Pinos Altos	21	2,000	6,500	8,500
Stevens, David Maryland	San Miguel: Antón Chico	27	7,000	1,500	8,500
Spiegelberg, Manuel Prussia	Santa Fe: Santa Fe	23	300	8,000	8,300
Miller, T. G. Louisiana	Doña Ana: La Mesa	33	2,200	6,000	8,200
Gould, Louis Poland	Santa Fe: Santa Fe	38	100	8,000	8,100
Aleck, José Spain	Doña Ana: Mesilla	32	3,000	5,000	8,000
Lucas, James Missouri	Doña Ana: Mesilla	34	3,000	5,000	8,000
Sledd, Joshua Virginia	Doña Ana: Mesilla	50	5,500	2,000	7,500
Barela, Nestor Mexico	Doña Ana: Mesilla	32	2,000	5,000	7,000
Green, H. H. Chicago	Mora: Santa Gertrudis	38	—	6,000	6,000
Zoller, John Baden Baden	Doña Ana: Las Cruces	36	2,000	4,000	6,000

Woodman, [J.] New York	San Miguel: El Burro	36	2,000	3,500	5,500
Estes, George Virginia	Santa Fe: Santa Fe	41	250	5,000	5,250
Hayes, M. Missouri	San Miguel: Las Vegas	37	1,000	4,000	5,000
Deus, Charles Germany	Taos: Culebra	41	1,900	3,000	4,900
Constante, Antonio Perú	Doña Ana: Las Cruces	47	4,000	200	4,200
Beaubien, Charles Canada	Mora: San Fernando	59	3,000	1,000	4,000
Beaubien, Jean Baptiste Montreal, Canada	Mora: Río Colorado	48	2,000	2,000	4,000
Magruder, C. B. Maryland	Santa Fe: Santa Fe	44	1,000	3,000	4,000
Maxwell, Ferdinand Illinois	Mora: San Fernando	43	—	4,000	4,000
Sachs, M. Germany	Valencia: Los Lunas	37	1,000	3,000	4,000
Wesche, Charles Prussia	Santa Fe: Santa Fe	29	—	4,000	4,000
Rhoman, W. B. Ohio	Doña Ana: Pinos Altos	24	100	3,500	3,600
Bent, Alfred Taos	Mora: El Rancho	23	1,000	2,000	3,000
Bernadet, José Miguel Cataluña, Spain	Mora: Las Golondrinas	34	1,000	2,000	3,000
de Valois, Mariano Mexico	Doña Ana: Santa Rita	59	—	3,000	3,000
Hart, Charles —	Mora: El Rancho	40	1,000	2,000	3,000
Latapie, Jean France	Mora: San Fernando	30	—	3,000	3,000
Massell, Thomas Missouri	Doña Ana: La Mesa	40	500	2,000	2,500
Mousan, Jules Germany	Doña Ana: Pinos Altos	26	1,500	1,000	2,500
Noel, Gustavus France	Santa Fe: Santa Fe	42	1,500	1,000	2,500
Woodson, James B. Virginia	Taos: Conejos	39	310	2,000	2,310
Easterday, H. E. Virginia	Taos: Culebra	42	500	1,800	2,300
Duper, Christian Germany	Doña Ana: Ft. Fillmore	33	600	1,500	2,100
Carey, Robert St. Louis	Mora: El Rancho	42	1,000	1,000	2,000
Francisco, John M. Virginia	Taos: Culebra	40	—	2,000	2,000
[Heppin], Charles Rhode Island	Doña Ana: Mesilla	49	1,500	500	2,000

Thornton, Willis Kentucky	Doña Ana: Mowry City	56	—	2,000	2,000
Mignault, Teodoro Canada	Mora: San Fernando	39	—	1,800	1,800
Muller, Frederik Prussia	Mora: San Fernando	30	—	1,800	1,800
Proffit, William Missouri	Mora: El Rancho	43	600	1,000	1,600
Seligman, B. Hesse	Santa Fe: Santa Fe	22	—	1,500	1,500
Grandert, William Hanover	Mora: San Antonio	28	—	1,300	1,300
Moreau, Agustín France	Doña Ana: Mesilla	48	1,000	300	1,300
Bordeaux, Victor France	Socorro: El Pago	37	250	1,000	1,250
Valle, Frank Missouri	Doña Ana: Pinos Altos	29	—	1,150	1,150
Carter, [?] Virginia	Doña Ana: Pinos Altos	53	—	1,000	1,000
Debus, Wendel Hesse	Santa Fe: Santa Fe	41	—	1,000	1,000
Haas, G. Switzerland	Doña Ana: Pinos Altos	46	—	1,000	1,000
Hastings, G. M. Missouri	Doña Ana: Pinos Altos	40	500	500	1,000
Rite, Charles Bavaria	Mora: San Fernando	26	—	1,000	1,000
Schewrick, L. Bavaria	Mora: San Fernando	24	—	1,000	1,000
Winslow, Henry Georgia	Bernalillo: Albuquerque	43	—	1,000	1,000
Buckman, S. F. New York	Valencia: Cubero	30	—	650	650
Harrison, John England	San Miguel: Antón Chico	43	600	—	600
Schwarkoff, Maurice Bohemia	Santa Fe: Santa Fe	21	—	400	400
Spiegelberg, Solomon Prussia	Santa Fe: Santa Fe	35	—	300	300
Morris, George M. Virginia	Socorro: Socorro	33	—	200	200
Martinez, [Chaffee] France	Doña Ana: Las Cruces	60	—	100	100
Curtis, Edward Virginia	Santa Fe: Santa Fe	27	—	—	—
Hammond, G. H. Tennessee	Doña Ana: Ft. Fillmore	33	—	—	—
Mitchell, W. Maryland	San Miguel: El Tecolote	32	—	—	—
Reese, B. L. Missouri	San Miguel: El Tecolote	32	—	—	—

Non-Hispano Merchants Listed in the 1870 Census
(Sorted according to total assets)

Name	County of Residence: Precinct or Town	Age	Real Estate ($)	Personal Estate ($)	Total Assets ($)	Stated Origin	Listed Occupation
Johnson, James	Santa Fe: Santa Fe	45	210,000	30,000	240,000	Maryland	wholesale merchant
Maxwell, Lucien	Colfax: Precinct 3	56	150,000	20,000	170,000	Illinois	merchant (retired)
Moore, William	Mora: La Quinta	51	20,000	100,000	120,000	New York	retail merchant, groceries & dry goods
Porter, Henry M.	Colfax: Precinct 1	29	70,000	20,000	90,000	Pennsylvania	banker & grocer
Spiegelberg, Lebman	Santa Fe: Santa Fe	29	2,000	75,000	77,000	Prussia	wholesale & retail merchant
Birmbaum, Henry	Mora: Mora	42	4,000	70,000	74,000	Hesse	retail merchant, groceries & dry goods
Rosenbaum, Louis	Doña Ana: Las Cruces	41	—	60,000	60,000	Prussia	dry goods merchant & retailer
Koch, Diedrich B.	Santa Fe: Santa Fe	35	21,000	36,000	57,000	Aldenburg	wholesale merchant
Bull, Thomas	Doña Ana: Mesilla	43	20,000	35,000	55,000	Ohio	dry goods merchant & wholesaler
Lesenicky, Henry	Doña Ana: Las Cruces	35	4,000	50,000	54,000	Prussia	dry goods merchant & retailer
Zeckendorf, Aaron	Bernalillo: Albuquerque	35	2,000	50,000	52,000	Hanover	wholesale merchant
Staab, Abraham	Santa Fe: Santa Fe	31	—	50,000	50,000	Prussia	wholesale & retail merchant
Grzelachowsky, A.	San Miguel: Las Vegas	46	11,400	35,791	47,191	Poland	dealer in general merchandise
Metriger, Frank	Mora: Mora	51	22,100	24,350	46,450	Prussia	retail merchant, groceries & dry goods
Seligman, Bernard	Santa Fe: Santa Fe	32	25,000	20,000	45,000	Hesse	wholesale merchant & retailer
Watrous, Samuel B.	Mora: La Quinta	61	23,500	21,000	44,500	Vermont	retail merchant
Dent, John	Mora: La Quinta	53	10,000	30,000	40,000	Pennsylvania	retail merchant
Lemon, John	Doña Ana: Mesilla	38	25,000	15,000	40,000	Pennsylvania	dry goods merchant, wholesaler & retailer
LaRue, J. A.	Las Vegas: San Miguel	39	—	34,243	34,243	Canada	dealer in general merchandise
Huning, J.	Bernalillo: Albuquerque	41	13,000	20,000	33,000	Prussia	wool merchant
Keyser, Meyer	Santa Fe: Santa Fe	36	12,000	20,000	32,000	Saxony	wholesale merchant & retailer
Spiegelberg, Willi	Santa Fe: Santa Fe	25	2,000	30,000	32,000	Prussia	wholesale & retail merchant
Reynolds, Joseph	Doña Ana: Mesilla	45	5,500	25,000	30,500	Ireland	dry goods merchant & retailer

Huning, Charles	Bernalillo: Albuquerque	37	10,000	20,000	30,000	Hanover	merchant & druggist
Dold, Andrés	San Miguel: Las Vegas	45	16,000	13,320	29,320	Germany	dealer in general merchandise
Gould, Louis	Santa Fe: Santa Fe	48	25,500	3,000	28,500	Poland	wholesale & retail merchant
Gitskey, George	Colfax: Precinct 1	30	25,000	2,500	27,500	Prussia	clothing dealer
Bernard, Joab	San Miguel: Las Vegas	38	5,250	21,245	26,795	Virginia	dealer in general merchandise
Dold, John	San Miguel: Las Vegas	40	2,000	24,150	26,150	Germany	merchant (retired)
Webster, David	Taos: El Rancho	41	6,000	20,000	26,000	New York	general merchant & retailer
Franz, Ehrhardt	Valencia: Los Lunas	35	7,000	18,000	25,000	Hanover	dry goods merchant & retailer
Lea, Adolph	Doña Ana: Leasburg	45	9,000	16,000	25,000	at sea	dry goods merchant & retailer
Hayce, May	San Miguel: Las Vegas	48	13,500	10,527	24,027	Missouri	dealer in general merchandise
Joseph, Antonio	Taos: San Fernando	26	10,000	12,000	22,000	Missouri	general merchant & retailer
Stapp, William B.	Colfax: Precinct 1	36	2,000	20,000	22,000	Illinois	retail merchant
Thayer, Charles	Santa Fe: Santa Fe	45	7,000	15,000	22,000	Massachusetts	merchant
Griggs, James E.	Doña Ana: Mesilla	34	5,500	15,000	20,500	New Jersey	dry goods merchant & retailer
Muller, Frederick	Taos: San Fernando	41	13,300	7,000	20,300	Germany	general merchant & retailer
Hunter, James	Santa Fe: Santa Fe	43	20,000	—	20,000	Kentucky	merchant
Newshenn, Robert	Grant: Mimbres	29	2,000	18,000	20,000	Illinois	dry goods merchant wholesaler & retailer
Letcher, Adolph	San Miguel: Las Vegas	41	—	18,700	18,700	Hanover	dealer in general merchandise
Pendaries, John	San Miguel: Las Vegas	45	11,700	6,320	18,020	France	retail grocer
Wedeles, Hugo	Mora: Mora	31	7,000	10,000	17,000	Bavaria	retail merchant, groceries & dry goods
Dowlin, Paul	Lincoln: Precinct 2	40	10,000	5,000	15,000	Pennsylvania	lumber merchant
Geck, Louis	Doña Ana: Doña Ana	52	5,000	10,000	15,000	Poland	dry goods merchant & retailer
Hecht, Jacob	San Miguel: Las Vegas	30	—	15,000	15,000	New York	dealer in general merchandise
Middaugh, Asa	Lincoln: Precinct 2	29	8,000	7,000	15,000	Pennsylvania	grocer
Vase, Rufus	Lincoln: Precinct 3	36	5,000	10,000	15,000	California	wholesale dry goods merchant
Raymond, Vaina	Socorro: Contadera	23	500	14,000	14,500	Switzerland	general merchant
DeHague, Joseph	San Miguel: Tecolote	36	4,000	9,000	13,000	Illinois	dealer in general merchandise
Maxwell, George	Doña Ana: Las Cruces	31	5,000	8,000	13,000	New York	dry goods merchant & retailer

Name	Location	Age				Origin	Occupation
Russell, Richard	San Miguel: Tecolote	31	4,000	9,000	13,000	Canada	dealer in general merchandise
Stephenson, Horace	Doña Ana: La Mesa	36	11,500	1,500	13,000	Mexico	dry goods merchant & retailer
Fritz, Emil	Lincoln: Fort Stanton	38	10,500	2,000	12,500	Germany	wholesale merchant
Murphy, Lawrence	Lincoln: Fort Stanton	35	10,500	2,000	12,500	Ireland	wholesale merchant
Grundyman, [Vinna]	Doña Ana: Las Cruces	31	10,000	2,000	12,000	Switzerland	dry goods merchant & retailer
Martinet, [Chaffee]	Doña Ana: Las Cruces	68	3,000	9,000	12,000	Italy	dry goods merchant & retailer
Goke, Henry	San Miguel: Sapillo	27	4,300	6,590	10,890	Prussia	dealer in general merchandise
Springer, Harry	Bernalillo: Albuquerque	39	150	10,000	10,150	Bavaria	retail merchant
Debus, Vandal	Santa Fe: Santa Fe	51	—	10,000	10,000	Hesse	wholesale merchant & retailer
Lowestein, Benjamin	Mora: Mora	40	5,000	5,000	10,000	Hesse	retail & dry goods merchant
Wheeler, Samuel	Santa Fe: Santa Fe	29	7,000	3,000	10,000	New York	wholesale merchant & retailer
Welsch, Charles	San Miguel: Las Vegas	39	—	9,510	9,510	Prussia	dealer in general merchandise
Eldadt, Nathan (Nicholas)[a]	Río Arriba: San Juan	30	300	9,000	9,300	Prussia	merchant
Clark, Louis[b]	Río Arriba: San Juan	35	1,000	8,000	9,000	Prussia	retail & dry goods merchant
Colman, Joseph	Colfax: Precinct 1	34	3,000	6,000	9,000	Prussia	dry goods merchant
Mignault, Theodore	Mora: Mora	46	1,500	7,500	9,000	Canada	retail merchant, groceries & dry goods
Huning, Louis	Valencia: Belén	36	1,500	6,000	7,500	Hanover	dry goods merchant & retailer
Barneville, John	Doña Ana: Doña Ana	37	3,000	4,000	7,000	Illinois	dry goods merchant & retailer
McMartin, Samuel	Mora: Loma Parda	45	4,000	3,000	7,000	Canada	retail merchant
Knauer, Ferdinand	San Miguel: Las Vegas	40	4,000	2,900	6,900	Prussia	dealer in general merchandise
Joseph, Juan B.	Taos: San Fernando	23	4,000	2,500	6,500	Missouri	general merchant & retailer
Rosenwald, Emanuel	San Miguel: Las Vegas	32	—	6,400	6,400	Bavaria	dealer in general merchandise
Grant, William	Grant: Ralston City	38	3,000	3,000	6,000	Scotland	dry goods merchant & retailer
Messick, [Eric] F.	Colfax: Precinct 1	36	400	5,000	5,400	Maryland	retail merchant
Pape, Gorgous	Taos: San Fernando	45	1,200	4,200	5,400	France	cattle merchant
Blazer, Daniel	Lincoln: Precinct 4	45	3,000	2,000	5,000	Iowa	lumber merchant
Carter, Charles	Mora: Golondrinas	29	2,500	2,500	5,000	Bohemia	retail merchant
Clouthier, Joseph	Taos: San Fernando	34	1,000	4,000	5,000	Canada	general merchant & retailer

[Dufralde], Pedro	Doña Ana: Mesilla	40	300	4,700	5,000	France	dry goods merchant
Hyman, Rinaldo	Santa Fe: Santa Fe	27	—	5,000	5,000	Russia	merchant & retailer
Michaelis, Aaron	Santa Fe: Santa Fe	28	—	5,000	5,000	Prussia	merchant
Trudell, Charles	Socorro: La Joya	39	1,000	4,000	5,000	Berlin	general merchant
Webb, Sidney M.	Grant: Mimbres	33	2,000	3,000	5,000	Ohio	dry goods retailers
Nelson, Andrés	Albuquerque: Bernalillo	29	—	4,600	4,600	Denmark	wool merchant
Dickson, Robert	Lincoln: Precinct 4	41	3,000	1,500	4,500	Alabama	lumber merchant
Nesmith, George	Lincoln: Precinct 4	35	3,000	1,500	4,500	Ohio	lumber merchant
Huning, Henry	Valencia: Cubero	28	250	4,000	4,250	Prussia	dry goods merchant & retailer
Chisom, P. W.	Lincoln: Precinct 3	35	1,500	2,500	4,000	Texas	wholesale dry good merchant
Grisdorf, Alejandro	Santa Fe: Santa Fe	21	—	4,000	4,000	Prussia	wholesale & retail merchant
Maxwell, Ferdinand	Taos: El Rancho	59	3,000	1,000	4,000	Illinois	merchant (retired)
Schiffer, Herman	Colfax: Precinct 1	25	1,000	3,000	4,000	Bavaria	dry goods merchant
Bourgignon, Philip	Socorro: Limitar	42	2,000	1,500	3,500	Hesse	general merchant
Schwartz, Jacob	Valencia: Los Lunas	36	400	3,000	3,400	Austria	dry goods merchant & retailer
Stern, Isidore	San Miguel: Las Vegas	29	—	3,400	3,400	Prussia	dealer in general merchandise
Barth, Solomon	Valencia: Cubero	28	300	3,000	3,300	Prussia	dry goods merchant & retailer
Dougherty, James	Mora: San Antonio	26	2,000	1,025	3,025	Ireland	retail merchant, groceries & dry goods
Boiseller, Julius	Lincoln: Precinct 4	33	—	3,000	3,000	France	retail dry good merchant
Burns, Thomas D.	Río Arriba: Abiquiú	28	—	3,000	3,000	Ireland	retail merchant
Desmarais, Frederick	San Miguel: Las Vegas	30	1,550	1,450	3,000	Canada	dealer in general merchandise
Ely, Simeon	Doña Ana: Picacho	24	1,000	2,000	3,000	Ohio	dry goods merchant & retailer
Geofrian, Octave	San Miguel: Las Vegas	32	1,550	1,450	3,000	Canada	dealer in general merchandise
Hopkins, Caleb	Colfax: Precinct 1	40	1,000	2,000	3,000	Illinois	retail merchant
McCulloch, Jim B.	Colfax: Precinct 1	26	1,000	2,000	3,000	Pennsylvania	retail merchant
Seligman, Adolf	Colfax: Precinct 1	27	2,000	1,000	3,000	Hesse	dry goods merchant
Woods, James B.	Grant: Pinos Altos	26	100	2,900	3,000	Arkansas	dry goods merchant & retailer
Warden, John	Mora: Golondrinas	36	300	2,400	2,700	Ohio	retail merchant
Obermeyer, Hermann	Mora: San Antonio	40	1,000	1,550	2,550	Prussia	retail merchant, groceries & dry goods
Constant, Louis	Santa Fe: Santa Fe	53	2,500	—	2,500	Missouri	merchant
Jeaneret, Jules	Doña Ana: Mesilla	37	500	2,000	2,500	Switzerland	dry goods merchant and retailer

Olendorf, Meyer	Mora: Mora	29	2,000	500	2,500	Prussia	retail merchant, groceries & dry goods
Harrison, John	San Miguel: Antón Chico	52	530	1,500	2,030	England	dealer in general merchandise
Audital, Arnold	Doña Ana: Las Cruces	21	—	2,000	2,000	Switzerland	dry goods merchant & retailer
Baker, Henry	San Miguel: San José	32	—	2,000	2,000	Prussia	merchant in dry goods
Bassie, Alexander	Grant: Ralston City	35	—	2,000	2,000	Canada	retail grocer
Gould, Aaron	Santa Fe: Santa Fe	25	—	2,000	2,000	Poland	merchant & retailer
Hattenback, Isaac	Colfax: Precinct 1	32	1,000	1,000	2,000	Prussia	dry goods merchant
Ilfeld, Herman	Santa Fe: Santa Fe	28	—	2,000	2,000	Prussia	store clerk
Merletti, Juan B.	Taos: San Fernando	45	500	1,500	2,000	Italy	general merchant & retailer
St. John, Marshall	Grant: Mimbres	33	1,000	1,000	2,000	New York	dry goods retailer
Thompson, William	Grant: Pinos Altos	38	—	2,000	2,000	Tennessee	dry goods merchant & retailer
Boquet, John	Santa Fe: Pojoaque	46	1,500	400	1,900	France	retail merchant
Grant, William	Bernalillo: Albuquerque	45	800	1,000	1,800	Prussia	retail merchant
Kohn, Louis	San Miguel: Sapillo	41	1,500	200	1,700	Bavaria	merchant (retired)
Mercure, Henry	Río Arriba: Tierra Amarilla	48	500	1,200	1,700	Canada	retail merchant
Fisher, M.	Taos: Picuris	30	—	1,500	1,500	Prussia	merchant
Sulzbacher, Louis	Mora: Ocate	27	400	1,000	1,400	Bavaria	retail grocer
Brewert, Elias	Socorro: Polvareda	47	—	1,200	1,200	Michigan	general merchant
Jeffords, Thomas	Socorro: Polvareda	34	—	1,200	1,200	New York	general merchant
Moreno, Charles	Grant: Pinos Altos	44	100	1,000	1,100	Italy	dry goods merchant & retailer
Bibo, Nathan	Valencia: Seboyeta	27	500	500	1,000	Prussia	dry goods merchant & retailer
Carver, Albert	Colfax: Precinct 1	30	1,000	—	1,000	Massachusetts	retail merchant
Keene, Charles L.	Grant: Fort Bayard	28	—	1,000	1,000	Hanover	dry goods merchant & retailer
Knox, David	Grant: Fort Bayard	38	—	1,000	1,000	Virginia	dry goods merchant & retailer
Moses, Stephen	Río Arriba: Abiquiú	23	—	1,000	1,000	New Hampshire	retail merchant
Rosenstein, Simon	Santa Fe: Santa Fe	54	1,000	—	1,000	Hanover	wholesale merchant & retailer
Friedman, Julius	Taos: San Fernando	34	300	400	700	Silesia	general merchant & retailer
Hefner, Augustus	Grant: Ralston City	23	200	500	700	Illinois	dry goods merchant & retailer
Libel, George	Grant: Ralston City	22	—	800	800	Canada	retail grocer
Fortune, Therese	Socorro: Socorro	45	—	600	600	Ireland	general merchant
Bibo, Samuel	Valencia: Seboyeta	19	—	500	500	Prussia	dry goods merchant & retailer
Bibo, Simon	Valencia: Seboyeta	23	—	500	500	Prussia	dry goods merchant & retailer

Name	Location	Age				Origin	Occupation
Lowestein, Solomon	Lincoln: La Cueva	39	—	500	500	Hessia	retail grocer
Zigmond, Richard	Grant: Silver City	42	300	200	500	Canada	dry goods merchant & retailer
Valentín, Luis	San Miguel: San José	38	300	—	300	France	merchant (retired)
Ilfeld, Noah	Santa Fe: Santa Fe	20	—	200	200	Prussia	store clerk
Eldadt, Marcus	Río Arriba: San Juan	27	—	—	—	Prussia	retail merchant
Frankenthal, Simon	Mora: San Antonio	30	—	—	—	Prussia	retail merchant, groceries & dry goods
Hersch, Joseph	Santa Fe: Santa Fe	55	—	—	—	Russia	merchant & retailer
Ilfeld, Charles	San Miguel: Las Vegas	23	—	—	—	Prussia	dealer in general merchandise
Koste, Henry	Mora: Mora	30	—	—	—	Prussia	retail merchant, groceries & dry goods
McMartin, Adam	Mora: Loma Parda	33	—	—	—	Canada	retail merchant
Meyer, Frederick	Mora: Mora	37	—	—	—	Germany	retail merchant, groceries & dry goods
Olendorf, [Pastoll]	Mora: Mora	26	—	—	—	Prussia	retail merchant, groceries & dry goods
Rohman, Anthony	Mora: Mora	67	—	—	—	Bavaria	retail merchant, groceries & dry goods
St Vrain, Ceran	Mora: Mora	67	—	—	—	Illinois	retail merchant, groceries & dry goods
St Vrain, Vicente	Mora: Mora	43	—	—	—	New Mexico	retail merchant, groceries & dry goods
Wedeles, Sigmund	Mora: Mora	34	—	—	—	Bavaria	retail merchant, groceries & dry goods
Zuckenberg, Marcus	San Miguel: Las Vegas	23	—	—	—	Prussia	dealer in general merchandise

[a]Enumerators listed him twice — once as Nathan, another time as Nicholas.

[b]Census enumerators listed him twice. As a county resident his assets were reported to be $1,000 in real estate and $8,000 in personal estate; as a resident of the San Juan Pueblo his assets were $4,000 both for real and personal estate.

Appendix 5
Hispano Freighters Listed in the 1870 Census
(Sorted alphabetically)

Name	County of Residence: Precinct or Town	Age	Real Estate ($)	Personal Estate ($)	Total Assets ($)
Abeita, Antonio	Santa Fe: Santa Fe	33	3,500	2,500	5,000
Amador, Martín	Doña Ana: Mesilla	33	7,000	7,000	14,000
Aragón, José	San Miguel: Antón Chico	38	400	1,022	1,422
Armijo, Gerónimo	Socorro: La Joyita	18	—	—	—
Baca, Fernando	San Miguel: El Tecolotito	25	500	775	1,275
Baca, José	Socorro: Precinct 1	26	1,000	1,000	2,000
Baca, Luciano	Santa Fe: Santa Fe	31	1,500	1,500	3,000
Baca, Mariano	Socorro: La Joya	27	300	700	1,000
Baca, Pascual	San Miguel: Antón Chico	36	1,000	1,300	2,300
Baca, Rómulo	Socorro: Las Nutrias	30	1,000	1,000	2,000
Baca y Ortiz, Manuel	San Miguel: Las Vegas	29	500	1,000	1,500
Barela, Esteban	Bernalillo: Los Ranchos	27	500	1,800	2,300
Chávez, Dionisio	Valencia: Gabaldones	35	200	2,000	2,200
Chávez, Ermenegildo	Doña Ana: Mesilla	35	5,000	1,500	6,500
Chávez, Pablo	Valencia: Casa Colorada	36	500	1,600	2,100
Chávez, [Reducindo]	Valencia: Tomé	49	500	1,200	1,700
Contreras, José	Socorro: La Joya	26	500	—	500
Contreras, Matías	Socorro: La Joya	35	1,000	2,000	3,000
Córdoba, Tomás	Socorro: La Joya	36	200	800	1,000
Delgado, Ismael	San Miguel: Las Vegas	38	200	300	500
García, Blas	Bernalillo: Corrales	30	200	1,000	1,200
García, Ponce	Valencia: Casa Colorada	26	150	200	350
González, Antonio	Socorro: Alamosita	30	300	1,200	1,500
González, Estanislao	Socorro: Contadera	37	100	1,200	1,300
González, Juan	Santa Fe: Santa Fe	45	1,000	2,000	3,000
González, Santiago	Socorro: Contadera	69	1,000	8,000	9,000
Gutiérrez, Tomás	Bernalillo: Los Griegos	30	1,000	4,000	5,000
Jaramillo, Abraham	Valencia: Los Lunas	39	1,000	5,000	6,000
Jaramillo, Laureano	Valencia: Tomé	27	800	1,800	2,600
[Loyola], Pascual	Socorro: Alamosita	44	400	—	400
Lucero, Fernández	Santa Ana: Cochití	28	500	500	1,000
Luna, Jesús	Socorro: Limitar	23	—	5,800	5,800
Luna, Jesús María	Valencia: Los Lunas	32	1,000	3,000	4,000
Luna, Patrocinio	Valencia: Jarales	26	—	1,500	1,500

Luna, Santiago	Valencia: Los Lunas	34	1,000	3,000	4,000
Luna, Santiago	Valencia: Los Lunas	34	1,000	3,600	4,600
Martín, Ramón	Santa Fe: Santa Fe	60	840	800	1,640
Martín, Rómulo	Santa Fe: Santa Fe	29	—	600	600
Martínez, Nicolás	San Miguel: Antón Chico	25	200	300	500
Montoya, Anastasio	Valencia: Tomé	38	1,000	1,000	2,000
Montoya, Feliciano	Santa Ana: Cochití	26	500	500	1,000
Montoya, Francisco	Santa Fe: Santa Fe	36	300	1,000	1,300
Olguín, Jesús de la Cruz	Socorro: Valverde	26	—	—	—
Otero, Narciso	San Miguel: Las Vegas	29	100	1,060	1,160
Pino, Francisco	Socorro: Precinct 1	30	400	100	500
Rael, Candelario	San Miguel: Antón Chico	30	200	500	700
Rivera, Juan	San Miguel: Las Vegas	47	351	4,464	4,815
Romero, Esquipulo	Santa Ana: Lemitas	30	—	1,500	1,500
Romero, Miguel	Valencia: Los Lunas	40	500	4,000	4,500
Romero, Nicanor	Valencia: Gabaldones	29	—	1,000	1,000
Romero, Toribio	Valencia: Los Lunas	42	500	4,000	4,500
Sainz, Casimiro	Valencia: Casa Colorada	24	—	500	500
Sainz, Pilar	Valencia: Casa Colorada	25	200	1,000	1,200
Salas, Bernabel	Valencia: Manzano	40	500	1,000	1,500
Salas, Felix	Valencia: Tomé	34	300	500	800
Salas, Higinio	Valencia: Gabaldones	40	500	1,000	1,500
Salazar, Aniceto	San Miguel: Sapello	34	300	200	500
Salazar, Antonio	Valencia: Los Lunas	33	300	1,000	1,300
Salazar, Jesús	Valencia: Precinct 1	34	1,000	500	1,500
Salazar, José Rómulo	Valencia: Tomé	47	600	3,000	3,600
Salazar, Manuel	Valencia: Los Lunas	35	600	376	976
Salazar, Manuel	Valencia: Tomé	33	300	1,000	1,300
Sánchez, Anastasio	San Miguel: Tecolote	31	300	300	600
Sánchez, Desiderio	Valencia: Gabaldones	37	2,000	6,000	8,000
Sánchez, José	Valencia: Gabaldones	30	—	—	—
Sánchez, Juan	San Miguel: Antón Chico	40	500	1,250	1,750
Sánchez, Manuel	Valencia: Precinct 1	35	1,000	3,000	4,000
Trujillo, Andrés	San Miguel: Las Vegas	60	300	200	500
Ulibarri, José F.	San Miguel: Chaperito	47	500	2,000	2,500
Vigil, Martín	Valencia: Gabaldones	36	400	1,200	1,600
Yrizarri, Manuel	Bernalillo: Los Ranchos	29	1,000	3,000	4,000

Notes

1. Fort Collins, Colorado State University, Special Collections, Mexican Archives of New Mexico (hereafter MANM), roll 23, frames 705–10.

2. Pino was not using the term "capitalist" as we would today (to describe one who is involved in an economic system characterized by private ownership of goods, by investments that are determined by private decisions rather than by state control, and by prices, production, and distribution of goods that are determined mainly by the free market), but simply to describe one who owned capital. Unwittingly, by choosing the word "capitalist" instead of other more frequently used terms, such as *comerciantes*, *negociantes*, *habitantes*, or *residentes*, Pino predicted the nature of the mercantile system that would characterize New Mexico.

3. Nearly all of the studies published focus exclusively on the route between Missouri and Santa Fe, "foreign" traders and freighters, and the period prior to the Mexican War (1821–46). Jack Rittenhouse's fine *The Santa Fe Trail: A Historical Bibliography* (Albuquerque: University of New Mexico Press, 1971) is entirely devoted to materials pertinent to the trail.

4. The terms "New Mexican" and "Hispano" are used interchangeably to identify individuals with Hispanic names living and working in New Mexico. It is not always possible to establish if individuals were born in the province, but for the purpose of this study, such distinctions are not always necessary. Likewise, the terms "Anglo" and "foreigner" are used to identify traders whose last names are indicative of non-Hispanic origins.

5. Few scholars have examined New Mexicans in the context of the Santa Fe Trail. However, David A. Sandoval has completed a dissertation, "Trade and the *Manito* Society in New Mexico, 1821–1848" (University of Utah, 1978), which addresses some of the issues raised in this study. He has also written a series of articles on New Mexican merchants: "Who is Riding the Burro Now? A Biblio-

graphical Critique of Scholarship on the New Mexico Trader," *The Santa Fe Trail: New Perspectives*, ed. David Wetzel, *Essays and Monographs in Colorado History* 6 (1987): 75–92; "Montezuma's Merchants: Mexican Traders on the Santa Fe Trail," in *Adventure on the Santa Fe Trail*, ed. Leo Oliva (Topeka: Kansas State Historical Society, 1988), 37–60; and "Gnats, Goods, and Greasers: Mexican Merchants on the Santa Fe Trail,"*Journal of the West* 28 (April 1989): 22–31. Jere Krakow is another scholar who has examined New Mexican merchants in "Hispanic Influence on the Santa Fe Trail," *Courier* (October 1991): 21–23. Marc Simmons also made available to me a copy of "The Mexican Side of the Santa Fe Trail," a paper he presented at Rendezvous 1980, Larned, Kansas, 28 March 1980. Maurilio E. Vigil examines those merchants who operated out of Las Vegas ("New Mexicans, Las Vegas, and the Santa Fe Trail," *Wagon Tracks* 10 [February 1996]: 17–22). William Patrick O'Brien stresses that regardless of their ethnic origin cooperation was essential among merchants associated with the Santa Fe trade ("Independence, Missouri's Trade with Mexico, 1827–1860: A Study in International Consensus and Cooperation" [Ph.D. diss., University of Colorado, 1994], 5–15, 169, 252–56).

6. According to dependency theory, uneven development is caused by the expansion of developed states into undeveloped areas. As developed states expand, they rely on resources from undeveloped regions to further their own development. First, this entails direct seizure of territory and resources; then, capitalist trade (Thomas D. Hall, *Social Change in the Southwest, 1350–1880* [Lawrence: University Press of Kansas, 1989], 12; Jorge Larrain, *Theories of Development: Capitalism, Colonialism, and Dependency* [Cambridge, UK: Polity Press, 1989], 14–15, 109–15, 117–211).

7. For an examination of the equally complex commercial activities of Missouri merchants, see O'Brien, "Independence," 217–49. Lewis E. Atherton was aware of the need to expand the geographic boundaries of the trail, as he noted that "the annual Santa Fe caravans carried goods that often originated in American seaboard cities and from abroad, and that much of the proceeds from such trade returned to those same points" ("The Santa Fe Trader as Mercantile Capitalist," *Missouri Historical Review* 77 [October 1982]: 2). Unfortunately Atherton's work focuses exclusively on Anglo merchants before the Mexican War and ignores the trade with Mexico.

8. Mark Gardner, "Locomotives, Oxen, and Freight: The Last Decade of the Santa Fe Trail," summary of a presentation proposed for the Western History Association Meeting, Albuquerque, New Mexico, October 1994; Darlis A. Miller notes the magnitude of the expenditures incurred by the United States Army Quartermaster's Department for supplies, labor, and transportation during the 1860s (*Soldiers and Settlers: Military Supply in the Southwest, 1861–1885* [Albuquerque: University of New Mexico Press, 1989], 349–55).

9. William J. Parish, *The Charles Ilfeld Company: A Study of the Rise and Decline of Mercantile Capitalism in New Mexico*, Harvard Studies in Business History 20 (Cambridge: Harvard University Press, 1961), passim; "The German Jew and the Com-

mercial Revolution in Territorial New Mexico, 1850–1900," *New Mexico Historical Review* 35 (1960): 1–29, 129–51. I have discovered that when I describe the commercial activities of the New Mexican merchants, other scholars wonder if these New Mexicans might have been crypto-Jews. It is a possibility in some cases, although subtle anti-Semitism is also present in certain of the documents. (See chapter 6, particularly note 51.)

10. Sandra Jaramillo has found a few examples from Río Arriba where women asserted their rights to their property (Personal communication, October 1995).

11. This has been documented for the previous century for trading families in the French settlements along the Mississippi River (Susan Calafate Boyle, "Did She Generally Decide? Women in Ste. Genevieve, 1750–1805," *The William and Mary Quarterly* 64 [October 1987]: 777–89).

12. William G. Robbins, "Laying Siege to Western History: The Emergence of New Paradigms," in *Trails: Toward a New Western History*, ed. Patricia Nelson Limerick, Clyde A. Milner II, and Charles E. Rankin, 182–214 (Lawrence: University of Kansas Press, 1991), 198.

CHAPTER ONE

1. Pedro Bautista Pino's book, *Exposición sucinta y sencilla de la provincia de Nuevo México*, originally published in 1812, is printed in its original form in *Three New Mexico Chronicles*, ed. and trans. H. Bailey Carroll and J. Villasana Haggard, 211–61 (New York: Arno Press, 1967), 224–25.

2. Ross Harold Frank maintains that the Bourbon reforms during the second half of the eighteenth century fostered the growth of the local New Mexican economy and its integration into the larger regional commercial system of northern Mexico ("From Settler to Citizen: Economic Development and Cultural Change in Late Colonial New Mexico, 1750–1820" [Ph.D. diss., University of California, Berkeley, 1992]).

3. Frances V. Scholes, "The Supply Service of the New Mexican Missions in the Seventeenth Century," *New Mexico Historical Review* 5 (1930): 93–115, 186–210, 386–404; Max L. Moorhead, *New Mexico's Royal Road: Trade and Travel on the Chihuahua Trail* (Norman: University of Oklahoma Press, 1958), 34–35, 40–43; John O. Baxter, *Las Carneradas: Sheep Trade in New Mexico, 1700–1860* (Albuquerque: University of New Mexico Press, 1987), 79; Alfred Barnaby Thomas, ed. and trans., *Forgotten Frontiers: A Study of the Spanish Indian Policy of Don Juan Bautista de Anza, Governor of New Mexico, 1777–1787* (Norman: University of Oklahoma Press, 1932), 178, 180, 345; Ralph Emerson Twitchell, comp., *The Spanish Archives of New Mexico*, 2 vols. (New York: Arno Press, 1976) (hereafter SANM), 1: 1299, 1342. The two other pre-Columbian routes were the West Mexican Interior Trail, and the Mexican Coastal Trail. These trails greatly facilitated the spread of Mesoamerican culture, agriculture, and religion (Larry Walsh, "A Public Report," in *Archaeological Survey Project on El Camino Real de Tierra Adentro* [New Mexico State Historic

Preservation Division, 1991], 2, 7–8). For a brief discussion of the breakdown of trade patterns and their impact on Pueblo society before the arrival of the Spanish, see T. D. Hall, *Social Change*, 43–48.

4. Scholes, "Mission Supply Service," 187–88; Moorhead, *Royal Road*, 28–35; SANM, 1: 1342; Walsh, "Public Report," 7–8.

5. Scholes, "Mission Supply Service," 188; Moorhead, *Royal Road*, 34, 49. Frank indicates that in 1787 there was a proposal for increasing the frequency of the caravans to twice a year, but the second convoy was temporarily suspended shortly after. Walsh states that by the middle of the eighteenth century a civil caravan service was instituted on an annual basis ("Public Report," 9). Zebulon Pike reported that by 1806 the caravan left twice a year (Frank, "From Settler to Citizen," 248–49).

6. James E. Ivey, "In the Midst of a Loneliness: The Architectural History of the Salinas Missions," Southwest Cultural Resources Center, Professional Paper No. 15. Second Printing (Santa Fe, NM: National Park Service, 1991), 206. For a general description of the local products that were being exported, see Lansing Bartlett Bloom, "A Trade Invoice of 1638," *New Mexico Historical Review* 10 (1935): 242–48. Frank claims that the value and volume of New Mexican manufactures exported between 1780 and 1820 were substantial, the value surpassing 100,000 pesos a year ("From Settler to Citizen," 248–54). If this were indeed the case, it would mean that the production and export of efectos del país would have declined dramatically throughout the 1820s, 1830s, and 1840s since the value of all of the combined shipments to Mexico during those decades amounted to less than 80,000 pesos.

7. SANM, 2: 327, 456, 514, 1304, 1324; Henri Folmer, "Contraband Trade Between Louisiana and New Mexico in the Eighteenth Century," *New Mexico Historical Review* 16 (1941): 249–74, "The Mallet Expedition of 1739 Through Nebraska, Kansas, and Colorado to Santa Fe," *The Colorado Magazine* 16 (1939): 161–73; Abraham P. Nasatir, *Borderland in Retreat: From Spanish Louisiana to the Far Southwest* (Albuquerque: University of New Mexico Press, 1976), 86–106; Marc Simmons, *New Mexico: A Bicentennial History* (New York: W. W. Norton and Company, 1977), 79–81; Luis Navarro García, "The North of New Spain as a Political Problem in the Eighteenth Century," in *New Spain's Far Northern Frontier: Essays on Spain in the American West, 1540–1821*, ed. David J. Weber (Albuquerque: University of New Mexico Press, 1979), 205; R. L. Duffus, *The Santa Fe Trail* (New York: Longmans, Green, and Co., 1930), 19–27; Moorhead, *Royal Road*, 55–56.

8. After 1795 there appears to have been a growing number of Frenchmen coming to Santa Fe (SANM, 2: 1888, 1942, 2010, 2023, 2090, 2484, 2565, 2646); Isaac Joslin Cox, "Opening the Santa Fe Trail," *Missouri Historical Review* 25 (1930): 30–66. Noel M. Loomis and Abraham P. Nasatir *(Pedro Vial and the Roads to Santa Fe* [Norman: University of Oklahoma Press, 1967], 110–136) provide a detailed account of the diplomatic, political, and economic factors leading to increased French presence in the New Mexican territory. See also George Ulibarri, "The Chouteau–

DeMun Expedition to New Mexico, 1815–1817," *New Mexico Historical Review* 36 (1961): 263–73; William E. Foley and C. David Rice, *The First Chouteaus: River Barons of Early St. Louis* (Urbana: University of Illinois Press, 1983), 176.

9. SANM, 2: 1871, 1900, 1925 (32), 2009, 2291, 2340, 2714; Donald Dean Jackson, ed., *The Journals of Zebulon Montgomery Pike: With Letters and Related Documents,* 2 vols. (Norman: University of Oklahoma Press, 1966); Cox, "Opening the Trail," 46–66; Loomis and Nasatir, *Pedro Vial,* 12–13, 137–261.

10. For Anza's claim, see A. B. Thomas, *Forgotten Frontiers,* 367; Navarro García, "North of New Spain"; SANM, 2: 1187, 1322, 1333; George P. Hammond, "The Zuñiga Journal, Tucson to Santa Fe: The Opening of a Spanish Trade Route, 1788–1795," *New Mexico Historical Review* 6 (1931): 40–65. For Mares's trip, see Loomis and Nasatir, *Pedro Vial,* 288–315. Joseph Miguel's expedition is mentioned in SANM, 2: 1490. For a reference to Amangual's trip, see SANM, 2: 2139; Loomis and Nasatir, *Pedro Vial,* 459–534.

11. Loomis and Nasatir, *Pedro Vial,* provides the most complete account of the extensive travels of Pedro Vial; SANM, 2: 1187, 1321, 1322, 1323, 1333, 1953; Simmons, *New Mexico,* 95–96.

12. Frank hypothesizes that during the Bourbon period New Mexico became part of a growing inter-regional economy centered in Chihuahua, with important nodes in Parral, Durango, and the northern line of presidios ("From Settler to Citizen," 20).

13. For an excellent summary of the impact of Indian attacks on the province's economy, see Frank, "From Settler to Citizen," 34–64.

14. Spanish documents referred to the Indians as *naciones bárbaras, indios bárbaros, salvajes,* or *gentiles.* Spaniards, Mexicans, Americans, and the Indians themselves participated in slave trading, a nefarious activity that continued to be quite common at least through the 1850s. See Leland Hargrave Creer, "Spanish-American Slave Trade in the Great Basin, 1800–1853," *New Mexico Historical Review* 24 (1949): 171–83; Marc Simmons, *The Little Lion of the Southwest: A Life of Manuel Antonio Chaves* (Chicago: Swallow Press, 1973), 34–37; T. D. Hall, *Social Change,* 123–28, 168–69.

15. For proceedings against "embarrassing" and illegal trading, see SANM, 2: 185, 339, 340, 402, 403, 414, 429, 497, 530, 740, 912, 913, 920, 1393, 2511; A. B. Thomas, *Forgotten Frontiers,* 300–301, 306; William B. Griffen, *Utmost Good Faith: Patterns of Apache-Mexican Hostilities in Northern Chihuahua Border Warfare, 1821–1848* (Albuquerque: University of New Mexico Press, 1988), 6–7; Navarro García, "North of New Spain," 210–12; A. B. Thomas, *Forgotten Frontiers,* 380; SANM, 1: 1393, 1670a, 1953; Foley and Rice, *River Barons,* 123. Loomis and Nasatir claimed that the Spaniards did not want to rid New Mexico of the Indian menace, for most of the Indians made periodic trips to the settlements to conduct fairs of their own and traded valuable furs for trinkets (*Pedro Vial,* 16–17).

16. Loomis and Nasatir, *Pedro Vial,* 77–78, 80. The Spanish Archive of New Mexico contains a large number of records documenting the resources spent in

buying gifts and trying to pacify the various tribes (SANM, 2: 1025, 1228, 1287a, 1303a, 1320, 1366, 1395, 1400, 1410, 1428, 1513, 1633, 1769, 2076). After 1800 hostilities seem to have risen, and by 1806 the Navajo chiefs were demanding gifts (SANM, 2: 1985; Griffen, *Good Faith*, 12–18; Frances Leon Swadesh, *Los Primeros Pobladores: Hispanic Americans of the Ute Frontier* [Notre Dame: University of Notre Dame Press, 1974], 24–25, 163–70).

   17. Frank, "From Settler to Citizen," 42–43; Duffus, *Santa Fe Trail*, 27; William deBuys, *Enchantment and Exploitation: The Life and Hard Times of a New Mexico Mountain Range* (Albuquerque: University of New Mexico Press, 1985), 69, 75, 94, 97; Creer, "Slave Trade," 171–83; Simmons, *New Mexico*, 85–86; A. B. Thomas, *Forgotten Frontiers*, 306. Taos remained the most important fur-trading center in the southern Rockies throughout the 1820s and 1830s (deBuys, *Enchantment and Exploitation*, 94; Lansing Bartlett Bloom, "New Mexico under Mexican Administration, 1821–1846," *Old Santa Fe* 1 [July 1913]: 39–40; Marc Simmons, "Trade Fairs and Markets in New Mexico: Tracing the Roots of Trading from the Aztecs to the Spanish Culture," *Inside Santa Fe and Taos* [July 1993]).

   18. Peter Gerhard, *The Northern Frontier of New Spain* (Princeton: Princeton University Press, 1982), 161–243; Oakah L. Jones, *Nueva Vizcaya: Heartland of the Spanish Frontier* (Albuquerque: University of New Mexico Press, 1988), 117–47; Baxter, *Las Carneradas*, 42–43; Marc Simmons, *Spanish Government in New Mexico* (Albuquerque: University of New Mexico Press, 1968), 12–13, 72–73; Moorhead, *Royal Road*, 49–54. In 1805 the viceroy decreed that all goods bartered by New Mexicans at the annual fair in the San Bartolomé Valley (today's Valle de Allende) would be free from the payment of *alcabala* (excise tax) (L. B. Bloom, "Mexican Administration," (1913): 40).

   19. David A. Sandoval notes that *"gachupín"* is a Nahuatl term that means "one who wears spurs" (Review of *Comerciantes, Arrieros, y Peones: The Hispanos and the Santa Fe Trade*, by Susan Calafate Boyle, *Folio* [November 1995]: 12–13). Nevertheless, the term remains an apt one in this context since Spanish merchants were perceived as oppressors throughout the Spanish empire in Latin America.

   20. Enrique Florescano, "The Hacienda in New Spain," in *Colonial Spanish America*, ed. Leslie Bethell (London: Cambridge University Press, 1987), 275–76; Henry Bamford Parkes, *A History of Mexico* (Boston: Houghton Mifflin Company, 1969), 100–104.

   21. Florescano, "Hacienda in New Spain," 276; Lillian E. Fisher, "Commercial Conditions in Mexico at the End of the Colonial Period," *New Mexico Historical Review* 7 (1932): 143–64; Parkes, *History of Mexico*, 104.

   22. MANM, roll 9, frames 1142–43; Moorhead, *Royal Road*, 49–52; Jones, *Nueva Vizcaya*, 122, 186–88; Baxter, *Las Carneradas*, 43.

   23. Murdo J. Macleod ("Aspects of the Internal Economy," in *Colonial Spanish America*, ed. Leslie Bethell, 315–60 [Cambridge, UK: Cambridge University Press, 1987], 359–60) discusses how the *peso fuerte* or *peso de a ocho*, a silver coin divided into eight reales, was often cut with a cold chisel in two parts to make *tostones*, or in eight

"bits" or reales; A. B. Thomas, *Forgotten Frontiers*, 113–14; Loomis and Nasatir, *Pedro Vial*, 5; Hubert H. Bancroft, *History of Arizona and New Mexico, 1530–1888* (San Francisco: History Company, 1889), 277–78; SANM, 2: 247; Moorhead, *Royal Road*, 50.

24. Moorhead documented the extent of New Mexicans' increasing economic dependence on Chihuahua's merchants, particularly as they obtained contracts to supply the garrison at New Mexico (*Royal Road*, 52–54).

25. Florescano, "Hacienda in New Spain," 275–77; Marc Simmons, ed. and trans., *Fray Juan Agustín de Morfi's Account of Disorders in New Mexico, 1778* (Isleta, NM: Historical Society of New Mexico, 1977), 14–21. The practice of mortgaging crops years in advance would continue through the nineteenth century (see chapter 7, this work, and particularly the Rafael Armijo Papers [Santa Fe, New Mexico, New Mexico State Records Center and Archives (hereafter SRC)]).

26. Moorhead, *Royal Road*, 49.

27. Every European government during the sixteenth, seventeenth, and eighteenth centuries, followed mercantilism. This economic policy meant that the state directed all economic activities within its borders, theoretically subordinating private profit to public good. In particular, governments sought to increase national wealth by discouraging imports and encouraging exports.

28. Fisher, "Commercial Conditions," 145; Charles C. Cumberland, *Mexico: The Struggle for Modernity* (New York: Oxford University Press, 1968), 84–112; Parkes, *History of Mexico*, 100–104; Loomis and Nasatir, *Pedro Vial*, 5–6.

29. Macleod, "Internal Economy," 340–41; Parkes, *History of Mexico*, 100.

30. Macleod, "Internal Economy," 340–41; Fisher, "Commercial Conditions," 146–47; Parkes, *History of Mexico*, 100. For a detailed discussion of the taxation in the Spanish colonies, see C. H. Haring, *The Spanish Empire in America* (New York: Harcourt, Brace and World, 1947), 256–78.

31. Fisher, "Commercial Conditions," 146–47; Haring, *Spanish Empire*, 256–78; Macleod, "Internal Economy," 340–43; Parkes, *History of Mexico*, 100–101.

32. Fisher, "Commercial Conditions," 147.

33. Fisher, "Commercial Conditions," 147; Macleod, "Internal Economy," 342–45; Parkes, *History of Mexico*, 100–101; Simmons, *Spanish Government*, 90–111.

34. Frank, "From Settler to Citizen," 86–154.

35. Frank, "From Settler to Citizen," 86–154.

36. Baxter, *Las Carneradas*, 44–60.

37. SANM, 2: 1844.

38. L. B. Bloom, "Mexican Administration," 47–49; David J. Weber, *The Mexican Frontier, 1821–1846: The American Southwest Under Mexico* (Albuquerque: University of New Mexico Press, 1982), 16–17; Simmons, *New Mexico*, 105–6. For a description of the political system as it operated in New Mexico between 1821 and 1846, see Ralph Emerson Twitchell, *Leading Facts of New Mexican History* (Albuquerque: Horn and Wallace), 2: 9–16.

39. New Mexico was one of the *Provincias Internas* until 1824. In that year it was

joined to the provinces of Chihuahua and Durango to form the *Estado Interno del Norte*. The people of Durango protested vehemently, so finally Chihuahua and Durango were made into states, while New Mexico came to be a territory of the Mexican republic. With the constitution of 1836 the territory was changed into a department (Twitchell, *Leading Facts*, 2: 7–8; Weber, *Mexican Frontier*, 25).

40. Pino was also selected as New Mexico's representative in 1820 but was unable to make the trip to Spain due to lack of financial resources (SANM, 2: 2937, 2940, 2993; Weber, *Mexican Frontier*, 18–19; Simmons, *New Mexico*, 105–6; Pino, *Exposición*, in Carroll and Haggard, *Three Chronicles*, 224–25.

41. Pino listed *bayetones* (large woolen ponchos), *sargas* (serge), *frazadas* (blankets), *sarapes*, *bayetas* (baize), *sayales* (coarse woolen cloth), *gergas* (another type of coarse woolen cloth), *medias de algodón* (cotton stockings), and *mantelería* (table linen) (*Exposición*, in Carroll and Haggard, *Three Chronicles*, 219).

42. Pino, *Exposición*, in Carroll and Haggard, *Three Chronicles*, 227.

43. Pino, *Exposición*, in Carroll and Haggard, *Three Chronicles*, 223–24; Moorhead, *Royal Road*, 64.

44. Pino also noted the lack of doctors, surgeons, and even that of a pharmacy (*Exposición*, in Carroll and Haggard, *Three Chronicles*, 228–29).

CHAPTER TWO

1. MANM, roll 3, frames 1068–69.

2. New Mexicans were quite serious about autonomy. In 1822 electors from fourteen *alcaldías* (municipal districts) met in Santa Fe and elected seven *vocales* (representatives) to serve in the diputación. There was no authorization to do this; nevertheless, these representatives met on a regular basis for over a year until the Mexican Congress formally sanctioned their existence (Weber, *Mexican Frontier*, 19).

3. *El Fanal*, 6 January 1835, pp. 5–6.

4. Hira de Gortari Rabiela, "La minería durante la guerra de independencia y los primeros años del México independiente, 1810–1824," in *The Independence of Mexico and the Creation of the New Nation*, ed. Jaime E. Rodríguez O., 129–61 (Los Angeles: UCLA Latin American Center Publication, 1989). According to Lucas Alamán average silver production between 1815 and 1820 fluctuated between 6 million and 11 million pesos, quoted in Rabiela "La minería," 145. Stanley C. Green (*The Mexican Republic: The First Decade, 1823–1832* [Pittsburgh: University of Pittsburgh Press, 1987], 112–13, 128–29) shows that in the 1820s the value of silver production averaged 8.3 million pesos, but between 1822 and 1827 the mean dropped to 3.8 million.

5. Lenders could charge an interest rate of 3 percent a month because capital had disappeared. Two-thirds of it had been the property of the gachupines, many of whom had returned to Spain taking their money with them. The others — accused of conspiring to restore Spanish authority — were to be expelled in 1829 (Harold Dana Sims, *The Expulsion of Mexico's Spaniards, 1821–1836* [Pittsburgh: University

of Pittsburgh Press, 1990], 38–41, 136–38, 152–53). José María Quiroz set the amount of capital flight at 786 million pesos (quoted in Barbara A. Tenenbaum, "Taxation and Tyranny: Public Finance during the Iturbide Regime, 1821–1823," in Rodríguez O., *Independence of Mexico*, 203). Government expenditures were often twice the revenue. Between 1821 and 1868 government income averaged 10.5 million pesos, its expenses 17.5 million (Parkes, *History of Mexico*, 178–79; Cumberland, *Mexico*, 136–45).

6. Charles A. Hale, *Mexican Liberalism in the Age of Mora, 1821–1853* (New Haven: Yale University Press, 1968), 254–57; Cumberland, *Mexico*, 169.

7. Albert William Bork, "Nuevos aspectos del comercio entre Nuevo Méjico y Misuri, 1822–1846" (Ph.D. diss., Universidad Nacional Autónoma de México, 1944), 11–12; Cumberland, *Mexico*, 170–71; Green, *Mexican Republic*, 115.

8. MANM, roll 1, frames 703–5.

9. Green, *Mexican Republic*, 135; Bork, "Nuevos aspectos," 11–12.

10. Green, *Mexican Republic*, 134–35; Hale, *Mexican Liberalism*, 255.

11. Hale, *Mexican Liberalism*, 257, 268–77. Taxation of foreign trade presented two major problems which promoted conflict and instability — supervision of collections and international trade fluctuations. First, given the high cost of transportation in nineteenth-century Mexico, the ports and border crossings were relatively far from the capital and other centers of population. If high costs of supervising the collection of foreign trade taxes allowed customs officials to pilfer from the treasury, the national government's dependence on trade taxes collected in the periphery threatened the government's fiscal basis. The national government's main source of income was highly vulnerable to dissidents who found it easy to appropriate custom revenues to pay their own supporters. Second, dependence on taxation of foreign trade meant that revenues were subject to the vicissitudes of economic fluctuations as well. With total revenues largely dependent on international trade and business cycles, a decline in foreign trade produced government revenue shortfalls (Donald Fithian Stevens, *Origins of Instability in Early Republican Mexico* (Durham, NC: Duke University Press, 1991), 12, 17–18.

12. Josiah Gregg, *The Commerce of the Prairies*, ed. Max L. Moorhead (Norman: University of Oklahoma Press, 1954), 13–14; Twitchell, *Leading Facts*, 2: 103; Weber, *Mexican Frontier*, 125–26; Michael L. Olsen and Harry C. Myers, "The Diary of Pedro Ignacio Gallegos Wherein 499 Soldiers Following the Trail of Comanches Met William Becknell on his First Trip to Santa Fe," *Wagons Tracks: Santa Fe Trail Association Quarterly* 1 (November 1992): 15–20.

13. Quoted in Weber, *Mexican Frontier*, 128.

14. Moorhead, *Royal Road*, 195–96.

15. *The Franklin Intelligencer*, 8 May 1824, p. 2, col. 3.

16. *The Franklin Intelligencer*, 18 June 1825. The same concerns were expressed in the 4 November issue (p. 3). David Lavender, *Bent's Fort* (Lincoln: University of Nebraska Press, 1972), 61–64.

17. MANM, roll 6, frames 459–71; for a detailed listing of Beaubien's merchan-

dise, see frames 469–70; for Wilson's, see frame 471; for Harrison's, see MANM, roll 14, frames 191–200. For a comparison between earlier and later shipments, see MANM, roll 4, frames 1213–28; roll 7, frames 743–57; roll 8, frames 1341–53; roll 10, frames 367–82; roll 12, frames 1133–60; roll 14, frames 176–319; roll 15, frames 1018–43; roll 17, frames 1108–23; roll 21, frames 367–97; roll 24, frames 767–802; and roll 27, frames 620–43.

18. The records for 1826–28 identify the specific amount of duties paid by each merchant (MANM, roll 6, frames 472–514). There is no evidence of the duties exacted during other years. The *aduana* (custom house) documents show that by 1835 in addition to the derecho de consumo custom officials were collecting *derecho de reserva* and *derecho de alcabala*, but the rates were not indicated, only the actual sums collected (MANM, roll 21, frame 135). James Josiah Webb, *Adventures in the Santa Fe Trade, 1844–1847*, ed. Ralph P. Bieber (Glendale, CA: The Arthur H. Clark Company, 1931), 80–84; Gregg, *Commerce*, 79–80, 265–68.

19. Tenenbaum, "Taxation and Tyranny," 201–14.

20. Green, *Mexican Republic*, 135–38; Bork, "Nuevos aspectos," 40–47. It should also be noted that the mark-up of 100 or 120 percent was not unusual. See chapter 4 for a look at contraband and chapter 5 for a discussion of the rates wholesale merchants charged retailers.

21. MANM, roll 1, frames 724–25. Weber, *Mexican Frontier*, 149. Excessive regulation of products, like tobacco, also continued to be the rule (MANM, roll 1, frames 565–68).

22. Before 1830 only those New Mexicans carrying foreign merchandise had to obtain guías (MANM, roll 10, frames 513–74).

23. Sandoval's "Trade" was the first attempt to analyze the role of New Mexicans through the study of guías. See also Gregg, *Commerce*, 265–67; Moorhead, *Royal Road*, 139; Susan Calafate Boyle, "*Comerciantes, Arrieros, y Peones*: The Hispanos and the Santa Fe Trade," Southwest Cultural Resources Center, Professional Paper No. 54 (Santa Fe, NM: National Park Service, 1994), particularly chapter 11. Customs officials were expected to follow extremely complex procedures following the arrival of caravans from the United States. For the instructions issued to the Taos administrators, see MANM, roll 4, frames 776–78.

24. Starting in 1831 the customs office at Santa Fe began to record the foreign merchandise introduced by all merchants. It is not clear if officials were required to do so, but in general these documents lack the consistency of the guías and are often missing (MANM, roll 14, frames 182–87; roll 21, frames 142–271; roll 28, frames 730–60; roll 32, frames 1598–610; roll 34, frames 1171–210; and roll 41, frames 811–15). For Parkman's manifest, see MANM, roll 14, frames 182–87; for his guía, see roll 14, frames 243–49.

25. MANM, roll 1, frames 724–25. At times New Mexicans were unwilling to perform their jobs according to the legal stipulations, and authorities in Mexico City were forced to insist that proper procedures be followed (MANM, roll 17, frames 762–93). With the exception of tornaguías, which were issued in other custom

houses, there is no evidence that regular communications were maintained with either terrestrial or maritime customs.

26. Requests for additional revenues became quite regular as political instability and conflict within Mexico increased; MANN, roll 1, frames 1098–99; roll 3, frames 758–59; roll 12, frame 1091; roll 22, frame 940; roll 23, frame 592; roll 24, frames 663, 671, 674; roll 25, frame 820; roll 26, frame 336; roll 30, frame 669; and roll 38, frame 608.

27. "La miseria de estas gentes llega a tal grado que me consta que ya se han comenzado a alimentarse con cueros de reses" (MANM, roll 1, frames 1098–99).

28. "Extrañan muchísimo no saber para que se dirigen estas contribuciones tan anuales" (MANM, roll 3, frames 758–59).

29. Daniel Tyler, "The Personal Property of Manuel Armijo, 1829," *El Palacio* 80 (1974): 45–48.

30. MANM, roll 22, frames 940–76, 982–83.

31. Manuel Armijo wrote to Pérez on 16 and 21 May 1837, advising him that Mariano Chávez only had 600 pesos in cash and would be unable to meet his 1,500-peso assessment (MANM, roll 23, frames 353, 360, 592–96). Janet Lecompte, *Rebellion in Río Arriba, 1837* (Albuquerque: University of New Mexico Press, 1985), 11–21.

32. MANM, roll 17, frame 645. Concern about the dire economic circumstances that they faced appear in many documents. See MANM, roll 17, frames 743–57, 762–64, 774–76.

33. MANM, roll 22, frame 1075. There are numerous examples of public employees receiving their salaries months after they were due (MANM, roll 22, frames 1061, 1079, 1082).

34. MANM, roll 21, frame 568.

35. MANM, roll 22, frames 1035, 1096, 1097, 1098; roll 24, frames 663, 671, 674–75; roll 26, frames 336–41; roll 25, frames 820–49; roll 30, frame 669; and roll 38, frame 608. In 1836 American Thomas Rowland lent the New Mexico treasury almost 1,000 pesos to pay for uniforms for the troops (MANM, roll 22, frame 1096); during the same year, Subcomisario Francisco Sarracino provided almost 5,000 pesos to pay for officials' salaries and supplies for the troops (MANM, roll 22, frames 1097, 1098); however, the records show that in general New Mexican ricos contributed a substantial portion of these funds (roll 24, frames 663, 674–75).

36. MANM, roll 22, frames 1091–92.

37. MANM, roll 21, frames 847–52; Daniel Tyler, "The Mexican Teacher," *Red River Valley Historical Review* 1 (1974): 207–21.

38. MANM, roll 1, frames 1475–81; roll 3, frames 219–85. Some of the census information is not reliable. The documents show a lot of errors in adding the reported figures, they often contain blank categories, and some of the information is suspect. It is also not clear from the census if those who listed themselves as teachers were actually working in that capacity.

39. MANM, roll 7, frames 2–5, 52. There is no record of any action on the part of officials in Mexico City to address educational issues in New Mexico.

40. MANM, roll 19, frames 646–48; Weber, *Mexican Frontier*, 111–14; Lecompte, *Rebellion*, 9–10.

41. Lecompte, *Rebellion*, 10. Pino noted that some men were ruined in a single campaign, trading their clothing for ammunition or selling their children into peonage to perform their military duty (*Exposición*, in Carroll and Haggard, *Three Chronicles*, 227).

42. MANM, roll 23, frames 705–10; Baxter, *Las Carneradas*, 92–95; Frank D. Reeve, ed., "The Charles Bent Papers," *New Mexico Historical Review* 30 (1955): 344, 348–50.

43. Weber believes that the Indians were successful in their raids against Hispano communities because the rapid influx of Americans had upset the balance of power and weakened old alliances based on trade (*Mexican Frontier*, 92).

44. These patterns appear to have been equally applicable to many other regions along the northern Mexican frontier (Weber, *Mexican Frontier*, 94–95). For growing tensions between foreigners and New Mexicans, see MANM, roll 23, frames 406–9, 622–23.

45. MANM, roll 1, frames 260–61.

46. MANM, roll 6, frame 947.

47. For examples of Navajo stealing, see MANM, roll 5, frames 491, 574–76.

48. MANM, roll 9, frames 627, 632, 654, 658, 665, 834–35, 866–68; roll 10, frame 941.

49. MANM, roll 9, frames 805–6, 815–16, 831–33.

50. MANM, roll 9, frames 1083–112.

51. MANM, roll 13, frames 481, 559–83, 600.

52. MANM, roll 14, frames 975–78.

53. MANM, roll 18, frame 356.

54. MANM, roll 21, frames 660–82; roll 38, frame 540.

55. MANM, roll 22, frames 772–800, 809–26, comprise lists of men eligible for the militia between the ages of fourteen and sixty, and they often indicate the type of weapons they had available. In 1836 many of them showed *flechas* (arrows). Officials also published lists of men who had to march with the regular troops in the campaign against the Indians.

56. MANM, roll 5, frames 1322–25; roll 8, frames 387–438, 440–503.

57. The wording of the petition by Andrés Archuleta is, "como siempre ha sido estilo" (MANM, roll 27, frame 1031; roll 41, frames 548–51). Swadesh, *Primeros Pobladores*, 62–63; Weber, *Mexican Frontier*, 281; Simmons, *Spanish Government*, 185.

58. "Sin dinero no hay tropas y faltando éstas está fuera de duda que peligra mi provincia" (MANM, roll 3, frame 1068).

59. "No han faltado disidentes malvados que en mi provincia andan diseminando la especie de que le estaría mejor agregarse a los Estados Unidos del Norte" (MANM, roll 3, frame 1069).

60. MANM, roll 3, frames 1071–74. There is no record of the extent of the funds, if any, released by this authorization.

61. The letter was signed by Juan Diego Sena, Antonio Sena, and Francisco Baca y Ortiz (MANM, roll 4, frames 702–4). For a concise discussion of the problems which plagued the judicial system, see Weber, *Mexican Frontier,* 37–40.

62. Letter signed by A. Armijo in 1828 stresses the "hambre y miseria a que se hallan reducidos estos habitantes" (the hunger and misery to which the inhabitants have been reduced) (MANM, roll 7, frame 1181). For Pino's letter, see MANM, roll 8, frames 1119–26. For continuous problems with the judicial system, see Weber, *Mexican Frontier,* 37–40.

63. MANM, roll 9, frames 1142–43. There is no record of official acknowledgment of Alarid's request.

64. MANM, roll 13, frames 601, 613.

65. MANM, roll 13, frames 393–94, 601, 613, 630–42. It is not clear why this plan never received much attention; Santiago Abreu, the jefe político at the time decided to *archivar* (archive) the project (MANM, roll 13, frame 642).

66. MANM, roll 13, frame 635.

67. MANM, roll 23, frames 705–10.

68. "Dijimos en el artículo de que se trata después de quejarnos de esta indiferencia, que el Estado por conservarse rompería los vínculos que lo unen con la Nación Mexicana y se uniría a la República del Norte para salir de la abyección a que lo tiene reducido la guerra de los bárbaros y el abandono del Gobierno general" (*El Fanal,* 6 January 1835, p. 56). *El Fanal* was published between 29 September 1834 and 22 September 1835. Many of its editorials were quite critical of the central government, and the paper was closed as a result. *El Noticioso,* its replacement, explained in its editorial of 2 October 1835 the reasons for the closure. Rejoicing at the demise of the "subversive" *El Fanal,* it read "pues los editores de aquel periódico a fuerza de presentar al Supremo Gobierno general ante sus conciudadanos como un padrastro cruel, acaso alguna vez conseguirían alarmar a estos pacíficos paisanos. Las incesantes declamaciones de El Fanal eran reducidas a persuadir que el alto gobierno no atiende con igual zelo al centro de la República que a sus extremos, no advirtiendo o afectando no advertir que si no sobran los recursos para extinguir la guerra desoladora que nos aflige, es porque tampoco hay los suficientes para cubrir las vastas atenciones que pesan sobre el erario federal. Hace el Gobierno supremo . . . cuanto está en la esfera de su posibilidad para atender a aquel objeto y por consiguiente exigirle más de un modo irritante es procurar el trastorno del orden; más los señores redactors de El Fanal jamás tomaron en consideración la crítica posición del gobierno para denostarlo casi en todos sus números, porque no ha disuelto como al humo a las hordas de los salvajes: lejos de esto incitan a la rebelión invocando principios del derecho público con que alucinan a los incautos" (the editors of that newspaper, in trying to depict the Supreme Government before the citizenry as a cruel stepfather, perhaps sometimes would succeed in alarming these peaceful coun-

trymen. The never-ending claims of *El Fanal* were limited to persuade the people that the government does not pay equal attention to the core of the republic as to its edges, not realizing or pretending not to realize that if there are not enough resources to extinguish the devastating war that afflicts us, it is because there are insufficient funds to cover the vast number of responsibilities that have to be taken care of by the public treasury. The government . . . does everything possible to take care of this, and to demand more in an irritating fashion is to look for upheaval and disorder; but the editors of *El Fanal* never took into consideration the critical situation of the government and insulted it in every issue because it has not easily solved the Indian problem; far from this they [editors] incite a rebellion invoking civil rights with which they hallucinate the innocent).

69. *El Fanal*, 6 January 1835, p. 56.

70. Thomas Esteban Chávez, "The Trouble with Texans: Manuel Alvarez and the 1841 'Invasion,'" *New Mexico Historical Review* 53 (1978): 133–44.

CHAPTER THREE

1. The road to Chihuahua (and the interior of Mexico) was called the Camino Real, el Camino Real de Tierra Adentro, and the Chihuahua Trail.

2. The records indicate that between 1821 and 1838 the only Hispano who traveled east to purchase manufactures directly in the United States was Manuel Escudero, a merchant from Chihuahua; see chapter 5.

3. *Franklin Intelligencer*, 25 January 1825, p. 3; 18 June 1825, p. 3. Some scholars, like T. D. Hall (*Social Change*, 150), argue that reporting about a saturated New Mexican market was an attempt on the part of Missourians to discourage competition, but the traders themselves complained that selling for a profit was quite difficult.

4. The first surviving guías issued in July 1825 demonstrate that initially shipments were fairly small and consisted of a wide array of goods (MANM, roll 4, frames 1213–28). By the 1830s the volume and value of the merchandise had increased considerably, although there was a proportional decline in the variety of items (MANM, roll 11, frames 1133–60; roll 14, frames 188–319; roll 15, frames 1018–41; roll 17, frames 1107–23; roll 19, frames 226–94; roll 21, frames 273–398; roll 24, frames 767–802; roll 25, frames 1429–67; roll 27, frames 620–43; roll 28, frames 753–99; roll 30, frames 315–24; roll 32, frames 1630–63; roll 34, frames 1202–71; roll 37, frames 392–535; and roll 40, frames 282–358). Webb bemoaned the fact that after more than three weeks and close to four hundred miles on the road, he had only been able to sell $350 worth of goods (*Adventures*, 116).

5. Gerhard, *Northern Frontier*, 24; Moorhead, *Royal Road*, 64–65. Figures on the population of Nueva Vizcaya vary, as Jones reports 190,159 for the census of 1821 (*Nueva Vizcaya*, 245). Missouri newspapers also advertised the advantages of these markets (*Franklin Intelligencer*, 28 May 1825, p. 1; 4 November 1825, p. 3).

6. These patterns continued until the Mexican War in 1846 (Robert W. Frazer,

ed. *Over the Chihuahua and Santa Fe Trails, 1847–1848: George Rutledge Gibson's Journal* (Albuquerque: University of New Mexico Press and New Mexico Historical Society, 1981), 8. After 1846 changes resulted because Mexican duties made importation of efectos del país uneconomical, but trading did not come to a halt. For a brief discussion of commercial exchange between New Mexican merchants and their Mexican counterparts, see chapters 6 and 7.

7. Gregg computed the distance between Missouri and Santa Fe several times; in all cases the total was less than eight hundred miles (the distance between Santa Fe and Mexico City is about 1,660 miles), and he also commented on the poor quality of the drinking water (*Commerce*, 217, 275); "el ideal carácter del territorio que se tenía que recorrer entre Misuri y Nuevo Mexico en comparación con el paisaje tan difícil de naturaleza en gran parte de la ruta interna" (Bork, "Nuevos aspectos," 13).

8. Chantal Cramaussel documents that the preference for traveling in groups, even if it entailed traveling longer routes, dates from early in the colonial period ("Historia del camino real de tierra adentro y sus empalmes de Zacatecas a El Paso" [paper delivered at El Camino Real de Tierra Adentro: Historia y Cultura, Coloquio Internacional, Valle de Allende, Chihuahua, Mexico, 7–9 June 1995]). Gibson seldom made positive comments about native New Mexicans (Frazer, *Over the Trails*, 14–15). He commented that women accompanied the men on trading trips, an observation that was confirmed by other travelers (ibid., 15).

9. Gregg, *Commerce*, 305; MANM, roll 23, frame 900; John Adam Hussey, "The New Mexico-California Caravan of 1847–1848," *New Mexico Historical Review* 18 (1943): 8–9.

10. Of the 511 dated guías, eight were issued in January, ten in February, two in March, one in April, fourteen in July, 216 in August, 143 in September, seventy-four in October, thirty-eight in November, and five in December (see appendix 1); Gregg's description of his trip to Chihuahua follows the norm—leaving on 22 August, it took him about forty days to arrive at his destination (1 October) (*Commerce*, 268, 277–78).

11. See appendix 1.

12. William B. Napton, *Over the Santa Fe Trail, 1857* (Santa Fe: Stagecoach Press, 1964), 16.

13. Alvin R. Sunseri, "The Hazards of the Trail," *El Palacio* 81 (Fall 1975): 29–38. George R. Gibson, traveling north with very light wagons, noted that his caravan was able to travel twice the distance as when there were full loads, but he seldom made more than twenty-five miles in a day (Frazer, *Over the Trails*, 12–13, 15, 28, 30, 33–36).

14. Gregg, *Commerce*, 288–89; for the names of arrieros listed in the guías, see appendix 1.

15. Frazer, *Over the Trails*, 17.

16. Philip St. George Cooke, "A Journal of the Santa Fe Trail," *Mississippi Valley Historical Review* 12 (1935): 72–98, 227–55.

17. Gregg, *Commerce*, 128–29; Moorhead, *Royal Road*, 87.

18. Lavender, *Bent's Fort*, 94.

19. Quoted in Sunseri, "Hazards," 33.

20. Mules did not carry all the goods sent to the Mexican territory, and some of the merchandise was hauled in wagons pulled by oxen. However, it appears that until the Mexican War pack mules were the favored mode of transportation. Clara Elena Suárez presents an excellent description of Mexican freighting at the end of the eighteenth century in "La arriería en el camino real de tierra adentro a fines del siglo XVIII" (paper presented at El Camino Real de Tierra Adentro: Historia y Cultura, Coloquio Internacional, Valle de Allende, Chihuahua, Mexico, 7–9 June 1995); see also Jose Ortiz y Pino III, *Don José: The Last Patrón* (Santa Fe: Sunstone Press, 1981), 5; Erasmo Gamboa, "The Mexican Mule Pack System of Transportation in the Pacific Northwest and British Columbia," *Journal of the West* 29 (1990): 16–28; Gregg, *Commerce*, 319; Moorhead, *Royal Road*, 86; Janet Lecompte, *Pueblo Hardscrabble Greenhorn: The Upper Arkansas, 1832–1856* (Norman: University of Oklahoma Press, 1978), 81; L. Walsh, "A Public Report," 4–5. Gregg asserts that even the nomenclature of the apparatus had been adopted by the army (*Commerce*, 129).

21. Suárez, "La arriería," passim; Gamboa, "Mexican Mule Pack System," 17–18; Moorhead, *Royal Road*, 86–87.

22. John Keast Lord, quoted in Gamboa, "Mexican Mule Pack System," 18.

23. Moorhead, *Royal Road*, 87–89; Gamboa, "Mexican Mule Pack System," 18.

24. Gregg, *Commerce*, 286; Moorhead, *Royal Road*, 87; Gamboa, "Mexican Mule Pack System," 19.

25. *Sacramento Daily Union*, 30 October 1860 (the information comes from a reprinted article, which originally appeared in the St. Louis *Republican*).

26. Some experts believe that a tercio was a unit of weight of approximately 150 to 200 pounds; others believe it refers to a three-part load (Marc Simmons, Personal communications, January to February 1996). Still, it is not possible to establish with certainty at this time whether bultos, fardos, cajones, baúles, or piezas represented standard measurements of volume or weight, or they reflect packing strategies.

27. Subcomisario Francisco Sarracino admitted that the scribe had made an honest error in recording the merchandise of Eduardo Ara on 29 November 1835 (MANM, roll 21, frame 377).

28. For the cuaderno de guías reference, see MANM, roll 34, frame 1215; for the guía itself, see roll 36, frame 1267.

29. MANM, roll 34, frame 1205.

30. MANM, roll 34, frames 1208, 1215.

31. For Tomás Baca, see MANM, roll 21, frames 278, 302, 311, 320; roll 22, frame 1180; and roll 30, frame 319; for Vicente Baca, see roll 10, frame 328; roll 12, frame 1155; and roll 30, frame 320; for Francisco García, see roll 21, frame 277; and roll 37, frame 402; for José Montaño, see roll 21, frames 304, 307, 314, 336; and roll 32, frame 1651.

32. See appendix 1. The number and possibly the bulk of the shipments sent by Hispanos were greater than those sent by Anglos, although the value was smaller.

For example, surviving records indicate that in 1835 there were nineteen Anglo shipments and thirty-one Hispano; in 1836, thirty-four Anglo and eleven Hispano; in 1837, twenty-four Anglo and twenty-five Hispano (almost even); in 1838, twelve Anglo and forty Hispano; in 1839, thirty-two Anglo and seventy-seven Hispano; in 1840, six Anglo and seventy-four Hispano; and in 1843, twelve and seventy-two respectively. Gregg does not distinguish between American and New Mexican loads but also notes the growth in value of the merchandise sent to Mexico by way of the Royal Road after 1831 (*Commerce*, 332).

33. MANM, roll 32, frames 1206, 1639, 1648, 1652, 1660.

34. Antonio Barreiro noted that "New Mexicans trade quite actively with the neighboring provinces exporting annually flocks of sheep, hides, piñón nuts, coarse woolen goods, tobacco and other articles. Some have contracts in Durango for the delivery of fifteen thousand sheep or more for which they received nine or more reales" (*Ojeada sobre Nuevo Mexico*, 287 [Barreiro's report is printed in its original form in Carroll and Haggard, *Three Chronicles*, 263–318]). It is not clear if, and how, New Mexicans ever carried tobacco to the interior of Mexico, as its production and sale had been an important government monopoly throughout the colonial period. For the excessive regulations associated with the tobacco monopoly, see MANM, roll 1, frames 565–68.

35. Their last names were Archuleta, Armijo, Baca, Chávez, Gutiérrez, Luna, Ortiz, Otero, Perea, Pino, Saavedra, Salas, Salazar, Sandoval, Valdez, and Yrizarri. One of the best studies of socioeconomic conditions in New Mexico is Baxter's, *Las Carneradas*, which devotes an excellent chapter (89–110) to the period prior to the Mexican War; see also Edward Norris Wentworth, *America's Sheep Trails* (Ames, IA: Iowa State College Press, 1948), 112–35.

36. The few surviving records for 1842 do not include any shipments of sheep, but surviving tornaguías and guías issued in Mexico appear to indicate that trading might not have been too different from that of previous years. Felipe Chávez's papers at the University of New Mexico and at the State Records Center and Archives at Santa Fe clearly demonstrate the importance of the sheep trade at least through the 1870s. For a more detailed discussion of the sheep trade to California, see chapter 4; Baxter, *Las Carneradas*, 111–50; Donald Chaput, *Francois X. Aubry: Trader, Trailmaker and Voyageur in the Southwest, 1846–1854* (Glendale, CA: The Arthur H. Clark Company, 1975), 113–22, 137–49; Walker D. Wyman, "F. X. Aubry: Santa Fe Freighter, Pathfinder, and Explorer," *New Mexico Historical Review* 7 (1932): 1–31.

37. In 1839 Juan Silva carried two bundles of domestic merchandise valued at 35 pesos 2 reales (MANM, roll 21, frame 327). The same day Anastasio Sandoval took fourteen bundles assessed at 38 pesos (MANM, roll 21, frame 327). Two weeks later Juan Bautista Montoya hauled four bundles worth 46 pesos (MANM, roll 21, frame 334). For Santillanes's pase, see MANM, roll 25, frame 1460. There were others whose loads were not appraised and who were likely to have carried goods not in excess of the above sums.

38. This assessment appears extremely low and might be a mistake (MANM, roll 32, frame 1660).

39. MANM, roll 32, frames 1648, 1652, 1654, 1656, 1658, 1660.

40. MANM, roll 15, frames 828–35; for samples of exemption requests, see roll 21, frames 897–98; roll 23, frames 705–10; roll 25, frame 804.

41. Juan Armijo carried twelve hundred common blankets in August 1839 (MANM, roll 21, frame 325); Manuel Armijo took eighteen hundred common blankets at the same time (roll 21, frame 325); he had carried twenty tercios of blankets in 1835 (roll 21, frame 274); Juan Bautista Baca took 460 blankets in 1836 (roll 21, frame 294); others, like Antonio Sandoval, and Julián and Juan Tenorio, carried smaller quantities (roll 21, frames 324, 308, 309); for Felipe Romero's shipment, see MANM, roll 25, frame 1445.

42. See appendix 1.

43. For Agapito Albo, see MANM, roll 19, frame 323; roll 21, frame 318. For Manuel Armijo, see MANM, roll 21, frames 274, 275, 294, 299, 301, 303, 305, 325, 348, 349, 354; roll 37, frame 393; roll 40, frame 282. The fact that the guías include no information on Armijo's shipments of foreign goods to Mexico, particularly after 1839, is a good indication that a sizable proportion of the trading activities was not recorded by the aduana officials.

44. MANM, roll 21, frames 278, 279, 302, 311, 346; roll 22, frame 1180; roll 30, frame 319; and roll 34, frame 1206.

45. MANM, roll 30, frame 320; roll 37, frames 397, 398; and roll 40, frames 314, 316.

46. MANM, roll 21, frames 279, 311, 332, 1206, 1207; roll 34, frames 1206, 1207. Pedro Córdoba is another merchant who appeared to have increased his relatively small investment. He made three trips in 1838, 1844, and 1845. He specialized in domestic merchandise and augmented the size and value of his shipments each year (MANM, roll 21, frame 312; roll 37, frame 401; and roll 40, frame 332).

47. MANM, roll 21, frames 297, 314, 337, 360; roll 27, frame 643.

48. For Diego Gómez, see MANM, roll 21, frame 361; roll 34, frame 1214; roll 37, frame 407. For Salvador López, see MANM, roll 21, frames 312, 355. For José Dolores Durán, see MANM, roll 21, frames 312, 353. For Juan Miguel Mascarenas, see roll 21, frame 326; roll 25, frame 1467; roll 34, frame 1208; roll 40, frame 324. For Blas Lucero, see MANM, roll 21, frames 304, 333; roll 34, frame 1207. For Mariano Lucero, see MANM, roll 21, frame 305; roll 34, frame 1215. For Pedro Antonio Lucero, see MANM, roll 21, frames 329, 352; roll 34, frame 1209; roll 37, frame 403. There were many others who appear to fall in this category: Francisco Antonio Mestas made trips in 1839, 1840, 1843, and 1844 (roll 21, frames 329, 361; roll 34, frames 1207; and roll 37, frame 403); José Nicolás Montoya, in 1839, 1840, and 1841 (roll 21, frame 338, 352; roll 30, frame 320); Antonio Matías Ortiz, in 1839, 1840, 1843, and 1844 (roll 21, frames 323, 354; roll 34, frame 1207; and roll 37, frame 396); Isidro Ortiz, in 1839 and 1840 (roll 21, frames 335, 360); Antonio Alejandro Pacheco, in 1838 and 1839 (roll 21, frames 313, 327; roll 25, frame 1449);

Blas Padilla, in 1839, 1840, and 1845 (roll 21, frames 327, 354); Manuel Antonio Sánchez, in 1835, 1837, and 1839 (roll 21, frames 283, 303, 328); Jesús María Silva, in 1840, 1844, and 1845 (roll 21, frame 348; roll 28, frame 762; roll 37, frames 397, 398; and roll 40, frames 286, 321); Juan Tenorio, in 1838 and 1839 (roll 21, frames 309, 333); Julián Tenorio, in 1838, 1840, and 1844 (roll 21, frames 308, 309, 357; roll 37, frame 399); Ignacio Díaz Valdez, in 1843 and 1844 (roll 34, frames 1271; roll 37, frames 396, 397).

49. See appendix 1.

50. MANM, roll 21, frame 305; roll 34, frame 1205; roll 40, frame 283; roll 21, frame 317; and roll 21, frame 316.

51. MANM, roll 21, frame 356; roll 37, frame 402; roll 24, frame 759; and roll 34, frame 1209.

52. C. Gregory Crampton, and Steven K. Madsen, *In Search of the Spanish Trail: Santa Fe to Los Angeles, 1829–1848* (Salt Lake City: Gibbs-Smith Publisher, 1994); Albuquerque, New Mexico, University of New Mexico, Center of Southwest Research, Antonio Armijo Journal.

53. MANM, roll 21, frame 334; roll 34, frame 1202; and roll 37, frames 403, 405.

54. Hussey, "Caravan," 1–16.

55. It is not possible to establish if García and Sánchez were from New Mexico. Sánchez received guías 3 and 6. Garcia's guía has not survived, but it is listed in the cuaderno (MANM, roll 6, frames 463, 465, 474, 475, 477). For a complete listing of all surviving information on guías issued to Hispanos in New Mexico and pertinent tornaguías, see appendix 1.

56. Jesús Contreras purchased one tercio of foreign goods from Solomon Houck on 2 August 1832 (MANM, roll 15, frame 1028); José Francisco Ortiz, from Z. Nolan on 14 October 1828 (roll 8, frame 1342); José Francisco Valverde, from John E. Hardman on 3 October 1831 (roll 14, frame 250); Juan Vizcarra, from Louis Robidoux on 28 November 1831 (roll 14, frame 294); José María Zuloaga purchased foreign merchandise in the United States and "in the area" on 22 September 1845 (roll 40, frame 349); Vicente Baca (possibly arriero for Antonio Robidoux) bought one tercio of foreign merchandise in the country on 18 November 1829 (roll 10, frame 382); Juan Felipe Carrillo bought two piezas of foreign merchandise in Santa Fe on 16 October 1840 (roll 21, frame 360); José Manuel Sánchez bought two tercios of foreign merchandise locally on 4 September 1845 (roll 49, frame 285).

57. Their businesses probably extended to many communities in northern Mexico. Vicente Otero made a significant purchase in Chihuahua in 1832, paying 1,541 pesos in duties (MANM, roll 15, frame 1023); José Chávez dealt with wholesalers in Durango where in 1837 he purchased fifty pieces of foreign goods valued at $7,680 (MANM, roll 24, frame 802).

58. Juan Otero paid 100 percent surcharge on the merchandise he purchased from Manuel Alvarez (SRC, Manuel Alvarez Papers [hereafter MAP], roll 1, frames 458–61).

59. Few guías survive detailing shipments of foreign goods (see appendix 1). For

the most interesting ones, see MANM, roll 34, frame 1205; roll 37, frames 397, 472. For José's guías see roll 34, frames 1294, 1205; roll 37, frames 394, 398. For Mariano's, see roll 37, frame 395. For Antonio José Otero's, see roll 37, frames 392, 395, 396.

60. MANM, roll 34, frames 1233–40.

61. The documents record forty-seven consignments. The most popular consignees were José Cordero, Juan de Dios Márquez, Juan María Ponce de León, Ignacio Ronquillo, Juan Nepomuceno Urquide, Juan Yzurrieta, and Francisco Zuviría. For a complete list of these transactions, see appendix 1.

CHAPTER FOUR

1. Testimony of Francisco Pérez Serrano (MANM, roll 8, frame 514).

2. For the occupational census of 1822, see MANM, roll 3, frames 214–85; for the 1841 census, see roll 30, frames 339–401; for the 1844 census for La Cañada, see roll 37, frames 703–5. For the 1860 and 1870 census data, see Population Schedules, Eighth Census of the United States, Original Return of the Assistant Marshalls, Microfilm Edition, 14/6, rolls 712–16; Ninth Census of the United States, Original Return of the Assistant Marshalls, Microfilm Edition, 12/7, rolls 893–97; see chapter 8.

3. Records kept by Felipe Delgado, who operated the Chávez store at San Miguel del Vado indicate the wages paid (SRC, Delgado Papers, Dingee Collection, 1837–53). Of the 209 men involved in the 1847–48 convoy to California, fifty were boys under the age of sixteen (Hussey, "Caravan," 1–16); "José Librado Gurulé's Recollections, 1867," in *On the Santa Fe Trail*, ed. Marc Simmons, 120–33 (Lawrence: University Press of Kansas, 1986).

4. Moorhead, *Royal Road*, 184.

5. Charles Raber, "Personal Recollections of Life on the Plains from 1860 to 1868," *Collections of the Kansas State Historical Society* 16 (1925): 325; T. J. Sperry, "A Long and Useful Life for the Santa Fe Trail," *Wagon Tracks* 4 (May 1990): 14–17; Darlis A. Miller, "Freighting for Uncle Sam," *Wagon Tracks* 5 (November 1990): 11–15.

6. Miller, *Soldiers and Settlers*, 308–20, 357, 359–62, 365, 369, 372–73, 377; Mamie Bernard Aguirre, "Spanish Trader's Bride," *Westport Historical Quarterly* 4 (December 1968): 5–23; see chapter 8.

7. Richard L. Nostrand demonstrates that between 1790 and 1880 the New Mexican population greatly expanded. However, this expansion, though in part a result of increasing demand for local products, was mostly the result of the search for additional grazing lands, and it did not enhance the circumstances of most of the people who continued indebted to the wealthy ("The Century of Hispano Expansion," *New Mexico Historical Review* 62 [1987]: 361–86).

8. During the 1850s Rafael Armijo kept a notebook where he recorded the cash loans he made. Most borrowed small sums of money but were forced to mortgage

their future crops to secure these loans. In many instances, they mortgaged crops two or three years in advance (SRC, Rafael Armijo Papers). The 1860 and 1870 censuses indicate that few native New Mexicans declared any real or personal estate property.

9. Clarence L. VerSteeg, *The Formative Years, 1607–1763* (New York: Hill and Wang, 1964), 173–202; Susan Calafate Boyle, "Inequality and Opportunity: Wealth Distribution in Ste. Genevieve, 1757–1804" (paper delivered at the Social Science History Association Meeting, Washington, D.C., October 1983).

10. Gregg, *Commerce*, 332–33.

11. U.S. Congress. House of Representatives, *Drawback Act*, 13th Cong., 1st sess., 1845, Rept. 458 to accompany H. Rept. 58.

12. Gregg, *Commerce*, 154, see also 156, 268–69.

13. Gregg, *Commerce*, 159.

14. Reeve, "Bent Papers," *New Mexico Historical Review* 29 (1954): 234–39, 311–17; 30 (1955): 154–67, 252–54, 340–52; 31 (1956): 75–77, 157–64; 251–53.

15. Barton H. Barbour, ed., *Reluctant Frontiersman: James Ross Larkin on the Santa Fe Trail, 1856–1857* (Albuquerque: University of New Mexico Press, 1990), 103; Frazer, *Over the Trails*, 21.

16. John P. Bloom, "New Mexico Viewed by Anglo Americans, 1846–1849," *New Mexico Historical Review* 34 (1959): 182.

17. MANM, roll 15, frames 230–57; roll 16, frames 1000–1014; roll 20, frames 2–124, 126–50, 355–458, 522–30; roll 22, frames 3–5, 6–192; roll 23, frames 1046–75; roll 25, frames 262–368; roll 26, frames 602–50, 681–729; roll 28, frames 103–31; roll 29, frames 168–77, 289–320; roll 32, frames 2–12, 31–63; roll 33, frames 752–72; roll 35, frames 5–48, 227–57; roll 39, frames 3–37, 143–62; and roll 42, frames 453–90.

18. MANM, roll 36, frames 380–89.

19. MANM, roll 5, frames 1322–30, Case against Silvester Pratte for illegal hunting of beaver; roll 8, frames 387–417, Case against Vicente Guion for illegally owning three hundred pounds of beaver; roll 15, frames 162–70, Case against Ewing Young. For a colorful description of the fur traders' adventures in the New Mexican territory, see Lavender, *Bent's Fort*, 59–89.

20. MANM, roll 4, frames 707–8; roll 5, frames 1322–30; roll 6, frames 851–52, 1017–20; roll 7, frames 204–47; and roll 8, frames 372–418, 448–504; 1319–32.

21. MANM, roll 5, frames 1322–30; roll 8, frames 387–418, 1319–32.

22. MANM, roll 15, frames 162–70.

23. MANM, roll 15, frames 268–70.

24. MANM, roll 8, frames 504–672.

25. MANM, roll 13, 647–49.

26. MANM, roll 10, frames 565–72.

27. MANM, roll 1, frame 208; roll 8, frames 1349–53; roll 10, frames 545–46, 556–58; 565–72; roll 15, frames 909–10, 1007; roll 22, frame 505; roll 38, frame 90; and roll 39, frames 222–23.

28. MANM, roll 8, frames 440–503, 118, 1142; roll 13, frames 647–49; roll 14, frames 49–52; roll 15, frames 635–50, 835, 869–70; roll 16, frames 311–12, 998–99; roll 18, frames 400–401; roll 26, frames 675–78; and roll 39, frames 164–239.

29. Gregg, *Commerce,* 75

30. MANM, roll 23, frames 406–9, 622–23; roll 38, frames 511–14.

31. MANM, roll 8, frames 505–664.

32. MANM, roll 8, frames 505–32.

33. MANM, roll 8, frames 533–36.

34. MANM, roll 8, frames 538–52.

35. MANM, roll 8, frames 604–9.

36. MANM, roll 8, frames 611–30.

37. MANM, roll 8, frames 631–45.

38. MANM, roll 8, frames 645–60.

39. MANM, roll 8, frames 661–64.

40. MANM, roll 14, frames 49–52.

41. MANM, roll 13, frames 647–54.

42. MANM, roll 15, frames 620–23.

43. Appendix 1; Louise Barry, *The Beginning of the West: Annals of the Kansas Gateway to the American West, 1540–1845* (Topeka, KS: Kansas State Historical Society, 1972), 437, 449, 455, 475–76, 486, 565, 571.

44. Documents indicate that after 1839 wealthy New Mexicans regularly paid a substantial portion of the import duties collected by the Customs Office (MANM, roll 28, frames 698–719, 730, 736–38; roll 32, frames 1598–620; roll 34, frames 1171–99; roll 37, frames 413–58; and roll 41, frames 811–12), but the Armijos (Manuel, Juan, and Rafael) were not identified among those bringing merchandise in 1840 and 1842, nor were their names among the lists of those paying import duties.

CHAPTER FIVE

1. Damaso Robledo to Manuel Alvarez, 29 October 1846 (MAP, roll 1, frame 598).

2. *Council Grove (Kansas) Press,* 17 August 1863; ibid., 14 September 1863; MAP, roll 2, frame 557 includes a copy of Rhodes' announcement.

3. *Westport Border Star* (Missouri), 15 July 1859; ibid., 12 August 1859; Barry, *Beginning of the West,* 1037–38; *Missouri Republican* (St. Louis), 8 September 1858; ibid., 21 October 1858; ibid., 17 December 1858; ibid., 8 June 1859; ibid., 18 July 1859; ibid., 15 August 1859; Fort Dodge, Kansas, Fort Dodge Records, frame 227, 23 July 1867; frame 272, September 1867; Sister Lilliana Owens, "Jesuit Beginnings in New Mexico, 1867–1882," *Jesuit Studies—Southwest* 1 (n.d.): 32–35; "Preliminary Report of Survey of Inscriptions Along Santa Fe Trail in Oklahoma," *Chronicles of Oklahoma* 37 (Autumn 1960): 310–22. The inscriptions, however, do not reveal if the names belonged to owners or freighters.

4. The commercial activities of Felipe Chávez provide an excellent example of operations associated with the Santa Fe trade (see chapter 6 for the specific details).

5. Barry, *Beginning of the West*, 117.

6. Twitchell, *Leading Facts*, 1: 118; MANM, roll 5, frames 575–76, 846–47; Barry, *Beginning of the West*, 117, 132; James W. Covington, "Correspondence Between Mexican Officials at Santa Fe and Officials in Missouri: 1823–1825," *The Bulletin, Missouri Historical Society* (October 1959): 20–32; William R. Manning, *Early Diplomatic Relations Between the United States and Mexico* (New York: Greenwood Press, 1968), 177–86; Moorhead, *Royal Road*, 66.

7. *Franklin Intelligencer*, 9 June 1826, p. 3. Unfortunately, there are no official records listing the merchandise Escudero introduced in the Santa Fe custom house at the end of his trip.

8. MANM, roll 6, frame 486.

9. *Franklin Intelligencer*, 9 June 1826, p. 3.

10. MANM, roll 11, frame 346.

11. This is the last guía that records the introduction of foreign merchandise through Chihuahua (MANM, roll 24, frame 802).

12. MANM, roll 24, frames 1039–40.

13. U.S. Congress, House of Representatives, *To Establish Ports of Entry in Arkansas and Missouri, and to Allow Debenture*, 26th Cong., 1st sess., 1840, Rept. 540, serial 372, 14–16. On the other hand, fluctuations in the mining industry in Chihuahua might have caused a decrease in the demand for foreign goods.

14. MAP, roll 1, frames 458–61; roll 2, frame 618.

15. For Cordero's manifest, see MANM, roll 27, frames 603–12; for the guías, see roll 21, frames 341–42.

16. Barry, *Beginning of the West*, 383; information from surviving manifests and guías indicates that at least three leading New Mexican merchants participated in this trip: José and Mariano Chávez, and Antonio José Otero (MANM, roll 28, frames 698–99, 700–704, 730, 736–38, 750); see appendix 2 for a list of all surviving manifests presented by Hispano merchants.

17. MANM, roll 28, frames 710–50. It is difficult to estimate the value of foreign merchandise coming to Santa Fe because neither manifests nor guías generally include an assessment of the value of the goods; a comparison of the loads from this period with those from the 1860s and 1870s reveals that with time their size and value improved dramatically. Another notable Mexican who brought a substantial amount of merchandise from the United States that year was Francisco Elguea (eleven bultos), but unfortunately the value was not indicated.

18. Barry, *Beginning of the West*, 449, 455.

19. MANM, roll 34, frames 1176, 1182, 1203, 1204, 1205.

20. Moorhead, *Royal Road*, 124–25.

21. MANM, roll 27, 603–12, 613–18. The customs official sometimes referred to the derecho de internación as derecho de alcabala, which is technically incorrect; it

is not possible to ascertain how they assigned import duties; derecho de consumo was 15 percent of the derecho de internación (MANM, roll 28, frames 702, 730 738, 750).

22. MANM, roll 28, frames 699, 702–4. Gregg confirms that only five merchants traveled that year; he claims that only $50,000 worth of merchandise was shipped that year, the fourth lowest since 1822 (*Commerce*, 332). Information on the amount of import duties merchants paid in other years is sporadic and does not allow for a comparison.

23. Barry, *Beginning of the West*, 430, 438; Gregg, *Commerce*, 332.

24. Webb, *Adventures*, 111.

25. In 1841, believing that public sentiment in New Mexico favored Texas in its dispute with Mexico City, Texas Governor Mirabeau Buonaparte Lamar sent a party of over three hundred armed men across the Plains to assert Texas jurisdiction over New Mexico. Governor Manuel Armijo was warned of the Texans' intent and easily forced the surrender of the weary, hungry and thirsty Texans (Weber, *Mexican Frontier*, 266–69; Gregg, *Commerce*, 337–45).

26. MANM, roll 32, frames 1598–1603; see appendix 2.

27. MANM, roll 32, frames 1607–28; see appendix 2.

28. For Alvarez's manifest, see MANM, roll 32, frames 1604–6; for John McKnight, roll 32, frames 1590–91; for James Magoffin, roll 32, frames 1588–89; see appendix 2.

29. Gregg, *Commerce*, 332.

30. Marc Simmons's *Murder on the Santa Fe Trail: An International Incident, 1843* (El Paso: Texas Western Press, 1987) provides the most complete account of the incident in which Antonio José Chávez lost his life; Barry, *Beginning of the West*, 475–76.

31. MANM, roll 34, frame 1171; import duties had increased dramatically following the disposition of a decree issued on 27 June 1842, with some fabrics paying up to eighty reales (ten dollars) per vara. The special tax on knitted fabrics was dropped, and the derecho de consumo fluctuated between 15 and 20 percent (roll 34, frames 1176–99).

32. MANM, roll 34, frames 1180–81, 1190; see appendix 2.

33. MANM, roll 34, frames 1176–77, 1193–95.

34. MANM, roll 37, frames 413–17, 418–36, 437–42, 443–55, 456–58; see appendix 2.

35. MANM, roll 40, frames 287–92, 294–311, 322–23, 325–27, 349–51; for other guías issued to traders carrying foreign merchandise, see roll 40, frames 392, 393, 394, 395, 396, 397, 399, 400, 402, 408, 472.

36. Barry, *Beginning of the West*, 571, 580, 591, 600, 628, 638, 642, 685, 702, 827–28, 874.

37. Barry, *Beginning of the West*, 512–13, 527, 565; Lavender, *Bent's Fort*, 230–31; for the Armijo trip to New York, see *New York Weekly Tribune*, 15 November 1845, p. 4; see appendix 2.

38. *Pittsburgh Daily Commercial Journal*, 6 April 1846; ibid., 7 April 1846; ibid., 16

April 1846; Tom Thomas, "The Evolution of Transportation in Western Pennsylvania," unpublished manuscript, 1994, 56–59.

39. Gregg, *Commerce*, 331–32.

40. Walker D. Wyman, "Freighting: A Big Business on the Santa Fe Trail," *Kansas Historical Quarterly* 1 (November 1931): 19–25; *Missouri Republican*, 15 August 1859; O'Brien, "Independence," 103–4.

41. Cooke, "Journal," 254. Cooke is saying that he did not see ten wagons that belonged to Americans who resided in the United States. However, of the two hundred wagonloads that Cooke mentions, several belonged to Americans who lived in Mexico. For example, Henry Connelly, a naturalized Mexican citizen, partially owned twenty-two wagons on the trail that year (Mark Gardner, Personal communication, 1 November 1994).

42. Eugene T. Wells, "The Growth of Independence, Missouri: 1827–1850," *Bulletin of the Missouri Historical Society* 16 (1959): 33–46; Moorhead, *Royal Road*, 110; Barry, *Beginning of the West*, 438, 455, 486, 565; for Armijo's guías, see appendix 1.

43. A cart laden with foreign goods could carry $3,390 worth of merchandise; see MANM, roll 21, frame 352; roll 28, frames 730, 736–38.

44. *Westport Border Star*, 15 July 1859; ibid., 12 August 1859.

45. The years 1841 and 1842 were not good for keeping records associated with the Santa Fe Trail; in 1841 the Texan Santa Fe Expedition disrupted the trade and as a punishment the custom offices in Santa Fe and Chihuahua were closed for seven months between 7 August 1843 and 31 March 1844 (Gregg, *Commerce* 344; Moorhead, *Royal Road*, 124–25). For American guías in 1843, see MANM, roll 34, frames 1202, 1206, 1211, 1212, 1216; roll 37, frames 392, 405, 407; and roll 39, frames 287–92, 294–311. Possibly as a result of the Drawback Act passed by the United States Congress in 1845, American traders showed renewed interest in the trade. James Magoffin took $26,000 in merchandise; Albert Speyer, close to $70,000 (MANM, roll 40, frames 294–311). The late Myra Ellen Jenkins believed that overall the MANM records show that the Hispanos did not control the trade (Personal communication, 18 May 1992).

46. Sandoval, "Trade," passim.

47. Lewis E. Atherton, "James and Robert Aull — A Frontier Missouri Mercantile Firm," *Missouri Historical Review* 30 (1935), 3–27; "Business techniques in the Santa Fe Trade," *Missouri Historical Review* 34 (1940), 335–41; "Santa Fe Trader," 1–12.

48. Parish, *Mercantile Capitalism*, 3–10, 11–82; "German Jew," 3–29; 129–43.

49. Parish, "German Jew," 18–23; *Mercantile Capitalism*, 33–35.

50. Parish, "German Jew," 9.

51. Henry Connelly, George and Charles Bent, and other "foreign" merchants could have developed similar commercial techniques as Alvarez (Parish, "The German Jew," 5). Unfortunately, there have been no systematic studies of their mercantile activities.

52. The life of Manuel Alvarez has received a splendid treatment at the hands of Thomas E. Chávez, *Manuel Alvarez, 1794–1856: A Southwestern Biography* (Niwot:

University Press of Colorado, 1990). This biography, however, does not explore in sufficient detail Alvarez's economic activities. His extensive ledgers and correspondence in Spanish, French, and English deserve a more careful reading; they might provide a better understanding of the economic system that developed in New Mexico prior to the Mexican War. For a discussion of his transactions that involved other Santa Fe Trail merchants, see also O'Brien, "Independence," 231–47.

53. MAP, roll 1, frames 441–43.

54. Parish, "German Jew," 18.

55. MAP, roll 1, frames 458–61, 479, 480, 481.

56. MAP, roll 1, frames 1–102; roll 2, frames 557, 546, 618; O'Brien, "Independence," 231–47.

57. Parish, "German Jew," 19; MAP, roll 1, frames 441–43, 560–61, 574, 576, 594, 598, 600–601, 603, 634–35, 654–55, 694–95, 697, 723–24.

58. MAP, roll 1, frames 441–43, 576, 723–24.

59. MAP, roll 1, frames 594, 598, 600–601, 603, 694–95.

60. Parish, *Mercantile Capitalism*, 8.

61. Surviving stationery from the Perea family indicates that they owned at least one store in Bernalillo (SRC, Felipe Delgado Business Papers, 1864–1881); Webb, *Adventures*, 92–93.

62. In 1844 Simón Delgado wrote to his brother Pablo, "a estos individuos no les aflojen un momento hasta que te paguen el último medio" (don't let up until these individuals pay you the last cent) (SRC, Delgado Papers, Dingee Collection, 1837–1853, 1843–51).

63. SRC, Delgado Papers, Dingee Collection, 1837–53; SRC, Delgado Family Papers, Jenkins Collection, 1828–76; SRC, Felipe Delgado Business Papers, 1864–81.

64. A note on the back of one receipt said "Apunte de los carneros que tiene cuidando Nicolás Casados pertenecientes a esta tienda" (Number of sheep belonging to the store that Nicolás Casados is watching) (SRC, Delgado Family Papers, Jenkins Collection, San Miguel del Vado Accounts, 1837–53 [the document has no date]).

65. SRC, Delgado Papers, Dingee Collection, 1851–54; according to Agnes C. Laut, José Chávez was one of the foremost miners in New Mexico (*Pilgrims of the Santa Fe* [New York: Frederick A. Stokes Company, 1931], 272).

66. In 1854 Fernando Delgado sold 101 ounces of silver in St. Louis for which he received $360.09 (SRC, Delgado Papers, Dingee Collection, 1851–54); see chapter 6 for a more detailed discussion of Felipe Chávez's shipments outside New Mexico.

CHAPTER SIX

1. SRC, José Felipe Chávez Papers (hereafter FCSRC), folder 33, Felipe Delgado, 16 June 1906. This letter was addressed to José E. Chávez right after the death of José Felipe Chávez, his father.

2. Felipe Chávez played a very important role in the history of New Mexico during the nineteenth century. Substantial records survive to conduct a biographical study incorporating an in-depth analysis of both his business career and his private life. The present study does not include materials after 1880 and does not claim to have examined all of the Chávez records. For a brief summary of his life, see Tibo J. Chávez's "'*El Millonario*': Ambitious Merchant Cut Stylish Figure on Frontier," *New Mexico Magazine* (June 1989): 73–79.

3. His papers are at SRC, and at the Center for Southwest Research at the University of New Mexico in Albuquerque (José Felipe Chávez Papers [hereafter FCZIM]). The latter is part of the New Mexican merchants collection. Most of the documents used in this work come from box 1. To facilitate the identification of the individual documents, the folder number—as well as the author of the letter or invoice—is listed, followed by the date of the document. Felipe Chávez also became a powerful New Mexican political leader. He did not participate in politics, but used his influence to lobby the United States Congress on behalf of the community of Belén. He was also instrumental in the selection of territorial delegates to Washington (FCZIM, folder 42, correspondence with Henry Hilgert, 1865–71).

4. FCZIM, folder 66, Agustín de la Rúa, 2 December 1852. Felipe Chávez died in June 1906 (FCZIM, folder 33, Felipe Delgado, June 1906).

5. For example, the borrador for 1859 to 1863 included seventy-six letters addressed to W. H. Chick, P. Harmony, Edward James and William Henry Glasgow, Joseph Amberg, José Cordero, Henry Connelly, R. Bernard, William Smith, Antonio Castillo, Ambrosio Armijo, and others.

6. FCZIM, borrador 1859–63, letters to P. Harmony, 13 August 1859, 16 September 1859, 22 September 1859; letters to E. Glasgow, 29 August 1859; folder 39, E. Glasgow, 13 September 1859, P. Harmony, 15 December 1859; for the itemized list of the bolts of cloth Chávez purchased, see FCSRC, business papers, P. Harmony, 9 May 1856.

7. Parish, "German Jew," 18.

8. Walter Barrett, *The Old Merchants of New York City* (New York: Thomas R. Knox and Co., 1885), 226–27. For invoices, see FCSRC, business papers, P. Harmony, 26 April 1856, 30 April 1856; E. Glasgow, 10 May 1856, 21 May 1856; FCZIM, folder 39, P. Harmony, 26 April 1856, 2 May 1856; E. Glasgow, 21 May 1856; folder 41, P. Harmony, 14 May 1856. A month and a half later, Felipe arranged for the purchase of an additional sixteen thousand pounds of goods, this time from Kearney and Bernard, Westport, Missouri (FCZIM, folder 41, Kearney and Bernard, 6 June 1856).

9. FCSRC, business papers, P. Harmony, 16 June 1856, 30 April 1856, 13 December 1860; E. Glasgow, 6 May 1856. There are more than a hundred examples of these types of transactions. Edward James and William Henry Glasgow were among the leading Missouri mercantile firms that engaged in active trade with New Mexico and the northern Mexican provinces. See Mark L. Gardner, ed., *Brothers on the Santa*

Fe and Chihuahua Trails: Edward James Glasgow and William Henry Glasgow, 1846–1848 (Niwot: University of Colorado Press, 1993).

10. FCSRC, business papers, P. Harmony, 30 April 1859.

11. FCSRC, business papers, P. Harmony, 14 March 1860; FCZIM, folder 41, P. Harmony, 15 march 1860.

12. FCZIM, folder 31, W. H. Chick, 23 April 1863; folder 39, E. Glasgow, 31 March 1863.

13. Gardner, *Brothers*, 43–45.

14. FCSRC, business papers, E. Glasgow, 6 May 1856.

15. FCZIM, folder 31, Chick, Browne, and Co., 4–7 July 1871.

16. FCZIM, folder 31, Chick, Browne, and Co., 17 November 1873; folder 68, S. Davis and Co., 22 February 1876.

17. FCZIM, folder 31, Chick, Browne, and Co., 10 July 1872, 17 November 1873.

18. Robles's comments are very interesting. More than once he noted that sometimes the packaging of the merchandise was worth more than its contents: "Las pomadas son de buena calidad y si se tira lo que adentro contienen, el pomo o botellita vale el dinero y un poco más" (Unguents are of high quality and after the contents are gone the tube or little bottle is worth the money, or even more) (FCSRC, business papers, A. Robles, 22 February 1860). FCSRC, business papers, A. Robles, 17 February 1860, 22 February 1860; FCZIM, folder 67, A. Robles, 21 February 1860, 26 February 1860.

19. FCZIM, folder 41, P. Harmony, 4 May 1859, 9 May 1859.

20. Robles did not continue as Chávez's agent after this trip, possibly because Harmony sent a very unflattering report on him. Robles's activities offended the Spanish entrepreneur and almost delayed the shipment of the order. According to Harmony, while his workers were trying to prepare the final invoice for shipment, numbering and checking the various loads, Robles would appear announcing the purchase of a new set of merchandise, which had to be packaged adequately, labeled, and included in the invoice. To accommodate the additional goods, the workers would have to stop their work on the invoice and shift their attention to the items Robles had bought. They were pressed for time since the merchandise had to be ready for shipment. Harmony admitted that in their hurry his workers had misnumbered various fardos. Chávez also complained that he had not received some of the shovels that Robles had purchased (FCSRC, business papers, P. Harmony, 1 August 1860).

21. FCZIM, folder 39, E. Glasgow, 30 June 1858.

22. FCZIM, folder 39, E. Glasgow, 17 May 1861, 31 March 1863.

23. FCZIM, folder 67, Charles Stern, 15 April 1867; FCSRC, miscellaneous documents 2, Cuno, Bohms, and Co., 20 February 1868; FCZIM, folder 67, Appleton, Noyes, and Co., 14 April 1868.

24. FCZIM, folder 68, E. Glasgow, 23 June 1871; folder 68, R. D. Wells, 23 June 1871; folder 68, A. Mellier, 21 June 1871; folder 68, B. and J. Slevin, 23 June 1871.

25. FCSRC, business papers, S. P. Shannon, June 1865.

26. FCZIM, folder 31, W. H. Chick and Co., 22 March 1867, 11 October 1869.

27. FCSRC, miscellaneous papers 2, Cuno, Bohms, and Co., 20 February 1868; FCZIM, folder 68, Bartels Brothers and Co., 26 September 1876; folder 21, Browne and Manzanares, 25 April 1879.

28. FCZIM, folder 68, P. Brother, 15 August 1871.

29. FCZIM, folder 67, A. Montoya, March 1860.

30. FCSRC, business papers, P. Harmony, 5 June 1859.

31. FCZIM, folder 39, E. Glasgow, 5 April 1862; FCSRC, business papers, E. Glasgow, 4 March 1860.

32. FCZIM, folder 31, W. H. Chick, 8 June 1869.

33. FCZIM, folder 31, Chick, Browne, and Co., 4–8 July 1871, 22 November 1871.

34. FCZIM, folder 21, F. Manzanares, 25 April 1878.

35. FCZIM, folder 21, V. Baca, 17 July 1878. Storage and commission fees were other expenses that had to be added to the cost of the merchandise. These charges could be fairly high at times (FCZIM, folder 31, W. H. Chick, 23 April 1863). FCSRC, business papers, W. H. Chick, 6 June 1863.

36. FCZIM, folder 41, P. Harmony, 28 September 1864.

37. FCSRC, business papers, Otero and Sellar, 22 September 1868.

38. FCZIM, folder 31, W. H. Chick, 26 June 1869.

39. There are a lot of documents that show this pattern (see FCZIM, folder 41, P. Harmony, 20 October 1863; folder 31, W. H. Chick and Co., 18 June 1869).

40. FCZIM, folder 39, E. Glasgow, 29 May 1862; folder 31, W. H. Chick, 8 June 1869, 18 June 1869; folder 39, E. Glasgow, 6 October 1879.

41. FCZIM, folder 31, W. H. Chick, 8 June 1869, 18 June 1869; FCSRC, business papers, Chick, Browne, and Co., 25 April 1872; business papers, W. C. Houston, Jr. and Co., 2 October 1880; FCZIM, folder 39, E. J. Glasgow, 6 August 1879; folder 68, Benjamin Walker, 21 May 1879.

42. FCSRC, business papers, P. Harmony, 16 June 1856.

43. FCSRC, business papers, P. Harmony, 14 July 1857.

44. FCZIM, folder 5, Nicolás Armijo, 2 February 1869, 2 March 1869, 9 March 1869, 15 November 1869; folder 13, 8 September 1872; folder 26, J. Francisco Chávez, 10 October 1865. Chávez's associates and friends also kept him informed of developments that could negatively affect his family and that required his attention. In 1871 the vicar of Denver wanted to discuss with Felipe's mother the inheritance of her recently deceased daughter. Delgado advised Chávez that the vicar had been named administrator of the estate, and that he (Delgado) had informed the vicar that Mrs. Chávez was not the guardian. Since the vicar insisted, Delgado felt it would be better for Mrs. Chávez if Felipe himself went to Santa Fe and spoke directly with the vicar (FCSRC, business papers, Pablo Delgado, 23 February 1871).

45. FCZIM, folder 27, Melquíades Chávez, 4 November 1867.

46. FCZIM, folder 24, Francisco Chávez II, 21 June 1879, 25 June 1879.

47. FCSRC, business papers, J. B. Rougemont, 28 March 1873, 20 October 1879; Nicolás Quintana, 21 June 1874; Gutiérrez addressed Felipe as *primo* (cousin) (FCSRC, miscellaneous papers, José Gutiérrez, 16 January 1868).

48. FCZIM, folder 33, Pablo Delgado, 12 May 1871; folder 68, Rita R. de Valencia, 22 May 1873; Luis M. Baca, 21 May 1877; Benito and Eleuterio Baca, 21 February 1879; folder 16, Benito and Eleuterio Baca, 3 March 1879; FCSRC, business papers, Jacob Amberg, 30 May 1869, A. Zeckendorf, 29 July 1867.

49. FCSRC, miscellaneous papers 2, J. Martín Amador, 3 February 1868; FCZIM, folder 33, Pablo Delgado, 30 July 1870. He also lent $3,000 to the Baca brothers and extended the loan for an additional year (FCZIM, folder 68, Baca Hermanos, 21 February 1879; folder 16, Baca Hermanos, 3 March 1879). Americans also borrowed (folder 33, Pablo Delgado, 12 May 1871).

50. FCSRC, business papers, A. Zeckendorf, 26 June 1867, 29 July 1867. It is possible that Chávez was anti-Semitic. While his correspondence does not reveal overt anti-Semitism, a letter from Antonio Robles, his trusted agent, shows strong anti-Jewish sentiment. Writing from New York on 26 February 1860, Robles told Chávez, "esta judillada is infernal, si Salomón no es judío, vive con ellos, y sigue las mismas huellas" (this bunch of Jews is infernal; if Salomón is not a Jew, he lives with them and follows the same tracks) (FCZIM, folder 67, Antonio Robles, 26 February 1860). The massive Felipe Chávez records include relatively few pieces of correspondence or transactions with Jews. This is unusual, since after the Mexican War the German Jewish merchants played a key role in the territorial economy and Chávez maintained close ties to most influential merchants.

51. FCZIM, folder 33, Felipe Delgado, 16 June 1906.

52. FCSRC, miscellaneous papers 2, José Felix Benavídez, 27 January 1868.

53. FCZIM, folder 31, W. H. Chick, 11 October 1869; folder 41, P. Harmony, 3 November 1865, 23 April 1867.

54. FCZIM, folder 39, E. Glasgow, 6 April 1860.

55. FCSRC, business papers, P. Harmony, 12 August 1859; José Cordero, 24 February 1860, 20 September 1862; FCZIM, folder 41, P. Harmony, 18 August 1859, 7 August 1861; folder 67, José Cordero, 11 September 1862.

56. FCZIM, folder 41, P. Harmony, 6 June 1861; folder 67, P. Harmony, 10 July 1861; FCSRC, business papers, P. Harmony, 10 July 1861.

57. FCSRC, business papers, Delino Hermanos, 16 September 1862.

58. FCZIM, folder 68, F. Maceyra, 26 April 1878.

59. FCZIM, folder 41, P. Harmony, 15 March 1860; folder 66, Alvarez Araujo, 29 November 1859; FCSRC, borrador, Felipe Chávez to P. Harmony, 5 October 1859.

60. FCSRC, business papers, Antonio José Otero, 8 July 1862; FCZIM, folder 41, Antonio José Otero, 3 December 1862.

61. It is possible that Pablo was also a partner. An invoice from the First National Bank of Santa Fe indicates that Pablo Delgado was making regular deposits on Felipe Chávez's account (FCSRC, business papers, [no name, ca. November 1872]).

62. FCSRC, business papers, P. Harmony, 10 January 1857.

63. FCZIM, folder 33, Simón Delgado, 4 February 1863, 10 February 1863, 25 March 1863, 15 September 1865; Pablo Delgado, 9 June 1869, 18 June 1869, 30 July 1870, 12 May 1871, 20 July 1871, 25 February 1872; FCSRC, business papers, Simón Delgado, 1 September 1861; W. H. Moore and Co., 1865; Pablo Delgado, 28 June 1870, 13 October 1870, 23 February 1871; FCZIM, folder 41, P. Harmony, 16 April 1867.

64. FCSRC, business papers, 1868, Pablo Delgado, 11 June 1868.

65. FCZIM, folder 21, F. Manzanares, 26 December 1868.

66. FCZIM, folder 33, Pablo Delgado, 9 May 1869. Amberg informed Chávez at the end of May that his partner (Gustave Elsberg) had cheated him, stolen all their property, and destroyed his reputation. He had even sold their store in Chihuahua. As soon as Amberg heard of this, he went to Chihuahua to take care of the situation. Amberg assured Chávez that he would pay everything he owed even before it was due (FCSRC, business papers, Jacob Amberg, 30 May 1869).

67. FCZIM, folder 33, Pablo Delgado, 9 May 1868, 18 June 1869.

68. FCZIM, folder 33. Unfortunately, it is not clear how much each partner invested in the operation initially; the one surviving invoice indicates that Chávez contributed $20,795.14, while Simón Delgado's share was substantially smaller, $3,827.65 (FCSRC, business papers, [no name], 1861, Simón Delgado, 1 September 1861).

69. FCZIM, folder 33, P. Delgado, 2 May 1872.

70. FCZIM, folder 33, Pablo Delgado, 30 July 1870; folder 39, Antonio José Otero, 9 January 1859; FCSRC, business papers, Pablo Delgado, 28 June 1870, 27 October 1870, 23 February 1871.

71. FCZIM, folder 39, E. Glasgow, 2 February 1861; folder 31, W. H. Chick, 3 October 1869.

72. FCSRC, business papers, A. Montoya, 12 July 1858.

73. FCZIM, folder 39. In 1871 he was still authorizing P. Harmony to make payments in gold, but the reasons for this specific request are not clear (FCZIM, folder 41, Theodore Herrmann, 18 April 1871).

74. The evidence is not conclusive. The only reference to the deposit of gold comes from one invoice (FCZIM, folder 33, W. H. Chick, 24 June 1871).

75. FCSRC, business papers, 1859. This was not unusual. In September 1861, on Chávez's behalf, Simón Delgado sent $15,400 in libranzas to P. Harmony in New York (FCSRC, business papers, S. Delgado, 1 September 1861). In 1864 P. Harmony gave him credit for $38,833.37 (FCZIM, folder 41, 1 October 1864).

76. FCZIM, folder 41, P. Harmony, 24 August 1863; folder 31, Chick, Armijo, and Co., 10 November 1867, 18 November 1867; FCZIM, folder 31, 18 October 1867.

77. FCSRC, business papers, P. Harmony, 31 October 1857; FCZIM, folder 66, P. Harmony, 29 September 1856.

78. Eighth Census of the United States, roll 712.

79. Ninth Census of the United States, roll 897.

80. FCZIM, folder 41, P. Harmony, 11 January 1871; folder 39, Glasgow Brothers, 1 January 1879; folder 21, Browne and Manzanares, 3 July 1879; Chick, Browne, and Co., 3 July 1879; FCSRC, business papers, bank statement for 1872; FCZIM, folder 41, P. Harmony, 31 December 1879. In November 1870 Manzanares wrote explaining that even though Chávez had been proposed as one of the directors of the National Bank to be established in Santa Fe, that would not be possible because all of the stock had been sold. It is interesting to note that three of the six directors were merchants from the Río Abajo: José Leandro Perea, Manuel Antonio Otero, and Frank A. Manzanares. The other three directors were S. B. Elkins, J. L. Johnson, and J. L. Griffin (FCSRC, business papers, 1870, Frank A. Manzanares, 18 November 1870). Unfortunately, due to changes in census format, it is not possible to establish if the family wealth continued to grow during the 1870s.

81. Most of the surviving partidos are in FCZIM, folder 59; folder 68, Luis M. Baca, 14 October 1878.

82. FCSRC, business papers, Edwin Edgar, 1 October 1869.

83. The first surviving record of Chávez shipping wool dates from 1869 (FCZIM, folder 31, W. H. Chick, 3 October 1869; FCSRC, business papers, Chick, Browne, and Co., 14 October 1872). Coordinating wool deliveries was also complex (FCZIM, folder 68, Luis M. Baca, 14 October 1878); sometimes, if only a small lot arrived at the railroad terminal, the middle-man would wait until he accumulated a larger amount to negotiate for a better price (FCSRC, business papers, Chick, Browne, and Co., 25 April 1872).

84. FCZIM, folder 31, W. H. Chick, 3 October 1869, 17 October 1869, 10 October 1870; folder 21, Browne and Manzanares, 2 April 1878; folder 25, Jesus Bonifacio Chávez, 10 September 1870; folder 39, Glasgow Brothers, 17 May 1878, 14 June 1878, 11 July 1878, 27 July 1878; folder 41, P. Harmony, 1 October 1878, 6 October 1878, 6 November 1878; folder 68, Luis M. Baca, 14 November 1878; FCSRC, business papers, Chick, Browne, and Co., 14 August 1872; business papers, Glasgow Brothers, 21 April 1879, 25 April 1879.

85. FCZIM, folder 41, P. Harmony, 31 December 1879.

86. FCZIM, folder 41, P. Harmony, 26 October 1879, 8 November 1879, 10 November 1879; folder 39, E. J. Glasgow, 2 October 1879.

87. FCZIM, folder 17, Vicente M. Baca, 29 April 1879.

88. FCSRC, business papers, P. Harmony, 5 June 1861; FCZIM, folder 41, P. Harmony, 6 June 1861.

89. FCSRC, business papers, Z. Staab and Brother, 14 June 1868.

90. FCZIM, folder 67, José Lobato account, 21 July 1868 to 20 May 1872; folder 68, José Miguel Baca account, 12 February 1868 to 24 June 1873; Rita R. de Valencia, 22 May 1873.

91. FCZIM, folder 67, Baca's partial account, January 1868 to June 1873.

92. FCSRC, business papers, 1868, Pablo Delgado, 27 October 1870, 13 November 1870.

93. FCZIM, folder 41, P. Harmony, 10 January 1864, 10 May 1864, 28 September 1864, 1 October 1864, 10 October 1864; folder, 67, A. Castillo, 8 October 1864; FCSRC, business papers, P. Harmony, 7 February 1865. The former was at 59 East 28th Street; the latter was at 36 East 29th Street.

94. FCSRC, business papers, P. Harmony, 1 December 1865; FCZIM, folder 41, P. Harmony, 6 May 1865, 10 May 1865, 3 October 1865.

95. FCSRC, business papers, P. Harmony, 5 April 1866, 5 October 1866.

96. FCZIM, folder 41, P. Harmony, 29 January 1866, 20 February 1866, 19 March 1867, 9 May 1867; FCSRC, business papers, P. Harmony, 28 December 1867. ˊ

97. FCZIM, folder 41, P. Harmony, 13 September 1869, 9 October 1869.

98. FCZIM, folder 41, P. Harmony, 8 March 1871, 6 May 1871, 11 July 1871.

99. FCZIM, folder 39, E. Glasgow, 1 January 1879; folder 41, P. Harmony, 22 July 1879, 28 October 1879.

CHAPTER SEVEN

1. Henry Hilgert to Felipe Chávez, 5 July 1867 (FCZIM, folder 42).

2. Jose Zubía to Manuel Delgado, 17 May 1844 (SRC, Delgado Papers, Dingee Collection, 1842–46); correspondence from José Leandro Perea (1865, 1877, and 1881) shows both Perea and Delgado doing favors for each other (SRC, Felipe Delgado Business Papers, 1864–81); Juan García to Martín Amador, a merchant from Las Cruces, 9 September 1877 (Las Cruces, New Mexico, New Mexico State University, Special Collections, Martín Amador Papers, box 15); Howard Roberts Lamar stresses the division between the "more conservative native forces advocating home rule and preservation of the status quo and their opponents who felt that New Mexico must move with the times" (*The Far Southwest, 1846–1912: A Territorial History* (New Haven: Yale University Press, 1966), 101. O'Brien indicates that cooperation was crucial to the success of non-Hispano merchants (see "Independence," passim). Merchants also realized the importance of cooperation to maintain efficient communications between the province and shipping points for trade goods. In 1851 more than sixty leading Hispano and non-Hispano entrepreneurs petitioned the United States government to expand the mail service between Santa Fe and Independence (MAP, roll 2, frames 1076–78).

3. Miscellaneous letters from H. Hilgert to Felipe Chávez, 1866–71 (FCZIM, folder 42); Lamar, *Far Southwest*, 87–134.

4. *History of New Mexico: Its Resources and People*, vol. 2 (Los Angeles: Pacific States Publishing Co., 1907), 536–37.

5. MANM, roll 28, frames 736–38; roll 32, frames 1607–28; roll 37, frames 456–58; see appendix 3; Eighth Census of the United States, rolls 712–16; Ninth Census of the United States, rolls 893–97; *Westport Border Star*, 15 July 1859, p. 3; ibid., 12 August 1859; R. G. Dunn and Company Collection, vol 1., 346.

6. MANM, roll 24, frame 794; roll 28, frames 772–73; roll 37, frame 396; FCZIM,

folder 39, Antonio José Otero, 9 January 1859; FCSRC, business papers, Antonio José Otero, 8 July 1862; FCZIM, folder 41, Antonio José Otero, 3 December 1862; FCZIM, folder 5, Manuel Antonio Otero, 10 January 1867; folders 6–11, numerous letters from Manuel Antonio writing from La Constancia.

7. Gross, Kelly, and Company to Manuel Antonio Otero, 22 December 1881 (Albuquerque, New Mexico, University of New Mexico, Center for Southwest Research, General Library).

8. Miller, *Soldiers and Settlers*, 131–32.

9. Miguel Antonio Otero, *My Life on the Frontier, 1864–1882: Incidents and Characters of the Period When Kansas, Colorado, and New Mexico Were Passing Through the Last of Their Wild and Romantic Years*, vol. 1 of *Otero: An Autobiographical Trilogy* (New York: Arno Press, 1974), 280–288; Lamar, *Far Southwest*, 104.

10. Otero, *Life on the Frontier*, 8–164; *History of New Mexico*, vol. 2, 537.

11. Otero, *Life on the Frontier*, 11–12.

12. Otero, *Life on the Frontier*, 87, 164. In return for ceding their lands, Indian tribes received yearly payments, known as annuities, from the United States government. See O'Brien, "Independence," 56–58.

13. Manuel Antonio Otero listed $10,000 in real estate and $154,550 in personal estate. José Leandro Perea was the richest with $225,000; he was followed by Mariano Yrizarri with $213,000, Cerain St. Vrain with $211,000, and W. H. Moore with $165,000 (Eighth Census of the United States, rolls 712–16; Ninth Census of the United States, rolls 893–97); see appendixes 3 and 4.

14. Otero, *Life on the Frontier*, 65; for credit reports on Otero, see R. G. Dunn and Co. Collection, vol. 1; for a discussion of Lewis Tappan's Mercantile Agency, the first credit-reporting firm in the United States, see O'Brien, "Independence," 130–132. Miguel Antonio Otero II followed his father's example and became a successful politician. President William McKinley appointed him governor of the territory of New Mexico in 1897. The first native New Mexican to occupy the post, he continued to act in that capacity until 1906. The literature on his political life is extensive, but there is little, if any, specific information on the family's economic activities (Lamar, *Far Southwest*, 197–201). The January 1992 issue of the *New Mexico Historical Review* is totally devoted to the career of Miguel Antonio Otero: Gerald D. Nash, "New Mexico in the Otero Era: Some Historical Perspectives," 1–12; María E. Montoya, "The Dual World of Governor Miguel A. Otero: Myth and Reality in Turn-of-the-Century New Mexico," 13–32; Cynthia Secor Welsh, "A 'Star Will Be Added': Miguel Antonio Otero and the Struggle for Statehood," 33–52; Jolane Culhane, "Miguel Antonio Otero: A Photographic Essay," 53–62. None of these publications addresses the business background of the Otero family.

15. Lamar includes a lot of information on the political activities of native New Mexicans like the Pereas, but does not address their economic activities (*Far Southwest*, 87, 90, 99, 134–35, 187–88, 192, 198–99). W. H. Allison, "Colonel Francisco Perea," *Old Santa Fe* 1 (1913), 209–22.

16. *Westport Border Star*, 12 August 1859, p. 3.

17. Simmons, "José Librado," in *Santa Fe Trail*, 120–33.

18. MANM, roll 28, frame 769; roll 34, frame 1232; roll 37, frame 524; R. G. Dunn and Co. Collection, vol. 1, 348.

19. Eighth Census of the United States, roll 712; Ninth Census of the United States, roll 893. Perea also participated in territorial politics and appears to have been strongly anti-American (Lamar, *Far Southwest*, 87, 90, 99). According to his granddaughter, at the time of his death in 1882 José Leandro owned $7 million. This information comes from a newspaper clipping, possibly from an Albuquerque newspaper (Albuquerque, New Mexico, University of New Mexico, Center for Southwest Research, General Library).

20. Lamar identified Perea as the president of the 1860 New Mexican Convention, which met in Santa Fe to consider Indian defense *(Far Southwest*, 99); for other references to Perea's anti-American feelings, see ibid., 87, 90, 91.

21. Eighth Census of the United States, roll 712; Ninth Census of the United States, roll 893.

22. E. Boyd Collection, box 11, folder 180.

23. R. G. Dunn and Co. Collection, vol. 1, 364.

24. R. G. Dunn and Co. Collection, vol. 1, 364; Eighth Census of the United States, roll 712; Ninth Census of the United States, roll 893; appendixes 3 and 4.

25. Eighth Census of the United States, roll 712; Ninth Census of the United States, roll 893; see appendix 3.

26. The documents examined during the course of this study do not permit an assessment of Governor Manuel Armijo's wealth; Janet Lecompte is working on a definitive biography of Manuel Armijo, and it is quite likely that her study will answer many questions regarding Armijo's business activities. For a study of two other members of the Armijo family (Rafael and Manuel) at the time of the Civil War and the impact of their support for the Confederacy, see Susan V. Richards, "From Traders to Traitors? The Armijo Brothers Through the Nineteenth Century," *New Mexico Historical Review* 69 (July 1994): 215–29.

27. *Westport Border Star*, 15 July 1859, p. 3.

28. *History of New Mexico*, 2: 537–40; Eighth Census of the United States, roll 712; Ninth Census of the United States, roll 893; R. G. Dunn and Co. Collection, vol. 1, 341; see appendix 3.

29. Richards, "Traders to Traitors?" 215–29; Eighth Census of the United States, roll 712; SRC, Rafael Armijo Papers, business papers, account book.

30. SRC, Rafael Armijo Papers, business papers, account book.

31. Albuquerque, New Mexico, University of New Mexico, Center for Southwest Research, John J. Gay Papers, items 12, 15, 16, 22.

32. Center for Southwest Research, John J. Gay Papers, item 10, 5 January 1859; item 11, 13 January 1859.

33. Center for Southwest Research, John J. Gay Papers, items 15 and 16, 18 February 1861; item 24, 17 March 1864; item 26, 8 April 1865; item 27, 15 April 1865; item 33, 8 November 1866; item 37, 14 June 1867; item 38, 8 July 1868; item

39, 8 August 1868; item 40, 1869. Richards, "Traders to Traitors?" 215–29; Parish, *Mercantile Capitalism*, 35–36, 38–45, "German Jew," 18–23, 139–42.

34. John O. Baxter has published the best study on Armijo, "Salvador Armijo: Citizen of Albuquerque, 1823–1879," *New Mexico Historical Review* 53 (July 1978): 219–37.

35. Baxter, "Salvador Armijo," 223–27; Eighth Census of the United States, roll 712; Ninth Census of the United States, roll 893.

36. *Westport Border Star,* 15 July 1859, p. 3; ibid., 12 August 1859, p. 3; Eighth United States Census, rolls 712–16; Ninth United States Census, rolls 893–97; appendix 3.

37. SRC, Delgado Papers, Dingee Collection, 1837–53, 1842–46, 1843–51; SRC, Felipe Delgado Business Papers, 1864–81; FCSRC, business papers, [ca. November 1872]; FCSRC, business papers, P. Harmony, 10 January 1857; FCZIM, folder 33, Simón Delgado, 4 February 1863, 10 February 1863, 25 March 1865, Pablo Delgado, 9 May 1869, 18 June 1869, 30 July 1870, 12 may 1871, 20 July 1871, 25 February 1872; FCSRC, business papers, Simón Delgado, 1 September 1861, Pablo Delgado, 8 June 1870, 13 October 1870. Felipe Delgado worked for Felipe Chávez until the latter's death in 1906 (FCZIM, folder 33, Felipe Delgado, 16 June 1906).

38. SRC, Delgado Papers, Dingee Collection, 1854; Eighth Census of the United States, rolls 712–16; Ninth Census of the United States, rolls 893–97; see appendix 3; for a discussion of the Felipe Chávez's assets, see chapter 6.

39. Eighth Census of the United States, rolls 712–16; Ninth Census of the United States, rolls 893–97; see appendix 3.

40. SRC, Delgado Papers, Jenkins Collection; SRC, Felipe Delgado Business Papers, 1864–81.

41. SRC, Felipe Delgado Business Papers, 1864–81.

42. SRC, Felipe Delgado Business Papers, 1864–81.

43. Internal conflict between Porfirio Díaz and Sebastián Lerdo de Tejada highlight the history of Mexico during the 1870s; Parkes, *History of Mexico*, 270–73, 281–322; Cumberland, *Mexico*, 194–96.

CHAPTER EIGHT

1. Miller, *Soldiers and Settlers*, 308–9. Aguirre and his brothers may also have worked as subcontractors in Arizona. Epifanio was killed in Arizona in 1870 (M. B. Aguirre, "Trader's Bride," 5–23). By 1870 William H. Moore had become the third-richest foreigner in New Mexico (see appendix 4).

2. Miller, *Soldiers and Settlers*, 308–9, 331–55 (this tabulation has been extracted from appendixes 1–14, 357–78). The same trend appears in Arizona and Texas.

3. The census reports for 1850 and 1880 do not include values for personal estate and preclude a long-term assessment and comparison of the economic assets of New Mexican merchants.

4. Eighth Census of the United States, rolls 712–16; Ninth Census of the United States, rolls 893–97; see appendix 3.

5. Eighth Census of the United States, rolls 712–16; Ninth Census of the United States, rolls 893–97; see appendix 3.

6. Eighth Census of the United States, rolls 712–16; Ninth Census of the United States, rolls 893–97; see appendix 3.

7. Eighth Census of the United States, rolls 712–16; Ninth Census of the United States, rolls 893–97; see appendix 3.

8. Eighth Census of the United States, rolls 712–16; Ninth Census of the United States, rolls 893–97; see appendix 3.

9. Eighth Census of the United States, rolls 712–16; Ninth Census of the United States, rolls 893–97; see appendix 3.

10. Eighth Census of the United States, rolls 712–16; Ninth Census of the United States, rolls 893–97; see appendix 4.

11. Eighth Census of the United States, rolls 712–16; Ninth Census of the United States, rolls 893–97; see appendix 4.

12. For a discussion of some of the problems associated with the use of census information, see Susan C. Boyle, *Social Mobility in the United States: Historiography and Methods* (New York: Garland Publishing, Inc., 1989), 115–16; Margaret Walsh, "The Census as an Accurate Source of Information: The Value of Mid-Nineteenth Century Manufacturing Returns," *Historical Methods Newsletter* 3 (September 1970): 4–13; Joel Perlman, "Using Census Districts in Analysis: Record Linkage and Sampling," *Journal of Interdisciplinary History* 10 (Autumn 1979): 279–89; Ian Winchester, "The Linkage of Historical Records by Man and Computer: Techniques and Problems," *Journal of Interdisciplinary History* 1 (Autumn 1970): 107–25; Theodore Hershberg, Alan Burstein, and Robert Dockhorn, "Record Linkage," *Historical Methods Newsletter* 9 (March–June 1976): 137–63.

13. Eighth Census of the United States, rolls 712–16; Ninth Census of the United States, rolls 893–97; appendixes 3 and 4.

14. Eighth Census of the United States, rolls 712–16; Ninth Census of the United States, rolls 893–97; appendixes 3 and 4.

15. Eighth Census of the United States, rolls 712–16; Ninth Census of the United States, rolls 893–97.

16. Nestor and Nicolás lived in Chihuahua for a decade between the late 1860s and 1870s. Between 1860 and 1870 the reported average age for New Mexico merchants rose from 36.37 to 38.53 years (Eighth Census of the United States, rolls 712–16; Ninth Census of the United States, rolls 893–97).

17. Eighth Census of the United States, rolls 712–16; Ninth Census of the United States, rolls 893–97. Although most of these individuals appeared to be reaching middle age, the accumulation of personal estate seems excessive for the conditions in a territory where the average personal estate that farmers reported was less than $100.

18. Eighth Census of the United States, rolls 712–16; Ninth Census of the

United States, rolls 893–97. Freighting was an occupation for younger men — only three freighters were over fifty years of age. The average age for freighters in 1870 was 34.34 years, more than four years younger than the merchants.

19. Eighth Census of the United States, rolls 712–16; Ninth Census of the United States, rolls 893–97; see appendix 5.

20. Eighth Census of the United States, rolls 712–16; Ninth Census of the United States, rolls 893–97.

21. Eighth Census of the United States, rolls 712–16; Ninth Census of the United States, rolls 893–97.

22. "Salazar and Gallegos," *Pace* (n.d.): 1–4. There is an extensive correspondence between Nicolás Armijo and Felipe Chávez which documents the commercial activities of the Armijo brothers in Mexico (see FCZIM, folder 5, Nicolás Armijo, 2 February 1869, 2 March 1869, 9 March 1869, 15 November 1869).

23. Both Valencia and Bernalillo Counties ceded their eastern third to San Miguel while Doña Ana and Socorro Counties relinquished a substantial portion of their territory to make possible the creation of Grant and Lincoln Counties. Eighth Census of the United States, rolls 712–16; Ninth Census of the United States, rolls 893–97; see appendixes 3 and 4; Warren A. Beck and Ynez D. Haase, *Historical Atlas of New Mexico* (Norman: University of Oklahoma Press, 1969), 34–38. Lamar discusses the lawlessness that characterized these newly created counties in the years after the Civil War (*Far Southwest*, 151–70).

24. Pedro Baca reported $19,000 in 1860, but only $12,000 in 1870; Guadalupe Miranda claimed $2,800 in 1860, but only $1,500 a decade later.

25. Eighth Census of the United States, rolls 712–16; Ninth Census of the United States, rolls 893–97; for a listing of New Mexican merchants included in the 1860 and 1870 censuses, see appendix 3. Darlis A. Miller presents the best analysis to date on cross-cultural marriages ("Cross-Cultural Marriages in the Southwest: The New Mexico Experience, 1846–1900," *New Mexico Historical Review* 57 [1982]: 335–59). See also Nancie L. González, *The Spanish-Americans of New Mexico: A Heritage of Pride* (Albuquerque: University of New Mexico Press, 1967), 80; Baxter, "Salvador Armijo," 229.

26. Richards, "Traders to Traitors?" 215–29; Center for Southwest Research, John J. Gay Papers, items 12, 15, 16, 22; Baxter, "Salvador Armijo," 218–37. For a more detailed account of the Armijos' activities, see chapter 7.

27. The correspondence of Felipe Chávez at this time indicates that many merchants were in great fear of suffering major losses as a result of the hostilities (FCZIM, folder 41, P. Harmony, 28 September 1864; FCSRC, business papers, Otero and Sellar, 22 September 1868).

28. Lamar, *Far Southwest*, 134; the Missouri *Westport Border Star* published a register of the men, wagons, and stock that passed Council Grove during the months of June and July 1859: more than fifteen hundred men and one thousand wagons traveled to New Mexico carrying almost three thousand tons of merchandise (15 July 1859, p. 3; 12 August 1859, p. 3). According to the *Trinidad Chronicle*

News some of wagons trains were so long in the late 1860s and early 1870s that it took two or three days for their teams to pass through Uncle Dick Wootton's toll gate (quoted in Honora DeBusk Smith, "Early Life in Trinidad and the Purgatory Valley" [Master's thesis, Colorado College, 1930], 29).

CONCLUSION

1. A quick examination of John M. Kingsbury's correspondence reveals a striking similarity with that of Felipe Chávez (Jane Lenz Elder and David J. Weber, eds., *Trading in Santa Fe: John M. Kingsbury's Correspondence with James Josiah Webb, 1853–1861* [Courtesy of the authors, manuscript submitted for publication]).

APPENDIX ONE

1. All of the information here comes from MANM. Roll, frame, and date are included for each entry.

APPENDIX TWO

1. All of the information here comes from MANM. Roll and frame are included for each entry. The first year for which there are surviving manifests of merchandise introduced by Americans into New Mexico is 1831 (MANM, roll 14, frames 176–87).

Glossary

acero: steel

acto: act, decree

administrador: administrator

aduana: customs house

ad valorem: levied according to assessed value

aforo: appraisal

aguardiente: alcoholic spirit

alambique: still

alcabala: excise tax

alcalde: mayor, magistrate

alcaldía: municipal district

algodón: cotton

almacén: warehouse

almirantazgo: import duty

almojarifazgo: customs fee

almud: dry measure about 1.5 pints

alpaca: wool, cloth

anta: elk skin

aparejo: pack saddle

aprehensor: apprehender

arancel: tariff, customs duty

arbitrio: municipal or excise tax

archivar: archive

arma: arm, weapon

arriero: muleteer

artículo: article

atajo: team of pack mules

audiencia: Spanish colonial high court
autoridad: authority
avería: tax to cover transportation costs
ayuntamiento: town council

bala: bolt of cloth
barril: barrel
barrio: neighborhood
baúl: trunk
bayeta: baize
bayetón: large woolen poncho
bestia: animal such as horse, cow, sheep, or goat
bien: property
bono: bond, note
borrador: onion-skin notebooks containing carbon copies of correspondence
buey: ox
de bula santa cruzada: tax on indulgences
bulto: bundle
burro de carga: donkey able to carry a load

caballo: horse
cabra: goat
caja: box, chest
cajita: little box
cajón: big box, chest
Camino Real: Royal Road
Camino Real de Tierra Adentro: the Royal Road to Chihuahua and the interior of
    Mexico
cantidad: amount, quantity
cantina: large wallet or leather box; canteen
carga: load, burden
cargamento: cargo, shipment
carnero: ram, wether
carro: cart
casa: house
castor: beaver
cátedra: college-level class
caza: hunting
chicle: chewing gum
chile colorado: red pepper
cibolero: buffalo hunter
cíbolo: buffalo, buffalo skin
ciudadano: citizen

colcha: quilt, bedspread
comerciante: merchant
comercio: commerce
comiso (ley de):   law that stipulates procedures for the seizure or confiscation of goods
común: common
conchilla: seashell
conductor: driver of a caravan
consulado: merchant guild
consumo: consumption
contrabando: smuggled goods, contraband
cordobán: tanned goat skin
cordón: string of people or animals
corona: blanket used with the saddle
corte: a piece of cloth or fabric larger than a remnant
Cortes: Spanish legislative body (includes equivalent of House of Representatives and Senate)
costal: large sack for grain
costurera: seamstress
cuaderno de guías: notebook where *guías* were recorded
cuenta: account; bead

decreto: decree
denunciante: denouncer
derecho: right; duty
derecho de consumo: consumption fee
derecho de fundidor: smelting charge
derecho de internación: tariff, import duty
derecho de reserva: literally, reserve duty; charged by New Mexico customs to merchants
destino: destination
diezmo: tithe
diligencia: errand
dinero: money
Diputación Provincial: provincial delegation to Congress
diputado: representative to Congress; deputy
Dirección General de Hacienda: Treasury Department
districto: district
documento: document
donde me convenga: where it suits me
douceur: gift

efectos: goods, effects, merchandise
efectos del país: local merchandise

efectos extranjeros: foreign merchandise
empaque: packaging
empleado: employee
escribiente: scribe
estado: state, condition; government
estanco: monopoly on tobacco
expender: to sell
extranjero: foreign
extraordinario: extraordinary

factura: receipt
fanega: grain measure of about 1.6 bushels
fardo: bundle
feria: fair
fiador: guarantor
fierro: iron
flecha: arrow
fletero: freighter
fraudulenta introducción: illegal entry
frazada: blanket
frazada corriente: common blanket
frazada camera: blanket for the bed, bedspread
frontera: frontier

gachupín: Spanish-born merchant who settles in Latin America (Nahuatl term
     that means "one who wears spurs," i.e. oppressor)
gamuza: deer skin
gasto: expense
genízaros: non-Pueblo Indian captive rescued by the Spanish settlers from various
     nomadic tribes
gentil: heathen, pagan
gobierno: government
grano: grain; monetary unit (12 *granos*=1 *real*)
gruesa: gross
grupera: leather band; part of the pack saddle
guantes: gloves
guía: commercial passport that itemized articles shipped between the various
     Mexican provinces

habitante: inhabitant
hacendado: owner of real estate, farm and/or cattle ranch
herramienta: tool

importación: import
importe: amount
indiana: calico
indio: Indian
interino: provisional, temporary
interna: interior, internal

jefe político: political chief
jerga (also *gerga*): coarse woolen cloth
juez de paz: justice of the peace
juez: judge
junta: council, board
jurisdicción: jurisdiction

labrador: farmer
lana: wool
letra de cambio: letter of exchange; draft
letra de crédito: written order to pay; draft
letrado: lawyer
libranza: written order to pay; draft
lienzo: linen

maestro: teacher
mahón: nankeen
manito: abbreviation of *hermanito;* literally, little brother or friend (term used in New Mexico)
manta: coarse cotton fabric
mantelería: table linen
máquina: machine
marítima: maritime
mayordomo: steward
media: sock, stocking
mejicano: Mexican
media añata: half of the first year's salary of officials
mercería: haberdashery
mesada: tax on appointive offices
milicia: militia
millonario: millionaire
modista: dressmaker
moneda: coin; currency
mula: mule

nación bárbara: hostile Indian tribe
naipes: playing cards
negociante: trader, merchant
negocio: business; deal
nota: note, bond, bill
nulidad: error that nullifies a legal act
nutria: beaver

oficio: official document
orden de pago: order to pay
oso: bear
otros puntos en el camino: other points along the road
oveja: sheep

palmeo: trade tax based on the bulk of the merchandise
paño: type of cloth
pañuelo: scarf, handkerchief
papel: paper; official document
partida: shipment, consignment
partido: administrative unit; pastoral institution that dominated the sheep industry in New Mexico
partidario: individual who signed an agreement to care for sheep belonging to someone else
pasaporte: passport
pase: pass; permission to carry small amount of merchandise between provinces
patrón: boss, master
peón: laborer
peso: monetary unit
peso a precios antiguos: bookkeeping monetary unit worth 4 *reales*
peso a precio de proyecto: bookkeeping monetary unit worth 6 *reales*
peso de la tierra: bookkeeping monetary unit worth 2 *reales*
peso de plata: silver *peso*
piel: skin
pieza: piece; unit
piloncillo: Mexican brown sugar in small pylon-shaped cakes
piñón: pinyon, pine nut
población: population
préstamo forzoso: forced loan
primo: cousin
promotor fiscal: district attorney
promovedor: promoter
proveniente: coming from

provincia: province
público: public
pueblo: town; people
puesto: post, place
punto: spot, place

quintal: weight measurement equal to about 130 pounds in early-nineteenth-century system of weights and measures
quinto: royalty on bullion; literally, a fifth

rancho: ranch
real: monetary unit (8 *reales*=1 *peso*)
rebozo: shawl
recargo: surcharge, surtax
recibo: receipt
remesa: remittance
remitente: sender
rico: wealthy individual
rúbrica: signature; category

sabanilla: linen bedspread
salvaje: savage, Indian
sarape de niño: child's sarape
sarape: shawl or blanket worn as an outer garment
sarape corriente: common sarape
sarga: serge
sayal: coarse woolen cloth
sastre: tailor
segundo: second
sisa: excise on food
sobremesa: tablecloth
sombrero: hat
subcomisario: deputy sheriff
subscripción: subscription
subsidio extraordinario: extraordinary subsidy
sujeto: subject
Supremo Poder Ejecutivo: Supreme Executive Power

tejido: weaving
tercio: bale, bundle; each of the bundles in a mule load; third
territorio: territory
tierra de pan llevar: irrigated land

tornaguía: document indicating that merchandise taken into Mexico had been delivered
trabajo: work

vaca: cow
valor: value; bond, stock
vara: unit of measurement close to 1 yard
vino: wine
vocal: deputy
voluntaria: voluntary
Vuestra Excelencia: Your Excellency

yegua: mare

Bibliography

PRIMARY SOURCES

Manuscript Materials

Fort Collins, Colorado. Colorado State University. Special Collections.
    Mexican Archives of New Mexico, Microfilm Edition (MANM).
    Spanish Archives of New Mexico, Microfilm Edition (SANM).
Cambridge, Massachusetts. Harvard University. Special Collections, Baker
    Library.
    R. G. Dunn and Company Collection.
Santa Fe, New Mexico. New Mexico State Records Center and Archives (SRC).
    Ray Juan de Aragón Papers.
    Manuel Alvarez Papers (MAP).
    Rafael Armijo Papers.
    E. Boyd Collection.
    Felipe Chávez Papers (FCSRC).
    Delgado Papers. Dingee Collection.
    Delgado Family Papers. Jenkins Collection.
    Felipe Delgado Business Papers.
    History File 181. Blankets/Weaving.
    Read Collection.
    Twitchell Collection.
Las Cruces, New Mexico. Territorial Archives of New Mexico, Microfilm Edition.
Las Cruces, New Mexico. New Mexico State University. Special Collections.
    Martín Amador Papers.
Socorro, New Mexico. Socorro County Historical Society.
    Antonio Abeita y Armijo Papers.

El Paso, Texas. University of Texas at El Paso. Special Collections.
  Archivos del Ayuntamiento de Chihuahua, Microfilm Edition.
  Chihuahua (State) Periodicals, Microfilm Edition.
Albuquerque, New Mexico. University of New Mexico, Center for Southwest Research.
  Antonio Armijo Journal.
  Antonio Armijo Papers.
  Anita Ailer Ayala Papers.
  Borrego-Ortega Papers.
  José Felipe Chávez Papers (FCZIM).
  John J. Gay Papers.
  Gross, Kelly and Company Papers.
  Miguel Antonio Lovato Papers.
  Antonio José Martínez Papers.
  Perea Brothers Mercantile Papers.
  Jack D. Rittenhouse Papers.
  Secundino Romero Papers.
  Pedro Silva Papers.
Fort Dodge, Kansas.
  Fort Dodge Records, Microfilm Edition.

Government Publications

De Valois, Mariano. Letter to the House, 26th Cong., 1st sess., Edward Cross, representative of Arkansas, 20 April 1840, 13–16.
U.S. Congress. House. *Drawback Act.* 13th Cong., 1st sess., 1845. Rept. 458 to accompany H. Rept. 58.
———. *Manuel X. Harmony Petition.* 30th Cong., 1st sess., 1848. Rept. 540.
———. *To Establish Ports of Entry in Arkansas and Missouri, and to Allow Debenture.* 26th Cong., 1st sess., 1840. Rept. 540. Serial 372.
Denver, Colorado. National Archives.
  Internal Revenue Assessment Lists for the Territory of New Mexico, M-782, RG 58.
  Population Schedules. Eighth Census of the United States. Original Returns of the Assistant Marshalls, Microfilm Edition, 14/6, rolls 712–16.
  ———. Ninth Census of the United States. Original Returns of the Assistant Marshall, Microfilm Edition, 12/7, rolls 893–97.

Newspapers

Antorcha Federal (Chihuahua).
Council Grove (Kansas) Press.
El Fanal (Chihuahua).

El Noticioso (Chihuahua).
Franklin (Missouri) Intelligencer.
St. Louis Missouri Republican.
Santa Fe New Mexican.
New York Weekly Tribune.
Maryland Niles' National Register.
Pittsburgh Daily Commercial Journal.
Sacramento Daily Union.
Santa Fe Gazette.
Trinidad (Colorado) Chronicle News.
New Orleans Weekly Picayune.
Westport (Missouri) Border Star.

SECONDARY SOURCES

Books

Acuña, Rodolfo. *Occupied America: A History of Chicanos.* 2d ed. New York: Harper and Row, 1981.

Aguirre, Yginio. *Echoes of the Conquistadores: History of a Pioneer Family in the Southwest.* Casa Grande, AZ: Privately printed, 1983.

Almada, Francisco R. *Resúmen de la historia del estado de Chihuahua.* Mexico: Libros Mexicanos, 1955.

Atherton, Lewis Eldon. *The Frontier Merchant in Mid-America.* Columbia: University of Missouri Press, 1971.

Bancroft, Hubert H. *History of Arizona and New Mexico, 1530–1888.* San Francisco: The History Company, 1889.

Barbour, Barton H., ed. *Reluctant Frontiersman: James Ross Larkin on the Santa Fe Trail, 1856–1857.* Published in cooperation with the Historical Society of New Mexico. Albuquerque: University of New Mexico Press, 1990.

Barnes, Thomas C., Thomas H. Naylor, and Charles W. Polzer. *Northern New Spain: A Research Guide.* Tucson: University of Arizona Press, 1981.

Barrett, Walter. *The Old Merchants of New York City.* New York: Thomas R. Knox and Co., 1885.

Barry, Louise. *The Beginning of the West: Annals of the Kansas Gateway to the American West, 1540–1854.* Topeka, KS: Kansas State Historical Society, 1972.

Bartlett, John Russell. *Personal Narrative of Explorations and Incidents in Texas, New Mexico, Sonora, and Chihuahua.* Chicago: Río Grande Press, 1965.

Baxter, John O. *Las Carneradas: Sheep Trade in New Mexico, 1700–1860.* Albuquerque: University of New Mexico Press, 1987.

Beachum, Larry M. *William Becknell, Father of the Santa Fe Trade.* El Paso: Texas Western Press, 1982.

Beck, Warren A., and Ynez D. Haase. *Historical Atlas of New Mexico*. Norman: University of Oklahoma Press, 1969.

Beers, Henry P. *Spanish and Mexican Records of the American Southwest*. Tucson: University of Arizona Press, 1979.

Bethell, Leslie, ed. *Colonial Spanish America*. Cambridge, UK: Cambridge University Press, 1987.

Bolton, Herbert Eugene. *Athanaze de Mézieres and the Louisiana-Texas Frontier, 1768–1780*. 2 vols. Cleveland: Arthur H. Clark Co., 1914.

——. *Texas in the Middle Eighteenth Century: Studies in Spanish Colonial History and Administration*. Berkeley: University of California Press, 1915.

Bork, Albert William. "Nuevos aspectos del comercio entre Nuevo Méjico y Misuri, 1822–1846." Ph.D. diss., Universidad Nacional Autónoma de Méjico, 1944.

Boyle, Susan C. *Social Mobility in the United States: Historiography and Methods*. New York: Garland Publishing, Inc., 1989.

Brown, William E., coord. *The Santa Fe Trail*. U.S. Department of the Interior, National Park Service, 1963.

Browne, Linda Fergusson, ed. *Trader on the Santa Fe Trail: The Memoirs of Franz Huning*. Albuquerque: Calvin Horn Publisher, 1973.

Bryant, H. B., and H. D. Stratton. *Book-Keeping: Complete Exposition of the Science of Accounts in the Application to the Various Departments of Business: Including Complete Sets of Book Wholesale and Retail Merchandising*. New York: Ivison, Phinney, Blakeman and Company, 1865.

Carroll, H. Bailey, and J. Villasana Haggard, eds. and trans. *Three New Mexico Chronicles*. New York: Arno Press, 1967.

Castillo, Pedro, and Alberto Camarillo, eds. *Furia y muerte: Los bandidos chicanos*. Los Angeles: Aztlán Publications, 1973.

Chaput, Donald. *Francois X. Aubry: Trader, Trailmaker and Voyageur in the Southwest, 1846–1854*. Glendale, CA: The Arthur H. Clark Company, 1975.

Charles, Ralph. "Development of the Partido System in the New Mexico Sheep Industry." Master's thesis, University of New Mexico, 1940.

Chávez, Fray Angélico. *Archives of the Archdiocese of Santa Fe, 1678–1900*. Washington, D.C.: Academy of American Franciscan History, 1957.

——. *Origins of New Mexico Families in the Spanish Colonial Period*. 2d. ed. Albuquerque: University of Albuquerque Press in collaboration with Calvin Horn Publisher, 1973.

Chávez, Thomas E. *Manuel Alvarez, 1794–1856: A Southwestern Biography*. Niwot: University Press of Colorado, 1990.

——, ed. *Conflict and Acculturation: Manuel Alvarez's 1842 Memorial*. Santa Fe: Museum of New Mexico Press, 1988.

Cleland, Robert G. *This Reckless Breed of Men: The Trappers and Traders of the Southwest*. Albuquerque: University of New Mexico Press, 1976.

Cobos, Ruben. *A Dictionary of New Mexico and Southern Colorado Spanish*. Santa Fe: Museum of New Mexico Press, 1983.

Connor, Seymour V., and Jimmy M. Skaggs. *Broadcloth and Britches: The Santa Fe Trade*. College Station: Texas A & M University Press, 1977.

Crampton, C. Gregory, and Steven K. Madsen. *In Search of the Spanish Trail: Santa Fe to Los Angeles, 1829–1848*. Salt Lake City: Gibbs-Smith Publisher, 1994.

Cumberland, Charles C. *Mexico: The Struggle for Modernity*. New York: Oxford University Press, 1968.

deBuys, William. *Enchantment and Exploitation: The Life and Hard Times of a New Mexico Mountain Range*. Albuquerque: University of New Mexico Press, 1985.

De Thoma, Francisco. *Historia popular de Nuevo Méjico, desde su descubrimiento*. New York: American Book Company, 1896.

Drumm, Stella M., ed. *Down the Santa Fe Trail and into Mexico: the Diary of Susan Shelby Magoffin, 1846–1847*. New Haven: Yale University Press, 1927.

Duffus, R. L. *The Santa Fe Trail*. New York: Longmans, Green, and Co., 1930.

Dunbar, Roxanne Ortiz. *Roots of Resistance: Land Tenure in New Mexico, 1680–1980*. Los Angeles: Chicano Studies and American Indian Studies Center, UCLA, 1980.

Elder, Jane Lenz, and David J. Weber, eds. *Trading in Santa Fe: John M. Kingsbury's Correspondence with James Josiah Webb, 1853–1861*. Courtesy of the authors. Manuscript submitted for publication.

Espinoza, Gilberto, Tibo J. Chávez, and Carter M. Waid. *El Río Abajo*. Portales, NM: Bishop Publishing Co., n.d.

Fierman, Floyd S. *Guts and Ruts: The Jewish Pioneer on the Trail in the American Southwest*. New York: Ktav Publishing House, 1985.

Foley, William E., and C. David Rice. *The First Chouteaus: River Barons of Early St. Louis*. Urbana: University of Illinois Press, 1983.

Folmer, Henri. *Franco-Spanish Rivalry in North America, 1524–1763*. Spain in the West Series, VII. Glendale: Arthur H. Clark Company, 1953.

Foote, Cheryl J. *Women of the New Mexico Frontier, 1846–1912*. Niwot: University Press of Colorado, 1990.

Frank, Ross Harold. "From Settler to Citizen: Economic Development and Cultural Change in Late Colonial New Mexico, 1750–1820." Ph.D. diss., University of California, Berkeley, 1992.

Frazer, Robert W., ed. *Over the Chihuahua and Santa Fe Trails, 1847–1848: George Rutledge Gibson's Journal*. Albuquerque: University of New Mexico Press and New Mexico Historical Society, 1981.

Froebel, Julius. *Seven Years' Travel in Central America, Northern Mexico, and the Far West of the United States*. London: Richard Bentley, 1849.

Gardner, Mark L., ed. *Brothers on the Santa Fe and Chihuahua Trails: Edward James Glasgow and William Henry Glasgow, 1846–1848*. Niwot: University of Colorado Press, 1993.

Garrard, Lewis H. *Wah-To-Yah and the Taos Trail: or Prairie Travel and Scalp Dances, with a Look at Los Rancheros from Mulesback, and the Rocky Mountains Campfire.* Norman: University of Oklahoma Press, 1955.

Gerhard, Peter. *The Northern Frontier of New Spain.* Princeton: Princeton University Press, 1982.

González, Nancie L. *The Spanish Americans of New Mexico: A Heritage of Pride.* Albuquerque: University of New Mexico Press, 1967.

González, Manuel G. *The Hispanic Elite of the Southwest.* Southwestern Studies Series. No. 86. El Paso: Texas Western Press, 1989.

Green, Stanley C. *The Mexican Republic: The First Decade, 1823–1832.* Pittsburgh: University of Pittsburgh Press, 1987.

Greenleaf, Richard E., and Michael C. Meyer. *Research in Mexican History: Topics, Methodology, Sources: A Practical Guide to Field Research.* Lincoln: University of Nebraska Press, 1973.

Gregg, Kate L. *The Road to Santa Fe: The Journal and Diaries of George Champlin Sibley.* Albuquerque: University of New Mexico Press, 1952.

Gregg, Josiah. *The Commerce of the Prairies.* Edited by Max L. Moorhead. Norman: University of Oklahoma Press, 1954.

Griffen, William B. *Utmost Good Faith: Patterns of Apache-Mexican Hostilities in Northern Chihuahua Border Warfare, 1821–1848.* Albuquerque: University of New Mexico Press, 1988.

Gutiérrez, Ramón A. *When Jesus Came, the Corn Mothers Went Away: Marriage, Sexuality, and Power in New Mexico, 1500–1846.* Stanford: Stanford University Press, 1991.

Hale, Charles H. *Mexican Liberalism in the Age of Mora, 1821–1853.* New Haven: Yale University Press, 1968.

Hall, Thomas D. *Social Change in the Southwest, 1350–1880.* Lawrence: University Press of Kansas, 1989.

Haring, C. H. *The Spanish Empire in America.* New York: Harcourt, Brace and World, 1947.

History of New Mexico: Its Resources and People. 2 vols. Los Angeles: Pacific States Publishing Co., 1907.

Horgan, Paul. *Great River: The Río Grande in North American History.* 2 vols. New York: Holt, Rinehart and Winston, 1954.

Horsman, Reginald. *Race and Manifest Destiny: The Origins of American Racial Anglo-Saxonism.* Cambridge, MA: Harvard University Press, 1977.

Hulbert, Archer Butler, ed. *Southwest on the Turquoise Trail: The First Diaries on the Road to Santa Fe.* Denver: Denver Public Library, 1933.

Jackson, Donald, ed. *The Journals of Zebulon Montgomery Pike: With Letters and Related Documents.* 2 vols. Norman: University of Oklahoma Press, 1966.

Jenkins, Myra Ellen. *Calendar of the Mexican Archives of New Mexico, 1821–1846.* Santa Fe: State of New Mexico Records Center, 1970.

Johansen, Robert W. *To the Halls of the Montezumas: The Mexican War in the American Imagination.* New York: Oxford University Press, 1985.

Johansen, Bruce, and Roberto Maestas. *El Pueblo: The Gallegos Family's American Journey, 1503–1980.* New York: Monthly Review Press, 1983.

Jones, Oakah L. *Los Paisanos: Spanish Settlers in the Northern Frontier of New Spain.* Norman: University of Oklahoma Press, 1979.

———. *Nueva Vizcaya: Heartland of the Spanish Frontier.* Albuquerque: University of New Mexico Press, 1988.

Karnes, Thomas L. *William Gilpin, Western Nationalist.* Austin: University of Texas Press, 1970.

Lamar, Howard Roberts. *The Far Southwest, 1846–1912: A Territorial History.* New Haven: Yale University Press, 1966.

Lane, Lydia Spencer. *I Married a Soldier.* Albuquerque: University of New Mexico Press, 1964.

Larrain, Jorge. *Theories of Development: Capitalism, Colonialism, and Dependency.* Cambridge, UK: Polity Press, 1989.

Laut, Agnes C. *Pilgrims of the Santa Fe.* New York: Frederick A. Stokes Company, 1931.

Lavender, David. *Bent's Fort.* Lincoln: University of Nebraska Press, 1972.

Lawrence, Eleanor Frances. "The Old Spanish Trail from Santa Fe to California." Master's thesis, University of California, Berkeley, 1930.

Lecompte, Janet. *Pueblo Hardscrabble Greenhorn: The Upper Arkansas, 1832–1856.* Norman: University of Oklahoma Press, 1978.

———. *Rebellion in Río Arriba, 1837.* Albuquerque: University of New Mexico Press, 1985.

Limerick, Patricia Nelson. *The Legacy of Conquest: The Unbroken Past of the American West.* New York: W. W. Norton, 1987.

Limerick, Patricia Nelson, Clyde A. Milner II, and Charles E. Rankin, eds. *Trails: Toward a New Western History.* Lawrence: University Press of Kansas, 1991.

Loomis, Noel M., and Abraham P. Nasatir. *Pedro Vial and the Roads to Santa Fe.* Norman: University of Oklahoma Press, 1967.

López y Rivas, Gilberto. *The Chicanos: Life and Struggles of the Mexican Minority in the United States.* New York: Monthly Review Press, 1974.

———. *La Guerra del 47 y la resistencia popular a la ocupación.* Ciudad de Méjico: Nuestro Tiempo, 1976.

Loyola, Sister Mary. *American Occupation of New Mexico, 1821–1852.* New York: Arno Press, 1976.

Manning, William R. *Early Diplomatic Relations Between the United States and Mexico.* New York: Greenwood Press, 1968.

Mayer, Brantz. *Mexico: Aztec, Spanish, and Republican.* Hartford, CT: S. Drake and Co., 1852.

Meier, Matt S., and Feliciano Rivera. *A Bibliography for Chicano History.* San Francisco: R. and E. Research Associates, 1972.

———.*The Chicanos: A History of Mexican Americans.* New York: Hill and Wang, 1972.

Meketa, Jacqueline Dorgan. *Legacy of Honor: The Life of Rafael Chacón, A Nineteenth-Century New Mexican.* Albuquerque: University of New Mexico Press, 1986.

Miller, Darlis A. *Soldiers and Settlers: Military Supply in the Southwest, 1861–1885.* Albuquerque: University of New Mexico Press, 1989.

Minge, Ward Alan. "Frontier Problems in New Mexico Preceding the Mexican War, 1840–1846." Ph.D. diss., University of New Mexico, 1965.

Moorhead, Max L. *The Apache Frontier: Jacobo Ugarte and Spanish-Indian Relations in Northern New Spain, 1769–1791.* Norman: University of Oklahoma Press, 1968.

———. *New Mexico's Royal Road: Trade and Travel on the Chihuahua Trail.* Norman: University of Oklahoma Press, 1958.

Napton, William B. *Over the Santa Fe Trail, 1857.* Santa Fe: Stagecoach Press, 1964.

Nasatir, Abraham P. *Borderland in Retreat: From Spanish Louisiana to the Far Southwest.* Albuquerque: University of New Mexico Press, 1976.

Nasatir, Abraham P. *Before Lewis and Clark: Documents Illustrating the History of the Missouri, 1785–1804.* 2 vols. St Louis: Historical Documents Foundation, 1952.

New Mexico: Land of Enchantment. Washington, D.C.: GPO, 1941.

Noble, David Grant, ed. *Santa Fe: History of an Ancient City.* Santa Fe: School of American Research Press, 1989.

O'Brien, William Patrick. "Independence, Missouri's Trade with Mexico, 1827–1860: A Study in International Consensus and Cooperation." Ph.D. diss., University of Colorado, Boulder, 1994.

Oglesby, Richard E. *Manuel Lisa and the Opening of the Missouri Fur Trade.* Norman: University of Oklahoma Press, 1963.

Oliva, Leo E. *Soldiers on the Santa Fe Trail.* Norman: University of Oklahoma Press, 1967.

Olivera, Ruth R., and Liliane Crete. *Life in Mexico Under Santa Ana, 1822–1855.* Norman: University of Oklahoma Press, 1991.

Olmstead, Virginia. *New Mexico Spanish and Mexican Colonial Censuses: 1790, 1823, 1845.* Albuquerque: New Mexico Genealogical Society, 1975.

Ortiz y Pino, José, III. *Don José, The Last Patrón.* Santa Fe: Sunstone Press, 1981.

Otero, Miguel. *My Life on the Frontier, 1864–1882: Incidents and Characters of the Period When Kansas, Colorado, and New Mexico Were Passing Through the Last of Their Wild and Romantic Years.* Vol. 1 of *Otero: An Autobiographical Trilogy.* New York: Arno Press, 1974.

Pahissa, Angela Moyano. *El comercio de Santa Fe y la Guerra del 47.* Ciudad de Méjico: Secretaría de Educación Pública, 1976.

Palmer, Gabrielle G., ed. *El Camino Real de Tierra Adentro*. Cultural Resources Series. No. 11. New Mexico: Bureau of Land Management, 1993.

Parish, William J. *The Charles Ilfeld Company: A Study of the Rise and Decline of Mercantile Capitalism in New Mexico*. Harvard Studies in Business History 20. Cambridge, MA: Harvard University Press, 1961.

Parkes, Henry Bamford. *A History of Mexico*. Boston: Houghton Mifflin Company, 1969.

Pattie, James Ohio. *Personal Narrative of James O. Pattie*. Missoula: Mountain Press Publishing Company. 1988.

Pérez de Villagrá, Gaspar. *History of New Mexico*. Translated by Gilberto Espinoza. Los Angeles: The Quivira Society, 1933. Republished. New York: Arno Press, 1967.

Pitt, Leonard. *The Decline of the Californios: A Social History of the Spanish-Speaking Californios, 1846–1890*. Berkeley: University of California Press, 1966.

Polzer, C. W., and Thomas H. Polzer. *Northern New Spain: A Research Guide*. Tucson: University of Arizona Press, 1981.

Powell, Philip W. *Tree of Hate: Propaganda and Prejudice Affecting United States Relations with the Hispanic World*. New York: Basic Books, 1971.

Rabiela, Hira de Gortari. "La minería durante la guerra de independencia y los primeros años del México independiente, 1810–1824." In *The Independence of Mexico and the Creation of the New Nation*, edited by Jaime E. Rodríguez O., 129–61. Los Angeles: UCLA Latin American Center Publication, 1989.

Rittenhouse, Jack D. *The Santa Fe Trail: A Historical Bibliography*. Albuquerque: University of New Mexico Press, 1971.

Robinson, Cecil. *With the Ears of Strangers: The Mexican in American Literature*. Tucson: University of Arizona Press, 1963.

Robinson, Cecil. *Mexico and the Hispanic Southwest in American Literature*. Tucson: University of Arizona Press, 1977.

Rodriguez O., Jaime E., ed. *The Independence of Mexico and the Creation of the New Nation*. Los Angeles: UCLA Latin American Center Publication, 1989.

Russell, Marian Sloan. *Land of Enchantment: Memoir of Marian Russell Along the Santa Fe Trail*. Albuquerque: University of New Mexico Press, 1981.

Sandoval, David A. "Trade and the *Manito* Society in New Mexico, 1821–1848." Ph.D. diss., University of Utah, 1978.

Segale, Sister Blandina. *At the End of the Santa Fe Trail*. Columbus, Ohio, 1932.

Simmons, Marc. *The Little Lion of the Southwest: The Life of Manuel Antonio Chaves*. Chicago: Swallow Press, 1973.

——. *Murder on the Santa Fe Trail: An International Incident, 1843*. El Paso: Texas Western Press, 1987.

——. *New Mexico: A Bicentennial History*. New York: W. W. Norton and Company, 1977.

——. *Spanish Government in New Mexico*. Albuquerque: University of New Mexico Press, 1968.

———, ed. *On the Santa Fe Trail.* Lawrence: University Press of Kansas, 1986.

———, ed. and trans. *Fray Juan Agustín de Morfi's Account of Disorders in New Mexico, 1778.* Isleta, NM: Historical Society of New Mexico, 1977.

Simmons, Marc, and Joan Myers. *Along the Santa Fe Trail.* Albuquerque: University of New Mexico Press, 1986.

Sims, Harold Dana. *The Expulsion of Mexico's Spaniards, 1821–1836.* Pittsburgh: University of Pittsburgh Press, 1990.

Skaggs, Jimmy M., and Seymour V. Connor. *Broadcloth and Britches: The Santa Fe Trade.* College Station, TX: Texas A & M University Press, 1977.

Smith, Honora DeBusk. "Early Life in Trinidad and the Purgatory Valley." Master's thesis, Colorado College, 1899.

Stevens, Donald Fithian. *Origins of Instability in Early Republican Mexico.* Durham, NC: Duke University Press, 1991.

Stocking, Hobart E. *The Road to Santa Fe.* New York: Hastings House Publishers, 1971.

Stoddard, Amos. *Sketches, Historical and Descriptive of Louisiana.* Philadelphia: Matthew Carey, 1812.

Storrs, Augustus, and Alphonso Wetmore. *Santa Fe Trail First Reports: 1825.* Houston: Stagecoach Press, 1960.

Sunder, John E., ed. *Matt Field on the Santa Fe Trail.* Collected by Clyde and Mae Reed Porter. Norman: University of Oklahoma Press, 1960.

Sunseri, Alvin R. *Seeds of Discord: New Mexico in the Aftermath of the American Conquest, 1846–1861.* Chicago: Nelson-Hall, 1979.

Swadesh, Frances Leon. *Los Primeros Pobladores: Hispanic Americans of the Ute Frontier.* Notre Dame: University of Notre Dame Press, 1974.

———. *20,000 Years of History: A New Mexico Bibliography.* Santa Fe: Sunstone Press, 1973.

Thomas, Alfred Barnaby, ed. and trans. *Forgotten Frontiers: A Study of the Spanish Indian Policy of Don Juan Bautista de Anza, Governor of New Mexico, 1777–1787.* Norman: University of Oklahoma Press, 1932.

Thomas, Tom. "The Evolution of Transportation in Western Pennsylvania." Unpublished manuscript, 1994.

Thorndale, William, and William Dollarhide. *Map Guide to the U.S. Federal Censuses, 1790–1920.* Baltimore: Genealogical Publishing Co., 1987.

Tobias, Henry J. *A History of the Jews in New Mexico.* Albuquerque: University of New Mexico Press, 1990.

Twitchell, Ralph Emerson. *History of the Military Occupation of the Territory of New Mexico from 1846 to 1851 by the Government of the United States.* Chicago: Río Grande Press, 1963.

———. *Leading Facts of New Mexican History.* 2 vols. Albuquerque: Horn and Wallace, 1963.

———. *Old Santa Fe: The Story of New Mexico's Ancient Capital.* Chicago: Río Grande Press, 1963.

———, comp. *The Spanish Archives of New Mexico.* 2 vols. Reprint of the 1914 edition published by Torch Press, Cedar Rapids, Iowa. New York: Arno Press, 1976.

Tyler, Daniel. *Sources for New Mexico History, 1821–1848.* Santa Fe: Museum of New Mexico Press, 1984.

Ulibarri, Richard Onofre. "American Interest in the Spanish-Mexican Southwest, 1803–1848." Ph.D. diss., University of Utah, 1963.

Utley, Robert M. *Fort Union and the Santa Fe Trail.* El Paso: Western Press, 1989.

Valdes, Daniel T. *A Political History of New Mexico.* Manuscript on deposit at Colorado State University Library (1971).

VerSteeg, Clarence L. *The Formative Years, 1607–1763.* New York Hill and Wang, 1964.

Vestal, Stanley. *The Old Santa Fe Trail.* Boston: Houghton Mifflin Company, 1939.

Vigil, Maurilio E. *Los Patrones: Profiles of Hispanic Political Leaders in New Mexico History.* Washington, DC: University Press of America, 1980.

Walker, Henry Pickering. *The Wagonmasters: High Plains Freighting from the Earliest Days of the Santa Fe Trail to 1880.* Norman: University of Oklahoma Press, 1966.

Walter, Paul A. *Biography of Colonel José Francisco Chávez.* No. 31. Santa Fe: Historical Society of New Mexico, 1926.

Webb, James Josiah. *Adventures in the Santa Fe Trade, 1844–1847.* Edited by Ralph P. Bieber. Glendale, CA: The Arthur H. Clark Company, 1931.

Weber, David J. *Arms, Indians, and the Mismanagement of New Mexico.* Southwestern Studies Series. No. 77. El Paso: Texas Western Press, 1986.

———. *The Mexican Frontier, 1821–1846: The American Southwest Under Mexico.* Albuquerque: University of New Mexico Press, 1982.

———. *The Spanish Frontier in North America.* New Haven: Yale University Press, 1992.

———. *The Taos Trappers: The Fur Trade in the Far Southwest.* Norman: University of Oklahoma Press, 1971.

———, ed. *The Extranjeros: Selected Documents from the Mexican Side of the Santa Fe Trail, 1825–1828.* Santa Fe: Stagecoach Press, 1967.

———. *New Spain's Far Northern Frontier: Essays on Spain in the American West, 1540–1821.* Albuquerque: University of New Mexico Press, 1979.

Wentworth, Edward Norris. *America's Sheep Trails.* Ames, IA: Iowa State College Press, 1948.

White, Richard. *"It's Your Misfortune and None of My Own": A New History of the American West.* Norman: University of Oklahoma Press, 1991.

Wislizenus, A. *A Memoir of a Tour to Northern Mexico.* Washington, 1848.

Young, Otis. *The First Military Escort on the Santa Fe Trail 1829: From the Journal and Reports of Major Bennet Riley and Lieutenant Philip St. George Cooke.* Glendale, CA: The Arthur H. Clark Company, 1952.

Zeleny, Carolyn. *Relations Between the Spanish-Americans and Anglo-Americans in New Mexico.* New York: Arno Press, 1974.

Articles

Aguirre, Mamie Bernard. "Spanish Trader's Bride." *Westport Historical Quarterly* 4 (December 1968): 5–23.

Allison, W. H. "Colonel Francisco Perea." *Old Santa Fe* 1 (1913): 209–22.

Aragón y Perea, Julián. "A Brief Memoir." *New Mexico Historical Review* 46 (November 1971): 351–55.

Armstrong, Ruth. "San Miguel: Port of Entry on the Santa Fe Trail." *New Mexico Magazine* 46 (February 1968): 10–13.

Atherton, Lewis E. "Business Techniques in the Santa Fe Trade." *Missouri Historical Review* 34 (1940): 335–41.

———. "James and Robert Aull — A Frontier Missouri Mercantile Firm." *Missouri Historical Review* 30 (1935): 3–27.

———. "The Santa Fe Trader as Mercantile Capitalist." *Missouri Historical Review* 77 (1982): 1–12.

Baxter, John O. "Salvador Armijo: Citizen of Albuquerque, 1823–1879." *New Mexico Historical Review* 53 (1978): 219–37.

Beers, Henry Putney. "Military Protection of the Santa Fe Trail to 1843." *New Mexico Historical Review* 12 (1937): 113–33.

Bender, Averam B. "Military Transportation in the Southwest, 1848–1860." *New Mexico Historical Review* 32 (1957): 123–50.

Bernard, William R. "Westport and the Santa Fe Trade." *Kansas Historical Collections* 9 (1905–6): 552–65.

Bieber, Ralph P. "Letters of James and Robert Aull." *Missouri Historical Society Collections* 5 (1928): 286–87.

———. "The Papers of James J. Webb, Santa Fe Merchant, 1844–1861." *Washington University Studies* 11 (1924): 255–305.

Bloom, John P. "New Mexico Viewed by Anglo Americans, 1846–1849." *New Mexico Historical Review* 34 (1959): 165–98.

Bloom, Lansing Bartlett. "The Chihuahua Highway." *New Mexico Historical Review* 12 (1937): 209–16.

———. "The Death of Jacques D'Eglise." *New Mexico Historical Review* 2 (1927): 369–80.

———. "Ledgers of a Santa Fe Trader." *New Mexico Historical Review* 21 (1946): 135–39.

———. "New Mexico under Mexican Administration, 1821–1846." *Old Santa Fe* 1 (July 1913): 3–49; 2 (1914): 118–28, 351–80.

———. *Old Santa Fe: A Magazine of History, Archaeology, Genealogy and Biography* 2 (April 1915).

———. "A Trade Invoice of 1638." *New Mexico Historical Review* 10 (1935): 242–48.

Bolton, Herbert Eugene. "New Light on Manuel Lisa and the Spanish Fur Trade." *Quarterly of the Texas State Historical Association* 17 (1903): 61–66.

Boyle, Susan Calafate. "*Comerciantes, Arrieros, y Peones*: The Hispanos and the

Santa Fe Trade." Southwest Cultural Resources Center, Professional Papers. No. 54. Santa Fe, NM: National Park Service, 1994.

———. "Did She Generally Decide? Women in Ste. Genevieve, 1750–1805." *The William and Mary Quarterly* 64 (October 1987): 777–89.

———. "Inequality and Opportunity: Wealth Distribution in Ste. Genevieve, 1757–1804." Paper delivered at the Social Science History Association Meeting, Washington, D.C., October 1983.

Bradford Prince, L. "Bacas, Chávezes and Armijos had been rulers of New Mexico." *Historical Sketches of New Mexico*. New York and Kansas City, 1883, 285.

Brading, D. A. "Bourbon Spain and its American Empire." In *Colonial Spanish America*, edited by Leslie Bethell, 112–62. Cambridge, UK: Cambridge University Press, 1987.

Callon, Milton W. "The Merchant-Colonists of New Mexico." In *Brand Book of the Denver Westerners*. Vol. 21., 3–26. Denver: The Denver Westerners Inc., 1966.

Carlson, Alvar Ward. "New Mexico Sheep Industry: 1850–1900: Its Role in the History of the Territory." *New Mexico Historical Review* 44 (1969): 25–50.

Carpenter, Helen. "A Trip Across the Plains in an Ox Wagon, 1857." In *Ho for California! Women's Overland Diaries from the Huntington Library*, edited by Sandra L. Myres. San Marino: Huntington Library, 1980.

Chávez, Fray Angélico. "New Names in New Mexico." *El Palacio* 64 (1957): 298.

Chávez, Thomas Esteban. "The Trouble with Texans: Manuel Alvarez and the 1841 'Invasion.'" *New Mexico Historical Review* 53 (1978): 133–44.

Chávez, Tibo J. "'El Millonario': Ambitious Merchant Cut Stylish Figure on Frontier." *New Mexico Magazine* (June 1989): 73–79.

Clum, Joseph P. "Santa Fe in the "70s." *New Mexico Historical Review* 2 (1927): 380–86.

Connelley, William E. "Documents: A Journal of the Santa Fe Trail." *Mississippi Valley Historical Review* 12 (1926): 98, 241–50.

Cooke, Philip St. George. "A Journal of the Santa Fe Trail." *Mississippi Valley Historical Review* 12 (1935): 72–98, 227–55.

Covington, James W. "Correspondence Between Mexican Officials at Santa Fe and Officials in Missouri: 1823–1825." *The Bulletin, Missouri Historical Society* (October 1959): 20–32.

Cox, Isaac Joslin. "Opening the Santa Fe Trail." *Missouri Historical Review* 25 (1930): 30–66.

Cramaussel, Chantal. "Historia del camino real de tierra adentro y sus empalmes de Zacatecas a El Paso." Paper delivered at El Camino Real de Tierra Adentro: Historia y Cultura, Coloquio Internacional, Valle de Allende, Chihuahua, Mexico, 7–9 June 1995.

Creer, Leland Hargrave. "Spanish-American Slave Trade in the Great Basin, 1800–1853." *New Mexico Historical Review* 24 (1949): 171–83.

Culhane, Jolane. "Miguel Antonio Otero: A Photographic Essay." *New Mexico Historical Review* 67 (1992): 53–62.

Culmer, Frederic A. "Marking the Santa Fe Trail." *New Mexico Historical Review* 9 (1934): 78–93.

Douglas, Walter B. "Manuel Lisa." *Missouri Historical Collections* 3 (1911): 233–68, 367–407.

Ebright, Malcolm. "Manuel Martínez's Ditch Dispute: A Study in Mexican Period Custom and Justice." *New Mexico Historical Review* 54 (1979): 21–34.

Fierman, Floyd S. "The Staabs of Santa Fe: Pioneer Merchants in New Mexico Territory." *Río Grande History* 13 (1983): 2–23.

Fisher, Lillian E. "Commercial Conditions in Mexico at the End of the Colonial Period." *New Mexico Historical Review* 7 (1932): 143–64.

Florescano, Enrique. "The Hacienda in New Spain." In *Colonial Spanish America*, edited by Leslie Bethell, 250–85. Cambridge, UK: Cambridge University Press, 1987.

Folmer, Henri. "Contraband Trade Between Louisiana and New Mexico in the Eighteenth Century." *New Mexico Historical Review* 16 (1941): 249–74.

———. "The Mallet Expedition of 1739 Through Nebraska, Kansas, and Colorado to Santa Fe." *The Colorado Magazine* 16 (1939): 161–73.

Foote, Cheryl J. "Selected Sources for the Mexican Period, 1821–1848, in New Mexico." *New Mexico Historical Review* 59 (1984): 81–89.

Francis, E. K. "Padre Martinez: A New Mexican Myth." *New Mexico Historical Review* 31 (1956): 265–89.

Frazer, Robert W. "Purveyors of Flour to the Army: Department of New Mexico, 1849–1861." *New Mexico Historical Review* 47 (1972): 213–39.

Gamboa, Erasmo. "The Mexican Mule Pack System of Transportation in the Pacific Northwest and British Columbia." *Journal of the West* 29 (1990): 16–28.

Gardner, Mark. "Locomotives, Oxen, and Freight: The Last Decade of the Santa Fe Trail." Summary of a presentation proposed for the Western History Association Meeting, Albuquerque, New Mexico, October 1994.

Gianini, Charles A. "Manuel Lisa." *New Mexico Historical Review* 2 (1927): 323–33.

Goodrich, James W. "Revolt at Mora, 1847." *New Mexico Historical Review* 47 (1972): 49–60.

Greever, William S. "Railway Development in the Southwest." *New Mexico Historical Review* 32 (1957): 151–203.

Gutiérrez, Ramón A. "Honor, Ideology, Marriage Negotiation, and Class-Gender Domination in New Mexico, 1690–1846." *Latin American Perspective* 12 (1985): 81–104.

Hall, G. Emlen. "Juan Estevan Pino, 'Se Los Coma': New Mexico Land Speculation in the 1820s." *New Mexico Historical Review* 57 (1982): 27–42.

Hall, G. Emlen, and David J. Weber. "Mexican Liberals and the Pueblo Indians." *New Mexico Historical Review* 58 (1983): 5–32.

Hammond, George P. "The Zuñiga Journal, Tucson to Santa Fe: The Opening of a Spanish Trade Route, 1788–1795." *New Mexico Historical Review* 6 (1931): 40–65.

Harvey, Charles. "The Story of the Santa Fe Trail." *Atlantic Monthly* 104 (December 1909): 774–85.

Hershberg, Theodore, Alan Burstein, and Robert Dockhorn. "Record Linkage." *Historical Methods Newsletter* 9 (1976): 137–63.

Hill, Joseph J. "The Old Spanish Trail." *Hispanic American Historical Review* 4 (1921): 444–73.

———. "Spanish and Mexican Exploration and Trade Northwest from New Mexico into the Great Basin, 1765–1853." *Utah Historical Quarterly* 3 (1930): 3–23.

———. "An Unknown Expedition to Santa Fe in 1807." *Mississippi Valley Historical Review* 6 (1920): 560–62.

Homes, Kenneth L. "The Benjamin Cooper Expeditions to Santa Fe in 1822 and 1823." *New Mexico Historical Review* 38 (1963): 139–50.

Hussey, John Adam. "The New Mexico-California Caravan of 1847–1848." *New Mexico Historical Review* 18 (1943): 1–16.

Ivey, James E. "In the Midst of a Loneliness: The Architectural History of the Salinas Missions." Southwest Cultural Resources Center, Professional Papers. No. 15. Second Printing. Santa Fe, NM: National Park Service, 1991.

Krakow, Jere. "Hispanic Influence on the Santa Fe Trail." *Courier* (October 1991): 21–23.

Latimer, Roman L. "Spiegelberg Brothers: Bankers and Merchants to New Mexico Territory." *Numismatic Scrapbook Magazine* 38.432 (February 1972): 118–44.

Lawrence, Eleanor Frances. "Mexican Trade Between Santa Fe and Los Angeles, 1830–1848." *California Historical Society Quarterly* 10 (1931): 27–39.

Lecompte, Janet. "Manuel Armijo's Family History." *New Mexico Historical Review* 48 (1973): 251–58.

López, Larry S. "Sample Partido Contracts." *New Mexico Historical Review* 52 (1977): 111–16.

Macleod, Murdo J. "Aspects of the Internal Economy." In *Colonial Spanish America*, edited by Leslie Bethell, 315–60. Cambridge, UK: Cambridge University Press, 1987.

Maloney, Alice Bay. "The Richard Campbell Party of 1827." *California Historical Society Quarterly* 18 (1939): 347–54.

McNitt, Frank. "Navajo Campaigns and the Occupation of New Mexico, 1847–1848." *New Mexico Historical Review* 42 (1968): 173–94.

Meyer, Doris L. "Early Mexican-American Responses to Negative Stereotyping." *New Mexico Historical Review* 53 (1978): 75–91.

Miller, Darlis A. "Cross-cultural Marriages in the Southwest: The New Mexico Experience, 1846–1900." *New Mexico Historical Review* 57 (1982): 335–59.

———. "Freighting for Uncle Sam." *Wagon Tracks* 5 (1990): 11–15.

Mills, T. B. "Report on the Internal Commerce of the United States." Reprinted in *Wagon Tracks* 2 (1987): 12–13.

Minge, Ward Alan. "The Last Will and Testament of Don Seferino Martínez." *New Mexico Quarterly* 33 (1963): 33–56.

Montoya, María E. "The Dual World of Governor Miguel A. Otero: Myth and Reality in Turn-of-the-Century New Mexico." *New Mexico Historical Review* 67 (1992): 13–32.

Moorhead, Max L. "Spanish Transportation in the Southwest, 1540–1846." *New Mexico Historical Review* 32 (1957): 107–22.

Muehl, Ruth D. "The Time of My Life: Women Who Loved the Trek." *American Heritage* 37 (1985): 92–93.

Murphy, Lawrence R. "Rayado: Pioneer Settlement in Northeastern New Mexico, 1848–1857." *New Mexico Historical Review* 46 (1971): 37–57.

Murphy, Lawrence R. "The Beaubien and Miranda Land Grant: 1841–1846." *New Mexico Historical Review* 42 (1967): 27–47.

———. "The United States Army in Taos, 1847–1852." *New Mexico Historical Review* 47 (1972): 33–48.

Myres, Sandra L. "Mexican Americans and Westering Anglos: A Feminine Perspective." *New Mexico Historical Review* 57 (1982): 317–34.

Nasatir, Abraham P. "Jacques Clamorgan: Colonial Promoter of the Northern Border of New Spain." *New Mexico Historical Review* 22 (1942): 101–12.

———. "Jacques D'Eglise on the Upper Missouri, 1791–1795." *Mississippi Valley Historical Review* 14 (1927): 47–71.

Nash, Gerald D. "New Mexico in the Otero Era: Some Historical Perspectives." *New Mexico Historical Review* 67 (1992): 1–12.

Navarro García, Luis. "The North of New Spain as a Political Problem in the Eighteenth Century." In *New Spain's Far Northern Frontier: Essays on Spain in the American West, 1540–1821*, edited by David J. Weber, 203–215. Albuquerque: University of New Mexico Press, 1979.

Noggle, Burt. "Anglo Observers of the Southwest Borderlands, 1825–1890: The Rise of a Concept." *Arizona and the West* 1 (1959): 105–41.

Nostrand, Richard L. "The Century of Hispano Expansion." *New Mexico Historical Review* 62 (1987): 361–86.

Olch, Peter D. "Bleeding, Purging, and Puking in the Southwestern Fur Trade and Along the Santa Fe Trail, 1800–1850." In *Adventure on the Santa Fe Trail*, edited by Leo E. Oliva, 11–35. Topeka: Kansas State Historical Society, 1988.

Olsen, Michael, and Harry C. Myers. "The Diary of Pedro Ignacio Gallegos Wherein 499 Soldiers Following the Trail of Comanches Met William Becknell on his First Trip to Santa Fe." *Wagon Tracks* 1 (1992): 15–20.

Owens, Sister Lilliana. "Jesuit Beginnings in New Mexico, 1867–1882." *Jesuit Studies — Southwest* 1 (n.d.): 32–35.

Paredes, Raymund A. "The Mexican Image in American Travel Literature, 1831–1869." *New Mexico Historical Review* 52 (1977): 5–30.

Parish, William J. "The German Jew and the Commercial Revolution in Territorial New Mexico, 1850–1900." *New Mexico Historical Review* 35 (1960): 1–29, 129–51.

———. "Sheep Husbandry in New Mexico." *New Mexico Historical Review* 37 (1962): 201–13, 259–308; 38 (1963): 56–77.

Perlman, Joel. "Using Census Districts in Analysis: Record Linkage and Sampling." *Journal of Interdisciplinary History* 10 (Autumn 1979): 279–89.

Perrine, Fred S. "Military Escorts on the Santa Fe Trail." *New Mexico Historical Review* 2 (1927): 175–93, 269–304; 3 (1928): 265–300.

"Preliminary Report of Survey of Inscriptions Along Santa Fe Trail in Oklahoma." *Chronicles of Oklahoma* 37 (Autumn 1960): 308–22.

Puckett, Fidelia Miller. "Ramón Ortiz: Priest and Patriot." *New Mexico Historical Review* 25 (1950): 265–95.

Raber, Charles. "Personal Recollections of Life on the Plains from 1860 to 1868." *Collections of the Kansas State Historical Society* 16 (1925): 316–40.

Reeve, Frank D., ed. "The Charles Bent Papers." *New Mexico Historical Review* 29 (1954): 234–39, 311–17; 30 (1955): 154–67, 252–54, 340–52; 31 (1956): 75–77, 157–64; 251–53.

Reno, Philip. "Rebellion in New Mexico." *New Mexico Historical Review* 40 (1965): 197–211.

Richards, Susan V. "From Traders to Traitors? The Armijo Brothers Through the Nineteenth Century." *New Mexico Historical Review* 69 (July 1994): 215–29.

Richardson, William H. "William H. Richardson's Journal of Doniphan's Expedition." *Missouri Historical Review* 2 (1928): 331–60; 4 (1928): 511–42.

Ríos-Bustamante, Antonio José. "New Mexico in the Eighteenth Century: Life, Labor and Trade in La Villa de San Felipe de Albuquerque, 1706–1790." *Aztlán* 7 (1976): 357–90.

Rowland, Buford. "Report of the Commissioners on the Road from Missouri to New Mexico, October 1827." *New Mexico Historical Review* 14 (1939): 213–29.

"Salazar and Gallegos." *Pace* (n.d.): 1–4.

Sandoval, David A. "Gnats, Goods, and Greasers: Mexican Merchants on the Santa Fe Trail." *Journal of the West* 28 (April 1989): 22–31.

———. "Montezuma's Merchants: Mexican Traders on the Santa Fe Trail." In *Adventure on the Santa Fe Trail*, edited by Leo Oliva, 37–60. Topeka: Kansas State Historical Society, 1988.

———. Review of *Comerciantes, Arrieros, y Peones: The Hispanos and the Santa Fe Trade*, by Susan Calafate Boyle. *Folio* (November 1995): 12–13.

———. "Who is Riding the Burro Now? A Bibliographical Critique of Scholarship on the New Mexico Trader." *The Santa Fe Trail: New Perspectives*, edited by David Wetzel. *Essays and Monographs in Colorado History* 6 (1987): 75–92.

Scholes, Frances V. "The Supply Service of the New Mexico Missions in the Seventeenth Century." *New Mexico Historical Review* 5 (1930): 93–115, 186–210, 386–404.

Secor Welsh, Cynthia. "A 'Star Will Be Added': Miguel Antonio Otero and the Struggle for Statehood." *New Mexico Historical Review* 67 (1992): 33–52.

Settle, Raymond W., and Mary Lund Settle. "The Early Careers of William Bradford Waddell and William Hepburn Russell: Frontier Capitalists." *Kansas Historical Quarterly* 26 (1960): 355–82.

Simmons, Marc. "A Hispano View of the Santa Fe Trail." *New Mexico Magazine* 57 (1980): 12–13.

———. "The Mexican Side of the Santa Fe Trail." Paper delivered at Rendezvous 1980, Larned, Kansas, 28 March 1980.

———. "New Mexico's Spanish Exiles." *New Mexico Historical Review* 59 (1985): 75–94

———. "The Santa Fe Trail As High Adventure." In *Adventure on the Santa Fe Trail*, edited by Leo E. Oliva, 1–10. Topeka: Kansas State Historical Society, 1988.

———. "Trade Fairs and Markets in New Mexico: Tracing the Roots of Trading from the Aztecs to the Spanish Culture." *Inside Santa Fe and Taos* (July 1993).

———. "Women on the Santa Fe Trail: Diaries, Journals, Memoirs. An Annotated Bibliography." *New Mexico Historical Review* 61 (1986): 233–43.

Smith, Ralph A. "Contrabando en la Guerra con los Estados Unidos." *Historia mexicana* 11 (1962): 361–81.

Snow, David H. "Purchased in Chihuahua for Feasts." In *El Camino Real de Tierra Adentro*, edited by Gabrielle G. Palmer, 133–46. Cultural Resources Series. No. 11. New Mexico: Bureau of Land Management, 1993.

Sperry, T. J. "A Long and Useful Life for the Santa Fe Trail." *Wagon Tracks* 4 (May 1990): 14–17.

Spiegelberg, Flora. "Reminiscences of a Jewish Bride of the Santa Fe Trail." *Jewish Spectator* 2 (1937): 21–22.

Steinberg, Ruth. "José Jarvet, Spanish Scout and Historical Enigma." *New Mexico Historical Review* 67 (July 1992): 227–49.

Stephens, F. F. "Missouri and the Santa Fe Trade." *Missouri Historical Review* 10 (1916): 233–62; 11 (1917): 289–312.

Stevens, Harry R. "A Company of Hands and Traders: Origins of the Glenn-Fowler Expedition of 1821–1822." *New Mexico Historical Review* 46 (1971): 181–222.

Suárez, Clara Elena. "La arriería en el camino real de tierra adentro a fines del siglo XVIII." Paper delivered at El Camino Real de Tierra Adentro: Historia y Cultura, Coloquio Internacional, Valle de Allende, Chihuahua, Mexico, 7–9 June 1995.

Sunseri, Alvin R. "The Hazards of the Trail." *El Palacio* 81 (Fall 1975): 29–38.

Tenenbaum, Barbara A. "Taxation and Tyranny: Public Finance during the Iturbide Regime, 1821–1832." In *The Independence of Mexico and the Creation of the New Nation*, edited by Jaime E. Rodríguez O., 201–14. Los Angeles: UCLA Latin American Center Publication, 1989.

Thomas, Alfred B. "Documents Bearing Upon the Northern Frontier of New Mexico, 1818–1819." *New Mexico Historical Review* 4 (1929): 146–64.

Thomas, Alfred B. "The Yellowstone River, James Long and Spanish Reaction to American Intrusion into Spanish Dominions, 1818–1819." *New Mexico Historical Review* 4 (1929): 164–87.

Timmons, W. H. "The El Paso Area in the Mexican Period, 1821–1848." *Southwestern Historical Quarterly* 84 (1980): 1–28.

Tjarks, Alicia V. "Demographic, Ethnic and Occupational Structure of New Mexico: The Census Report of 1790." *The Americas* 35 (1978): 45–88.

Tyler, Daniel. "Anglo-American Penetration of the Southwest: The View from New Mexico." *Southwestern Historical Quarterly* 75 (1972): 325–38.

———. "Governor Armijo's Moment of Truth." *Journal of the West* 11 (1972): 307–16.

———. "Gringo Views of Governor Manuel Armijo." *New Mexico Historical Review* 45 (1970): 23–46.

———. "The Mexican Teacher." *Red River Valley Historical Review* 1 (1974): 207–21.

———. "The Personal Property of Manuel Armijo, 1829." *El Palacio* 80 (1974): 45–48.

Ulibarri, George. "The Chouteau-DeMun Expedition to New Mexico, 1815–1817." *New Mexico Historical Review* 36 (1961): 263–73.

Utley, Robert M. "Fort Union and the Santa Fe Trail." *New Mexico Historical Review* 36 (1961): 36–48.

Van Cleave, Errett. "Credit on the Santa Fe Trail: Business Pioneering in Pueblo Regions." *Credit and Financial Management* 41 (1939): 16–17.

Vigil, Maurilio E. "New Mexicans, Las Vegas, and the Santa Fe Trail." *Wagon Tracks* 10 (1996): 17–22.

Wadleigh, A. B. "Ranching in New Mexico, 1886–1890." *New Mexico Historical Review* 27 (1952): 1–28.

Wagoner, J. J. "Development of the Cattle Industry in Southern Arizona, 1870s and 80s." *New Mexico Historical Review* 26 (1951): 204–24.

Wallace, William S. "Stagecoaching in Territorial New Mexico." *New Mexico Historical Review* 32 (1957): 204–10.

Walsh, Larry. "A Public Report." In *Archaeological Survey Project on El Camino Real de Tierra Adentro.* New Mexico State Historic Preservation Division, 1991.

Walsh, Margaret. "The Census as an Accurate Source of Information: The Value of Mid-Nineteenth Century Manufacturing Returns." *Historical Methods Newsletter* 3 (September 1970): 4–13.

Webb, James J. "The Papers of James J. Webb, Santa Fe Merchant, 1844–1861." *Washington University Studies* 9.2 (1924): 255–305.

Weber, David J. "American Westward Expansion and the Breakdown of Relations between *Pobladores* and '*Indios Bárbaros*' on Mexico's Far Northern Frontier, 1821–1846." *New Mexico Historical Review* 56 (1981): 221–38.

———. "Mexico's Far Northern Frontier, 1821–1854: Historiography Askew." *Western Historical Quarterly* 7 (1976): 279–93.

——. "The New Mexico Archives in 1827." *New Mexico Historical Review* 61 (1986): 53–61.

——. "'Scarce More Than Apes': Historical Roots of Anglo-American Stereotypes of Mexicans in the Border Region." In *New Spain's Far Northern Frontier: Essays on Spain in the American West, 1540–1821,* edited by David J. Weber, 293–307. Albuquerque: University of New Mexico Press, 1979.

——. "The Spanish Legacy in North America and the Historical Imagination." *Western Historical Quarterly* 23 (February 1992): 5–24.

——. "Turner, the Boltonians and the Borderlands." *American Historical Review* 91 (1986): 66–81.

——, ed. "A Letter from Taos, 1826." New Mexico Historical Review 41 (1966): 155–64.

——. "William Becknell as a Mountain Man: Two Letters." *New Mexico Historical Review* 46 (1971): 253–60.

Wells, Eugene T. "The Growth of Independence, Missouri: 1827–1850." *Bulletin of the Missouri Historical Society* 16 (1959): 33–46.

Wilson, John P. "How the Settlers Farmed: Hispanic Villages and Irrigation Systems in Early Sierra County, 1850–1900." *New Mexico Historical Review* 63 (1988): 333–56.

Winchester, Ian. "The Linkage of Historical Records by Man and Computer: Techniques and Problems." *Journal of Interdisciplinary History* 1 (Autumn 1970): 107–25.

Winther, Oscar Osburn. "The Southern Overland Mail and Stagecoach Line, 1857–1861." *New Mexico Historical Review* 32 (1957): 81–106.

Woodward, Arthur. "Adventuring to Santa Fe: The Book of the Muleteers." *New Mexico Historical Review* 17 (1942): 288–93.

Wyman, Walker D. "Freighting: A Big Business on the Santa Fe Trail." *Kansas Historical Quarterly* 1 (November 1931): 17–37.

——. "F. X. Aubry: Santa Fe Freighter, Pathfinder, and Explorer." *New Mexico Historical Review* 7 (1932): 1–31.

Index